EYEBLINK CLASSICAL CONDITIONING
VOLUME 1:
Applications in Humans

EYEBLINK CLASSICAL CONDITIONING
VOLUME 1:
Applications in Humans

edited by

Diana Woodruff-Pak
Temple University

Joseph E. Steinmetz
Indiana University

KLUWER ACADEMIC PUBLISHERS
Boston / Dordrecht / London

Distributors for North, Central and South America:
Kluwer Academic Publishers
101 Philip Drive
Assinippi Park
Norwell, Massachusetts 02061 USA
Telephone (781) 871-6600
Fax (781) 871-6528
E-Mail <kluwer@wkap.com>

Distributors for all other countries:
Kluwer Academic Publishers Group
Distribution Centre
Post Office Box 322
3300 AH Dordrecht, THE NETHERLANDS
Telephone 31 78 6392 392
Fax 31 78 6546 474
E-Mail <services@wkap.nl>

Electronic Services <http://www.wkap.nl>

Library of Congress Cataloging-in-Publication Data

Eyeblink classical conditioning / edited by Diana Woodruff-Pak, Joseph E. Steinmetz.
p. cm.
Contents: v. 1. Applications in humans.
Includes bibliographical references and index.
ISBN 0-7923-7727-3 (acid-free paper)
1. Neuropsychological tests. 2. Clinical neuropsychology. 3. Eyelid conditioning. I. Woodruff-Pak, Diana S., 1946- II. Steinmetz, Joseph E., 1955-

RC386.6.N48 E94 1999
153.1'526--dc21

99-049487

Printed on acid-free paper.
Printed in the United States of America

TABLE OF CONTENTS

LIST OF CONTRIBUTORS

Robert E. Clark
VA Medical Center
3350 La Jolla Village Drive
University of California
San Diego, CA 92161-0002

Irene Daum
Neuropsychology
Faculty of Psychology
Ruhr-University of Bochum
D-44780 Bochum Germany

Carol O. Eckerman
Department of Psychology
Duke University
Box 90086
Durham, NC 27708-0086

Sushmita S. Ghose
Department of Psychology
Indiana University
1101 E. 10th Street
Bloomington, IN 47405-7007

Isidore Gormezano
Department of Psychology
University of Iowa
Iowa City, IA 52242

John T. Green
Department of Psychology
Temple University
1701 N. 13th Street
Philadelphia, PA 19122

Dragana Ivkovich
Department of Psychology
Duke University
Box 90086
Durham, NC 27708-0086

Richard B. Ivry
Department of Psychology
3210 Tolman Hall
University of California
Berkeley, CA 94720-1650

Norman A. Krasnegor
National Institute of Child Health
and Human Development
6100 Executive Blvd, 4B05
Bethesda, MD 20892

Susan K. Lemieux
Temple Univ. School of Medicine
Department of Diagnostic Imaging
3401 N. Broad Sreet
Philadelphia, PA 19122

Richard M. McFall
Department of Psychology
Indiana University
1101 E. 10th Street
Bloomington, IN 47405-7007

Regina McGlinchey-Berroth
Brockton/West Roxbury
VA Medical Center
1400 VFW Parkway
West Roxbury, MA 02132

Anthony Randal McIntosh
Rotman Research Institute
Bay Crest Center
3560 Bathurst Street
Toronto, Ontario M6A 2E1 Canada

Nestor A. Schmajuk
Department of Psychology
Duke University
Durham, NC 27706

Bernard G. Schreurs
Behavioral Neuroscience Unit
National Institutes of Health
Building 36, Room B205
Bethesda, MD 20892

Markus M. Schugens
Neuropsychology
Faculty of Psychology
Ruhr-University of Bochum
D-44780 Bochum Germany

Lonnie L. Sears
Department of Pediatrics
University of Louisville
School of Medicine
334 E. Broadway
Louisville, KY 40292

Larry R. Squire
VA Medical Center
3350 La Jolla Village Drive
University of California
San Diego, CA 92161-0002

Mark E. Stanton
U.S. Environmental Protection Agency
Neurotoxicology Division MD -74B
Research Triangle Park, NC 27711

Joseph E. Steinmetz
Department of Psychology
Indiana University
1101 E. 10th Street
Bloomington, IN 47405-7007

Helge R. Topka
Department of Neurology
University of Tübingen
Neuklinikum, Hoppe-Selyler Str 3
72076 Tübingen Germany

Jo Anne Tracy
Department of Psychology
Indiana University
1101 E. 10th Street
Bloomington, IN 47405-7007

Diana S. Woodruff-Pak
Department of Psychology
Temple University and
1701 N. 13th Street
Philadelphia, PA 19122

1 PAST, PRESENT, AND FUTURE OF HUMAN EYEBLINK CLASSICAL CONDITIONING

Diana S. Woodruff-Pak
Temple University

Joseph E. Steinmetz
Indiana University

INTRODUCTION

Associative learning is a fundamental form of human cognition. A model paradigm of associative learning about which there is an extensive knowledge base both in neurobiological and behavioral science is eyeblink classical conditioning. Based on a foundation of behavioral neuroscience research initiated in non-human mammals, classical conditioning of the nictitating membrane (NM)/eyeblink response has become the best-documented learning paradigm in all mammals, including humans. As documented in this volume on human applications and its companion volume on animal models, the neural circuitry for classical eyeblink conditioning is similar in all mammals, including humans.

Now that fundamental neural circuitry and neurobiological mechanisms as well as behavioral attributes have been demonstrated to be similar in all mammals, there is renewed interest in this classical method for studying associative learning in humans. This volume on human applications identifies some of the domains in which the elaborate and well-understood model of eyeblink classical conditioning can be put to use. Highlighted are a wealth of insights to be gained from investigating human learning with a neurobiologically well-characterized behavioral paradigm.

In this chapter we introduce the eyeblink classical conditioning paradigm with is variety of procedures and present a history of just over a 100 years worth of progress in human eyeblink classical conditioning research. We then outline briefly the neural structures and circuitry essential for this form of associative learning and discuss the structures normally engaged in modulating the rate of learning. The role of this model in a number of theoretical domains in cognitive science and cognitive neuroscience is addressed along with insights gained in life span developmental approaches and in neurological diseases and psychopathology.

Driven by neurobiological research in animal models that elucidated the basis in which this form of associative learning occurs, human eyeblink conditioning has seen a revival. Here we present background on the development of this paradigm with its array of procedures and outline some of the promising new directions to be elaborated in subsequent chapters.

CLASSICAL CONDITIONING PROCEDURES

A basic principle in classical conditioning is the association of a neutral stimulus with a reflex-eliciting stimulus. The stimulus that causes the reflex induces the response naturally and thus is called the unconditioned stimulus (US). Organisms reflexively blink when their cornea is stimulated by an air puff or when a mild shock is administered to the skin around the eye. The air puff and the shock therefore constitute USs. A moderately loud sound or the onset of a light do not normally cause a blink. These are considered to be neutral stimuli with regard to the elicitation of an eyeblink reflex. Tones and lights are the most common examples of what is used in eyeblink classical conditioning as a conditioned stimulus (CS). It is the repeated association of the CS with the US that results in associative learning. For example, a tone CS turns on, and half a second later a corneal air puff US turns on. The organism learns, in many cases in the absence of conscious awareness, that the CS signals the onset of the US. The organism then begins to perform the reflexive response (an eyeblink in our example) to the CS in addition to the US. Performance of the reflexive response to the CS is what is learned. In eyeblink conditioning, the organism blinks to the CS. This learned response is called the conditioned response (CR).

There are many features of classical conditioning that make it attractive as a means to study associative learning. One advantage is that there are a number of classical conditioning procedures. An investigator has the advantage of being able to experiment with one form of classical conditioning and then build upon the knowledge base by using more complex classical conditioning procedures.

The simplest and most frequently used classical conditioning procedure was named by the scientist who introduced classical conditioning, Ivan Pavlov. He called it the delay classical conditioning procedure, using the term, "delay" to represent the fact that the CS was followed by the US after a short delay. The typical delay eyeblink classical conditioning procedure uses a pure tone such as a 1 kHz tone at 80 dB SPL as the CS and a corneal air puff of around 5 psi as the US. The interval between the CS and US is the same for every trial of a session, and the CS-US intervals most commonly used for human eyeblink conditioning studies range between 400 and 750 ms. In the delay classical conditioning procedure, the CS and US overlap.

Pavlov used the term, "trace" to characterize a classical conditioning procedure in which the CS turns on and then off, a period of time elapses, and then the US comes on. The idea was that a memory trace of the CS would have to form to bridge the blank time interval before the US. The trace procedure imposes a temporal separation between the offset of a CS and the onset of a US. Imposing an empty time period typically lengthens the interval between the CS and the US. Thus, trace and delay procedures usually vary in two ways: (1) the length of the CS-US interval and (2) the overlap of the CS and US. The CS and US coterminate in the delay procedure, but the CS is off for some time period before US onset in the trace procedure.

The discrimination procedure uses two CSs. The CS+ is always followed by the US, whereas the CS- is never followed by the US. The organism learns to discriminate between the CS+ and the CS-. There is an increase in the number of CRs to the CS+, and there are no CRs or a diminution of CRs to the CS-. Discrimination reversal occurs when the contingencies of the CS+ and the CS- are reversed. The previous

CS+ becomes the CS-, and the previous CS- becomes the CS+. Figure 1 illustrates the delay, trace, and discrimination/reversal classical conditioning procedures.

Most of the research discussed in this volume uses the classical conditioning procedures shown in Figure 1 or some combination of these procedures. However, we must stress that many additional classical conditioning procedures remain to be explored in human eyeblink conditioning research. For example, when he takes a

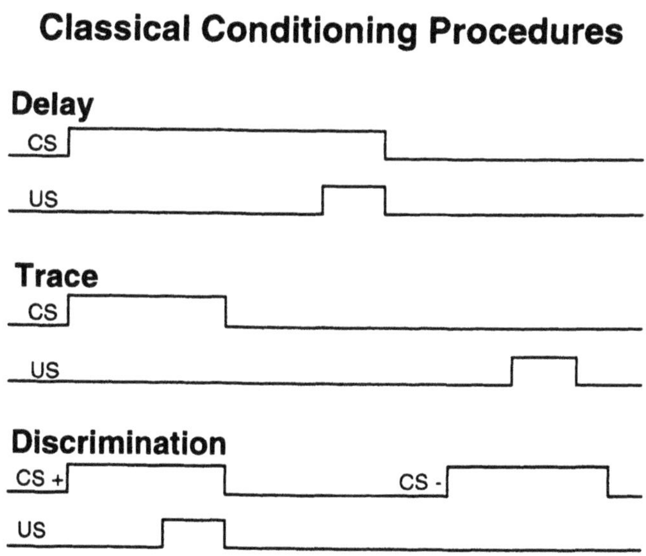

Figure 1. Examples of typical classical conditioning procedures. In the delay procedure the conditioned stimulus (CS) and unconditioned stimulus (US) overlap, whereas in the trace procedure the CS is turned off, there is a blank "trace" period, and the US is turned on after the trace interval. In a discrimination procedure, one CS called the CS+ is always followed by the US, but the CS- is never followed by the US. The discrimination reversal procedure (not shown) is used after the discrimination procedure has been used and involves reversing the contingencies so that the former CS- becomes the CS+ and the former CS+ becomes the CS-.

neural networks approach to human eyeblink conditioning in Chapter 2 of this volume, Schmajuk considers some other classical conditioning procedures tested in animals but not humans. We are simply at the beginning of an exploration of the potential of eyeblink classical conditioning to elucidate human associative learning. In a recent review of the research literature on the role of the cerebellum and hippocampus in eyeblink classical conditioning in mammals, Green and Woodruff-Pak (in press) identified the many classical conditioning procedures and the published eyeblink conditioning studies in these tasks. What became most evident was the number of procedures that have yet to be investigated with human eyeblink classical conditioning.

Throughout this volume the many attributes of classical conditioning will become evident. We mention some of them here. One advantage of classical conditioning procedures is that the learned response can be separated from the reflexive motor response. In the CR we have a relatively pure measure of learning that can be measured apart from the motoric aspects of the response. Thus, if we have a neurological condition that affects the blink reflex, we can avoid making the mistake of concluding that patients with that condition are impaired in the capacity to learn in the eyeblink classical conditioning paradigm by looking at the unconditioned response (UR) as well as the CR. Schugens and his associates comment more on classical conditioning and motor responses in their chapter in this volume.

Another attribute of classical conditioning that has made eyeblink conditioning so valuable to neuroscientific approaches is the precision in timing in this model. The CS and US are precisely timed, making the responses precisely timed. The CR and the UR can be predicted in time. When measuring responses from the vast network in the brain, it is essential to know when to expect a response. Knowledge about when the response occurs assists in locating where in the brain activation associated with the response occurs. Understanding the functional aspects involved in timing a response also add to knowledge about how components of the brain orchestrate behavior. Green and associates discuss this attribute and the role of timing in responding in Chapter 5 in this volume.

The fact that eyeblink classical conditioning is such a useful model for the investigation of associative learning has generated another advantage to researchers adopting this approach. There is an abundance of data collected in the eyeblink classical conditioning paradigm in non-human mammals and humans. Indeed, more data have been collected in the eyeblink classical conditioning paradigm in rabbits and in humans than in any other classical conditioning model. There is a wealth of knowledge about eyeblink conditioning that permits investigators to build and to go beyond rudimentary understanding of associative learning.

A BRIEF HISTORY

The history of the study of classical conditioning is relatively long, beginning late in the nineteenth century. Although he received the Nobel Prize in 1904 for his research on the physiology of digestion in dogs, Ivan Petrovitch Pavlov had already turned his attention to the work most frequently associated with his name. He devoted most of the last portion of his career to investigating formally the phenomenon of classical conditioning. Pavlov's procedures using a bell as the CS and meat powder as the US to elicit salivation as the CR still serve as the prime example for classical conditioning. First in Germany and later in the United States, investigators moved from studying the slower autonomic nervous system responses such as salivation to assessment of conditioning in the somatic nervous system using the eyeblink response. In the United States, Ernest Hilgard was among the first researchers to conduct studies on human eyeblink conditioning using techniques that might not be approved by contemporary human subject institutional review boards. Instead of an air puff, Hilgard used a paddle to smack the subject in the face. Of course, this large wooden US-eliciting device was effective in producing an eyeblink UR. As illustrated in Figure 2, more recent techniques use mild air puffs to elicit the blink UR.

One of the great values of Hilgard's work was to establish the close correspondence in properties of the conditioned eyeblink response in humans and other animals. He suggested that the underlying neuronal mechanisms of memory storage and retrieval may be the same in all mammals, including humans. Data collected over 60 years after he stated this insight have proved Hilgard to be correct.

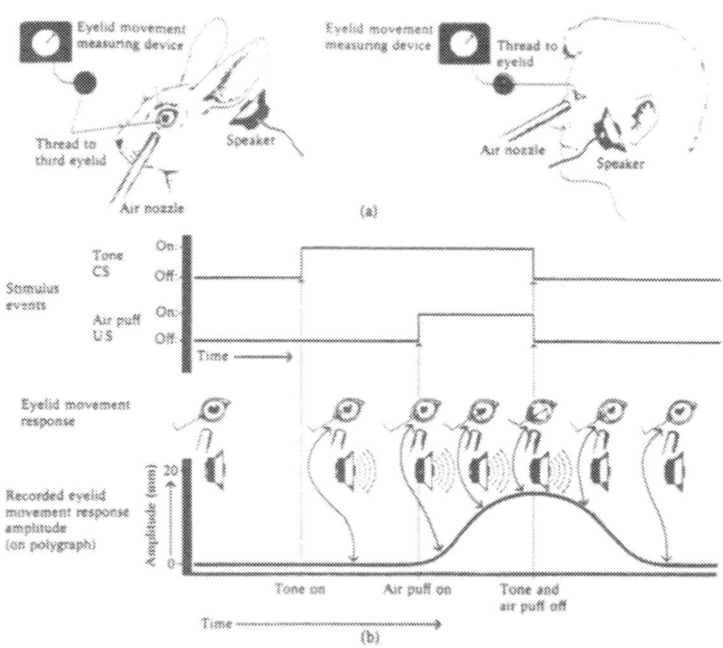

Figure 2. There are close parallels in the methodology and behavior of data collection in the eyeblink classical conditioning paradigm in rabbits and humans. This figure, or one similar, has been used in introductory psychology textbooks for decades. From: PSYCHOLOGY 2E by Lindzey et al. © 1978 by Worth Publishers. Used with permission.

Wide Adoption of the Eyeblink Classical Conditioning Model

Several investigators such as Alan Wagner recognized the utility of rabbits as a species for eyeblink classical conditioning research, but it was Isidore Gormezano who first published eyeblink conditioning studies in the rabbit and introduced measurement of the nictitating membrane extension response. Extensive behavioral research has been carried out using this animal preparation as reviewed in the companion volume to this volume, *Eyeblink Classical Conditioning: Volume II – Animal Models* (Woodruff-Pak & Steinmetz, 2000).

By far, more parametric data concerning eyeblink classical conditioning have been collected using rabbits than any other species. Much of the general literature on classical conditioning is based on data collected in the rabbit nictitating membrane paradigm and with the human eyeblink conditioning paradigm. What is exciting at present is that the eyeblink conditioning paradigm is so useful that investigators are adapting it to freely moving rats. The rat model is not only much more cost-effective to use, but rats have a wider behavioral repertoire thus making comparisons of eyeblink conditioning with other associative learning experiences possible. The number of studies testing eyeblink conditioning in rats may approach the number of studies using rabbits in the next decade. Furthermore, the mouse model of eyeblink classical conditioning has been established so that the developments in molecular genetics that are best worked out in mice can now be coupled with the powerful eyeblink classical conditioning model.

From the work of Hilgard and Gormezano and their collaborators and students, the parallels between animal and human eyeblink classical conditioning have been demonstrated empirically for decades. These empirical demonstrations of similarities in learning between animals and humans have not simply been buried in scientific journals gathering dust on library shelves. The parallel use of human and rabbit subjects in studies of eyeblink classical conditioning has been taught to thousands, perhaps even hundreds of thousands of introductory psychology students. The illustration of the classical conditioning paradigm using rabbits and humans was included in the first edition and in subsequent editions of a popular introductory psychology textbook for 25 years (Figure 2). If salivation to a bell is the archetype of classical conditioning, blinking to a tone is the prototype.

The Research Literature on Human Eyeblink Classical Conditioning

The investigation of this prototypical form of classical conditioning has a history spanning an entire century. The earliest human eyeblink classical conditioning study was published in a German physiology journal in the nineteenth century (Zwaardemaker & Lans, 1899). The second article, published by Weiss in 1910 was also in a German journal. An early article in English relevant to eyeblink conditioning was published by Dodge in 1913, but the article addresses the blink reflex rather than classical conditioning. Cason was the first to publish on the conditioned eyeblink response, and he had four publications on this topic between 1922 and 1925 in the *American Journal of Psychology* and in the *Journal of Experimental Psychology*.

In an attempt to identify all published research on human eyeblink classical conditioning in the twentieth century up to 1985, Gormezano collected a bibliography that he kindly shared with researchers interested in this topic (Gormezano, personal communication, February 1, 1989). With his permission, we include this bibliography that has proved to be extremely useful in teaching as well as research as an Appendix to this volume.

The Gormezano bibliography of human eyeblink classical conditioning includes a total of 507 publications cited between 1899 and 1985. The Gormezano bibliography identifies the decade of the 1930s as the period when a number of researchers became active in investigating human eyeblink conditioning, with 62 published articles generated in that decade. Research activity increased on the topic in the subsequent decades of the 1940s through the 1960s, with the peak year being 1967 with 38 published articles. Between 1964 and 1967 alone, 134 articles appeared. However, for a period in the 1970s and 1980s, the rate of publication on human eyeblink classical conditioning declined. On the one hand, an extensive body of knowledge had been generated accurately characterizing this form of behavior. In addition, there was concern about the role of voluntary responding in human eyeblink conditioning and the degree to which actual learning was being assessed.

It was during this relative inactive period in the history of human eyeblink classical conditioning that the model was under intense scrutiny from a neurobiological perspective in animals. In the decades of the 1970s and 1980s, the role of the hippocampus and cerebellum and the essential neural pathways for this form of learning were discovered. The knowledge base concerning eyeblink classical conditioning in behavioral neuroscience provided a platform for research with human eyeblink classical conditioning that began the resurgence documented in the various chapters in this volume.

NEURAL STRUCTURES AND CIRCUITRY IN HUMAN EYEBLINK CLASSICAL CONDITIONING

The initial discoveries of hippocampal and cerebellar involvement in eyeblink classical conditioning in rabbits occurred in the laboratory of Richard F. Thompson. In hundreds of experiments in Thompson's laboratory and in many other laboratories throughout the world, the initial results have been replicated and extended and reported in the companion volume, *Eyeblink Classical Conditioning: Volume II – Animal Models* (Woodruff-Pak & Steinmetz, 2000). Dramatic behavioral and neural parallels in eyeblink classical conditioning exist between rabbits and other mammals including monkeys, cats, rats, and mice. At present, there is almost complete identification of the neural circuitry underlying this form of learning and memory. The essential site of the plasticity for learning resides in the ipsilateral cerebellum, and the hippocampus plays a modulatory role. Mounting evidence indicates that the parallels in neurobiology and behavior extend to humans.

The Cerebellum in Human Eyeblink Conditioning

In Chapter 9 of this volume, the evidence for an essential cerebellar role in eyeblink classical conditioning in humans is presented. Cerebellar lesions in humans that include deep cerebellar nuclei permanently prevent acquisition of CRs. Patients with conditions known to impair cerebellar function such as autism (see Chapter 7) or ataxia-telangiectasia (Mostofsky, Green, Meginley, Christensen & Woodruff-Pak, in press) perform abnormally on eyeblink classical conditioning.

Cerebellar cortical lesions slow the rate of acquisition but do not prevent it entirely in non-human mammals. A role for cerebellar cortex in human eyeblink classical conditioning is suggested in studies that employ eyeblink conditioning along with other behavioral tasks for which cerebellar cortex is essential. For example, one such task, timed-interval tapping predicted performance on eyeblink classical conditioning in two separate samples (Woodruff-Pak & Jaeger, 1998; Woodruff-Pak, Papka & Ivry, 1996). Dual-task studies of eyeblink conditioning in normal adults who also simultaneously perform tasks such as timed-interval tapping demonstrate impaired CR acquisition (Papka, Ivry & Woodruff-Pak, 1995). The dual-task research on eyeblink conditioning is reviewed in Chapter 5 of this volume. Tasks sharing the same substrate such as the cerebellar cortex in the case of timed-interval tapping and eyeblink classical conditioning interfere with one another when performed simultaneously. Tasks with non-cerebellar substrates such as word-stem completion priming show no interference when performed with eyeblink conditioning (Green, Small, Downey-Lamb & Woodruff-Pak, in press).

Other brain structures that are consistently activated during eyeblink classical conditioning in humans and non-human mammals include the striatum and the hippocampus. The striatum plays a role in the timing of the CR (Woodruff-Pak & Papka, 1996) and the hippocampus is normally engaged during acquisition and can modulate the rate of acquisition. Chapter 3 in this volume on PET and Chapter 4 on functional MRI address activations in many brain structures in brain imaging investigations of eyeblink classical conditioning in humans. The most consistent of the observations across the various experiments and imaging methodologies is that the cerebellum and hippocampus are activated during human eyeblink classical conditioning.

The Hippocampus in Human Eyeblink Conditioning

PET studies in humans described in Chapter 3 of this volume identified activations in hippocampus during eyeblink conditioning using the delay procedure in young adults. Data collected using the delay eyeblink conditioning procedure with event-related functional MRI that can parse individual trials by trial-type identified bilateral activation in the hippocampus during trials with CRs and during trials with only URs (Lemieux & Woodruff-Pak, 1999). These results indicate a striking resemblance in the hippocampal responses in human and non-human animal studies in the delay eyeblink classical conditioning procedure.

Additional parallels between human eyeblink classical conditioning and eyeblink conditioning in other mammals involve lesions of the hippocampus. As elaborated in Chapter 10 in this volume, bilateral lesions of the hippocampus do not impair acquisition in the delay eyeblink conditioning procedure. This result has been documented in rabbits for decades (e.g., Schmaltz & Theios, 1972). In the trace classical conditioning procedure, when the CS-US interval exceeds a critical length, acquisition is impaired by hippocampal lesions. The critical interval appears to be shorter in rabbits than it is in humans. Clark and Squire (1998, 1999 and Chapter 11 in this volume) demonstrated that awareness becomes critical for acquisition in the long-trace procedure.

In addition to its role in the long-trace procedure, the hippocampus also plays a modulatory role in the delay eyeblink classical conditioning procedure affecting the rate of acquisition. Although the hippocampus is not essential for acquisition in the delay procedure, disruption or facilitation of the hippocampal activity affects the rate of conditioning. Scopolamine administration disrupts eyeblink conditioning in humans (Bahro, Schreurs, Sunderland & Molchan, 1995; Solomon et al., 1993). In Alzheimer's disease, when the hippocampal cholinergic system is severely disrupted, the rate of acquisition of CRs is severely impaired (see Chapter 8).

OVERVIEW OF EYEBLINK CLASSICAL CONDITIONING: APPLICATIONS IN HUMANS

The knowledge base on neural substrates and mechanisms involved in eyeblink conditioning make it an ideal paradigm for testing theories and brain mechanisms of learning and memory. New applications for the model that will be presented in this volume span a variety of theoretical perspectives and neurological conditions. Among the theoretical perspectives touched by eyeblink classical conditioning are neural network methods of theory-building, theories of brain memory systems, theories of human brain function, and theories in psychopathology.

Neural Network Methods of Theory-Building

The neural network approach is a means by which behavioral theory and brain models can be merged. Complex behavioral interactions and complex brain mechanisms are described using neural network techniques in terms of nonlinear dynamics. Computers are used to solve the differential equations required to formalize neural network models and make predictions about behavior. With this approach, psychological theories and models of the brain can be developed together.

For some years Schmajuk has used neural network approaches to classical eyeblink conditioning in animal models (Schmajuk, 1997). He has been extremely successful in carrying out experiments in rats to extend the empirical results from the NM/eyeblink classical conditioning paradigm in rabbits. He then interprets these results using neural networks models. The beauty of Schmajuk's approach is that he makes use of behavioral data and what he calls a "top-down" approach as well as neurophysiological and anatomical data for a "bottom-up" approach. Basing his neural network models on actual brain circuits, Schmajuk has advanced understanding about medial-temporal lobe structures as well as the cerebellum in eyeblink conditioning.

Chapter 2 in this volume makes a novel contribution in that Schmajuk moves from learning in rats and rabbits to human learning. In Chapter 2 there is the application of contemporary cognitive science techniques and mathematical models to human eyeblink conditioning. These computerized neural network models can be used to explain previously collected data as well as to predict human behavior in different experimental conditions. The power and potential of the neural network approach to human eyeblink conditioning is apparent.

Theories of Brain Memory Systems

A fundamental question concerning the human ability to learn and remember is whether this ability is comprised of multiple systems or is essentially a unitary phenomenon. Many cognitive neuroscientists have provided empirical support for the existence of two (or more) distinct memory systems within the brains of mammalian species (Baddeley, 1992; Nissen, Knopman & Schacter, 1987; Schacter, 1987; Squire, 1987, 1992). Larry Squire named these two forms of learning and memory *declarative* and *nondeclarative* and stated that eyeblink classical conditioning in the delay procedure is a quintessential example of nondeclarative learning. The definitions for these two forms of learning and memory used in Chapter 11 by Clark and Squire are, "Declarative memory provides the capacity for conscious recollection of facts and events. Nondeclarative memory is inaccessible to conscious recollection but is expressed through performance as skills, habits, and certain forms of classical conditioning." Simple delay eyeblink classical conditioning is nondeclarative because medial-temporal lobe circuits are not essential and because acquisition of CRs occurs even when the subject is unaware that learning is occurring.

Brain memory systems are defined in terms of: (a) the cognitive processes by which learning and memory occur and (b) by the neural structures that support those functions. From the cognitive perspective, the subjective awareness of "trying to learn" is typically present on declarative tasks (Shiffrin & Schneider, 1977). In contrast, nondeclarative learning occurs primarily through the performance of a given task. On a nondeclarative task, the subject is not always aware that learning is occurring, but when tested subsequently, the subject's performance is improved.

Different brain circuits subserve declarative and nondeclarative learning and memory. Medial-temporal lobe/diencephalic circuits are critical for declarative learning and memory (Squire, 1992). In contrast, medial-temporal lobe/diencephalic circuits are not essential for nondeclarative learning and memory (e.g., Cohen & Squire, 1980; Corkin, 1968; Milner, 1965). Whereas there is likely one major circuit for declarative learning and memory, different nondeclarative tasks are subserved by different brain memory systems. For example, the cerebellum is essential for eyeblink classical conditioning (e.g., Topka, Valls-Sole, Massaquoi, & Hallett, 1993). Motor skill learning engages motor cortex (e.g., Grafton et al., 1992). Occipital cortex is essential for repetition priming (Gabrieli et al., 1995).

Several chapters in this volume provide contributions to theories of brain memory systems. Documentation of the essential role of the human cerebellum in eyeblink classical conditioning is presented by Schugens, Topka, and Daum in Chapter 9. Using various neurological patient populations, Schugens and associates summarize for humans what Lavond and Crawford (2000) in their chapter in Volume 2 summarize for animals using lesion studies. For all eyeblink classical conditioning procedures, the cerebellum is essential. In patients with diseases of motor systems that do not involve the cerebellum (e.g., Parkinson's disease), eyeblink classical conditioning is normal.

In Chapter 10, McGlinchey-Berroth documents the nondeclarative quality of delay eyeblink classical conditioning by discussing the studies that demonstrate that patients with bilateral lesions in the medial-temporal lobes condition relatively normally using this procedure. McGlinchey-Berroth makes a good case for the fact that some forms of eyeblink classical conditioning, such as the trace procedure, can be considered to be declarative with the medial-temporal lobes essential for learning to occur. It is in the long-trace procedure when the interval between the CS and US is one second that this impairment is most apparent.

A widely held view based on studies of repetition priming was that nondeclarative learning and memory was stable in normal aging (see Chapter 8). On the other hand, declarative memory is clearly impaired in old age. Research with eyeblink conditioning using the delay procedure demonstrated large age-related deficits. These results supported the perspective that nondeclarative learning and memory is not a unitary form. Aging affects the different brain substrates of the various nondeclarative tasks differently, making it likely that behavior would show different age functions on the different nondeclarative measures. The occipital cortex is relatively spared in normal aging and even in Alzheimer's disease, but the cerebellum loses volume over the adult age span. The age-related deficit in cerebellar volume, likely representing age-associated loss of Purkinje cells is probably responsible for impaired eyeblink conditioning in older adults.

Older adults are also less aware than young adults that conditioning is occurring and that they have produced CRs. It is possible that age differences in eyeblink conditioning occur in part because older adults are less aware. However, it is more likely that the lower levels of awareness expressed by older adults on post-conditioning questionnaires stem from the fact that they produce fewer CRs.

Chapter 11 by Clark and Squire focuses on the feature of awareness as it is associated with the declarative/nondeclarative distinction. These researchers were the first to demonstrate clearly that it is when the length of the CS-US interval in the trace procedure extends to one second, that acquisition for amnesic patients does not occur. In normal adults, awareness of the CS-US relationship is also necessary in the long-trace interval for acquisition to occur. Chapter 11 also provides an example of how researchers can combine complex classical conditioning procedures to test human cognition. Clark and Squire used the trace procedure embedded in a discrimination procedure to test conditioning and awareness in older adults and patients with amnesia.

To explain why the medial-temporal lobes become essential when the trace interval exceeds a period around one second long, Green, Ivry, and Woodruff-Pak in Chapter 5 suggest a timing hypothesis. The cerebellum is effective in timing short intervals, but intervals of a second or longer may exhaust the cerebellar networks' retention capacity. Medial-temporal lobe associative capacity may be required to span the gap between the CS and US so that the two stimuli can be associated. From this perspective, the distinction between declarative and nondeclarative in eyeblink classical conditioning procedures rests on the capability of various brain circuits to hold and associate stimulus input.

Theories of Human Brain Function

The advent of imaging techniques has opened a new realm of opportunity to explore brain and behavior relationships. Given that so much is known about the eyeblink classical conditioning circuitry, using the model with brain imaging has benefits for the field of imaging as well as for the understanding of human associative learning.

We know, for example, that the hippocampus is activated during eyeblink conditioning in the simple delay procedure even though learning occurs normally in the absence of the hippocampus. There is a tendency in cognitive neuroscience to attribute an essential role to any structure that is activated during a cognitive task. Lemieux and Woodruff-Pak (1999) observed bilateral hippocampal activation during CR and UR alone trials. The result is quite similar to what electrophysiologists have observed when recording pyramidal cells in CA1 in rabbits. It is an expected result for neuroscientists familiar with animal data on eyeblink conditioning, but it is a surprising result to researchers expecting activations only in structures contributing directly to the learning.

McIntosh and Schreurs make a similar point in Chapter 3 on functional networks engaged in eyeblink conditioning. In particular, they stress their results with PET in which activations in prefrontal cortex were observed during simple delay eyeblink classical conditioning. In animal lesion studies, acquisition of CRs does not require frontal cortex, again emphasizing the fact that activations appear in regions beyond those that are essential.

On the one hand, studies with PET and human eyeblink conditioning demonstrated the correspondence with animal studies in brain regions activated. However, PET studies also depict the distributed nature of brain functions related to learning. In Chapter 3, McIntosh and Schreurs highlight the fact that many contemporary theories have emphasized that brain function emerges from the interactions of specialized regions. In Chapter 3 the perspective is that learning associations results in changes in interactions among several brain areas.

Theory and Integration in Psychopathology

The authors of Chapter 12, McFall, Tracy, Ghose, and Steinmetz have a challenging agenda for the base of knowledge currently available on eyeblink classical conditioning. They see a potential foundation in eyeblink conditioning for the integration of clinical science and cognitive neuroscience in the study of psychopathology. In addition to providing an eloquent rationale for the utility of learning paradigms used in experimental psychology for the exploration of mechanisms of psychopathology, they present data on the application of eyeblink conditioning to an obsessive-compulsive population of subjects.

EYEBLINK CONDITIONING AND LIFE-SPAN DEVELOPMENT

The three chapters on development effectively cover data collected on eyeblink classical conditioning over the entire life-span. Infancy is addressed in Chapter 6, and the infancy and childhood research literature are thoroughly presented in Chapter 7. Chapter 8 traces eyeblink conditioning from young adulthood to old age. Thus, the book includes a thorough review of the human developmental eyeblink conditioning literature. Pulling together the results on human eyeblink conditioning over the life span, it is most interesting that there appears to be an inverted U-shaped curve in rate of acquisition in the delay procedure at a 350 to 500 ms CS-US interval. At the early and later periods of the life span, organisms require longer CS-US intervals for optimal conditioning. The rate of conditioning is relatively slow in infancy, especially at shorter CS-US intervals. Conditioning improves gradually to reach an optimal rate around the age of eight years. Beginning in the decade of the 40s, the rate of conditioning slows, and longer CS-US intervals are required for optimal conditioning. Sears and Steinmetz point out in Chapter 7 that structural and functional brain imaging studies of the cerebellum indicate that progressive developmental events, such as formation of synapses and dendritic processes occur up to the age-range of seven to nine years, paralleling the apparent shift in the optimal rate of conditioning. In Chapter 8, Woodruff-Pak presents anatomical MRI data indicating decreases in cerebellar volume in normal aging. Thus, developmental and aging effects on eyeblink classical conditioning may be the result of changes in the cerebellum.

Ivkovich and her colleagues in Chapter 6 present recent results and techniques for assessing eyeblink conditioning in normal 4- and 5-month-old infants. In our companion volume on animals we include a chapter by Goodlett and associates on conditions analogous to fetal alcohol exposure that cause infant rats to be impaired in eyeblink conditioning. The close parallels in animal and human species on eyeblink conditioning have the implications that testing eyeblink conditioning in infancy may have significant pediatric applications in humans.

Eyeblink conditioning in normal childhood contrasted to abnormal development is described in Chapter 7 by Sears and Steinmetz who contribute a chapter on eyeblink conditioning in autism. The material on autism and the presentation of relevant mutant mouse data to interpret the results provides yet another example of the power of moving between research with humans and non-human mammals in a model with striking parallels between species.

The life-span developmental perspective is completed with Chapter 8 by Woodruff-Pak on eyeblink conditioning in normal aging and Alzheimer's disease. Whereas the data presented in Chapters 6, 7, and 8 on infancy, childhood development, autism, and normal aging emphasize the role of the cerebellum, the data on eyeblink conditioning in Alzheimer's disease implicate the critical modulatory role of the hippocampus.

EYEBLINK CONDITIONING AND DISEASES OF THE NERVOUS SYSTEM

An approach that is adopted in many of the chapters of this volume is the use of patient populations to test hypotheses about associative learning. Neurological patients have provided insights critical for extending the understanding of the neural circuitry essential in eyeblink classical conditioning from animals to humans. At present, Chapters 3 on imaging with PET and Chapter 4 on functional MRI do not include data on patients because the techniques are in the early stages of application to eyeblink classical conditioning. As such, they have only been used during conditioning of normal young adults. However, the potential to understand neurological disease processes as well as the potential to understand more about the neural basis of eyeblink classical conditioning will soon be realized when these techniques are applied to patient populations.

By establishing techniques and normative data on human infant development and eyeblink classical conditioning, Ivkovich and colleagues describe their work in Chapter 6 that is the basis for the investigation of abnormal development. In Chapter 7, Sears and Steinmetz present some of the value of the developmental application by reviewing data on the normal development of eyeblink classical conditioning in childhood and the differences observed in autistic children. There is an enormous potential to apply this well-characterized behavioral and neurobiological model to elaborate our understanding of normal and abnormal development. Extending eyeblink conditioning age functions over the life span in Chapter 8, Woodruff-Pak documents the age-related decline and discusses poor conditioning in another neurological population, patients with Alzheimer's disease.

In Chapter 9, Schugens, Topka, and Daum discuss eyeblink conditioning in neurological patients with motor impairments such as cerebellar lesions and Parkinson's disease and memory impairments such as amnesia. Insights from patients with amnesia of different neurological etiologies are presented by McGlinchey-Berroth in Chapter 10. These patients have been tested with several conditioning procedures to elaborate on the structures that affect eyeblink conditioning in its various forms. Studies with amnesic patients from a number of laboratories are reported and combined with their own work in Chapter 11 by Clark and Squire who present insights about the role of awareness in classical conditioning.

Theory-building in abnormal psychology is addressed by McFall and colleagues in Chapter 12. These investigators view eyeblink classical conditioning as having tremendous potential application to psychopathology. They provide an example by testing the relationship between obsessive-compulsivity and the rate of conditioning. Whereas it had been predicted that individuals with obsessive-compulsive tendencies would classically condition more rapidly, there was previously no empirical test of the theory. Chapter 12 emphasizes the power of such an experimental approach for clinical science.

SUMMARY AND CONCLUSIONS

There is tremendous power in applying the extensive neurobiological and behavioral knowledge base of eyeblink classical conditioning to investigations of human learning and memory. In this volume we present some of these applications. In this chapter we point out the value of the long history of investigation using this paradigm and identify eyeblink classical conditioning procedures and their unique strengths for the study of associative learning. A second overview from a different perspective is provided in Chapter 2 that presents neural network approaches developed in animal models and applied to human associative learning.

Cognitive neuroscience approaches to eyeblink conditioning in normal adults is the next focus of the volume with chapters using classic cognitive neuroscience techniques: PET, fMRI, and dual-task methodology. Chapter 3 on PET emphasizes the complexity of studying the human brain during cognition, even when the task is relatively simple such as in the delay eyeblink classical conditioning procedure. Chapter 4 on fMRI emphasizes the promise of this technique in the relative absence of data published on eyeblink conditioning and fMRI. Improved spatial and temporal resolution of this imaging technique has the potential to identify brain activations during single conditioning trials. Dual-task and repeated measures methodology is the approach presented in Chapter 5. This chapter provides clear evidence for the critical role the cerebellum plays in timing of responding. The chapter also emphasizes the utility of assessing timing in the attempt to understand associative learning.

Eyeblink conditioning over the life span is the topic of the third section of this volume. The combined perspective of the three chapters in this section covers the entire life span. Infancy is addressed in Chapter 6 that presents the careful and detailed methodology required to assess eyeblink classical conditioning in young infants. Chapter 7 covers eyeblink classical conditioning during normal development in childhood and early adolescence as well as is abnormal development in the case of autism. Abnormalities in the cerebellum in autism affect the timing of the CR, again underscoring the value of assessing response timing as emphasized in Chapter 5. The rest of the life span from late adolescence to old age is covered in Chapter 8. Both normal aging and eyeblink classical conditioning and neuropathology as in the case of Alzheimer's disease are covered.

Contributions of abnormal groups to theoretical and empirical understanding are stressed in the fourth section of this volume in four chapters on neurological or psychiatric populations. Neurological patients with motor impairments are discussed with regard to eyeblink conditioning in Chapter 9 that emphasizes the critical role of the cerebellum for acquisition of CRs. Chapter 10 on classical conditioning and amnesia presents the perspective of spared or impaired conditioning, depending on the conditioning procedure used. With the delay procedure, bilateral medial-temporal lobe lesions do not affect acquisition, but with the long-trace procedure acquisition is impaired. Conditioning in amnesic patients and age-matched adults with regards to participants' awareness of learning is the topic for Chapter 11. It is in this chapter (and also in Chapters 8 and 10) that we see how eyeblink classical conditioning procedures can be either declarative or nondeclarative. The role of eyeblink classical conditioning in clinical science is addressed in Chapter 12 that concludes the volume with an optimistic view of the potential of this paradigm. The authors contend that eyeblink classical conditioning is such a powerful tool that its utility will make clinicians and cognitive neuroscientists unite in the endeavor to understand and treat various forms of psychopathology.

REFERENCES

Baddeley, A. (1992). Working memory. *Science, 255*, 556-559.

Bahro, M., Schreurs, B.G., Sunderland, T., & Molchan, S.E. (1995). The effects of scopolamine, lorazepam, and glycopyrrolate on classical conditioning of the human eyeblink response. *Psychopharmacology, 122*, 395-400.

Cason, H. (1922). The conditioned eyelid reaction. *Journal of Experimental Psychology, 5*, 153-195.

Cason, H. (1923). A note on the conditioned eyelid reaction. *Journal of Experimental Psychology, 6*, 82-83.

Cason, H. (1924). The concept of backward association. *American Journal of Psychology, 35*, 217-221.
Cason, H. (1925). General aspects of the conditioned response. *Psychological Review, 32*, 285-331.
Clark, R.E., & Squire, L.R. (1998). Classical conditioning and brain systems: The role of awareness. *Science, 280*, 77-81.
Clark, R.E., & Squire, L.R. (1999). Human eyeblink classical conditioning: Effects of manipulating awareness of the stimulus contingencies. *Psychological Science, 10*, 14-18.
Cohen, N.J., & Squire, L.R. (1980). Preserved learning and retention of pattern analyzing skill in amnesia: Dissociation of knowing how and knowing that. *Science, 210*, 207-209.
Corkin, S. (1968). Acquisition of motor skill after bilateral medial temporal-lobe excision. *Neuropsychologia, 6*, 255-265.
Dodge, R. (1913). The refractory phase of the normal wink reflex. *American Journal of Psychology, 24*, 1-7.
Gabrieli, J.D.E., Fleischman, D.A., Keane, M.M., Raminger, S., Rinaldi, J., Morrell, F., & Wilson, R. (1995). Double dissociation between memory systems underlying explicit and implicit memory in the human brain. *Psychological Science, 6*, 76-82.
Grafton, S.T., Mazziotta, J.C., Presty, S., Friston, K.J., Frackowiak, R.S.J., & Phelps, M.E. (1992). Functional anatomy of human procedural learning determined with regional cerebral blood flow and PET. *Journal of Neuroscience, 12*, 2542-2548.
Green, J.T., Small, E.M., Downey-Lamb, M.M., & Woodruff-Pak, D.S. (in press). Dual task performance of eyeblink classical conditioning and visual repetition priming: Separate brain memory systems. *Neuropsychology.*
Green, J.T., & Woodruff-Pak, D.S. (in press). Eyeblink classical conditioning: Hippocampal formation is for neutral stimulus associations as cerebellum is for association-response. *Psychological Bulletin.*
Lemieux, S.K. & Woodruff-Pak, D.S. (1999). An event-related functional MRI study of eyeblink classical conditioning in young adults. *Society for Neuroscience Abstracts, 25.*
Milner, B. (1965). Visually guided maze learning in man: Effect of bilateral hippocampal, bilateral frontal, and unilateral cerebral lesions. *Neuropsychologia, 3*, 339-351.
Mostofsky, S.H., Green, J.T., Meginley, M., Christensen, J.R., & Woodruff-Pak, D.S. (in press). Conditioning in identical twins with ataxia-telangiectasia. *Neurocase.*
Papka, M., Ivry, R.B., & Woodruff-Pak, D.S. (1995). Selective disruption of eyeblink classical conditioning by concurrent tapping. *Neuroreport, 6*, 1493-1497.
Nissen, M.J., Knopman, D.S., & Schacter, D.L. (1987). Neurochemical dissociation of memory systems. *Neurology, 37*, 789-794.
Schacter, D.L. (1987). Implicit memory: History and current status. *Journal of Experimental Psychology: Learning, Memory, and Cognition, 13*, 501-518.
Schmajuk, N.A. (1997). *Animal Learning and Cognition: A Neural Network Approach.* Cambridge, UK: Cambridge University Press.
Schmaltz, L.W., & Theios, J. (1972). Acquisition and extinction of a classically conditioned response in hippocampectomized rabbits (*oryctolagus cuniculus*). *Journal of Comparative and Physiological Psychology, 79*, 328-333.
Shiffrin, R.M., & Schneider, W. (1977). Controlled and automatic human information processing: II. Perceptual learning, automatic attending, and a general theory. *Psychological Review, 84*, 127-190.
Solomon , P.R., Groccia-Ellison, M., Flynn, D., Mirak, J., Edwards, K.R., Dunehew, A., & Stanton, M.E. (1993). Disruption of human eyeblink conditioning after central cholinergic blockade with scopolamine. *Behavioral Neuroscience, 107*, 271-279.
Squire, L.R. (1987). *Memory and Brain.* NY: Oxford University Press.
Squire, L.R. (1992). Memory and the hippocampus: A synthesis from findings with rats, monkeys, and humans. *Psychological Review, 99*, 195-231.
Topka, H., Valls-Sole, J., Massaquoi, S.G., & Hallett, M. (1993). Deficit in classical conditioning in patients with cerebellar degeneration. *Brain, 116*, 961-969.
Weiss, O. (1910-1911). Die zeitliche Dauer Des Lidschlages. *Zsch F Psychol U Physiol D Sinnesorg, 45, Abstract II*, 307-312.
Woodruff-Pak, D.S., & Papka, M. (1996). Huntington's disease and eyeblink classical conditioning: Normal learning but abnormal timing. *Journal of the International Neuropsychological Society, 2*, 323-334.
Woodruff-Pak, D.S., Papka, M., & Ivry, R.B. (1996). Cerebellar involvement in eyeblink classical conditioning in humans. *Neuropsychology, 10*, 443-458.
Woodruff-Pak, D.S., & Steinmetz, J. E. (Eds.) (2000). Eyeblink Classical Conditioning: Volume II -

Animal Models. Boston: Kluwer Academic Publishers.
Zwaardemaker, H., & Lans, L.J. (1899). Uber ein Stadium relativer Unerregparkeit als Ursache des intermitterenden Charakters des Lidschlagreflexes. *Centbl F Physiol, 13*, 325-329.

2 NEURAL NETWORK APPROACHES TO CLASSICAL CONDITIONING

Nestor A. Schmajuk
Duke University

INTRODUCTION

In recent years, the functional anatomy of human eyeblink conditioning has been described using positron-emission tomography techniques (Blaxton, Zeffiro, Gabrieli, Bookheinmer, Carrillo, Theodore & Disterhoft, 1996; Logan & Grafton, 1995; Mcintosh & Schreurs, this volume; Molchan, Sunderland, Mcintosh, Herscovitch & Schreurs, 1994). The data support functions related to learning of brain regions that include cerebellar, hippocampal, ventral striatum, thalamic and cortical regions. But what are these functions?

In the past, I have addressed a similar question by portraying neural network models of animal classical conditioning and then proposing how elements in the model correspond to different brain regions and circuits. In building the neural network my colleagues and I made use, not only of behavioral data (a top-down approach), but also of neurophysiological and anatomical evidence (a bottom-up approach). These models include Schmajuk and DiCarlo's (1992) configural model of classical conditioning, Schmajuk, Lam, and Gray's (1996) attentional model, and Buhusi and Schmajuk's (1996) attentional-configural model.

Schmajuk and DiCarlo (1992) described classical conditioning in terms of a real-time, multilayer network that portrays stimulus configuration. The network [a] incorporates a layer of "hidden" units positioned between input and output units, [b] includes inputs that are connected to the output directly as well as indirectly through the hidden-unit layer, and [c] employs a biologically plausible backpropagation procedure to train the hidden-unit layer. In the multilayer network, the information coming from the input units is recoded by the hidden units into internal representations that are regarded as configural stimuli. Therefore, a conditioned stimulus (CS) presented at the input accrues a *direct* association with the unconditioned stimulus (US) at the output, and becomes *configured* with other CSs in hidden units that in turn become associated with the US at the output. The model defines the interaction between CS-US associations and configural stimuli-US associations. Schmajuk and DiCarlo (1992) showed that the model can describe a large number of classical conditioning paradigms. Recently, Schmajuk, Lamoureux, and Holland (1998; Lamoureux, Buhusi & Schmajuk, 1998) demonstrated that a version of the Schmajuk and DiCarlo (1992) model describes most of the features of occasion setting. Furthermore, Buhusi and Schmajuk (1999) combined the Schmajuk and DiCarlo

(1992) configural model with the Grossberg and Schmajuk (1989) model of timing, in order to describe the temporal and associative properties of simple conditioning, compound conditioning, and occasion setting.

The Schmajuk-DiCarlo (1992) configural model correctly describes neural activity in hippocampus and medial septum during classical conditioning. In addition, the model is very successful at describing the effects of nonselective as well as selective hippocampal lesions in numerous conditioning paradigms, including occasion setting (Schmajuk & Blair, 1993; Schmajuk & Buhusi, 1997). Whereas selective lesions of the hippocampus damage only the hippocampus proper, i.e., CA3 and CA1 regions; non-selective lesions of the hippocampal formation damage the dentate, hippocampus proper, subiculum, presubiculum, and entorhinal cortex.

In order to describe attentional phenomena not handled by the configural model, Schmajuk et al. (1996) presented an attentional model of classical conditioning that describes most of the features of latent inhibition. The network assumes that the effectiveness of a CS to establish associations with the US is proportional to a variable called Novelty, defined as proportional to the sum of the absolute value of the differences between predicted and observed amplitudes of all present stimuli, that is proportional to the sum of the individual novelty of every stimulus (CSs and USs) present in the environment. The model describes latent inhibition because Novelty and, therefore, CS effectiveness, decrease during CS preexposure.

Buhusi and Schmajuk (1996) combined the Schmajuk and DiCarlo (1992) and the Schmajuk et al. (1996) models into an attentional-configural model that proved capable of addressing an extensive number of classical conditioning paradigms, including detailed features of both occasion setting and latent inhibition. Importantly, the model was mapped onto the brain circuitry and, consequently, it was able to describe the effects of neurophysiological and pharmacological manipulations on conditioning.

In this Chapter I describe an updated mapping of the Buhusi and Schmajuk (1996) attentional-configural model, based on suggestions presented by Gray, Buhusi, and Schmajuk (1997) and Schmajuk, Buhusi, and Gray (1998) for the Schmajuk-Lam-Gray (1996) attentional model. I also describe some new results separately obtained with the configural and attentional models. Although the model was developed based on -- and applied to-- animal data, I show how it describes the functions of cerebellar, hippocampal, ventral striatum, and cortical regions in human eyeblink conditioning.

THE MODEL

The network illustrated here is a real-time model that portrays the temporal dynamics of classical conditioning. The dynamics of the model's variables are formalized by a set of differential equations that depict changes in the values of neural activities and connectivities as a function of time (see Appendix A in Buhusi & Schmajuk, 1996). Figure 1 shows a detailed diagram of the network that includes [a] a feedback system, [b] an attentional system, [c] a configural system, [d] a model of the environment, [e] a novelty system, and [f] a behavioral inhibition system.

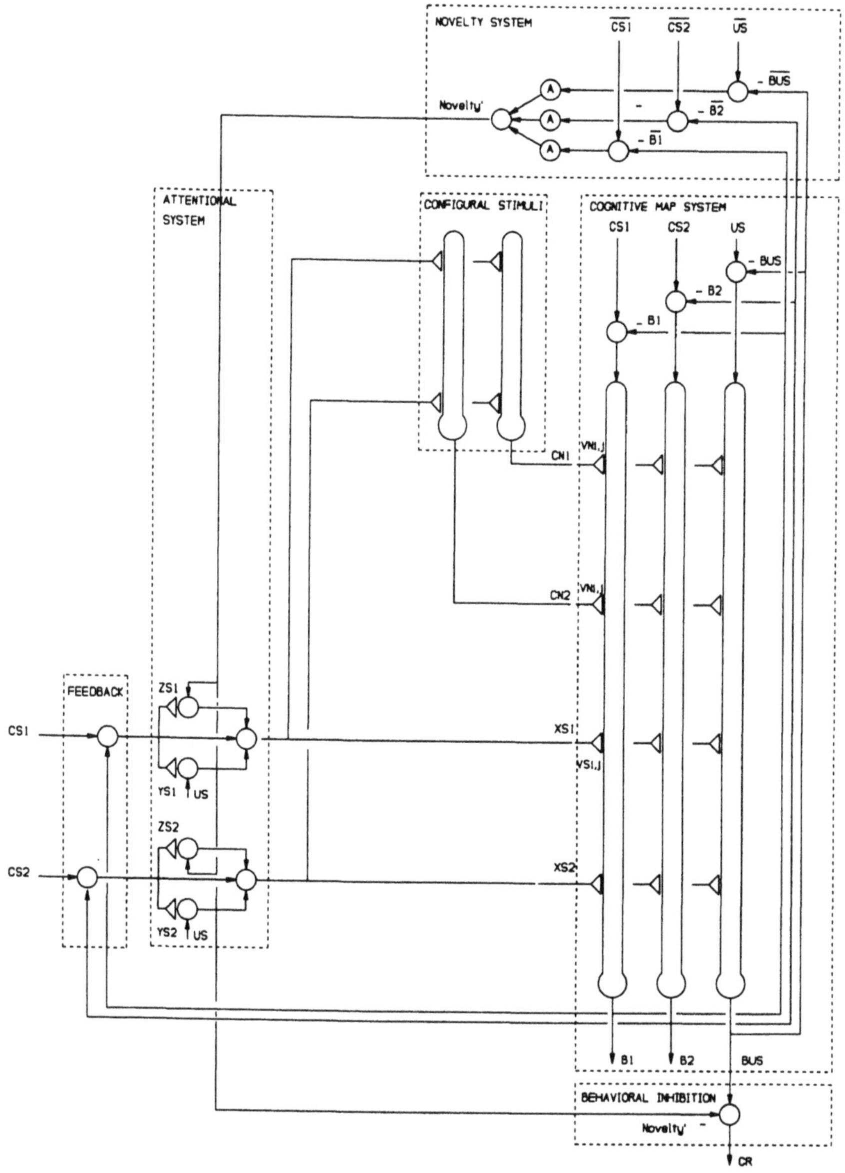

Figure 1. Diagram of the attentional-cognitive model. CS_i: conditioned stimulus; ZS_i, YS_i: attentional associations; XS_i: CS_i internal representation; XN_j: configural representation; VS_{ik}: XS_i-CS_k association; VS_{iUS}: XS_i-US association; VN_j: XN_j-US associations; VH_{ij}: XS_i-XN_j association; US: unconditioned stimulus; B_k: CS_k aggregate prediction; B_{US}: US aggregate prediction; $\overline{C}\,\overline{S}_k$: CS_k average observed value; $\overline{B}_k$: CS_k average predicted value. Arrows represent fixed synapses. Triangles represent variable synapses.

Feedback System

In order to allow a CS to establish associations with other CSs or the US even when separated by a temporal gap (trace conditioning), CS_1 and CS_2 activate a short-term memory trace, τ_i. τ_i increases over time to a maximum when CS_i is present and then gradually decays back to its initial value when CS_i is absent.

In order to infer novel predictions (cognitive mapping), the predictions of CS_1 and CS_2, namely B_1 and B_2, are added to τ_1 and τ_2 in the feedback system. This recurrent property allows the network to describe sensory preconditioning (Brogden, 1939) and second-order conditioning (Pavlov, 1927). In addition, this feedback loop allows the network to prolong the duration and increase the salience of its traces τ_1 and τ_2, therefore facilitating trace conditioning.

Attentional System

The outputs of the feedback system become associated with the total novelty, Novelty, detected by the system. This association is represented by attentional memory zs_i. When Novelty is relatively large, zs_i increases. When Novelty is relatively small, zs_i decreases.

Attentional memory, ys_i, reflects the association between the output of the feedback system and the US. The outputs of the attentional system, XS_i, proportional to both zs_i and ys_i, reach the model of the environment.

Configural System

In order to account for nonlinear protocols, the output of the attentional system, XS_i, becomes *configured* in a hidden layer. Stimulus configuration is achieved by adjusting XS_i-hidden unit associations (VH_{ij}: XS_i-XN_j associations). The outputs of the configural system, XN_j, are conveyed to the model of the environment.

Model of the Environment

The model of the environment receives inputs from the attentional system, XS_i, and inputs from the configural system, XN_j. XS_i becomes associated with the CSs and the US directly (VS_{ik}: XS_i-CS_k association; VS_{iUS}: XS_i-US associations), as well as indirectly through the hidden-unit layer (VN_j: XN_j-US associations). Both direct and indirect connections compete with each other to predict the CSs and the US.

Because attentional memories zs_i and ys_i control the magnitude of the internal representation XS_i, they indirectly control storage and retrieval of XS_i-CS_k and XN_j-US associations in the model of the world.

In general, the model of the environment consists of XS-CS, XS-US, XN-CS and XN-US associations stored in a recurrent autoassociative network (Kohonen, 1977). However, for simplicity, the Buhusi and Schmajuk (1996) version of the model does not include XN-CS associations.

The outputs of the model of the environment are the *aggregate predictions* of CS_k (a CS or the US), B_k. *Aggregate prediction* B_k is used to compute VS_{ik} and VN_j and reaches the feedback system to add to τ_k.

Novelty System

This system computes the total novelty detected by the system in the environment at a given time. Novelty is proportional to the sum of the absolute value of the difference between the average observed value of CS_k, $\overline{C}\,\overline{S}_k$: , and the average predicted value of CS_k, $\overline{B}_k$. The output of the novelty system reaches the attentional system, to control the values of zs_i and the behavioral inhibition system, to control the magnitude of the conditioned response (CR).

Behavioral Inhibition System

We assume that CR amplitude [a] increases proportionally to the magnitude of the prediction of the US, B_{US}, and [b] decreases in proportion to the magnitude of the OR. When applied to a taste aversion paradigm (Lubow, 1989, page 11), consumption decreases in proportion to both [a] B_{US} and [b] OR (Buhusi, Dunn, & Schmajuk, unpublished observations).

MAPPING OF THE MODEL ONTO THE BRAIN

Figure 2 presents how variables in the network described in Figure 1 are mapped onto the brain. The mapping is based on studies using different brain manipulations (including lesions, recordings, drug administration) during classical conditioning.

Cerebellum

Considering that classical conditioning of the eyeblink or nictitating membrane response is impaired after cerebellar lesions, we assume that XS_i-US and XN_j-US associations are stored in cerebellar areas, thereby controlling the generation of CRs. Simple stimuli, XS_i, and configural stimuli, XN_j, reach the pontine nuclei. In the cerebellum, these sensory representations are associated with the US representation conveyed by the dorsal accessory olive. The cerebellar output reflects the magnitude of $XS_i\ VS_{iUS}$ and $XN_j\ VN_j$ and generates a CR. $XS_i\ VS_{iUS}$ and $XN_j\ VN_j$ values are fed back to the dorsal accesory olive.

To the extent that the activity of pyramidal cells in the hippocampus reflects the temporal topography of the CR, and this neural activity depends on the integrity of cerebellar circuits (Sears & Steinmetz, 1990), Figure 2 shows that copies of $XS_i\ VS_{iUS}$ and $XN_j\ VN_j$ are relayed from the cerebellum to the entorhinal cortex and the

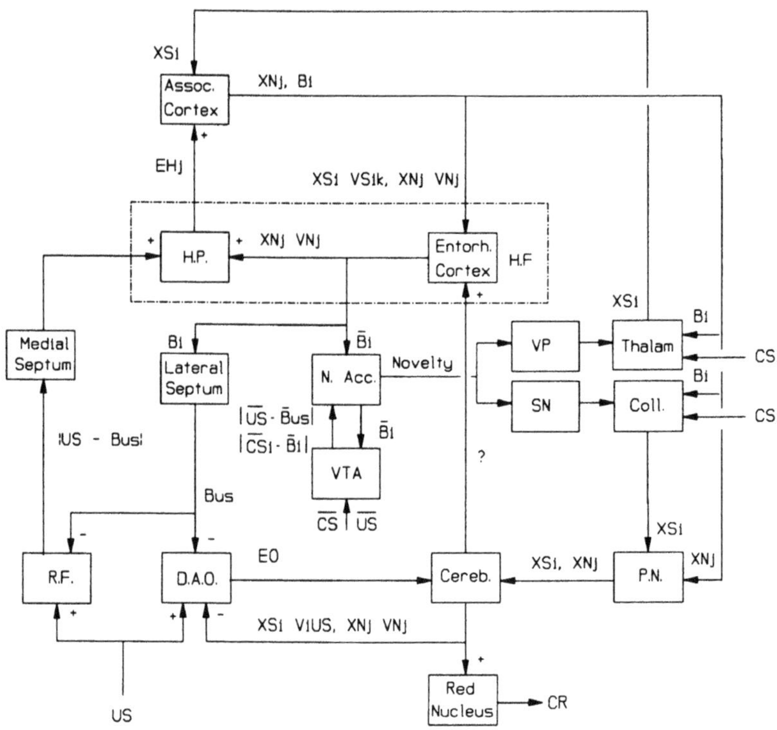

Figure 2. Mapping of the network onto a schematic diagram of the brain. CS_i: conditioned stimulus; US: unconditioned stimulus; XS_i: CS_i internal representation; XN_j: configural stimulus; VS_{ik}: XS_i-CS_k association; CR: conditioned response; B_k: CS_k aggregate prediction; B_{US}: US aggregate prediction; θ : theta rhythm; EO = (US - B_{US}) : output error; EHj = θ XN_j VN_j: hidden unit error. Assoc. Cortex: association cortex; Entorh. Cortex: entorhinal cortex; H.F.: hippocampal formation, H.P.: hippocampus proper; R.F.: reticular formation; D.A.O.: dorsal accessory olive; Cereb.: cerebellum; P.N.: pontine nucleus; Thalam.: thalamus; N.Acc.: nucleus accumbens; VP : ventral pallidus; S.Coll.: superior colliculi; VTA: ventral tegmental area. SN: substantia nigra.

hippocampus.

Figure 2 shows that, as suggested by Schmajuk and DiCarlo (1992), the hippocampus inhibits (through the lateral septum) the dorsal accessory olive, which conveys the US input to cerebellar areas. Therefore, the hippocampus controls the formation of XS_i-US and XN_j-US associations, and phenomena such as blocking, by inhibiting the dorsal accessory olive.

Hippocampal System

Schmajuk and Moore (1988) proposed that the hippocampus computes [a] the aggregate predictions of environmental events, B_k, including that of the US, B_{US}, and [b] the error signals needed to train the cortex. Whereas the aggregate predictions B_k regulate the *competition* among stimuli to establish associations with stimulus k, error signals modulate changes in the associations between conditioned stimuli.

Figure 2 shows that neural activity proportional to $XS_i\ VS_{ik}$ and $XN_j\ VN_j$ reaches the hippocampus through an yet uncertain cerebellar-entorhinal cortex pathway. This information is [a] summed to generate aggregate predictions, B_k, and [b] combined with the medial septal input θ to compute the error signal for hidden units, $EH_j = \theta\ XN_j\ VN_j$. B_{US} is used to determine the error signal, $(US - B_{US})$, that controls the association of different XSs and XNs with the US in the cerebellum. According to the model total hippocampal neural activity is proportional to $\Sigma_k B_k + \Sigma_j\ \theta\ XN_j\ VN_j$.

Selective Lesions of the Hippocampus Proper

Selective lesions of the hippocampus produced by ibotenic acid damage only the hippocampus proper, i.e., CA3 and CA1 regions. In the context of the model, lesions of the hippocampus proper can be described by assuming that [a] changes in cortical CS_i-CS_j associations are equal to zero and [b] the error term controlling changes in CS_i-hidden units associations is equal to zero (Schmajuk & Blair, 1993).

Buhusi and Schmajuk (1996) assumed that CS_i-CS_i associations, which produce habituation to CS_i by predicting itself, remain unaffected because lesions of the dorsal hippocampus do not impair habituation of the startle response (Leaton, 1981).

Nonselective Lesions of the Hippocampal Formation

Non-selective lesions of the hippocampus produced by aspiration or colchicine-kainic acid, that damage the dentate, hippocampus proper, subiculum, presubiculum, and entorhinal cortex, are best characterized as lesions of the hippocampal formation (Jarrard & Davidson, 1991). In the context of the configural model, Schmajuk and DiCarlo (1992) proposed that hippocampal formation lesions can be described by assuming that [a] aggregate predictions B_k are equal to zero and [b] changes in cortical CS_i-CS_j associations are equal to zero, and [c] the error term controlling changes in CS_i-hidden units associations is equal to zero.

Lateral Septum

Because neural activity in the lateral septum during acquisition of classical conditioning is similar to that recorded in hippocampal pyramidal cells (Berger & Thompson, 1978a), Schmajuk and DiCarlo (1992) proposed the existence of an excitatory hippocampal output (from CA3) to the lateral septum, proportional to B_k (see Figure 2).

Medial Septum

Axons of the medial septum project to the dentate gyrus, CA3, and to a lesser extent CA1 region, via the dorsal fornix and fimbria. Medial septal input has a major role in the generation of hippocampal theta rhythm and in controlling the responsiveness of pyramidal cells in CA1 and CA3 regions and of granule cells in the dentate gyrus. It has been suggested that medial septal "modulation" of dentate granule cells, CA1 and CA3 pyramidal cells is mediated through [a] a GABAergic inhibition of inhibitory interneurons and/or [b] a cholinergic excitation of pyramidal and granule cells (Bilkey & Goddard, 1975; Krnjevic, Ropert & Casullo, 1988; Rudell, Fox & Ranck, 1980; Stewart & Fox, 1990). Besides modulating pyramidal and granule cell activity, the medial septum controls the generation of LTP in perforant path-dentate gyrus synapses (Robinson & Racine, 1986; Robinson, 1986; Weisz, Clark & Thompson, 1984).

Figure 2 shows that, as suggested by Schmajuk and DiCarlo (1992), the reticular formation receives information about US and B_{US} and acts on the medial septum to control the value of theta, $\theta = |US - B_{US}|$. Figure 2 also shows that the hippocampus receives information related to θ from the medial septum.

Cholinergic System

Because medial septal "modulation" of dentate granule cells, CA1 and CA3 pyramidal cells is mediated through cholinergic activation of pyramidal and granule cells, we assume that scopolamine decreases and physostigmine increases the value of θ, and therefore of $EH_j = \theta\, XN_j\, VN_j$.

Association Cortex

Input-hidden unit associations and XS_i-CS_k associations are assumed to be stored in cortical areas. Hippocampal output is conveyed to association cortex to regulate stimulus configuration and the formation of XS_i-CS_k associations. Cortical lesions, which refer to the extensive removal of the neocortex, are described by making XS_i-CS_k and VH_{ij} equal to zero.

In Figure 2, association cortex projections to the pontine nuclei are responsible for conveying XN_j information to the cerebellum, where they become associated with the US. Entorhinal cortex provides the hippocampus with information about XS_i VS_{ik} and

$XN_j\ VN_j$.

Nucleus Acumbens

We assume that Novelty = $\Sigma_k \mid \overline{CS}_k - \overline{B}_k \mid$ is represented by the ventral tegmental area (VTA) input to the core of the nucleus accumbens (NA). Whereas $\overline{CS}_k$ input to the VTA might be provided by cholinergic neurons in the pendunculopontine tegmental nucleus (Dormont, Conde & Farin, 1998), $\overline{B}_k$ represents the hippocampal input that reaches the VTA through the shell of the NA.

As shown in Figure 2, the output of the NA reaches the thalamus through the ventral pallidus and the superior colliculi through the substantia nigra, in order to regulate attention, zs_i, to the input CSs.

Dopaminergic System

Gray et al. (1997) proposed that Novelty = $\Sigma_k \mid \overline{CS}_k - \overline{B}_k \mid$ is coded by the dopaminergic input from VTA to the accumbens (see also Schmajuk, Buhusi & Gray, 1998). Schmajuk et al. (1998) assumed that dopaminergic agonists (such as amphetamine) increase Novelty, and dopaminergic antagonists (such as haloperidol) decrease Novelty.

Summary

Table 1 summarizes how different variables in the attentional-configural model are mapped onto different brain regions. By assuming that the activation of the neural elements coding different model variables represents histograms of single neural activity, activation values of neural elements in the model (Figure 1) can be used to describe neural activity in the brain diagram (Figure 2).

HOW THE MODEL DESCRIBES ANIMAL DATA

This section illustrates how the model describes a broad range of experimental results from the animal learning literature, including neural activity in various brain areas, the effects of lesioning different brain regions, of pharmacological manipulations, and of long-term potentiation.

Neuronal Activity

In the brain-mapped model, the activity of neural elements represents activity of specific neural populations. Table 2 summarizes and compares simulated and experimental results.

Table 1. Mapping of the variables in the model for the eyeblink preparation

Symbol	Variable	Type	Location
CS_i	Observed value of the CS	Physical input	Environment
US	Observed value of the US	Physical input	Environment
OR	Orienting Response	Physical output	Environment
CR	Conditioned response	Physical output	Environment
τ_i	Short-term memory trace	Neural activity	Colliculus, thalamus
B_i	Aggregate prediction of CS_i	Neural activity	Entorhinal cortex, subiculum
B_{US}	Aggregate prediction of the US	Neural activity	Entorhinal cortex, subiculum
z_i	Attentional memory	Synaptic weight	Colliculus, thalamus
Novelty	Total novelty	Neural activity	Nucleus accumbens
X_i	Output of the attentional system	Neural activity	Colliculus, thalamus
V_{ik}	Association between X_i and stimulus k	Synaptic weight	Association cortex
V_{ii}	Association between X_i and stimulus i	Synaptic weight	Subcortical areas
V_{iUS}	Association between XS_i and the US	Synaptic weight	Cerebellum
$(CS_k - B_k)$	Output error for stimulus k	Neural activity	Reticular formation
$(US - B_{US})$	Output error for the US	Neural activity	Dorsal accessory olive
$\overline{CS}_k$	Average observed value of CS_k	Neural activity	Nucleus accumbens
$\overline{B}_k$	Average predicted value of CS_k	Neural activity	Nucleus accumbens
OR	Amplitude of the Orienting Response	Neural activity	Mesencephalic motor region
CR	Amplitude of the conditioned response	Neural activity	Red nucleus

Hippocampal Activity

Pyramidal cell activity is computed as $\Sigma_k B_k + \Sigma_j \theta XN_j VN_j$. Because both the CR and pyramidal activity are proportional to $\Sigma_i XS_i VS_{iUS} + \Sigma_j XN_j VN_j$, in agreement with empirical results (Berger & Thompson, 1978a; Berger, Rinaldi, Weisz & Thompson, 1983), pyramidal activity is positively correlated with the topography of the CR.

Simulated CR amplitude and hippocampal neural activity during the CS and US periods for normal animals show that, according to the attentional-configural model, changes in hippocampal activity during the US period precede both behavioral acquisition and extinction. These results are in agreement with experimental data (Berger & Thompson, 1978a; Berger et al., 1983; Berger & Thompson, 1982). However, in partial disagreement with empirical data (Berger & Thompson, 1982), simulated changes in pyramidal activity during the CS period precede behavioral changes during acquisition but not during extinction.

Medial Septal Neural Activity

In the model, medial septal neural activity is proportional to absolute difference between actual and predicted US values, $\theta = |US - B_{US}|$. Because the medial septum controls the generation of theta, hippocampal theta rhythm is also proportional to this value. In agreement with Berger and Thompson (1978b), because hippocampal activity is proportional to B_{US}, medial septal and hippocampal activity are negatively correlated during acquisition of classical conditioning.

Table 2. Simulations of neural activity compared with experimental results in different learning paradigms

Brain Region	Paradigm	Data	Model
Hippocampus	Acquisition	Increases	Increases
	CS Period	Increases-decreases	Increases-decreases
		Precedes Behavior	Precedes Behavior
	Extinction	Decreases	Decreases
	CS Period	Precedes Behavior	Succeeds Behavior*
	Acquisition	Increases	Increases
	US Period	Increases-decreases	Increases-decreases
		Precedes behavior	Precedes Behavior
	Extinction	Decreases	Decreases
	US Period	Precedes Behavior	Precedes Behavior
Lateral Septum	Acquisition	Increases	Increases
Medial Septum	Acquisition	Decreases	Decreases
Striatum	Acquisition		
	Early	Reflects US	Reflects US
	Late	Reflects CR	Reflects CR
Dorsal Accessory Olive	Acquisition	Decreases	Decreases

Note. ? = no available data, * = the model fails to describe accurately the experimental data.

Simulated medial septum neural activity during the US period for normal animals demonstrate that paired and unpaired cases show reductions in $|US - B_{US}|$ because the US is predicted by the CS in the paired case and by the sound of the US (an air puff) in the second case. Because the US is better predicted by the CS and the sound of the air puff than by the air puff alone, the final value of $|US - B_{US}|$ during the US period is smaller in the paired case than in the unpaired case. These simulation results are in agreement with experimental data (Berger & Thompson, 1978b).

Ventral Striatal Activity

As mentioned, we assume that Novelty = $\Sigma_k \mid \overline{C}\,\overline{S}_k - \overline{B}_k \mid$ is represented by the VTA input to the core of the NA, a part of the ventral striatum. White, Miller, White, Dike, Rebec & Steinmetz (1994) recorded neural activity in the rabbit's striatum during classical eyelid conditioning. Striatal neurons increased their responding to the US during the early phase of training and to the CR as training progressed. This pattern is well described by the model. At the beginning of training, $\overline{B}_{us}$ is very small and Novelty ~ | $\overline{C}\,\overline{S}_{us}$ |, that is, activity increases when the US is presented. As training progresses, $\overline{B}_{us}$ is large and Novelty ~ | - $\overline{B}_{us}$ |, that is, activity reflects the magnitude of the CR.

Brain Lesions

In the brain-mapped model, lesions of neural elements represent equivalent manipulations of specific neural populations in the brain. Lesions of the cerebellum are described by assuming that CS_i-US and CN_j-US associations are absent. Selective lesions of the hippocampus, obtained by ibotenic acid injections, are described by assuming that [a] the error term controlling changes in cortical CS_i-CS_j associations is equal to zero and [b] the error term controlling changes in CS_i-hidden units associations is equal to zero.

Non-selective lesions of the hippocampus, produced by aspiration or colchicine-kainic acid, are described by assuming that [a] aggregate predictions B_k are equal to zero and [b] changes in cortical CS_i-CS_j associations are equal to zero, and [c] the error term controlling changes in CS_i-hidden units associations is equal to zero. Cortical lesions, obtained by extensive removal of the neocortex, are described by making asociations VS_{ik}, VN_i and VH_{ij} equal to zero.

In this section we apply the brain-mapped model to the analysis of the effect of different brain lesions in the following cases: delay conditioning, acquisition and extinction series, trace conditioning, overshadowing and blocking, discrimination acquisition and reversal, conditioned inhibition and inhibitory conditioning, simultaneous and serial feature-positive discriminations (in which the stimuli act as simple CSs and occasion setters), negative patterning, positive patterning, contextual effects, sensory pre-conditioning, transitivity and symmetry, latent inhibition (acquisition and contextual effects). Whereas cerebellar lesions eliminate eyeblink conditioning, lesions of the hippocampus and the cortex have more subtle effects, many of them described by the model.

Simulated results are described for normal animals, and for animals with lesions of the hippocampus proper (HPL), hippocampal formation (HFL), and cortical regions (CL). Table 3 compares simulated and experimental results and also shows novel predictions.

Delay Conditioning

A considerable amount of data shows that lesions of several cerebellar areas permanently abolish the classically conditioned NM and eyeblink response in the rabbit and the rat (Thompson, 1986; Skelton, 1988). Acquisition of delay conditioning of the rabbit NM response has been reported to be slightly retarded or unaffected by bilateral cortical lesions (Oakley & Russell, 1972). Acquisition of trace conditioning of the rabbit NM response has been reported to be unaffected by cortical lesions (Yeo, Hardiman, Moore & Russell, 1984). There results are correctly addressed by the attentional-configural model.

Acquisition and Extinction Series

Consistent with Schmaltz and Theios (1972), the attentional-configural model shows that animals with lesions of the hippocampal formation display faster acquisition than normals in the first acquisition series using delay conditioning. In the normal case, and in agreement with Schmaltz and Theios (1972), the attentional-configural model predicts faster extinction over series. Also in agreement with Schmaltz and Theios' (1972) results in animals with lesions of the hippocampal formation, simulations show impairment in extinction over series. However, in disagreement with Schmaltz and Theios' (1972) data, the attentional-configural model shows impairment in the first series of extinction for animals with lesions of the hippocampal formation.

Trace conditioning

In animals, trace conditioning is sometimes (e.g., Solomon, Vander Schaaf, Thompson & Weisz, 1986; Moyer, Deyo & Disterhoft, 1990), but not always (e.g., Port, Romano, Steinmetz, Mikhail & Patterson, 1986; James, Hardiman & Yeo, 1987; Moyer et al., 1990), impaired by hippocampal lesions. Schmajuk and DiCarlo (1991) showed that in the absence of hippocampal feedback to the CS inputs, which enhance the amplitude and duration of the CS trace (τ_i), both animals with lesions of the hippocampus proper and of the hippocampal formation show impairments in trace conditioning. Computer simulations with the attentional-configural model show that, in the absence of the aggregate predictions of B_i (computed in the hippocampus), amplitude and duration of τ_i decrease thereby impairing trace conditioning.

Kim, Clark and Thompson (1995) reported that hippocampectomy impairs trace eyeblink conditioning in rabbits when the lesion is performed one day, but not one month, after training. Although we have not analyzed this particular case, Schmajuk et al. (1996) have applied the attentional model to the description of the effect of delayed testing on the magnitude of latent inhibition. In agreement with Kraemer, Randall and Carbary's (1991) data, the intact model shows latent inhibition at the one-day but not at seven- or 21-day retention intervals. The result shows that, as normal animals, the model is capable of processing information after training has been completed.

Overshadowing and Blocking

Consistent with Rickert, Bent, Lane and French's (1978) and Schmajuk, Spear and Isaacson's (1983), but not with Garrud, Rawlins, Mackintosh, Goodal, Cotton and Feldon's (1984) data, the attentional-configural model predicts that overshadowing is disrupted by lesions of the hippocampal formation. In addition, the model exhibits

Table 3. Simulated and experimental effects of brain lesions on different learning paradigms

	HFL		HPL		CL	
Paradigm	Data	Model	Data	Model	Data	Model
Delay Conditioning	+, 0	+	?	+	0	0
Trace Conditioning	+, 0, -	-	?	0	0	0
Extinction	0, -	-	?	-	0	0
Explicitly Unpaired Extinction	0	- *	?	-	?	-
Acquisition Series	-	-	?	-	?	-
Extinction Series	-	-	?	-	?	-
Blocking	0, -	-	?	0	0	0
Overshadowing	0, -	-	?	0	?	0
Simple Discrimination						
Acquisition	0	0	0	0	0	0
Reversal	-	-	?	0	+	0 *
Conditioned Inhibition	0	- *	?	0	0	0
Differential Conditioning	-	-	?	0	?	0
Occasion Setting		SEE TABLE 4				
Negative Patterning						
Acquisition	-	-	0	0	?	-
Retention	-	-	?	0	?	-
Positive Patterning						
Acquisition	?	-	0	0	?	-
Retention	?	-	?	0	?	-
Context Switching	-	-	?	0	?	-
Sensory Preconditioning	-	-	?	-	-	-
Transivity and Symmetry	-	-	?	-	-	-
Latent Inhibition		SEE TABLE 5				

Note. - = Deficit, + = Facilitation, 0 = No effect, ? = no available data, †: responding is stronger than in the data, * = the model fails to describe accurately the experimental data. HFL: hippocampal formation lesions, HPL: hippocampus proper lesions, CL: cortical lesions.

blocking in normal animals, animals with lesions of the hippocampus proper and animals with lesions of the cortex. In agreement with Rickert, Lorden, Dawson, Smyly and Callahan's (1979), Solomon's (1977), and Gallo and Candido's (1995), but not with Garrud et al.'s (1984) data, the attentional-configural model anticipates that lesions of the hippocampal formation eliminate blocking. In agreement with experimental data (Moore, personal communication, 1990), simulated results show that cortical lesions do not affect blocking.

Discrimination Acquisition and Reversal

According to the attentional-configural model, normal animals, animals with lesions of the hippocampus proper, animals with lesions of the hippocampal formation, and animals with lesions of the cortex show similar discrimination acquisition. These results agree with results obtained by Jarrard and Davidson (1991) for animals with lesions of the hippocampus proper, with results obtained by Berger and Orr (1983), Berger, Weikart, Bassett and Orr (1986), Port, Romano and Patterson (1986), and Weikart and Berger (1986) for animals with lesions of the hippocampal formation, and with results of Oakley and Russell (1975) for animals with lesions of the cortex.

In agreement with results obtained by Berger and Orr (1983), Berger et al. (1986), Buchanan and Powell (1980), Port et al. (1986), and Weikart and Berger (1986) the model describes a strongly impaired discrimination reversal in animals with lesions of the hippocampal formation. However, discrimination reversal is unimpaired in animals with lesions of the hippocampus proper, and animals with lesions of the cortex.

Conditioned Inhibition and Inhibitory Conditioning

In contrast to experimental results showing that conditioned inhibition is not affected by lesions of the hippocampal formation (Solomon, 1977), according to the attentional-configural model, the hippocampal formation case does not display conditioned inhibition. No data are available for conditioned inhibition in the hippocampus proper case. In agreement with Moore, Yeo, Oakley and Russell (1980) simulations display normal conditioned inhibition in the cortical lesion case.

According to the attentional-configural model, inhibitory conditioning is impaired in animals with lesions of the hippocampal formation because the aggregate prediction is needed in order to generate an inhibitory association between the second CS and the US (see Schmajuk & DiCarlo, 1992). The absence of inhibitory conditioning predicted by the model for the case of lesions of the hippocampal formation is consistent, however, with data showing that differential conditioning is impaired by lesions of the hippocampal formation (Micco & Schwartz, 1972).

Simultaneous and Serial Feature-Positive Discrimination

A CS may control the generation of CRs either as a "simple CS" (by signaling the occurrence of the US) or as an "occasion setter" (by modulating the responding generated by another CS). Schmajuk, Lamoreux and Holland (1998) suggested that, in the context of Schmajuk and DiCarlo's (1992) configural model, a CS acts as a simple conditioned stimulus through its direct connections with the US, and as an occasion setter through its indirect, configural connections (see Figure 1).

In a simultaneous feature-positive discrimination, animals learn to respond on simultaneous presentations of the feature and target ($CS_1 \rightarrow CS_2$) reinforced trials, but not on target (CS_2) nonreinforced trials. When the feature is as salient or more salient than the target, it acts as a simple CS. When the feature is less salient than the target, it acts as an occasion setter.

According to the attentional-configural model, simultaneous feature-positive discrimination is preserved in animals with lesions of the hippocampus proper, animals with lesions of the hippocampal formation, and animals with lesions of the cortex when the feature CS_1 is more salient than the target CS_2. The model also predicts that animals with lesions of the hippocampus proper and animals with lesions of the cortex, but not animals with lesions of the hippocampal formation, exhibit simultaneous feature-positive discrimination when the feature CS_1 is less salient than the target CS_2. These results are in agreement with Loechner and Weisz's (1987) data. No data are available for the effect of cortical lesions on simultaneous feature-positive discrimination.

According to the model, animals with lesions of the hippocampal formation are impaired to solve the discrimination when the feature is less salient than the target because the competition between the feature and the target to gain association with the US, mediated through B_{US}, is lacking.

In a serial feature-positive discrimination, animals learn to respond on serial presentations of the feature and target ($CS_1 \rightarrow CS_2$) reinforced trials, but not on target (CS_2) nonreinforced trials. In this case, the feature acts as an occasion setter.

According to the attentional-configural model, only normal animals and animals with lesions of the hippocampus proper exhibit serial feature-positive discrimination. These results are in agreement with Ross, Orr, Holland and Berger's (1984) data showing that acquisition of conditional discrimination is impaired in animals with lesions of the hippocampal formation, and with Jarrard and Davidson's (1991) observation that conditional discrimination is impaired in animals with lesions of the hippocampal formation but not in animals with lesions of the hippocampus proper.

According to the model, cortical lesioned animals are unable to solve a serial feature-positive discrimination because they lack the configural units necessary to allow the feature to function as an occasion setter, as required by the problem. In contrast, animals with lesions of the hippocampus proper can solve the discriminations because, although they are unable to retrain the configural units, some of their existent configural units allow the feature to function as an occasion setter and, therefore, to solve the problem. Animals with lesions of the hippocampal formation are impaired in serial feature-positive discriminations because, although potentially able to use their existent configural units, they lack the competition necessary to establish the correct associations with the US.

Table 4 summarizes the results obtained by Schmajuk and Buhusi (1997) for different types of discriminations in which the feature plays a role as a simple CS or an occasion setter.

Negative Patterning

The attentional-configural model shows that while simulated normal animals and animals with lesions of the hippocampus proper exhibit negative patterning, animals with lesions of the hippocampal formation and animals with lesions of the cortex do not. This result is in agreement with Rudy and Sutherland's (1989) results for animals with lesions of the hippocampal formation, and Gallagher and Holland's (1992) data for animals with lesions of the hippocampus proper.

Positive Patterning

The attentional-configural model shows that normal animals and animals with lesions of the hippocampus proper, but not hippocampal formation or cortical lesioned animals, exhibit positive patterning. In agreement with Gallagher and Holland (1992), animals with lesions of the hippocampus proper are not impaired at performing the task. No data are available for the effects of hippocampal formation lesions or cortical lesions on acquisition of positive patterning. According to the model, acquisition of positive patterning is impaired in animals with lesions of the cortex or the hippocampal formation because stimulus configuration is absent in both cases.

Contextual Effects

In agreement with Penick and Solomon (1991), the attentional-configural model predicts that normal animals show reduced responding when the context is switched, whereas animals with lesions of the hippocampal formation respond similarly in both contexts. The model predicts that animals with lesions of the hippocampus proper should show reduced responding after context switching, and that cortical lesioned animals should show similar responding in both contexts.

Sensory Preconditioning

Simulations with the attentional-configural model show that normal simulated animals, but not those with lesions hippocampal formation, hippocampus proper, or cortex, exhibit sensory preconditioning. According to the model, a CS_1-CS_2 association is acquired during the first phase, while a CS_1-US association is acquired in the second phase. On the test trial, CS_2 evokes a prediction of the CS_1, which in turn through the feedback systems evokes a prediction of the US. According to the model, hippocampal formation, hippocampus proper, and cortical lesioned animals do not show sensory preconditioning because cortical CS_1-CS_2 associations are not present. Port and Patterson (1984) found that fimbrial lesions eliminate sensory preconditioning, a result in accordance with the simulations for animals with lesions of the hippocampal formation. Simulations also agree with Thompson and Kramer's (1965) results, showing that cortical lesioned cats do not show sensory preconditioning.

Table 4. Simulated and experimental effects of brain lesions on several discrimination tasks. After Schmajuk and Buhusi (1997).

Paradigms	HFL		HPL		CL	
	Data	Model	Data	Model	Data	Model
SIMPLE CONDITIONING						
Simple Contextual Discrimination	0	0	?	0	?	0
Simple Discrimination	0	0	0	0	0	0
Simultaneous FP Discrimination with a nonsalient target	0	0	?	0	?	0
OCCASION SETTING						
Simultaneous FP Discrimination with a salient target	-	-	?	0	?	0
Serial FP Discrimination						
Acquisition	-	-	0	0	-	-
Retention	-	-	?	0	?	-
Transfer to a Trained/Extinguished Cue	*	*	0	0	*	*
Conditional Contextual Discrimination	-	- †	-	-	?	-
Conditional Motivational Discrimination	-	-	-	-	?	-

Note. - = Deficit, 0 = No effect, ? = no available data, * = the original discrimination is not learned. †: responding is stronger than in the experimental data. HFL: hippocampal formation lesions, HPL: hippocampus proper lesions, CL: cortical lesions.

Transitivity and Symmetry

Bunsey and Eichenbaum (1996) reported that rats with lesions of the hippocampal formation fail to demonstrate transitivity (the ability to generate inferences across stimulus pairs that share a common element) and symmetry (the ability to associate paired elements presented in the reverse of training order). The model describes transitivity as follows. During CS_1-CS_2 trials, $V_{1,2}$ associations increase, during CS_2-CS_3 trials, $V_{2,3}$ associations increase, and $V_{3,US}$ associations grow during CS_3 reinforced trials. When CS_1 (never presented with the US before) is presented by itself on a test trial, it activates the prediction of CS_2, B_2, which in turn activates prediction of CS_3,

B_3, which in turn activates the $V_{3,US}$ association, thereby generating a prediction of the US and a CR. According to the model, symmetry is simply the result of the simultaneous increase in $V_{2,1}$ and $V_{1,2}$ associations. In the absence of CS-CS associations that follow lesions of the hippocampal formation, the attentional-associational model is able to simulate the impairments in transitivity and symmetry.

Latent Inhibition

According to the model, latent inhibition is manifested because CS preexposure reduces Novelty, thereby reducing attention to the CS and retarding conditioning.

Acquisition of latent inhibition. Experimental data show that hippocampal lesions might impair, spare or even facilitate latent inhibition. Under the assumption that hippocampal lesions impair the computation of aggregate predictions, Buhusi et al. (1998) demonstrated through computer simulations (summarized in Table 5) that, depending on the behavioral protocol (i.e., procedure and total time of CS preexposure), Novelty in animals with hippocampal lesions might be larger, equal, or smaller (corresponding to smaller, equal, or larger latent inhibition) than in normal controls.

For instance, the attentional model correctly describes that lesions of the hippocampus proper impair latent inhibition when a "within-subject procedure" (WS) is used (Han, Gallagher & Holland, 1995), but facilitates latent inhibition when a "between-subject procedure with interspersed water presentations" (BW) is used (Reilly, Harley & Revusky, 1993). In the WS procedure, animals learn to predict the presence of the CS during CS preexposure. Because lesions of the hippocampus proper hinder the generation the CS prediction based on CX-CS associations, they cannot decrease Novelty as fast as normal animals, and latent inhibition is impaired. However, in the BW procedure, normal animals are able to predict the absence of the CS and the water when they are not presented, thereby increasing the value of Novelty, and decreasing latent inhibition. Because animals with lesions of the hippocampus proper are unable to predict the absence of CS and the water when they are not presented, Novelty is smaller in the lesioned animals, and latent inhibition is facilitated.

In sum, hippocampal lesions seem to interact with behavioral parameters to determine how latent inhibition is affected. This seems to be generally true for impairment (Han et al., 1995) vs. preservation (Honey & Good, 1993, Experiment 2) of latent inhibition. However, because the facilitatory effects of hippocampal lesions on latent inhibition have been reported only using a taste-aversion procedure, an alternative explanation is that latent inhibition facilitation is taste aversion specific. Therefore, Buhusi et al. (1998) suggested that the generality of the procedural explanation should be tested using a different preparation and substituting water by another stimulus: the between-subject with interspersed water presentations (WW) procedure should become a between-subject procedure with interspersed presentations of a salient nontarget cue.

Contextual effects on latent inhibition. Numerous studies (see Lubow, 1989) show that latent inhibition is disrupted by a change in the context from the CS preexposure phase to the conditioning phase. This effect is impaired by selective hippocampal

Table 5. Simulated and experimental effects of hippocampal lesions on latent inhibition under different experimental conditions (After, Buhusi, Gray and Schmajuk, 1998).

Reference	Lesion	Paradigm	Procedure	Total Time (s) of Preexposure	Data/Model
Ackil et al. (1969)	HFL	avoidance	BS	150	Impaired LI
Solomon and Moore (1975)	HFL	eyeblink	BS	225	Impaired LI
McFarland et al. (1978)	HFL	taste aversion	BS	30	Impaired LI
Schmajuk et al. (1994)	HFL	eyeblink	BS	225	Impaired LI
Kaye and Pearce (1987a,b)	HFL	foodcup entry	BS	720	Impaired LI
Honey and Good (1993)	HPL	foodcup entry	BS	720	Preserved LI
Han et al. (1995)	HPL	foodcup entry	WS	400	Impaired LI
Honey and Good (1993)	HPL	foodcup entry	WX	720	No CX effect
Reilly et al. (1993)	HPL	taste aversion	BW	7,200	Facilitated LI
Purves et al. (1995)	HFL	taste aversion	WW	7,200	Facilitated LI
Gallo and Candido (1995)	HFL	taste aversion	BW	900/5,400	Preserved LI
Christiansen and Schmajuk (1993)	HFL + HAL	eyeblink	BS	25	Restored LI
Yee et al. (1995)	HFL	CER + HAL	WS	450	Restored LI

Note: CER: Conditioned Emotional Response, WS: within-subject procedure, BS: between-subject procedure, WX: within-subject procedure with context change, WW: within-subject procedure with interspersed water presentations, BW: between-subject procedure with interspersed water presentations. HFL: hippocampal formation lesions, HPL: hippocampus proper lesions. HAL: haloperidol administration, LI: latent inhibition, CX: context..

lesions (Honey & Good, 1993, Experiment 3). Computer simulations with the attentional-configural model show that context changes disrupt latent inhibition in normal cases, but not in cases of lesions of the hippocampus proper or cortex. According to the model, latent inhibition is not disrupted by hippocampus proper and cortical lesions because the increase in Novelty that underlies the phenomenon in normal animals depends on CX-CS or CS-CX associations which are absent in lesioned animals (CX: context).

Pharmacological Manipulations

In the brain-mapped model, pharmacological manipulations of neural elements with agonists and antagonists represent equivalent manipulations of specific neurotransmitters in the brain.

Administration of Dopaminergic Agonists and Antagonists on Latent Inhibition

We assume that indirect DA agonists (e.g., amphetamine and nicotine) increase, and DA receptor antagonists (e.g., haloperidol and α-flupenthixol) decrease, the effect of Novelty on attention. Under these assumptions, Schmajuk et al. (1998) showed that the attentional model correctly describes (1) the impairment of latent inhibition by amphetamine when a strong US is used, (2) the impairment of latent inhibition by amphetamine when a nonsalient CS is used, (3) the impairment of latent inhibition by amphetamine administration when a short CS is used, (4) the facilitation of latent inhibition by α-flupenthixol when a weak US is used, (5) the facilitation of latent inhibition by haloperidol when a nonsalient CS is used, (6) the facilitation of latent inhibition by haloperidol with a strong US, and (7) the facilitation of latent inhibition by haloperidol with extended conditioning (see Table 6).

According to both attentional and attentional-configural models, latent inhibition is the result of the reduced Novelty, and the consequently reduced z_{CS} and X_{CS}, that follows CS preexposure. Therefore, (1) latent inhibition is impaired by amphetamine when a strong US (but not a weak US) is used because the strong US increases Novelty and amphetamine increases the effect of Novelty on z_{CS} during conditioning, (2) latent inhibition is impaired by amphetamine when a nonsalient CS (but not when a salient CS) is used because, during preexposure, Novelty decreases faster with a salient CS than with a nonsalient CS, (3) latent inhibition is impaired by amphetamine when a short CS (but not when a long CS) is used because, during preexposure, Novelty decreases more with a longer than with a shorter CS, (4) latent inhibition is facilitated by α-flupenthixol when a weak US (but not when a strong US) is used because, even if α-flupenthixol decreases the effect of Novelty on z_{CS}, Novelty is increased by the strong US during conditioning, (5) latent inhibition is facilitated by haloperidol when a nonsalient CS (but not a salient CS) is used because, even though Novelty does not decrease enough to show latent inhibition when a nonsalient CS is used, haloperidol decreases the effect of Novelty on z_{CS} during conditioning, and (6) latent inhibition is facilitated by haloperidol when the intensity of the US is strong enough to promote conditioning in either preexposed or non-preexposed animals. In sum, the attentional model accurately describe the interplay of [a] the behavioral factors (e.g., US strength, CS salience, CS duration, total time of preexposure, etc.) that influence the magnitude of the latent inhibition with [b] effect with the effect of DA agents. In sum, as in the case of hippocampal lesions, DA agents interact with behavioral procedures to determine how latent inhibition is affected.

<u>Combined effect of hippocampal lesions and haloperidol</u>. Interestingly, latent inhibition impairment by nonselective hippocampal lesions (Christiansen & Schmajuk, 1993) or selective retrohippocampal lesions is ameliorated by haloperidol (Yee, Feldon

& Rawlins, 1995). Computer simulations with the attentional and attentional-configural models demonstrate that, when latent inhibition is impaired by hippocampal formation lesions, it is reinstated by haloperidol administration, simulated by decreasing the value of Novelty (see Table 5).

Table 6. Simulated and experimental effects of the administration of dopaminergic agonists and antagonists on latent inhibition under different experimental conditions (After Schmajuk, Buhusi and Gray, 1998).

Reference	Drug	Condition	Data/Model
Killcross, Dickinson, Robbins (1994a)	Amphetamine	High US intensity Low US intensity	Disrupts LI Preserves LI
Ruob, Elsner, Weiner, and Feldon (1997)	Amphetamine	Low CS salience	Disrupts LI
Weiner, Tarrasch, Bernasconi, Broesen,	Amphetamine	Low CS salience, low and high US	Disrupts LI
Ruttimann, and Feldon (1998)	Amphetamine	High CS salience, low and high US	Preserves LI
De la Casa, Ruiz, and Lubow (1993)	Amphetamine	Short CS duration	Disrupts LI
De la Casa, Ruiz, and Lubow (1993)	Amphetamine	Long CS duration	Preserves LI
Killcross, Dickinson, and Robbins (1994b)	α-flupenthixol	Low US intensity	Facilitates LI
Ruob, Elsner, Weiner, and Feldon (1997)	Haloperidol	Low CS salience	Facilitates LI
Ruob, Weiner, and Feldon (1998)	Haloperidol	High US intensity	Facilitates LI
Ruob, Weiner, and Feldon (1998)	Haloperidol	Large number of conditioning trials	Facilitates LI

Administration of Cholinergic Agonists and Antagonists on Acquisition and Latent Inhibition

In our computer simulations, muscarinic cholinergic antagonists (such as scopolamine) decrease and muscarinic cholinergic agonists (such as physostigmine) increase the value of the errror for the hidden units EH_j.

Solomon, Solomon, Vander Shaaf and Perry (1983; see also Harvey, Gormezano & Cool-Hauser, 1983) reported that systemic administration of scopolamine severely retards acquisition of classical conditioning in rabbits with intact hippocampus. Although scopolamine administration impairs conditioning, it has no adverse effect on latent inhibition (Moore, Goodell & Solomon, 1976). Computer simulations with the attentional-configural show similar results.

Recently, Woodruff-Pak, Li, Hinchliffe and Port (1997) showed that administration of nefiracetam, a drug that promotes the release of acetylcholine, facilitates CR acquisition in older rabbits with intact hippocampus but not in older rabbits with bilateral hippocampectomy. Similar to these results, simulation results obtained for the administration of ACh agonists (such as physostigmine) indicate facilitation of acquisition. In addition to muscarinic agonists and antagonists, Woodruff-Pak, Li, Kazmi and Kem (1994) showed that administration of the nicotinic cholinergic antagonist mecamylamine disrupted eyeblink conditioning in young rabbits. Considering the role of nicotine as an indirect dopamine agonist, Schmajuk et al. (1998) showed that the attentional model can describe the facilitatory effect of nicotine on classical conditioning, i.e., the opposite result to that described with mecamylamine.

Effect of Long-Term Potentiation of Hippocampal Synapses

In the brain-mapped model, long-term potentiation (LTP) of the entorhinal-dentate pathway was simulated by a twenty-fold increase in the learning rate of the hidden units. Berger (1984) found that entorhinal cortex stimulation that produced LTP increased the rate of acquisition of a two-tone classical discrimination of the rabbit NM response. Schmajuk (1998) showed that according to the configural model, and in agreement with Berger (1984), discrimination acquisition proceeds faster in the LTP group than in the control group.

Summary

Table 2 summarizes how the attentional-configural model describes neural activity in different brain regions. Tables 3, 4, 5 and 6 show that the model is able to describe most of the effects of lesions of the hippocampus proper, the hippocampal formation, and the cortex in different classical conditioning paradigms. Table 3 indicates novel predictions generated by the model.

HOW THE MODEL DESCRIBES HUMAN DATA

Although the model has been mostly applied to animal data, some classical conditioning protocols have been studied both in animals and humans.

Delay Conditioning

As mentioned, lesions of several cerebellar areas permanently abolish the classically conditioned nictitating membrane and eyeblink response in the rabbit (Thompson, 1986) and eyeblink response in the rat (Skelton, 1988). Likewise, it has been reported that cerebellar lesions in humans impair eyeblink conditioning (Daum, Schugens, Ackermann, Lutzenberger, Dichgans & Birbaumer, 1993; Schugens, Topka & Daum, this volume; Solomon, Stowe, & Pendlebury, 1989; Lye, O'Boyle, Ramsden & Schady, 1988; Topka, Valls-Sole, Massaquoi & Hallett, 1993; Woodruff-Pak, Papka & Ivry, 1996; Chapter 9, this volume). Humans with hippocampal lesions show normal delay eyeblink conditioning (Woodruff-Pak, 1993; Gabrieli, McGlinchey-Berroth, Carrillo, Gluck, Cermak & Disterhoft, 1995; Chapter 10, this volume). The model can describe these results.

Trace Conditioning

Although humans show normal delay conditioning, they are impaired in trace conditioning (McGlinchey-Berroth, Carrillo, Gabrieli, Brawn & Disterhoft, 1998; see also Chapter 10, this volume). Again the model is competent in describing these results. Whereas in hippocampal lesioned animals, trace conditioning is impaired for interstimulus intervals (ITI) longer than 500 ms, humans with hippocampal lesions were impaired only with 1000 ms ITIs (Clark & Squire, 1998; Woodruff-Pak, 1993).

Trace Conditioning and Awareness

Gray (1995) proposed that the content of consciousness corresponds to the outputs of a comparator that compares the actual state of the organism's actual perceptual inputs with the predicted inputs. Gray et al. (1997) described conscious processing in terms of the attentional model. In the framework of the network, an environmental stimulus is processed in conscious mode when Novelty (represented by the VTA input to the core of the NA) and attention to the stimulus are large, and in unconscious mode otherwise. In the model, indirect DA agonists, such as amphetamine or nicotine, enhance the DA representation of Novelty, thereby increasing attention and engaging conscious processing of environmental stimuli. By contrast, DA receptor antagonists, such as haloperidol, reduce the DA representation of Novelty, thereby decreasing attention, and engaging unconscious processing of the stimuli.

Recently, Clark and Squire (1998; see Chapter 11, this volume) reported that amnesic patients with damage to the hippocampal formation and normal subjects were tested in delay and trace conditioning and then assessed for the extent to which they became aware of the relationship between the CS and the US. Amnesic patients acquired delay conditioning at a normal rate but failed to acquire trace conditioning. Normal subjects who show intact trace conditioning also show awareness of the CS-US relationship. Clark and Squire (1998, page 79) suggested that trace conditioning requires conscious knowledge because the CS-US interval makes it difficult to process the CS-US relationship in an automatic (nonconscious) way. Computer simulations with the attentional-configural model show that, in the normal case, Novelty and attention to the CS are greater in trace than in delay conditioning. According to the model, the failure of the hippocampal lesioned and amnesic patients to become aware of the CS-US relationship should be attributed to the fact that the CS trace is shorter after hippocampal lesions and attention to the CS is not increased under those circumstances. Therefore, simulation results suggest that the absence of conscious processing might not be the cause of the trace conditioning deficit and that instead, both deficits are the consequence of a decreased amplitude and duration of the CS trace, τ_i. The model can also be applied to the experiment in which subjects are explained the CS-US relationships and found to achieve a higher rate of conditioning. In this case, it is assumed that attentional memory, ys_i, to the CS starts at a higher value, which results in facilitated trace conditioning.

Conditional Discriminations

Daum, Channon, Polkey and Gray (1991) reported that lesions of the temporal lobe, which include the removal of the amygdala, uncus, parahippocampal gyrus, and part of the anterior hippocampus, impair an eyeblink conditional discrimination in humans. Subjects had to learn to respond on serial presentations of a light feature and a tone target (L1 → T) but not on serial presentations of another light feature and the tone target (L2 → T). In this case, the features act as occasion setters and, according to the attentional-configural model, lesions of the hippocampal formation impair the acquisition of the discrimination.

Administration of Muscarinic Cholinergic Antagonists

As in rabbits, administration of scopolamine impairs eyeblink conditioning in humans (Bahro, Schreurs, Sunderland & Molchan, 1995; Solomon, Groccia-Ellison, Flynn, Mirak, Edwards, Dunehew & Stanton, 1993). This effect is correctly described by the model.

Latent Inhibition and Schizophrenia

As mentioned, nonselective lesions of the hippocampus (Christiansen & Schmajuk, 1993) or selective retrohippocampal lesions (Yee, Feldon & Rawlins, 1995) impair latent inhibition, but latent inhibition is reinstated when treated with haloperidol. Similarly, acute schizophrenia may disrupt latent inhibition, but latent inhibition is reinstated by neuroleptic medication (Baruch, Hemsley & Gray, 1988). As shown above, the model correctly describes this interaction between hippocampal lesions and pharmacological manipulations.

CONCLUSION

A brain-mapped neural network that combines attentional and configural mechanisms is able to characterize the attributes of multiple classical conditioning paradigms and to describe the effects of many neurophysiological manipulations. As shown in Table 2, the attentional-configural model describes neural activity in several brain regions.

As shown in Table 3, the attentional-configural model has been applied to the description of the effects of [a] selective hippocampal lesions, [b] nonselective lesions of the hippocampus, and [c] cortical lesions, on multiple classical conditioning paradigms. Table 4 illustrates how the configural model correctly describes the effect of these lesions on discrimination paradigms in which stimuli can act as a simple CS or an occasion setter.

Table 5 shows that the model can offer a resolution for the apparently conflicting results of hippocampal selective and nonselective lesions on latent inhibition. Table 6 shows that the attentional model offers a description of the interaction between the procedural design and administration of dopaminergic drugs on latent inhibition.

One interesting conclusion from this series of studies is that it is difficult to describe the effect of brain manipulations on a general class of behaviors. Statements like "hippocampal lesions impair trace conditioning," or "hippocampal lesions impair latent inhibition," or "amphetamine impairs latent inhibition," were found to be erroneous generalizations. Many times, the effect of brain manipulations seems to be specific to the parametric conditions of the experiment, duration of the CS in the case of hippocampal lesions and trace conditioning, procedure and total time of preexposure in the case of hippocampal lesions and latent inhibition, and CS and US intensity and duration in the case of dopaminergic agents and latent inhibition. The specificity of these results is well captured by the neural network approaches described in this chapter.

We can now describe, in terms of the model, the functional anatomy of eyeblink conditioning in humans presented at the beginning of the chapter. According to the model, during eyeblink conditioning, the function of the cerebellar regions is the storage of associations between simple and configural stimuli with the US, hippocampal regions compute the aggregate predictions as well as the error function needed to train cortical areas, cortical regions store CS-CS and CS-configural associations, and the neural activity in the ventral striatum region represents Novelty used to determine the amount of attention derived to a certain CS.

Finally, although the combination of traditional and advanced technologies can bring an enormous amount of exciting information about how different regions in the human brain participate in eyeblink conditioning, our understanding of the functionality of these regions can only be achieved with the help of formal neural network models.

REFERENCES

Ackil, J., Mellgren, R.L., Halgren, C., & Frommer, G.P. (1969). Effects of CS preexposure on avoidance learning in rats with hippocampal lesions. *Journal of Comparative and Physiological Psychology, 69*, 739-747.

Bahro M, Schreurs BG, Sunderland T, & Molchan S.E. (1995). The effects of scopolamine, lorazepam, and glycopyrrolate on classical conditioning of the human eyeblink response. *Psychopharmacology, 122*, 395-400.

Baruch, I., Hemsley, D., & Gray, J.A. (1988). Differential performance of acute and chronic schizophrenics in a latent inhibition task. *Journal of Nervous and Mental Disease, 176*, 598-606.

Berger, T.W. (1984). Long-term potentiation of hippocampal synaptic transmission affects rate of behavioral learning. *Science, 224*, 627-630.

Berger, T.W., & Orr, W.B. (1983). Hippocampectomy selectively disrupts discrimination reversal conditioning of the rabbit nictitating membrane response. *Behavioral Brain Research, 8*, 49-68.

Berger, T.W., Rinaldi, P.C., Weisz, D.J., & Thompson, R.F. (1983). Single-unit analysis of different hippocampal cell types during classical conditioning of rabbit nictitating membrane response. *Journal of Neurophysiology, 50*, 1197-1219.

Berger, T.W., & Thompson, R.F. (1978a). Neuronal plasticity in the limbic system during classical conditioning of the rabbit nictitating membrane response. I. The hippocampus. *Brain Research, 145*, 323-346.

Berger, T.W., & Thompson, R.F. (1978b). Neuronal plasticity in the limbic system during classical conditioning of the rabbit nictitating membrane response. II. Septum and mammillary bodies. *Brain Research, 156*, 293-314.

Berger, T.W., & Thompson, R.F. (1982). Hippocampal cellular plasticity during extinction of classically conditioned nictitating membrane behavior. *Behavioral Brain Research, 4*, 63-76.

Berger, T.W., Weikart, C.L., Bassett, J.L., & Orr, E.B. (1986). Lesions of the retrosplenial cortex produce deficits in reversal learning of the rabbit nictitating membrane response: Implications for potential interactions between hippocampal and cerebellar brain systems. *Behavioral Neuroscience, 100*, 802-809.

Bilkey, D.K., & Goddard, G.V. (1985). Medial septal facilitation of hippocampal granule cell activity is mediated by inhibition of inhibitory interneurons. *Brain Research, 361*, 99-106.

Blaxton, T.A., Zeffiro, T.A., Gabrieli, J.D.E., Bookheinmer, S., Carrillo, M., Theodore, W.H., & Disterhoft, J.F. (1996). Functional mapping of human learning: A positron emission tomography activation study of eyeblink conditioning. *Journal of Neuroscience, 16*, 4032-4040.

Brogden, W.J. (1939). Sensory pre-conditioning. *Journal of Experimental Psychology, 25*, 223-232.

Buchanan, S.L., & Powell, D.A. (1980). Divergences in Pavlovian conditioned heart rate and eyeblink responses produced by hippocampectomy in rabbit (oryctolagus cuniculus). *Behavioral and Neural Biology, 30*, 20-38.

Buhusi, C.V., Gray, J.A, & Schmajuk, N.A. (1998). The perplexing effects of hippocampal lesions on latent inhibition: A neural network solution. *Behavioral Neuroscience, 112*, 316-351.

Buhusi, C., & Schmajuk, N.A. (1996). Attention, configuration, and hippocampal function. *Hippocampus, 6*, 621-642.

Buhusi, C.V., & Schmajuk, N.A. (1999). Timing in simple conditioning and occasion setting: A neural network approach. *Behavioral Processes, 45*, 33-57.

Bunsey, M., & Eichenbaum, H. (1996). Conservation of hippocampal memory function in rats and humans. *Nature, 379*, 255-257.

Christiansen, B.A., & Schmajuk, N.A. (1993). Latent inhibition: Effects of haloperidol and hippocampal lesions. *Abstracts of the Society of Neuroscience, 19*, 798.

Clark, R.E., & Squire, L. (1998). Classical conditioning and brain systems: role of awareness. *Science, 280*, 77-81.

Daum, I., Channon, S., Polkey, C.E., & Gray, J.A. (1991). Classical conditioning after temporal lobe lesions in man: Impairment in conditional discrimination. *Behavioral Neuroscience, 105*, 396-408.

Daum, I., Schugens, M. M., Ackermann, H., Lutzenberger, W., Dichgans, J., & Birbaumer, N. (1993). Classical conditioning after cerebellar lesions in humans. *Behavioral Neuroscience, 107*, 748-756.

De la Casa, L.G., Ruiz, G., & Lubow, R.E. (1993). Amphetamine-produced attenuation of latent inhibition is modulated by stimulus preexposure duration: implications for schizophrenia. *Biological Psychiatry, 33*, 707-711.

Dormont, J.F., Conde, H., & Farin, D. (1998). The role of the pedunculopotine tegmental nucleus in relation to a conditioned motor performance in the cat. I. Context-dependent and reiforcement-related single unit activity. *Experimental Brain Research, 121*, 401-410.

Gabrieli, J.D.E., McGlinchey-Berroth, R., Carrillo, M.C., Gluck, M.C., Cermak, L.S., & Disterhoft, J.F. (1995). Intact delay-eyeblink classical conditioning in amnesia. *Behavioral Neuroscience, 109*, 819-827.

Gallagher, P.C., & Holland, M. (1992). Preserved configural learning and spatial learning impairments in rats with hippocampal damage. *Hippocampus, 2*, 81-88.

Gallo, M., & Candido, A. (1995). Dorsal hippocampal lesions impair blocking but not latent inhibition of taste aversion learning in rats. *Behavioral Neuroscience, 109*, 413- 425.

Garrud, P., Rawlins, J.N.P., Mackintosh, N.J., Goodal, G., Cotton, M.M., & Feldon, J. (1984). Successful overshadowing and blocking in hippocampectomized rats. *Behavioural Brain Research, 12*, 39-53.

Gray, J.A. (1995). The contents of consciousness: a neuropsychological conjecture. *Behavioral & Brain*

Sciences, 18, 659-676.

Gray, J.A., Buhusi, C.V., & Schmajuk, N.A. (1997). The transition from automatic to controlled processing. *Neural Networks, 10*, 1257-1268.

Grossberg, S., & Schmajuk, N.A. (1989). Neural dynamics of adaptive timing and temporal discrimination during associative learning. *Neural Networks, 2*: 79-102.

Han, J-S., Gallahger, M., & Holland, P. (1995). Hippocampal lesions disrupt decrements but not increments in conditioned stimulus processing. *Journal of Neuroscience*.

Harvey, J.A., Gormezano I., & Cool-Hauser VA. (1983). Effects of scopolamine and methylscopolamine on classical conditioning of the rabbit nictitating membrane response. *Journal of Pharmacology & Experimental Therapeutics, 225*, 42-49.

Honey, R.C., & Good, M. (1993). Selective hippocampal lesions abolish the contextual specificity of latent inhibition and conditioning. *Behavioral Neuroscience, 107*, 23-33.

Jarrard, L.E., & Davidson, T.L. (1991). On the hippocampus and learned conditional responding: effects of aspiration versus ibotenate lesions. *Hippocampus, 1*, 107-117.

James, G.O., Hardiman, M.J., & Yeo, C.H. (1987). Hippocampal lesions and trace conditioning in the rabbit. *Behavioural Brain Research, 23*, 109-116.

Kaye, H., & Pearce, J. M. (1987a). Hippocampal lesions attenuate latent inhibition and the decline of the orienting response in rats. *The Quarterly Journal of Experimental Psychology, 39B*, 107-125.

Kaye, H., & Pearce, J.M. (1987b). Hippocampal lesions attenuate latent inhibition of a CS and a neutral stimulus. *Psychobiology, 15*, 293-299.

Killcross, A.S., Dickinson, A., & Robbins, T.W. (1994a). Amphetamine-induced disruptions of latent inhibition are reinforcer mediated -- Implications for animal models of schizophrenic attentional dysfunction. *Psychopharmacology, 115*, 185-195.

Killcross, A.S., Dickinson, A., & Robbins, T.W. (1994b). Effects of the neuroleptic α-flupenthixol on latent inhibition in aversely- and appetitively-motivated paradigms: evidence for dopamine-reinforcer interactions. *Psychopharmacology, 115*, 196-205.

Kim, J. J., Clark, R. E., &Thompson, R. F. (1995). Hippocampectomy impairs the memory of recently, but not remotely, acquired trace eyeblink conditioned responses. *Behavioral Neuroscience, 109*, 195-203.

Kohonen, T. (1977). *Associative memory*. Springer, Berlin Heidelberg, New York.

Kraemer, P.J., Randall, C.K., & Carbary, T.J. (1991). Release from latent inhibition with delayed testing. *Animal Learning and Behavior, 19*, 139-145.

Krnjevic, K., Ropert, N., & Casullo, J. (1988). Septohippocampal desinhibition. *Brain Research, 438*, 182-192.

Lamoureux, J. A., Buhusi, C.V., & Schmajuk, N.A. (1998). A real-time theory of Pavlovian conditioning: Simple CSs and occasion setters. In N.A. Schmajuk & P.C. Holland (Eds.). *Occasion Setting: Associative Learning and Cognition in Animals*, (pp. 383-424). Washington, DC.: American Psychological Association.

Leaton, R.N. (1981). Habituation of the startle response, lick suppression, and exploratory behavior in rats with hippocampal lesions. *Journal of Comparative and Physiological Psychology, 95*, 813-820.

Loechner, K.J., & Weisz, D.J. (1987). Hippocampectomy and feature-positive discrimination. *Behavioral Brain Research, 26*, 63-73.

Logan, C.G., & Grafton, S.T. (1995). Functional anatomy of human eyeblink conditioned determined with regional cerebral glucose metabolism and positron-emission tomography. *Proceedings of the National Academy of Sciences, 92*, 7500-7504.

Lubow, R.E. (1989). *Latent inhibition and conditioned attention theory*. Cambridge: Cambridge University Press.

Lye, R..H., O'Boyle, D.J., Ramsden, R.T., & Shady, W. (1988). Effects of unilateral cerebellar lesion in the acquisition of eye-blink conditioning in man. *Journal of Physiology, 403*, 58.

McFarland, D.J., Kostas, J., & Drew, W.G. (1978). Dorsal hippocampal lesions: Effects of preconditioning CS preexposure on flavor aversion. *Behavioral Biology, 2*, 398-404.

McGlinchey-Berroth, R., Carrillo, M.C., Gabrieli, J.D.E., Brawn, C.M., & Disterhoft, J.F. (1998). Impaired trace eyeblink conditioning in bilateral, medial,-temporal lobe amnesia. *Behavioral Neuroscience, 11*, 873-882.

Micco, D.J. & Schwartz, M. (1972). Effects of hippocampal lesions upon the developments of Pavlovian internal inhibition in rats. *Journal of Comparative and Physiological Psychology, 76*, 371-377.

Molchan, S. E., Sunderland, T., McIntosh, A. R., Herscovitch, P., & Schreurs, B.G. (1994). A functional anatomical study of associative learning in humans. *Proceedings of the National Academy of Sciences, 91*, 8122-8126

Moore, J.W., Goodell, N.A., & Solomon, P.R. (1976). Central cholinergic blockade by scopolamine and habituation, classical conditioning, and latent inhibition of the rabbit's nictitating membrane response. *Physiological Psychology, 4*, 395-399.
Moore, J.W., Yeo, C.H., Oakley, D.A., & Russell, I.S. (1980). Conditioned inhibition of the nictitating membrane response in decorticate rabbits. *Behavioural Brain Research, 1*, 397-409.
Moyer, J.R., Deyo, R.A., & Disterhoft, J.F. (1990). Hippocampectomy disrupts associative learning of the trace conditioned eye-blink response in rabbits. *Behavioral Neuroscience, 104*, 243-252.
Oakley, D.A., & Russell, I.S. (1975). Role of cortex in Pavlovian discrimination learning. *Physiology & Behavior, 15*, 315-321.
Pavlov, I.P. (1927). *Conditioned reflexes*. Oxford: Oxford University Press.
Penick, S., & Solomon, P.R. (1991). Hippocampus, Context, and Conditioning. *Behavioral Neuroscience, 105*, 611-617.
Port, R.L., & Patterson, M.M. (1984). Fimbrial lesions and sensory preconditioning. *Behavioral Neuroscience, 98*, 584-589.
Port, R.L., Romano, A.G., & Patterson, M.M. (1986). Stimulus duration discrimination in the rabbit: Effects of hippocampectomy on discrimination and reversal learning. *Physiological Psychology, 14*, 124-129.
Port, R.L., Romano, A.G., Steinmetz, J.E., Mikhail, A.A., & Patterson, M.M. (1986). Retention and acquisition of classical trace conditioned responses by rabbits with hippocampal lesions. *Behavioral Neuroscience, 100*, 745-752.
Purves, D., Bonardi, C., &, Hall, G. (1995). Enhancement of latent inhibition in rats with electrolytic lesions of the hipopcampus. *Behavioral Neuroscience, 109*, 366-370.
Reilly, S., Harley, C., & Revusky, S. (1993). Ibotenate lesions of the hippocampus enhance latent inhibition in conditioned taste aversion and increase resistance to extinction in conditioned taste preference. *Behavioral Neuroscience, 107*, 966-1004.
Rickert, E.J., Bent, T.L., Lane, P., & French, J. (1978). Hippocampectomy and the attenuation of blocking. *Behavioral Biology, 22*, 147-160.
Rickert, E.J., Lorden, J.F., Dawson, R., Smyly, E., & Callahan, M.F. (1979). Stimulus processing and stimulus selection in rats with hippocampal lesions. *Behavioral and Neural Biology, 27*, 454-465.
Robinson, G.B. (1986). Enhanced long-term potentiation induced in rat dentate gyrus by coactivation of septal and entorhinal inputs. *Brain Research, 379*, 56-62.
Robinson, G.B., & Racine, R.J. (1986). Interactions between septal and entorhinal inputs to the rat dentate gyrus: Facilitation effects. *Brain Research, 379*, 63-67.
Ross, R.T., Orr, W.B., Holland, P.C., & Berger, T.W. (1984). Hippocampectomy disrupts acquisition and retention of learned conditional responding. *Behavioral Neuroscience, 98*, 211-225.
Rudell, A.P., Fox, S.E., & Ranck, J.B. (1980). Hippocampal excitability phase-lock to theta rhythm in walking rats. *Experimental Neurology, 68*, 87-96.
Rudy, J.W., & Sutherland, R.J. (1989). The hippocampal formation is necessary for rats to learn and remember configural discriminations. *Behavioural Brain Research, 34*, 97-109.
Ruob, C., Elsner, J., Weiner, I., & Feldon, J. (1997). Amphetamine-induced disruption and haloperidol-induced potentiation of latent inhibition depend on the nature of the stimulus. *Behavioural Brain Research, 88*, 35-41.
Ruob, C., Weiner, I., & Feldon, J. (1998). Haloperidol-induced potentiation of latent inhibition: interaction with parameters of conditioning. *Behavioral Pharmacology, 9*, 245-253.
Schmajuk, N.A. (1998). LTP and information storage in cortex. *Behavioral and Brain Sciences, 20*, 629-631.
Schmajuk, N.A., & Blair, H.T. (1993). Stimulus configuration, spatial learning, and hippocampal function. *Behavioural Brain Research, 59*:103-117, 1993.
Schmajuk, N.A., & Buhusi, C.V. (1997). Occasion setting, stimulus configuration, and the hippocampus. *Behavioral Neuroscience, 111*, 235-258.
Schmajuk, N.A., Buhusi, C.V., & Gray, J.A. (1998). The pharmacology of latent inhibition: A neural network approach. *Behavioural Pharmacology, 9*, 711-730.
Schmajuk, N.A., & DiCarlo, J.J. (1991). A neural network approach to hippocampal function in classical conditioning. *Behavioral Neuroscience, 105*, 82-110.
Schmajuk, N.A., & DiCarlo, J.J. (1992). Stimulus configuration, classical conditioning, and the hippocampus. *Psychological Review, 99*, 268-305.
Schmajuk, N.A., Lam, Y.W., & Christiansen, B.A. (1993). Hippocampectomy disrupts latent inhibition of the rat eyeblink conditioning. *Physiology & Behavior, 55*, 597-601.

Schmajuk, N.A., Lam, Y.W., & Gray, J.A. (1996). Latent inhibition: A neural network approach. *Journal of Experimental Psychology: Animal Behavior Processes, 22*, 321-349,1996.

Schmajuk, N.A., Lamoureux, J., & Holland, P.C. (1998). Occasion setting and stimulus configuration: A neural network approach. *Psychological Review, 105*, 3-32.

Schmajuk, N.A., & Moore, J.W. (1985) Real-time attentional models for classical conditioning and the hippocampus. *Physiological Psychology, 13*, 279-290.

Schmajuk, N.A., & Moore, J.W. (1988). The hippocampus and the classically conditioned nictitating membrane response: a real time attentional-associative model. *Psychobiology, 46*, 20-35.

Schmajuk, N.A., Spear, N.E.,, & Isaacson, R.L. (1983). Absence of overshadowing in rats with hippocampal lesions. *Physiological Psychology, 11*, 59-62.

Schmaltz, L.W., & Theios, J. (1972). Acquisition and extinction of a classically conditioned response in hippocampectomized rabbits (Oryctolagus cuniculus). *Journal of Comparative and Physiological Psychology, 79*, 328-333.

Sears, L.L., & Steinmetz, J. E. (1990). Acquisition of classical conditioned-related activity in the hippocampus is affected by lesions of the cerebellar interpositus nucleus. *Journal of Neuroscience Research, 27*, 681-692.

Skelton, R.W. (1988). Bilateral cerebellar lesions disrupt conditioned eyelid responses in unrestrained rats. *Behavioral Neuroscience, 102*, 586-590.

Solomon, P.R. (1977). Role of the hippocampus in blocking and conditioned inhibition of rabbit's nictitating membrane response. *Journal of Comparative and Physiological Psychology, 91*, 407-417.

Solomon P.R., Groccia-Ellison, M., Flynn, D., Mirak, J., Edwards, K.R., Dunehew, A., & Stanton, M.E. (1993). Disruption of human eyeblink conditioning after central cholinergic blockade with scopolamine. *Behavioral Neuroscience, 107*, 271-279

Solomon, P.R., & Moore, J.W. (1975). Latent inhibition and stimulus generalization of the classically conditioned nictitating membrane response in rabbits (Oryctolagus cuniculus) following dorsal hippocampal ablation. *Journal of Comparative and Physiological Psychology, 89*, 1192-1203.

Solomon, P.R., Solomon, S.D., Vander Schaaf, E., & Perry, H.E. (1983). Altered activity in the hippocampus is more detrimental to classical conditioning than removing the structure. *Science, 220*, 329-331.

Solomon, P.R., Stowe, G.T., & Pendlbeury, W.W. (1989). Disrupted eyelid conditioning in a patient with damage to cerebellar afferents. *Behavioral Neuroscience, 103*, 898-902.

Solomon, P.R., Vander Schaaf, E.R.., Thompson, R.F., & Weisz, D.J. (1986). Hippocampus and trace conditioning of the rabbit's classically conditioned nictitating membrane response. *Behavioral Neuroscience, 100*, 729-744.

Steward, M., & Fox, S.E. (1990). Do septal neurons pace the hippocampal theta rhythm? *Trends in Neuroscience, 13*, 163-168.

Thompson, R.F. (1986). The neurobiology of learning and memory. *Science, 233*, 941-947.

Thompson, R.F., & Kramer, R.F. (1965). Role of association cortex in sensory preconditioning. *Journal of Comparative and Physiological Psychology, 60*, 186-191.

Topka, H., Valls-Sole, J., Massaquoi, S. G., & Hallett, M. (1993). Deficit in classical conditioning in patients with cerebellar degeneration. *Brain, 116*, 961-969.

Weikart, C., & Berger, T.W. (1986). Hippocampal lesions disrupt classical conditioning of cross-modality reversal learning of the rabbit nictitating membrane response. *Behavioural Brain Research, 22*, 85-90.

Weiner, I., Tarrasch, R., Bernasconi, E., Broesen, L.M., Ruttimann, T.C., & Feldon, J. (1997). Amphetamine-induced disruption of latent inhibition is not reinforcer mediated. *Pharmacology Biochemistry and Behavior, 56*, 817-826.

Weisz, D.J., Clark, G.A., & Thompson, R.F. (1984). Increased responsivity of dentate granule cells during nictitating membrane response conditioning in rabbit. *Behavioral Brain Research, 12*, 145-154.

White, I.M., Miller, ,D.P., White, W., Dike, G.L., Rebec, G.V., & Steinmetz, J.E. (1994). Neuronal activity in the rabbit neostriatum during classical conditioning. *Experimental Brain Research, 99*, 179-190.

Woodruff-Pak, D.S. (1993). Eyeblink classical conditioning in H.M.: Delay and trace paradigms. *Behavioral Neuroscience, 107*, 911-925.

Woodruff-Pak, D.S., Li, Y.-T., Hinchliffe, R.M., & Port, R.L. (1997). Hippocampus in delay eyeblink classical conditioning: Essential for nefiracetam amelioration of learning in older rabbits. *Brain Research, 747*, 207-218.

Woodruff-Pak, D.S., Li, Y.-T., Kazmi, A., & Kem, W.R. (1994). Nicotinic cholinergic system involvement in eyeblink classical conditioning in rabbits. *Behavioral Neuroscience, 108*, 486-493.

Woodruff-Pak, D.S, Papka, M., & Ivry, R.B. (1996). Cerebellar involvement in eyeblink classical conditioning in humans. *Neuropsychology, 10*, 443-458.
Yee, B.K., Feldon, J., & Rawlins, J.N.P. (1995). Latent inhibition in rats is abolished by NMDA-induced neuronal loss in the retrohippocampal region, but this lesion effect can be prevented by systemic haloperidol treatment. *Behavioral Neuroscience, 109*, 227-240.
Yeo, C.H., Hardiman, M.J., Moore, J.W., & Russell, I.S. (1984). Trace conditioning of the nictitating membrane response in decorticate rabbits. *Behavioural Brain Research, 11*, 85-88.

ACKNOWLEDGMENTS

This project was supported in part by an ONR contract to NAS.

3 FUNCTIONAL NETWORKS UNDERLYING HUMAN EYEBLINK CONDITIONING

Anthony Randal McIntosh
University of Toronto

Bernard G. Schreurs
National Institute of Neurological Disorders and Stroke

INTRODUCTION

The behavioral laws underlying classical conditioning of skeletal responses, such as eyeblink, are well-defined, making this paradigm especially attractive for studying human associative learning. Although animal studies of associative learning have provided considerable information about neurophysiological and neuroanatomical substrates, less is known about the neural systems involved in associative learning in humans. Many studies of classical conditioning of the rabbit nictitating membrane/eyelid response have focused attention on the cerebellum as a possible site underlying learning (Lavond, Kim & Thompson, 1993). Interestingly, evidence for clinical studies suggest that in humans, the cerebellum may also be crucial for eyeblink conditioning (Woodruff-Pak, 1997).

Study of human associative learning has been bolstered by developments in functional neuroimaging. With the ability to obtain activity measures from the entire brain while subjects are learning the association between the conditioned stimulus and unconditioned stimulus, tremendous strides have been made in the identification of the neural substrates in eyeblink conditioning. One of the most intriguing findings is the confirmation that even simple forms of learning seem to engage a distributed set of brain regions, suggesting that learning affects neural organization at several levels. The purpose of this chapter is to review some of the neuroimaging work on classical conditioning of human eyeblink response. While this research shows some commonality of neural substrates with those identified in animal studies; there are also some interesting differences that could reflect the potential cognitive mediation in classically conditioned responses. Conversely, the result may represent the multiple levels of association that can be formed in classical conditioning (Konorski, 1967; Wagner & Brandon, 1989).

We will focus on two of our own studies (Molchan, Sunderland, McIntosh, Herscovitch & Schreurs, 1994; Schreurs et al., 1997) and compare the results with work done by other groups. From there we will examine the possibility that learning an association results in changes in interactions among several brain areas which include cerebellum and prefrontal cortex. With the multiple levels of neural organization affected by learning, it is possible that different levels may interact with one another emphasizing that the formation of associations results from interactions among several brain areas (McIntosh & Gonzalez-Lima, 1998).

METHODOLOGICAL NOTES

The two primary studies to be considered were designed to explore the neural systems engaged in simple delay conditioning of the eyeblink response in humans. Both were designed to examine the acquisition and extinction of the response by using an initial unpaired phase, followed by a paired phase and then finally an extinction phase. Both studies used a tone conditioned stimulus (CS) and corneal air puff as the unconditioned stimulus (US). The studies differed in two dimensions: the side on which the air puff US was presented and how extinction was done. Some of the specifics are described below.

Behavioral Methods

Eyeblinks were detected using a low-torque, rotary potentiometer (Litton) coupled to the upper eyelid. The potentiometer together with a flexible tube which was positioned approximately 10 mm from the cornea (right for Study 1, left for Study 2), to deliver a 100-ms, 2-psi (1 psi = 6.89 kPa) air puff were attached to the right side (Study 1) and left side (Study 2) of a plastic mask, which served as the head-holding device for the PET scans[1]. The 2-psi air puff was strong enough to elicit an eyeblink reliably without being noxious. Earphones delivered the binaural 80-decibel, 1000-Hz, 500-ms tone CS.

A conditioned response (CR) was defined as any eyelid closure greater than 0.5 mm at least 150 ms after tone onset but before air puff onset. On explicitly unpaired extinction trials, a CR was defined as any eyelid closure exceeding 0.5 mm that occurred 150 ms after tone onset but before the end of the 1200-ms observation interval. Responses that occurred less than 150 ms after tone onset were scored as alpha responses (unconditioned responses to the tone) and not counted as CRs.

PET METHODS

Two PET scans to measure regional cerebral blood flow (rCBF) were performed during each of three different phases of stimulus presentation. The phases of stimulus presentation occurred in the following order: (1) explicitly unpaired presentations of the tone and air puff (unpaired control); (2) paired presentations of the tone preceding and coterminating with the air puff (classical conditioning); and (3) extinction. In the first study, extinction was achieved through successive CS-alone presentations and in the second study extinction entailed explicitly unpaired presentations of the tone and air puff. The change was made to provide the same number of tone and air puff presentations in each phase and so ensure greater comparability of the extinction phase with the unpaired control and paired phases. Consequently, in the second experiment, the number of tone and air puff presentations were the same for each of the three phases. Pairing began immediately after the second unpaired control scan and continued until the first extinction scan. Pairings were done between the two extinction scans to evaluate savings of the conditioned response. The timeline for the two experiments is shown in Table 1.

Table 1. Time course for eyeblink conditioning experiments

Scan	Time, Min	Event
1	1	Begin unpaired tone and air puff stimuli 30 s prior to scan; stimuli stop at scan end
2	13	Restart unpaired tone and air puff 30 seconds prior to scan
	14	Unpaired stimuli stop at scan end; paired tone and air puff begin
3	32	Paired stimuli continue
4	44	Paired stimuli continue
	55	Paired stimuli stop
5	56	Tone alone begins 30 seconds prior to scan
	57	Paired tone and air puff restarted after scan
	67	Paired stimuli stop
6	68	Tone alone begins 30 seconds prior to scan

PET scans were carried out with a Scanditronix PC2048-15B scanner (Scanditronix). Emission scans were obtained after a bolus intravenous injection of 40 mCi (1 Ci = 37 Gbq) of H215O (half-life of 123 s). Images were acquired over 60 s, starting when the bolus of radio tracer arrived in the head. Due to the near-linear relationship between rCBF and tissue counts accumulated over a brief scan period, the acquired images reflected relative changes in rCBF during different scan states. Six scans were conducted, separated by 12 min to allow for radioactive decay of the H215O to <2% peak levels, except for the second and third scans, which were 19 min apart to allow sufficient time for conditioning to occur.

Data Analysis

Most image analysis techniques focus on individual voxels and how their activity changes across different tasks. Because of the emphasis on functional systems, we used a multivariate analytic approach using partial least squares (PLS). Although univariate analyses were done in the original papers to complement PLS, we will focus on the results from PLS analysis. PLS was applied to look first at activity changes across the three phases of experiment and second in the functional connectivity of regions related to learning. A detailed mathematical description of PLS approaches can be found in McIntosh et al. (1996). A conceptual illustration can be made. For task-related activity changes, "task" PLS identifies an image wide pattern of activity, called the singular image[2] that maximally distinguishes conditions. In the present case, task PLS attempts to identify a singular image that would distinguish the paired phase from the unpaired and extinction phases of experiment. The second application of PLS is in the identification of task-dependent changes in functional connectivity. Functional connectivity is an empirical statement that two or more brain areas show some correlation in their response (Friston, 1994; Friston, Frith, Liddle & Frackowiak, 1993). These correlations can be examined region-by-region or, using PLS, between the one region and a collection of several others (McIntosh, Nyberg, Bookstein & Tulving, 1997). In this case the singular image represents the collection of regions that as a group show some task-dependent change in their functional connections with a reference, or seed, voxel. Statistical assessment of the PLS results is done at the image level using permutation tests, and voxel contributions are assessed for their reliability using bootstrapping.

Another outcome from the PLS analysis are scores from the singular image. The scores are the dot-product of the weights in the singular image and the subject's PET scan within each scan. Thus, there is one score for each subject in each scan. The scores index the degree to which a subject's image shows the pattern in the singular image, much in the same way a factor score operates in a factor analysis. The scores can be plotted by scan, in the case of task PLS, to show the variation in activity across the experiment. In the case of a seed voxel PLS, the correlation between the seed and scores within scan is plotted to show the task-dependency of the correlation pattern.

STUDY 1. LATERALITY OF LEARNING-RELATED CHANGES

The surprising outcome of this study was the widely distributed changes we observed that followed the acquisition and extinction of the conditioned response. While the study confirmed the involvement of the cerebellum in eyeblink conditioning, we did note several other regions that showed learning-related activity changes. One in particular, auditory cortex, confirms several animal learning studies that observed learning-related plasticity in sensory structures (Gonzalez-Lima, 1992; Weinberger, 1998).

Nine subjects acquired conditioned eyeblink responses over the course of tone-air puff pairings. By the first paired scan the average percent CRs was 47.7 and by a second paired scan the average percent CRs was 63.2. Paired presentations continued after the fourth scan and subjects achieved and asymptote of 73.7% CRs. During the tone-alone extinction phase, the percent CRs drop down to 40%, with six subjects extinguished completely.

The task PLS analysis identified two dominant singular images. The first effect was a linear change in rCBF across all six scans. Regions that showed this linear change likely reflect some adaptation or habituation independent of change in the associative relationship between the tone and air puff. A second singular image identified the collection of regions showing activity changes that mapped onto the three phases of experiment. The singular image and scores are shown in Figure 1. The singular image identifies areas that showed more activity during the paired phase (areas colored black) and those areas showing less activity during pairing (areas colored white). The scores from this image are plotted by scan showing that this activity pattern distinguished paired versus the unpaired phases. Areas showing increased rCBF during pairing included bilateral auditory cortices (although the extent of the activation of stronger on the left than the right), posterior cingulate, and left medial temporal lobe. The contribution of the left medial temporal was not noted in the original publication because a univariate analysis was used which is less sensitive to regional contributions in a distributed activity pattern. Regions showing

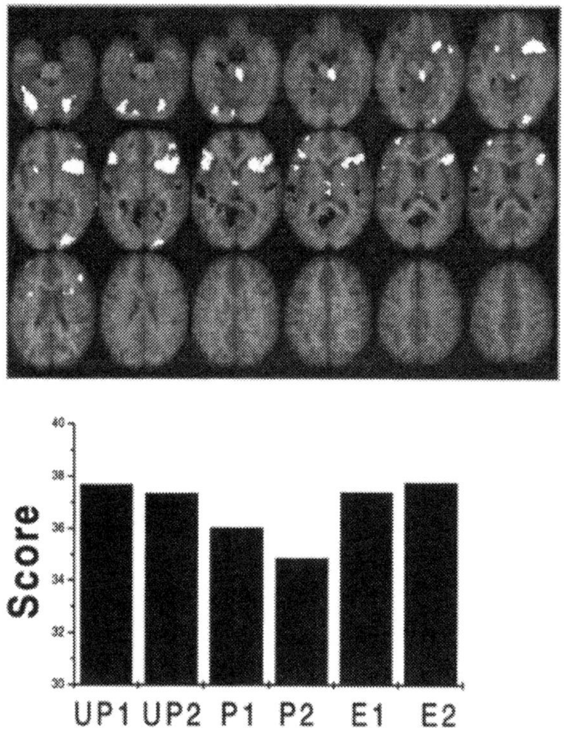

Figure 1. Singular image and plot of scores from task PLS analysis for Study 1. The variation in activity, depicted by the scores, distinguishes paired (P) from unpaired (UP) and extinction (E) scans, thus represents the acquisition of the conditioned response. The scores, plotted as scan means, represent the variation of the activity depicted in the image at the top of the figure. A more positive score represents relatively greater activity in areas shaded white and a more negative score means relatively more activity in areas shaded black. The areas that are most strongly related to the effect are shaded either white or black on an axial structural MRI. The MRI is in standard atlas space (Talairach & Tournoux, 1988). Slices start at -28mm from the AC-PC line at the top left slice and move in increments of 4mm to +36mm at the bottom right, and left is left and the top is anterior in the image.

decreased rCBF during pairing included bilateral cerebellum, midbrain, inferior right and left prefrontal cortices, and the right caudate. The bar plots in Figure 2 show the effects at key voxels identified in the singular image.

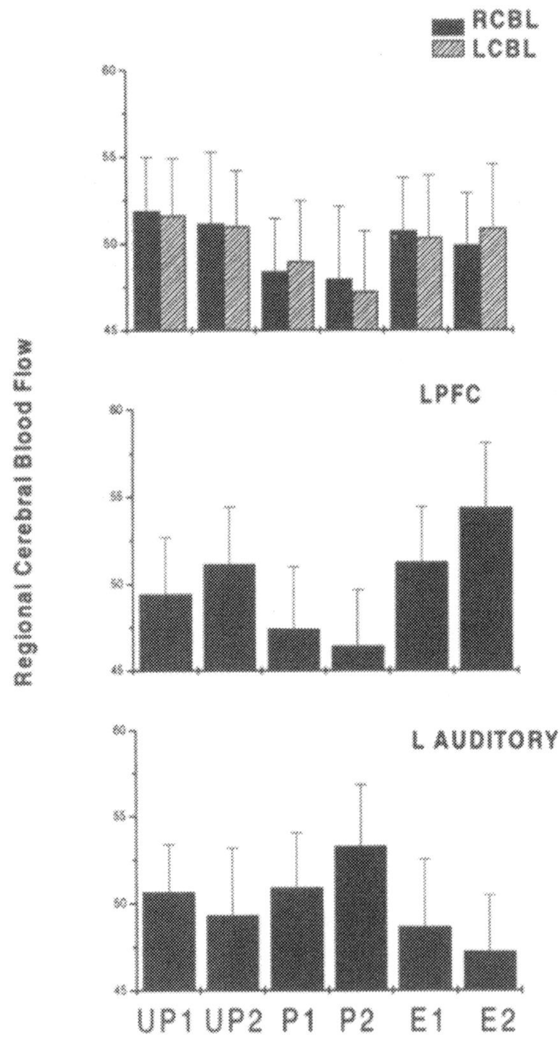

Figure 2. Bar plots (mean and standard error) for ratio-adjusted rCBF in the dominant voxels depicted in Figure 1. Right and left cerebellum (RCBL, coordinates: x = 24, y = -70, z = -24; LCBL, x = -26, y = -70, z = -28), and left prefrontal cortex (LPFC, x = -34, y= 24 , z = 0) show reduced rCBF during pairing. Left auditory cortex (Penhune, Zatorre, MacDonald & Evans, 1996) (x = -52, y = -18, z = 4) shows increased rCBF in the paired phase.

Aside from confirming the strong involvement of the cerebellum in eyeblink conditioning, the impressive result from this study was the rapid changes in evoked activity related to learning. All regions identified in the singular image showed changes in activity that mapped onto the acquisition and extinction of the CR. It emphasizes that neural plasticity spans several time scales. Neural plasticity is most often considered with respect to recovery from damage or prolonged training. Studies such as the one discussed presently emphasize a more transient plasticity that can track the behavioral relevance of stimuli. We shall return to this point below. A second important outcome was the distributed nature of the changes.

STUDY 2. REPLICATION

An interesting outcome in the previous study was the apparent asymmetry of response. The auditory cortex response was stronger in the left hemisphere and, although not obvious from the singular image in Figure 1, the caudate and cerebellar responses were stronger on the right. We hypothesized that this relative laterality may be related to the side the US was presented. The second study, therefore, assessed this laterality by a simple switch from the right to the left eye.

The behavioral quantification for Study 2 was somewhat more thorough than the first. Overall, there was a marked increase in CRs during the course of the experiment and a decrease in alpha responses (i.e., early tone-evoked responses) to a relatively low, stable level. In particular, during the two unpaired control scans, the tone elicited alpha responses of 43.5% and 22.7%, respectively, and responses that met the latency and amplitude criteria for conditioned responses occurred at a frequency of 11% and 6.7%, respectively. During the first three blocks of pairings, alpha responses decreased from 17.4% to 10.9% whereas conditioned responses showed significant acquisition, increasing from 35.7% during the first block to 59.8% by the third block. Acquisition of CRs continued, increasing from 49.5% to 62.5%. Conditioned responses asymptoted at approximately 61% during the next two blocks of paired trials. The first unpaired extinction scan yielded responding at a level of 39.5%. Responding during the final two blocks of paired training trials rose from 47% to 52.3%. The second unpaired extinction scan yielded 58% conditioned responses. There were two main behavioral differences between Studies 1 and 2: Study 1 showed higher percent CRs at asymptote and Study 2 showed somewhat less extinction. That latter result may reflect the use of explicitly unpaired extinction in Study 2.

As with the previous study, the PLS analysis identified two dominant singular images depicting independent experimental effects. The first image again reflects a linear change in activity across the six scans. There was remarkable overlap in the regions showing this change and those identified in the previous study. We noted that the same areas were identified in another study that examined these monotonic activity changes across three different experiments (Rajah, Hussey, Houle, Kapur & McIntosh, 1998). The correspondence suggests that such changes may be independent of the experimental manipulation and can be separated from learning-related changes. This is an important point since these non-specific effects that also express forward in time can easily confound learning studies. Learning studies are not easily counterbalanced.

For the present studies, the nonlinear change in associative value allowed us to separate learning effects from nonspecific effects (Grafton, Hazeltine & Ivry, 1995). In other cases, using a different set of scan conditions to start and end the study may help to distinguish effects (Honda et al., 1998; McIntosh, Lobaugh, Cabeza, Bookstein & Houle, 1998b).

The second singular image identified the same nonlinear change in activity that mapped onto the change in the association between the tone and air puff (Figure 3). As with the previous study, cerebellum, auditory cortex, left medial temporal areas, and inferior prefrontal cortices contributed to this activity pattern. There were however some interesting differences. The predominant changes in activity were observed in occipitotemporal cortices. Prefrontal involvement was more extensive but this may be due to the more extensive dorsal-ventral field of view in this study. The bar plots (Figure 4) for the comparable voxels identified from the first study show that activity changes in cerebellum, left prefrontal cortex, and right auditory cortex, followed a similar change in activity in the second study.

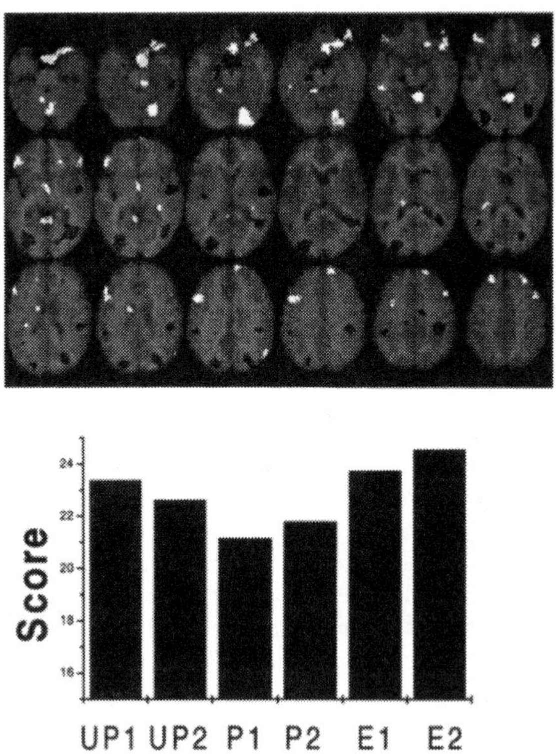

Figure 3. Singular image and plot of scores from task PLS analysis for Study 2. Convention is the same as Figure 1.

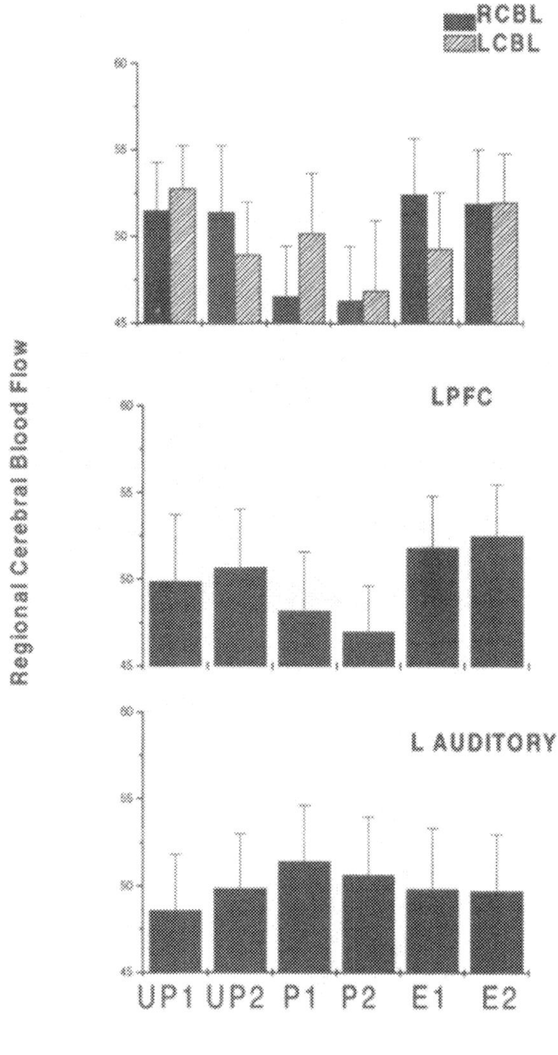

Figure 4. Bar plots (mean and standard error) for ratio-adjusted rCBF in the dominant voxels depicted in Figure 3. Right and left cerebellum (RCBL, coordinates: x = 10, y = -68, z = -24; LCBL, x = -10, y = -56, z = -28), and left prefrontal cortex (LPFC, x = -34, y= 24 , z = 0) show reduced rCBF during pairing. Left auditory cortex (Penhune et al., 1996) (x = 58, y = -12 z = 4) shows increased rCBF in the paired phase.

COMBINED ANALYSIS AND FUNCTIONAL CONNECTIONS OF PREFRONTAL CORTEX

The two tasks overlapped in several key regions. Both experiments confirmed the involvement of the cerebellum in acquisition and extinction of the CR. Both studies also showed strong involvement of auditory cortices and left medial temporal lobe structures. Interestingly the auditory cortex effect was strongest in the hemisphere contralateral to the air puff, while the medial temporal change was in the same side for both studies. The common effects were further evaluated by combining the two studies in a task PLS. The results from this analysis are shown in Figure 6 and the scores are plotted for each scan by experiment. Obvious from this plot is that subjects from Study 1 showed more activity variation across the experiment in areas identified in the singular image than subjects in Study 2. This is especially evident in the

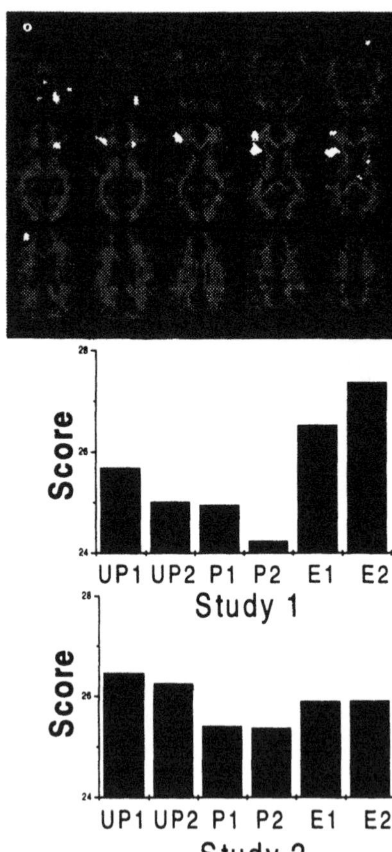

Figure 5. Singular image and scores from the combined task PLS analysis. Convention is the same as Figure 1. The variation in scores by scan is essentially the same for both studies although the scores are greater during extinction in Study 1 compared to Study 2.

extinction phase where subjects from Study 1 have greater scores than subjects in Study 2. The difference may reflect the lower levels of extinction in Study 2. The singular image identified areas that as a group showed variations in activity as the association changed in both studies (Figure 5). Bilateral middle temporal, posterior cingulate and left medial temporal lobe (all shaded black, thus negatively related to the pattern of scores) showed a common activity change with relatively higher rCBF during pairing. Right cerebellar cortex and striatum and left prefrontal cortex (all shaded white, thus positively related to the pattern of scores) showed less rCBF during pairing.

The common involvement of left prefrontal cortex is interesting in the context of imaging work on cognitive processes suggesting that learning, or encoding, of new information seems to recruit the left prefrontal regions more than the right prefrontal regions. This dissociation has been called the Hemispheric Encoding Retrieval Asymmetry model or HERA (Nyberg, Cabeza & Tulving, 1996; Tulving, Kapur, Craik, Moscovitch & Houle, 1994). Since the prefrontal cortices are ideally situated to receive information from multiple sensory modalities and to affect motor structures, their involvement in learning about and responding to the environment is perhaps not unexpected. The asymmetry is another matter. Some initial speculation suggested that the asymmetry observed in the HERA model may reflect the abundance of verbal material used in episodic memory studies (Kelley et al., 1998). However, our present observations suggest that this asymmetry may reflect some more fundamental difference in these two hemispheres. Since learning about the environment requires "binding" of new information, it may be that left prefrontal cortex is specialized for the formation of new sensorimotor associations. If this true, we would expect that the interactions to left prefrontal cortex should vary as the association is learned.

This hypothesis was evaluated by examining the functional connectivity of left prefrontal cortex (LPFC) across the two studies. Specifically, the expectation would be that the change in LPFC functional connections should map onto the change in the CS-US association. To maximize power for this analysis subjects from the two studies were combined. The first singular image from this analysis depicted common patterns of LPFC functional connectivity across the experiment. Remarkably, the second singular image (Figure 6) showed a change in functional connectivity that most strongly separated the paired from the unpaired and extinction phases. The bar graph in Figure 6 plots the correlations, converted to z-scores by division by their estimated standard error, of LPFC with the scores. Within the paired phase the strongest positive correlation between LPFC and the singular image score was in the second paired scan where subjects would have reached asymptote in learning. The bar plot shows the change in the correlation of the LPFC with the regions in the singular image. Regions within the singular image that were most strongly related positively to this pattern included cerebellum, midbrain, and left parahippocampal regions. Areas showing negative relation included the temporal poles, right prefrontal cortex, anterior cingulate, and bilateral regions deep within the superior temporal lobe near auditory cortex.

Since it seemed that the areas positively related to LFPC were close to areas showing decreased activity during pairing (i.e., cerebellum), one may expect these areas to also show the same pattern of changes in functional connectivity as LPFC.

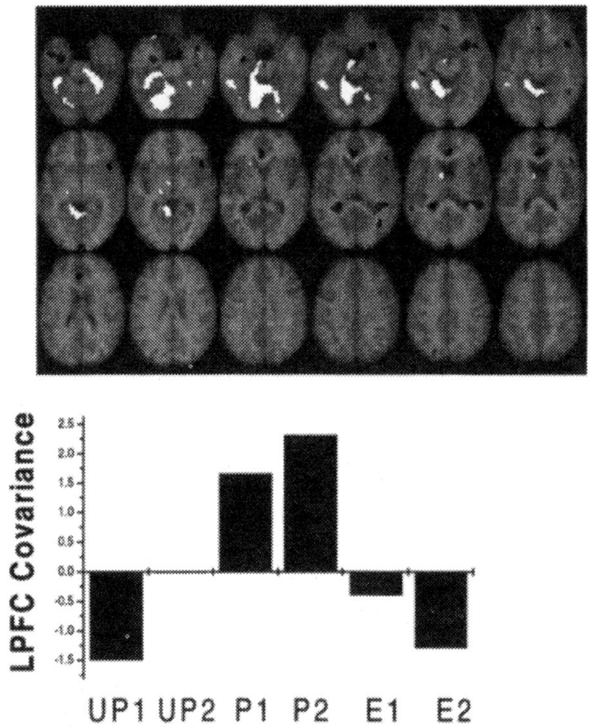

Figure 6. Singular image for the seed PLS analysis of functional connectivity. The image shows the areas with the strongest pattern of covariation with the left prefrontal cortex seed (coordinate: x = -34, y= 24 , z = 0). The bar plot shows the covariation of the LPFC seed with the scores from the image by scan. Covariation is positive during the paired phase and negative during unpaired and extinction phases. Thus, areas in white would show positive covariation with the prefrontal seed during the paired phase and black areas show negative covariation.

This was not the case. Out of all the areas identified by the task PLS, only LPFC showed a change in functional connectivity that could be mapped onto the change in the CS-US association.

One interpretation for these results is that the areas showing activity changes were not functionally connected until LPFC was engaged in the network responding to changing CS-US association. It is reasonable to expect the cerebellum, medial temporal, and auditory regions all show some learning-related modulation of activity since all regions show response plasticity. However, in the context of distributed and interacting neural systems, these regions may not become functionally bound until intermediate areas are engaged. Anatomical studies have demonstrated that all areas engaged in this task are connected to prefrontal cortices either directly, or through one intermediate synapse (Middleton & Strick, 1997; Pandya & Yeterian, 1990). Because most of these connections are reciprocal it follows that they also receive feedback from prefrontal cortices as the associations are learned. It is also possible that the prefrontal functional connectivity represents the "cognitive" component of the learned association. In the case of simple associations, the interactions of prefrontal cortex may not be critical, but as the complexity of the associations increase, prefrontal involvement is more central (Petrides, 1985; Petrides, 1997; Petrides, Alivisatos, Evans & Meyer, 1993).

COMPARISON WITH OTHER STUDIES

There are two PET studies of human eyelid conditioning (Blaxton et al., 1996; Logan & Grafton, 1995), which provide significant confirmation of some of our own data as well as identifying some differences. Logan and Grafton examined glucose metabolism and found increases in a number of regions including cerebellum, hippocampus, striatum, temporal gyrus, and the occipitotemporal fissure. Blaxton et al. examined rCBF and found increases in striatum, hippocampus, and decreases in cerebellum. Blaxton et al. also noted a decrease in LPFC as learning proceeded. A number of areas, most notably the cerebellum and hippocampus, were identified to be specifically involved during eyeblink conditioning in all of the imaging studies. Differences between studies could be related to several dimensions: imaging methods (e.g., glucose metabolism which has a longer scan period versus rCBF), different field of views, (the Logan and Grafton study positioned the PET camera more ventrally), behavioral paradigms (massed in the Blaxton et al. study versus continuous training in the two present studies) and conditioning levels may account for some of the between-study differences in brain areas and differences in the direction of changes observed in the imaging of human eyeblink conditioning. These factors may also combine with sampling different time windows during the acquisition of the conditioned response. It is possible that certain areas are recruited at different times during acquisition and may not be identified depending on what portion of the acquisition curve is sampled. These discrepancies could be remedied by using methods that affords better temporal resolution to follow the acquisition curve continuously (e.g., Evoked Response Potentials, functional Magnetic Resonance Imaging).

COMPARISON WITH OTHER LEARNING STUDIES

Several imaging studies of associative learning in humans have been published. A study comparable to those discussed above, but using leg flexion rather than eyeblink as the conditioned response, observed cerebellar, medial temporal and prefrontal activity changes as learning proceeded (Timmann et al., 1996). Other studies have examined learning of simple sensory associations (McIntosh, Cabeza & Lobaugh, 1998a; McIntosh et al., 1998b), aversive conditioning (Buchel, Morris, Dolan & Friston, 1998; LaBar, Gatenby, Gore, LeDoux & Phelps, 1998; Morris, Friston &

Dolan, 1997; Morris, Friston & Dolan, 1998), and implicit learning of motor sequences (Deiber et al., 1997; Grafton et al., 1995; Grafton et al., 1992; Jenkins, Brooks, Nixon, Frackowiak & Passingham, 1994; Seitz, Roland, Bohm, Greitz & Stone, 1990). Considered together, these studies emphasize two features of the neural systems engaged in learning. First, there is surprising overlap in regional involvement across studies that appear independent of the experimental specifics. For example, the striatum appears to be routinely engaged across almost all studies as associations are learned (Miskin & Petri, 1987). Frontal cortices, to a large extent, also seemed to be engaged routinely in implicit learning studies, although the location of the prefrontal area varies widely. The cerebellum is reported less frequently, but does seem to be engaged across several learning tasks. Importantly, cerebellar involvement does not seem to require an explicit motor response when learning-related activity measures are taken. The use of imaging in humans has demonstrated that the cerebellum seems to be engaged across a remarkably wide-range of tasks from motor functions to "higher-order" cognitive functions (Cabeza et al., 1997; Courchesne & Allen, 1997; Schmahmann, 1991).

It is tempting to suggest that the evolutionary expansion of prefrontal cortices has resulted in the unique engagement of prefrontal regions in associative tasks (e.g., Petrides, 1997). This is made more provocative when one considers that one of the other regions, besides prefrontal cortex (Pandya & Yeterian, 1990; Pandya & Yeterian, 1996), that has shown a disproportionate expansion in humans compared to other primates, is the cerebellum (Matano & Hirasaki, 1997; Rilling & Insel, 1998). The analysis of functional connectivity we report above demonstrates strong interactions between frontal and cerebellar regions in learning, and many imaging studies find co-activation of prefrontal and cerebellar regions in cognitive tasks. Does this mean that prefrontal-cerebellar interactions reflect cognitive mediation of simple associative behaviors or that cognitive processes use some of the same mechanisms as simple associative learning? The first perspective echoes the views in the 1960's and 70's when it was felt that human associative learning was distinct from associative learning in other species because of cognitive contamination. The second perspective revives early theoretical work in learning theory when it was felt that simple associative behaviors formed the foundation for higher-order cognition. At present, it seems that there may be truth to both of these statements, and it may result from the organization of the nervous system.

INTERACTING NEURAL SYSTEMS AND ASSOCIATIVE LEARNING

Two dominant organizational features of the brain, connectivity and plasticity, may be key to the understanding how the brain learns. Neurons are connected to one another both locally and at a distance. Most other systems in the body show some capacity for cell to cell communication, but the nervous system appears to be specialized for rapid transfer of signals. This means that a single change to the system is conveyed to several parts of the brain simultaneously and that some of this will feed back onto the initial site. There are obvious extremes to just how "connected" a system can be and the nervous system occupies some intermediate position. Local cell networks are highly interconnected, but not completely so, and this means that adjacent cells can have common and unique connections. The term "semiconnected" is used to designate this particular property of local cell networks[3]. The networks themselves can be thought of as semiconnectors, especially in as much as their function, as discussed below, is not only to mediate the signal between different cerebral regions but also to modulate the signal, in keeping with the specific properties of different semiconnectors. In information-theoretic terms, local cell networks (semiconnectors) act as noisy communication channels.

One consequence of the semiconnectivity of a local network is a certain degree of redundancy of responses (or degeneracy; Tononi, Sporns & Edelman, 1999). The concept of semiconnectivity allows, at the level of local circuits, for adjacent neurons to have similar response properties (e.g., orientation columns in primary visual cortex) whereas neurons slightly removed may possess overlapping, but not identical, response characteristics.

The connections between local ensembles are more sparse than the intra-ensemble connectivity. Estimates of the connections in the primate cortical visual system suggest that somewhere between 30-40% of all possible connections between cortical areas exist (Felleman & Van Essen, 1991). Recent simulation studies show that this sparseness is a computation advantage for the nervous system in that it allows for a high degree of flexibility in responses at the system level (Tononi, Sporns, & Edelman, 1992). Simply put, a system that has reciprocal and sparse connections, like the brain, is able to integrate a great deal more information than a system that is completely interconnected or one where regions are arranged hierarchically.

In addition to semiconnectivity, response plasticity seems to be a general feature of the brain. Neural plasticity is an established phenomenon. Following central or peripheral damage there is profound reorganization of the nervous system (Hubel & Wiesel, 1965; Merzenich et al., 1983; Pons et. al, 1991). Reorganization can also be observed after prolonged training (Karni et al., 1995). The plasticity considered here is more short-lived. Cells can show a rapid shift in response to afferent stimulation that is dependent on the context in which they fire. This transient response plasticity occurs over a much shorter time-scale compared to recovery from damage. Physiological investigation has consistently shown transient plasticity in the earliest parts of the nervous system (Morrell, 1961). If an auditory stimulus acquires some meaning, auditory cortex cells will respond more vigorously to the tone (Weinberger & Diamond, 1987). Even cells that did not respond to the tone prior to learning became more responsive to the tone after learning. Tuning curves that peaked at a different frequency, shifted towards that of the conditioned tone. Transient plasticity of responses in relation to learning and memory have been observed in several parts of the brain, from single cells in isolate spinal cord preparations (Wolpaw & Lee, 1989) to primary sensory and motor structures (Donoghue & Sanes, 1994; Recanzone, Schreiner & Merzenich, 1992). The changes can occur within a few stimulus presentations (Edeline, Pham & Weinberger, 1993; Molchan et al., 1994). Transient plasticity may be a ubiquitous property of the central nervous system (Wolpaw, 1997).

These two features mean that almost any structure in the brain has the biological capacity to participate in learning. This does not mean that all brain regions participate in all learning functions. Instead, each part of the brain has the necessary machinery to "learn" and "respond" to its afferent input. The critical feature is that a region can only respond to the information it receives, thus the constraints on which regions are engaged in learning about a particular situation is the anatomy. Brain areas are pluripotent or equipotent (Lashley, 1929), within the constraints of their anatomy.

Learning, at the level of overt behavior, seems to be a large-scale operation. A common observation from neuroimaging work is that most cognitive and behavior tasks tend to engage several widely-distributed regions (Cabeza & Nyberg, 1997). While some take this as an indication of the capriciousness of neuroimaging, it may be an accurate depiction of reality. The behavior typically measured, even something as simple as eyeblink conditioning, will actively engage brain regions allied with perception of the CS, those that respond to the US, and regions having the anatomical capacity form a CS-US link. Such anatomical convergence is evident along several points of the neuraxis (McIntosh & Gonzalez-Lima, 1998). All areas show response plasticity that relates to the formation of the association. What this means is that the process of learning can engage several levels of the nervous system.

At some level, this position seems to contradict demonstrations that certain regions appear critical to acquisition or expression of learned behaviors – usually through the use of lesion. The perspective of interacting neural systems in learning does not necessarily contradict these observations. Simply put, lesions indicate the regions that are "necessary" for an operation to take place while exploration of system activity/interactivity depict the "sufficient" systems. Most forms of associative learning appear to have multiple levels of representation. Behavioral studies have been able to reliably distinguish between different processes in learning (e.g., Konorski, 1967; Tait & Saladin, 1986; Wagner & Brandon, 1989), and it seems reasonable that these processes should be served by different neural systems or by changing interactions between the same neural systems. It is the process of learning that is the embodiment of these neural systems – learning is a nervous system specialization.

CONCLUSION

In this chapter, we have reviewed imaging work on human eyeblink conditioning to show the correspondence with animal studies and to emphasize the distributed nature of brain functions related to learning. The focus of much research has been on identification of critical sites for learned behaviors. These studies have provided valuable clues on the functional organization of behavior. Imaging work, and related methods that monitor brain activity such as electrophysiology, have the capacity to extend lesion studies by examining how these critical sites interact in the course of normal function. Many contemporary theories have emphasized that brain function emerges from the interactions of specialized regions (Friston, 1997; Mesulam, 1990; Tononi et al., 1992). No single method, however, is optimal for a complete investigation of brain function. The richness and complexity of nervous system function demands that the different approaches be regarded as complementary rather than contradictory.

NOTES

1. As an interesting aside, the apparatus made it impossible to scan individuals with large heads, so we limited the subject sample in both studies to females.
2. The name refers to the fact that the images derived through a singular value decomposition.
3. I am indebted to Endel Tulving for coming up with the term "semiconnected" to describe this feature of the brain.

REFERENCES

Blaxton, T.A., Zeffiro, T.A., Gabrieli, J.D.E., Bookheimer, S.Y., Carrillo, M.C., Theodore, W. H., & Disterhoft, J. F. (1996). Functional mapping of human learning: A PET activation study of eyeblink conditioning. *Journal of Neuroscience, 16*, 4032-4040.

Buchel, C., Morris, J., Dolan, R.J., & Friston, K.J. (1998). Brain systems mediating aversive conditioning: An event-related fMRI study. *Neuron, 20(5)*, 947-957.

Cabeza, R., Kapur, S., Craik, F.I.M., McIntosh, A.R., Houle, S., & Tulving, E. (1997). Functional neuroanatomy of recall and recognition: A PET study of episodic memory. *Journal of Cognitive Neuroscience, 9(2)*, 254-265.

Cabeza, R., & Nyberg, L. (1997). Imaging cognition: An empirical review of PET studies with normal subjects. *Journal of Cognitive Neuroscience, 9(1)*, 1-26.

Courchesne, E., & Allen, G. (1997). Prediction and preparation, fundamental funcitons of the cerebellum. *Learning and Memory, 4*, 1-35.

Deiber, M.P., Wise, S.P., Honda, M., Catalan, M.J., Grafman, J., & Hallett, M. (1997). Frontal and parietal networks for conditional motor learning: a positron emission tomography study. *Journal of Neurophysiology, 78(2)*, 977-91.

Donoghue, J.P., & Sanes, J.N. (1994). Motor areas of cerebral cortex. *Journal of Clinical Neurophysiology, 11(4)*, 382-396.

Edeline, J.M., Pham, P., & Weinberger, N.M. (1993). Rapid development of learning-induced receptive field plasticity in the auditory cortex. *Behavioral Neuroscience, 107(4)*, 539-551.

Felleman, D.J., & Van Essen, D.C. (1991). Distributed hierarchical processing in the primate cerebral cortex. *Cerebral Cortex, 1(1)*, 1-47.

Friston, K. (1994). Functional and effective connectivity: A synthesis. *Human Brain Mapping, 2(1&2)*, 56-78.

Friston, K.J. (1997). Imaging cognitive anatomy. *Trends in Cognitive Science, 1(1)*, 21-27.

Friston, K.J., Frith, C.D., Liddle, P.F., & Frackowiak, R.S.J. (1993). Functional connectivity: The principal-component analysis of large (PET) data sets. *Journal of Cerebral Blood Flow and Metabolism, 13*, 5-14.

Gonzalez-Lima, F. (1992). Brain imaging of auditory learning functions in rats: Studies with fluorodeoxyglucose autoradiography and cytochrome oxidase histochemistry. In F. Gonzalez-Lima, T. Finkenstaedt & H. Scheich (Eds.). *Advances in Metabolic Mapping Techniques for Brain Imaging of Behavioral and Learning Functions*, (Vol. 68, pp. 39-109). Dordrecht: Kluwer Academic Publishers.

Grafton, S.T., Hazeltine, E., & Ivry, R. (1995). Functional mapping of sequence learning in normal humans. *Journal of Cognitive Neuroscience, 7(4)*, 497-510.

Grafton, S.T., Mazziotta, J.C., Presty, S., Friston, K.J., Frackowiak, R.S.J., & Phelps, M.E. (1992). Functional anatomy of human procedural learning determined with regional cerebral blood flow and PET. *Journal of Neuroscience, 12(1)*, 2542-2548.

Honda, M., Deiber, M.P., Ibanez, V., Pascual-Leone, A., Zhuang, P., & Hallett, M. (1998). Dynamic cortical involvement in implicit and explicit motor sequence learning. A PET study. *Brain, 121(Pt 11)*, 2159-2173.

Hubel, D.H., & Wiesel, T.N. (1965). Binocular interaction in striate cortex of kittens reared with artificial squint. *Journal of Neurophysiology, 28(6)*, 1041-59.

Jenkins, I.H., Brooks, D.J., Nixon, P.D., Frackowiak, R.S.J., & Passingham, R.E. (1994). Motor sequence learning: A study with positron emission tomography. *Journal of Neuroscience, 14(6)*, 3775-3790.

Karni, A., Meyer, G., Jezzard, P., Adams, M.M., Turner, R., & Ungerleider, L.G. (1995). Functional MRI evidence for adult motor cortex plasticity during motor skill learning. *Nature, 377*, 155-158.

Kelley, W.M., Miezin, F.M., McDermott, K.B., Buckner, R.L., Raichle, M.E., Cohen, N.J., Ollinger, J.M., Akbudak, E., Conturo, T.E., Snyder, A.Z., & Petersen, S.E. (1998). Hemispheric specialization in human dorsal frontal cortex and medial temporal lobe for verbal and nonverbal memory encoding. *Neuron, 20(5)*, 927-36.

Konorski, J. (1967). *Integrative Activity of the Brain.* Chicago: University of Chicago Press.

LaBar, K.S., Gatenby, J.C., Gore, J.C., LeDoux, J.E., & Phelps, E.A. (1998). Human amygdala activation during conditioned fear acquisition and extinction: a mixed-trial fMRI study. *Neuron, 20(5)*, 937-45.

Lashley, K.S. (1929). *Brain Mechanisms and Intelligence.* New York: Hafner Publishing Co., Inc.

Lavond, D.G., Kim, J.J., & Thompson, R.F. (1993). Mammalian brain substrates of aversive classical conditioning. *Annual Review of Psychology, 44*, 317-342.

Logan, C.G., & Grafton, S.T. (1995). Functional anatomy of human eyeblink conditioning determined with regional cerebral glucose metabolism and positron-emission tomography. *Proceedings of the National Academy of Science, (USA), 92*, 7500-7504.

Matano, S., & Hirasaki, E. (1997). Volumetric comparisons in the cerebellar complex of anthropoids, with special reference to locomotor types. *American Journal of Anthropology, 103(2)*, 173-83.

McIntosh, A.R., Bookstein, F.L., Haxby, J.V., & Grady, C.L. (1996). Spatial pattern analysis of functional brain images using Partial Least Squares. *Neuroimage, 3*, 143-157.

McIntosh, A.R., Cabeza, R.E., & Lobaugh, N.J. (1998a). Analysis of neural interactions explains the activation of occipital cortex by an auditory stimulus. *Journal of Neurophysiology, 80*, 2790-2796.

McIntosh, A.R., & Gonzalez-Lima, F. (1998). Large-scale functional connectivity in associative learning: Interrelations of the rat auditory, visual and limbic systems. *Journal of Neurophysiology, 80*, 3148-3162.

McIntosh, A.R., Lobaugh, N.J., Cabeza, R., Bookstein, F.L., & Houle, S. (1998b). Convergence of neural systems processing stimulus associations and coordinating motor responses. *Cerebral Cortex, 8*, 648-659.

McIntosh, A.R., Nyberg, L., Bookstein, F.L., & Tulving, E. (1997). Differential functional connectivity of prefrontal and medial temporal cortices during episodic memory retrieval. *Human Brain Mapping, 5(4)*, 323-327.

Merzenich, M M., Kaas, J.H., Wall, J.T., Sur, M., Nelson, R.J., & Felleman, D.J. (1983). Progression of change following median nerve section in the cortical representation of the hand in areas 3b and 1 in adult owl and squirrel monkeys. *Neuroscience, 10*, 639-665.

Mesulam, M.M. (1990). Large-scale neurocognitive networks and distributed processing for attention, language, and memory. *Annals of Neurology, 28(5)*, 597-613.

Middleton, F.A., & Strick, P.L. (1997). Dentate output channels: motor and cognitive components. *Progress in Brain Research, 114*, 553-66.

Miskin, M., & Petri, H.L. (1987). Memories and habits: Some implications for the analysis of learning and retention. In L. R. Squire (Ed.), *Memory and the Brain, (pp. 287-296).* New York: Oxford University Press.

Molchan, S.E., Sunderland, T., McIntosh, A.R., Herscovitch, P., & Schreurs, B.G. (1994). A functional anatomical study of associative learning in humans. *Proceedings of the National Academy of Science, (USA), 91*, 8122-8126.

Morrell, F. (1961). Electrophysiological contributions to the neural basis of learning. *Physiological Review, 41*, 443-494.

Morris, J.S., Friston, K.J., & Dolan, R.J. (1997). Neural responses to salient visual stimuli. *Proceedings of the Royal Society B, 264(1382)*, 769-775.

Morris, J.S., Friston, K.J., & Dolan, R.J. (1998). Experience-dependent modulation of tonotopic neural responses in human auditory cortex. *Proceedings of the Royal Society B, 265(1397)*, 649-657.

Nyberg, L., Cabeza, R., & Tulving, E. (1996). PET studies of encoding and retrieval: The HERA model. *Psychonomic Bulletin and Review, 3*, 135-148.

Pandya, D.N., & Yeterian, E.H. (1990). Prefrontal cortex in relation to other cortical areas in rhesus monkey: Architecture and connections. In H. B.M. Uylings, C.G. Van Eden, J.P.C. De Bruin, M.A. Corner & M.G.P. Feenstra (Eds.), *Progress in Brain Research, (Volume 85, pp. 63-94).* Amsterdam: Elsevier Science Publishers.

Pandya, D.N., & Yeterian, E.H. (1996). Morphological correlations of human and monkey frontal lobe. In A.R. Damasio, H. Damasio & Y. Christen (Eds.), *Neurobiology of Decision Making, (pp. 13-46).* Berlin: Springer Verlag.

Penhune, V.B., Zatorre, R.J., MacDonald, J.D., & Evans, A.C. (1996). Interhemispheric anatomical differences in human auditory cortex: Probabalistic mapping and volume measurement from magnetic resonance scans. *Cerebral Cortex, 6*, 661-672.

Petrides, M. (1985). Deficits in associative-learning tasks after frontal- and temporal-lobe lesions in man. *Neuropsychologia, 23*, 601-614.

Petrides, M. (1997). Visuo-motor conditional associative learning after frontal and temporal lesions in the human brain. *Neuropsychologia, 35(7)*, 989-97.

Petrides, M., Alivisatos, B., Evans, A.C., & Meyer, E. (1993). Dissociation of human mid-dorsolateral from posterior dorsolateral frontal cortex in memory processing. *Proceedings in the National Academy of Science, (USA), 90(3)*, 873-877.

Pons, T., Garraghty, P.E., Ommaya, A.K., Kaas, E. Taub, E., & Mishkin, M. (1991). Massive cortical reorganization after sensory deafferentation in adult macaques. *Science, 252*, 1857-1860.

Rajah, M., Hussey, D., Houle, S., Kapur, S., & McIntosh, A.R. (1998). Task-independent effect of time on rCBF. *Neuroimage, 7(1)*, 314-325.

Recanzone, G.H., Schreiner, C.E., & Merzenich, M.M. (1992). Plasticity in the frequency representation of primary auditory cortex following discrimination training in adult owl monkeys. *Journal of Neuroscience, 13(1)*, 87-103.

Rilling, J.K., & Insel, T.R. (1998). Evolution of the cerebellum in primates: differences in relative volume among monkeys, apes and humans. *Brain, Behavior and Evolution, 52(6)*, 308-14.

Schmahmann, J.D. (1991). An emerging concept: The cerebellar contribution to higher function. *Archieves of Neurology, 48*, 1178-1187.

Schreurs, B.G., McIntosh, A.R., Bahron, M., Herscovitch, P., Sunderland, T., & Molchan, S.E. (1997). Lateralization and behavioral correlation of changes in regional cerebral blood flow with classical conditioning of the human eyeblink response. *Journal of Neurophysiology, 77*, 2153-2163.

Seitz, R.J., Roland, P.E., Bohm, C., Greitz, T., & Stone, E.S. (1990). Motor learning in man: A positron emission tomographic study. *Neuroreport, 1*, 57-60.

Tait, R.W., & Saladin, M.E. (1986). Concurrent development of excitatory and inhibitory associations during backwards conditioning. *Animal Learning and Behavior, 14*, 133-137.

Talairach, J., & Tournoux, P. (1988). *Co-Planar Stereotaxic Atlas of the Human Brain* (Mark Rayport, Trans.). New York: Thieme Medical Publishers, Inc.

Timmann, D., Kolb, F.P., Baier, C., Rijntjes, M., Muller, S.P., Diener, H.C., & Weiller, C. (1996). Cerebellar activation during classical conditioning of the human flexion reflex: A PET study. *Neuroreport, 7(12)*, 2056-60.

Tononi, G., Sporns, O., & Edelman, G. (1992). A measure of brain complexity: Relating functional segregation and integration in the nervous system. *Proceedings of the National Academy of Science, (USA), 91*, 5033-5037.

Tononi, G., Sporns, O., & Edelman, G.M. (1999). Measures of degeneracy and redundancy in biological networks. *Proceedings of the National Academy of Science, (USA), 96(6)*, 3257-3262.

Tulving, E., Kapur, S., Craik, F.I.M., Moscovitch, M., & Houle, S. (1994). Hemispheric encoding/retrieval asymmetry in episodic memory: Positron emission tomography findings. *Proceedings of the National Academy of Science, (USA), 91(6)*, 2016-2020.

Wagner, A.R., & Brandon, S.E. (1989). Evolution of a structured connectionist model of Pavlovian conditioning (AESOP). In S.B. Klein & R.R. Mower (Eds.), *Contemporary Learning Theories: Pavlovian conditioning and the Status of Learning Theory, (pp. 149-189)*. Hillsdale, NJ: Lawrence Erlbaum Association.

Weinberger, N.M. (1998). Physiological memory in primary auditory cortex: Characteristics and mechanisms. *Neurobiology of Learning and Memory, 70(1-2)*, 226-251.

Weinberger, N.M., & Diamond, D.M. (1987). Physiological plasticity in auditory cortex: Rapid induction by learning. *Progress in Neurobiology, 29(1)*, 1-55.

Wolpaw, J., & Lee, C. (1989). Memory traces in primate spinal cord produced by operant conditioning of H-reflex. *Journal Neuroscience, 61(3)*, 563-572.

Wolpaw, J.R. (1997). The complex structure of a simple memory. *Trends in Neurosciemce, 20(12)*, 588-94.

Woodruff-Pak, D.S. (1997). Classical conditioning. *International Review of Neurobiology, 41*, 341-66.

4 FUNCTIONAL MRI STUDIES OF EYEBLINK CLASSICAL CONDITIONING

Susan K. Lemieux and Diana S. Woodruff-Pak
Temple University

INTRODUCTION

Eyeblink classical conditioning is an ideal learning paradigm to investigate in humans using functional magnetic resonance imaging (fMRI). During the last 25 years, extensive progress has been made in identifying the neural structures and pathways engaged in this form of learning and memory (see Anderson & Steinmetz, 1994; Daum & Schugens, 1996; Lavond, Kim & Thompson, 1993; Steinmetz, 1999; Steinmetz & Thompson, 1991; Thompson & Krupa, 1994, Woodruff-Pak, 1997 for reviews and Lavond, 2000, Steinmetz, 2000, and Thompson, 2000 in the companion volume of this book). Many would argue that the neural basis of associative learning is more fully understood for eyeblink classical conditioning than for any other form of mammalian learning. Using fMRI with its many advantages as a neuroimaging technique, we can probe the neural basis of associative learning in humans by focusing on the structures known to be involved.

Theories and empirical data on learning in the cerebellum converged to enable focused predictions about the brain sites of plasticity in cerebellar cortex and deep nuclei in eyeblink conditioning (Thompson, 1986). The role of the medial-temporal lobes in learning and memory and in awareness of learning can also be addressed with complex eyeblink classical conditioning paradigms (Clark & Squire, 1998; Green & Woodruff-Pak, in press; La Bar & Disterhoft, 1998). The precision of single trial analysis and high spatial and temporal resolution permitted by fMRI enables testing of these theories in humans.

A number of chapters in this volume describe eyeblink conditioning data collected in patients with neurological lesions. These data argue strongly that the neural circuitry supporting eyeblink conditioning is similar in humans and other mammals. A logical extension of this research program is to confirm with imaging techniques, in healthy young adults, the locus of activated sites and to demonstrate the neurobiological changes underlying eyeblink conditioning as they occur.

The history of positron emission tomography (PET) applications to eyeblink classical conditioning is relatively long compared to the history of fMRI use in this paradigm. The first published study of eyeblink classical conditioning using PET appeared in 1994 (Molchan, Sunderland, McIntosh, Herscovitch & Schreurs, 1994) with several replications and extensions in the delay eyeblink classical conditioning paradigm (Blaxton et al., 1996; Logan & Grafton, 1995) and an extension to classical conditioning of leg flexion (Timmann et al., 1996). An extensive search of the literature identified only one other published abstract of a fMRI study of eyeblink classical conditioning (Ramnani, Toni, Josephs, Ashburner & Passingham, 1999) in addition to our own (Lemieux & Woodruff-Pak, 1999). In the absence of a large research literature to review, our aim in this chapter is to present techniques and research progress in using fMRI in studies of human eyeblink classical conditioning as well as to highlight the potential of fMRI in the investigation of the neurobiological basis of learning and memory.

IDENTIFYING EYEBLINK CLASSICAL CONDITIONING CIRCUITRY IN HUMANS

Positron emission tomography (PET) imaging studies of eyeblink classical conditioning identified the cerebellum as a site of physiological change during the acquisition of conditioned responses (CRs; see Chapter 3, this volume). PET imaging during eyeblink conditioning can identify sites that are activated during learning, but PET techniques also have limitations. For example, the spatial resolution of the PET images collected during eyeblink conditioning was relatively poor, making precise localization impossible. Furthermore, the temporal resolution in PET is limited so that the progression of learning could not be observed. Perhaps even more critical, in previous PET studies of eyeblink conditioning, it was not possible to separate individual trials in which CRs, unconditioned responses (URs), reflexive responses to the tone CS ("alpha responses"), and trials with baseline artifacts were produced. PET images in the published studies contain many trials, yet subjects in these studies were producing around 60% CRs. PET images of participants producing less than 100% CRs include a variety of trials with CRs and URs, URs alone, alpha responses, and pre-CS motor artifacts, all of which are dependent on different brain substrates. The neuroanatomical substrates of the actual learning (the production of CRs) are not clearly imaged because trials without the CR are merged with CR trials.

Disputes in the eyeblink conditioning literature have arisen regarding a cerebellar role in generating the CR versus the UR (e.g., Steinmetz et al., 1992; Welsh & Harvey, 1989), yet the temporal resolution of PET is not sufficient to separate CR with UR and UR-alone trials. Functional MRI studies of eyeblink conditioning have the following advantages over PET studies: (a) the brain circuitry for eyeblink conditioning is identified with some precision in non-human mammals so that superior spatial resolution of fMRI in humans can be fully utilized; (b) current fMRI techniques permit an examination of single trials and the ability to parse CRs, URs, alpha responses, and trials with baseline artifacts; (c) there is no radioactive injection required so repeated measurements required to observe learning unfold are less problematic; and (d) anatomical and functional images can be acquired in the same session for direct comparison with minimal misregistration.

Other sites of activation observed in PET studies of eyeblink conditioning included the hippocampus, the striatum, and the prefrontal cortex. Because the role that these structures play in conditioning may occur at different temporal intervals, we anticipate that the greater temporal precision of fMRI will enable us to understand better the neural sequence of events in conditioning.

In the case of the reported changes in the striatum, the timing of data collection might have been critical. In particular, Logan and Grafton (1995) found the striking result that bilateral activation in the ventral striatum was significantly correlated with learning. Other PET studies included scanning over early periods of acquisition, whereas Logan and Grafton (1995) scanned after subjects had received much more training. The CR topography analysis of Sears, Finn, and Steinmetz (1994) indicated that later in training when learning reached asymptotic levels, the timing of the CR was optimal in control subjects. Bilateral striatal activation apparent in the Logan and Grafton (1995) study might have occurred because brains were scanned later in acquisition when striatal input to cerebellum for optimal CR timing was most activated.

Whatever activity that occurs in striatum during eyeblink conditioning in normal subjects is apparently not essential for the production of CRs as patients with Huntington's disease and presumed degeneration in striatum acquire CRs as well as normal age-matched adults (Woodruff-Pak & Papka, 1996). However, the CRs in patients with Huntington's Disease have an earlier onset latency. White et al. (1994) recorded multiple-unit activity in the rabbit striatum during eyeblink conditioning and suggested that the striatum may play a role during later stages of conditioning in refining the timing of the CR. It is possible that the striatal activity observed in PET studies in humans during eyeblink conditioning was analogous to the responses electrophysiologically recorded in the rabbit neostriatum during conditioning by White et al. (1994). This activation may reflect signals from striatum to cerebellum about timing of the CR.

AN APPLICATION: VISUALIZATION OF ALZHEIMER'S DISEASE AS IT AFFECTS EYEBLINK CONDITIONING CIRCUITRY IN HUMANS

Functional imaging provides a dynamic perspective of the brain processing information. In the case of Alzheimer's Disease (AD) in which cognitive impairments characterize the disease, functional imaging may be useful for detecting the disease early in its course. Functional imaging also offers a medium for understanding the effects during development of the disease as it progresses in an individual. Many of the functional imaging studies of patients with AD which have been conducted thus far have used PET to examine brain metabolism and blood flow during the resting state. Other studies investigated the active state: manipulating and assessing cognition during PET or functional MRI image acquisition. These active studies which compare the responses of patients with AD and age-matched control subjects, have potential to differentiate the two groups. The potential for differentiation is maximized when the behavior tested during scanning has a high sensitivity for AD. Eyeblink classical conditioning is a behavior with a high sensitivity for AD (e.g. Solomon, Bein, Levine & Pendlebury, 1991; Woodruff-Pak, Finkbiner & Katz, 1989; Woodruff-Pak, Finkbiner & Sasse, 1990, Woodruff-Pak, Papka, Romano & Li, 1996).

Recently fMRI studies have been conducted to test the effects of AD on memory function, (Corkin, 1998; Small, Perera, DeLaPaz, Mayeux & Stern, 1999). Earlier research articles on fMRI and AD mention implications of fMRI in the diagnosis of AD rather than actually testing patients with probable AD (Moseley & Glover, 1995). Thus, to our knowledge, patients with probable AD have seldom been tested using fMRI. Functional MRI has advantages over PET in that it has greater spatial and temporal resolution. Another significant advantage is that fMRI does not require an injection of a radio-labeled tracer substance. The tracer injection is an essential component of PET methodology that may be especially problematic in older adults whose health status is marginal.

We predict that hippocampal disruption in eyeblink classical conditioning will be measurable as decreased fMRI response in AD in the hippocampus and especially in cerebellum. Disruption of the hippocampal cholinergic system interferes with acquisition of CRs in rabbits and humans, and hippocampal disruption likely results in severe impairment of eyeblink conditioning in patients with AD. Alzheimer's disease produces relatively mild pathology in the cerebellum that does not appear to involve the cerebellar circuitry essential for learning (Li, Woodruff-Pak & Trojanowski, 1994). However, like all aged adults, patients diagnosed with probable AD have Purkinje cell loss, a loss that is associated with poorer eyeblink conditioning (Chen et al., 1996; Woodruff-Pak, Cronholm & Sheffield, 1990; Woodruff-Pak & Trojanowski, 1996). In addition, probable AD patients have a disrupted hippocampal cholinergic system. Impairment in both of the brain structures involved in eyeblink conditioning results in a serious handicap in acquiring CRs that is probably detectable with fMRI. In addition there is an immediate clinical application for this knowledge. Since eyeblink conditioning has a high sensitivity for AD, fMRI studies of probable-AD patients should demonstrate the substrates responsible for poor conditioning in AD.

COMPARISON OF FMRI AND PET

As discussed above in the context of eyeblink classical conditioning, fMRI and PET are the two imaging modalities that are being widely used for human brain mapping. In the following sections fMRI is described, including the techniques that are being applied for studying conditioning. To begin, we compare fMRI and PET, then continue with further discussion of fMRI. Although the bases for the two techniques are quite different, they both rely on the underlying physiological changes that result from neuronal activation to localize active cortex. Therefore, if the experiments are carefully designed, data can be acquired for direct comparison.

To collect fMRI data that are comparable to PET data, two factors must be considered: the behavioral paradigm and the MRI data collection technique. First, the paradigm must be designed so that multiple trials contribute to each condition, because unlike PET data, fMRI data can be collected for single trials (Buckner, 1998; Duyn, Yang, Frank, Mattay & Hou, 1996; Friston et al., 1998a; Rosen, Buckner & Dale, 1998). Second, the MRI data collection method must be sensitive primarily to relative blood flow or volume changes as PET data are. Some fMRI acquisition methods are sensitive to changes in the metabolic rate of oxygen consumption as well as the blood flow and blood volume changes. (Bandettini et al., 1992; Kwong, 1992; Ogawa et al., 1993; Buxton, Wong & Frank, 1998).

Functional MRI data are collected using either commercial packages available from the scanner manufacturer or imaging software developed by investigators. The contrast, spatial resolution and temporal resolution of the fMRI data are determined by the pulse sequence and parameters such as field-of-view, matrix size and scan time. The pulse sequence determines the type of contrast in the magnetic resonance images. For example, T2-weighted fast-spin echo images have a high degree of contrast between gray and white matter while phase-contrast images can be used to visualize blood vessels. The pulse sequence is the interface between the user and the MRI scanning hardware. It allows the user to control the data collection by specifying the timing, shape, and amplitude for the excitation radio-frequency pulses and gradient pulses which are used for imaging. Pulse sequences are usually named with acronyms that describe how the magnetization is manipulated by the pulses or which type of contrast is generated.

If the fMRI data are acquired with a perfusion-sensitive pulse sequence, such as EPISTAR (Siewert et al., 1996) then both the fMRI and PET techniques detect changes in perfusion of the cortex to elucidate the areas activated by a task. The PET activation studies using radio-labeled water (H2O-15) measure changes in relative cerebral blood flow (rCBF). The fMRI perfusion studies use spin-tagging to detect changes in rCBF, (Detre et al., 1994; Siewert et al., 1996; Wong, Buxton & Frank, 1998).

More often, functional MRI studies use BOLD (Blood Oxygenation Level Dependent) contrast pulse sequences which measures changes in rCBF and also changes in the percentage of oxygenated hemoglobin (%HbO2) in the blood, (Bandettini, Wong, Hinks, Tikofsky & Hyde, 1992; Kwong, 1992, Ogawa et al., 1993). Studies using BOLD contrast are performed using pulse sequences that are the most sensitive to local susceptibility changes such as those caused by changes in %HbO2 like FLASH or EPI (Turner, Howseman, Rees, Josephs & Friston, 1998). The BOLD contrast is caused by the increased magnetic susceptibility of deoxygenated hemoglobin which results in lower MR signal intensity in less oxygenated blood. The increase in rCBF to activated cortex is larger than is required for the increase in metabolic rate so the MR signal intensity rises during activation in spite of the increase in deoxygenated blood. This unexpected result launched a flurry of theoretical and experimental studies designed to uncover the physiological mechanism of the signal changes observed in fMRI activation studies and to elucidate the connection between those changes and the underlying neuronal activity (Fox & Woldorff, 1994; Hajnal, Bydder & Young, 1995; Kiebel, Ashburner, Poline & Friston, 1997; Moseley & Glover, 1995; Rao et al., 1995; Weisskoff, 1995). Thus, the underlying physiology used for imaging activation differs somewhat between PET and fMRI data.

The criteria for stimuli presentation during imaging also differ between PET and fMRI. The regions which show PET signal changes during a task result from multiple repetitions of that task during acquisition. For example, a motor task might consist of multiple repetitions of finger-thumb opposition tapping. The PET signal changes generated by the neuronal activity are not large enough to detect single events. Thus the paradigm must be designed to generate sufficient neuronal activity during a single scan and that activity is integrated over the time course of the scan. The temporal resolution is determined by the time to acquire each image (40-70 seconds). Activation maps can be generated by subtracting the scans acquired during the task from the resting baseline scans, although often much more sophisticated techniques such as multivariate analysis are used, (see Chapter 3, this volume).

Comparable fMRI data can be acquired by repetition of the task for a block of time, with periods of rest used to acquire baseline images. The temporal resolution is determined by the time used to acquire the image (1-3 seconds). However, the task repetition integrates the neuronal activity so that each state has a longer temporal resolution as determined by the experimental design for the length of each block (15-30 seconds). Activation maps can be calculated by averaging together the data acquired during the task and averaging the data acquired during the resting baseline condition and then subtracting the two average images. This simple type of "blocked-trial" fMRI has been very successful in advancing our knowledge of the organization of the brain during sensorimotor tasks, visual tasks and cognitive tasks including attention, memory, learning, and executive function.

Significant advances in fMRI data analysis were a) the technique of correlation analysis (Bandettini, Jesmanowicz, Wong & Hyde, 1993), b) the calculation of the effect of the hemodynamic response function on the fMRI signal (Friston, Jezzard & Turner, 1994) and c) the code (Statistical Parametric Mapping, SPM) for a general linear model for fMRI analysis which was published and freely distributed (Friston, Holmes, Worsley, Poline, Frith & Frackowiak, 1995). Briefly, an analysis consists of: 1) generating a reference wave function - the reference can be calculated by convolution of the stimulation paradigm with the hemodynamic response function; 2) correlating the fMRI time course data pixel-by-pixel to the reference - the resulting correlation coefficents for each pixel indicate how closely that time course is modeled by the reference waveform; and 3) assessing the significance of the response of each voxel statistically.

During the last five years there has been further progress in fMRI data collection strategies and in the statistical analysis of the data sets. One of the most important developments has been single-trial or event-related fMRI (Bandettini et al., 1992; Buckner, 1998; Friston et al., 1998a; Kwong et al., 1992; Ogawa et al., 1993). Using this technique, individual events can be tagged with a behavioral response and either time-locked averaged or sampled at a higher effective trial frequency using random inter-trial intervals. Using these methods single-event fMRI data can be collected for paradigms such as eyeblink classical conditioning where averaging over trials with varying response is less informative. Images may be collected throughout the experiment or immediately after the stimulus as the hemodynamic response has a latency onset of about one second with the peak response occurring 5-6 seconds after the stimulus onset.

As described above, fMRI has significantly better temporal resolution than PET. The fMRI data also have significantly better spatial resolution. An fMRI data set is a time series of images of a selected volume. Each time point consists of a group of cross-sectional images or slices. The resolution is determined by the slice thickness, the field-of-view (FOV), and the imaging matrix size. For example, the spatial resolution of a scan taken with twelve 5 mm slices over a 240 mm FOV with a 64 x 64 matrix is FOV/matrix size so the pixels are 4 mm x 4 mm. Each volume element or voxel is 4 mm x 4 mm x 5 mm = 80 mm^3. The comparable benchmark for a PET scan would be voxels 7 mm x 7 mm x 7 mm = 343 mm^3.

FUNCTIONAL MRI USING BOLD CONTRAST

From the time that brain function was first imaged using MRI (Bandettini et al., 1992; Kwong et al., 1992; Ogawa et al., 1993), researchers have been working to understand the relationship between the MRI signal changes and the neurons activated during a task. Neither PET nor fMRI directly measure neuronal electrical activity (Jueptner & Weiller, 1995). In functional MRI, BOLD contrast is generated by changes in blood flow, blood volume, and percent of blood oxygenation as described above. Thus a model that linked those physiological changes to neuronal activation was needed.

Such a model was put forward (Friston, Jezzard & Turner, 1994) and has been extremely successful at describing fMRI results for single and blocked trials. This model, which takes into account the hemodynamics of the BOLD response, can be expressed as

$$M(t)=S(t)*h(t) + N(t) \qquad \text{Eq.1}$$

where S(t), the stimulus, is convolved with h(t), the hemodynamic response, and N(t) represents the noise. The model is generally useful as various forms for the hemodynamic response function and stimulus presentation can be easily integrated.

This model for the hemodynamic response can be used to estimate the response for a planned fMRI experiment. For eyeblink classical conditioning, the neuronal activity for the hippocampal cells in CA1 has been measured in rabbits in many laboratories, and a representative data set is shown in Figure 1a. The CA1 pyramidal cell activity and the predicted fMRI signal changes during CRs are shown in Figure 1a and Figure 1b. Measurements of multiple-unit action potentials in rabbits indicate that CA1 pyramidal cells fire during CRs and URs. For this calculation the hemodynamic response function was estimated following Friston using as Poisson function with a width of 8 seconds.

$$M(t) = \lambda_1^{\,t-t_0} e^{-\lambda} / (t - t_0)! \qquad \text{Eq. 2}$$

Recent work has focused on testing the linearity of the hemodynamic response and has shown that Equation 1 is an approximation to the response. Studies show that although the hemodynamic response function may be convolved with the stimulus to estimate the response for short periods of stimuli, that same hemodynamic response will underestimate the response for longer periods of stimulation (Friston, Josephs, Rees & Turner, 1998b; Glover, 1999; Mayhew et al., 1998; Vazquez & Noll, 1998). Also, an overshoot or undershoot is sometimes seen on the rising side of the hemodynamic response and a longer more pronounced undershoot may also be seen before complete return to baseline. The balloon model, a biochemical model that couples blood volume and oxygenation, predicts fMRI signal responses that demonstrate these effects (Buxton, Wong & Frank, 1998). More accurate predictions of the response to longer stimuli from measurements of the response to shorter stimuli can be obtained by use a modification to the balloon model (Glover, 1999).

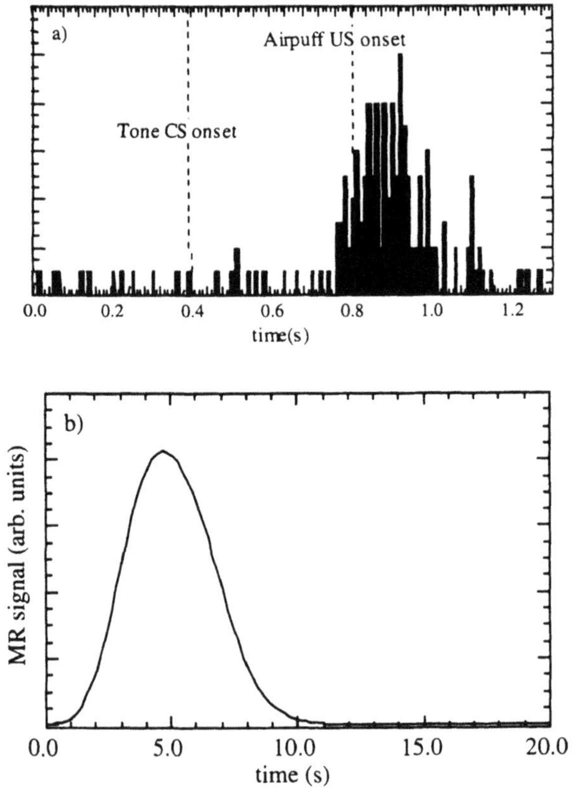

Figure 1. a) Multiple-unit recording from rabbit CA1 pyramidal cells during an eyeblink conditioning CR & UR. b) Estimated fMRI signal response as a result of the neural response. Note the difference in the time scales of these plots.

Measurements have been made of the hemodynamic response function by averaging the single event responses over many trials (Menon, Gati, Goodyear, Luknowsky & Thomas, 1998; Rosen et al., 1998). The response can be characterized by the following common features: the delay (defined as the time to onset after the stimlus) the time-to-peak (defined as the time from onset to peak intensity of the response) the width (defined as the time from onset to recovery to baseline) and the full width at half of the maximum of the peak intensity. An example of the time course for 10 averaged trials is shown in Figure 2. The stimulus duration was, for a block of time, 10 seconds in this example. A significant advantage of blocking trials in this manner is that the hemodynamic response continues to increase for the first 12 seconds after onset.

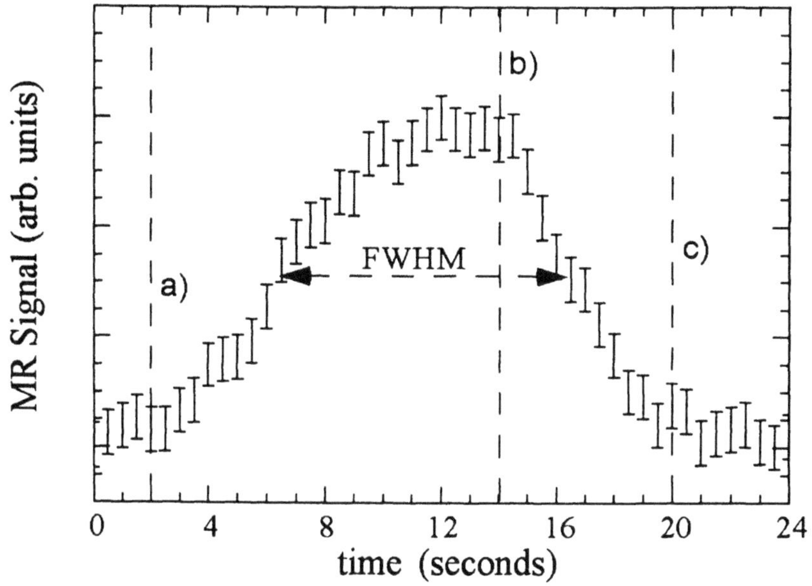

Figure 2. A representative time-locked average time course averaged over 10 single trials for sensorimotor cortex: a) delay, b) time-to-peak, and c) return to baseline. The width of the response is given by the full-width at half maximum, FWHM. The signal estimate was calculated using a stimulus duration of 10 seconds and an intertrial interval of 24 seconds. The signal-to-noise is about 7.

Ideally, as mentioned above, the BOLD signal contrast would result only from changes in the microvasculature responding to the increasing metabolic demand of neurons active during the task. In fact however, the draining macrovasculature shows high contrast as well (Frahm, Merboldt, Hanicke, Kleinschmidt & Boecker, 1994; Lee, Glover & Meyer, 1995). The feeding arteries and arterioles are basically fully oxygenated before activation so no BOLD changes appear on that side of the eloquent cortex. The draining veins and venules from the cortex are not fully oxygenated and thus may become more oxygenated during activation. Therefore, BOLD changes are seen in the activated cortex and on the draining side. A number of approaches can be used to minimize these effects (Bandettini, Wong, Jesmanowicz, Hinks & Hyde, 1994; Glover, Lemieux & Drangova, 1996; Hlustik, Noll & Small, 1998).

DATA ACQUISITION

Maximization of the signal-to-noise ratio for functional MRI data collection is accomplished through the choice of the magnetic field of the scanner, the radio-frequency coil and the pulse sequence. Although the main static magnetic field of the scanner is not an adjustable parameter, the higher signal-to-noise ratio of higher field scanners is an important consideration in scanner choice for a dedicated fMRI system (Turner et al., 1998). There is a significant advantage for BOLD contrast studies because the microsusceptiblity effects increase exponentially with field strength (Jack, Lee & Riederer, 1995). The improvement between the results at 4.0T as compared to 1.5T was a 70% higher number of activated voxels and a 20% higher average t score for the activated voxels (Yang et al., 1999). Most work is still conducted using 1.5 or 2 Tesla clinical imaging systems although many 3T and 4T scanners are installed in dedicated MRI laboratories.

The radio frequency coil is used to detect the magnetic resonance signal. Increases in signal-to-noise ratio for particular regions of the brain can be realized by using smaller surface coils, particularly in a phased array configuration which can cover more area. The signal-to-noise ratio increases linearly as the surface area enclosed by the coil decreases. The trade-off is between signal-to-noise ratio and radio-frequency penetration. The penetration is linearly related to the radius of the radio-frequency coil so small coils that work well for visual paradigms studying the occipital lobe will not work well for a study of the motor activation of the basal ganglia. The most commonly used coils in fMRI studies are quadrature detection birdcage head coils. These coils are the choice for clinical neuroimaging studies as they provide uniform signal throughout the entire brain. Surface coils can be used for improved signal-to-noise ratio in cortical areas closer to the surface such as occipital lobe imaging for studies of the visual cortex.

A variety of pulse sequences are available for fMRI studies; the most commonly used being echo-planar imaging (EPI) with BOLD contrast. Echo-planar imaging is fast, relatively motion-insensitive, and allows for whole brain scans as frequently as every 1-3 seconds depending on the slice thickness used. A variant of echo-planar imaging is called spiral imaging. Spiral imaging also permits acquisition of whole-brain volumes in 1-3 seconds and may be used in both 2D and 3D variations (Glover & Lai, 1998; Lai & Glover, 1998). Table 1 provides a summary of the most frequently used pulse sequences for fMRI (Bandettini et al., 1992; Bandettini et al., 1994; Detre et al., 1994; Edelmann et al., 1994; Glover & Lai, 1998; Hajnal et al., 1993; Hu & Kim, 1993; Kim, 1995; Kwong, 1995; Kwong et al., 1992; Lai & Glover, 1998; Noll, Cohen, Meyer & Schneider, 1995; Ogawa et al., 1993; Wong, Buxton & Frank, 1999; Yang et al., 1996). Several excellent reviews on fMRI data acquisition strategies are available (Aine, 1995; Duyn et al., 1996; Kim & Ugurbil, 1997; Turner et al., 1998).

FUNCTIONAL MRI DATA ANALYSIS

Each individual time course represents the changes in the MR signal for an individual volume element (voxel) of tissue during the experiment. The individual data points

Table 1. FMRI pulse sequences

Pulse Sequence	Contrast	References
Gradient echo	BOLD	Kwong et al., 1992; Bandettini,1992; Ogawa, 1993
Spin-echo	BOLD	Bandettini, 1994
spiral, 2D or 3D	BOLD	Noll, 1995; Yang, 1996; Glover, 1998; Lai, 1998
EPI	BOLD	Kwong, 1995
FLASH	BOLD	Hu, 1993
FAIR	rCBF	Kwong, 1992; Kim 1995
FLAIR	rCBF	Hajnal, 1993
spin-tagging	rCBF	Detre, 1992
QUIPPS	rCBF	Wong, 1996
EPISTAR	rCBF	Edelman, 1994

are therefore not independent. They are connected to each other both spatially and temporally by neurons and blood vessels. The division into little cubic elements is completely artificial - an artifact of the data acquisition. This fact, that each voxel may not be considered independently of the others, either spatially or temporally, is an integral feature of the data set that must not be neglected in the statistical analysis.

Typically, data sets are prepared for analysis in several steps designed to eliminate spurious activation and increase the functional signal to noise ratio. The data are corrected for motion using either a generally available package such as automated image registration (AIR; URL: http://bishopw.loni.ucla.edu/AIR3, (Woods, Grafton, Holmes, Cherry & Mazziotta, 1998a) or another technique. Next, the time courses are filtered to correct for any activity that occurs at low frequencies that are not task-related. The low frequency filtering is accomplished by either removing a linear or linear plus parabolic trend line or by Fourier transforming the data into the frequency domain and removing the lowest frequencies. Cardiac and respiratory activity can also be removed by filtering. A mask can be applied to eliminate from consideration any spurious activation outside the brain. The data may be smoothed both spatially and temporally to increase the signal-to-noise of the activation (Friston, Frith, Liddle & Frackowiak, 1991; Turner et al., 1998; Zarahn, Aguirre & D'Esposito, 1997).

After the data have been pre-processed, the statistical analyses are performed to detect significant activation. One method of extracting information from the data set is to consider each time series from each voxel individually. The response is modeled and then the data are compared to the model and a statistical measure of the model fit to the data is calculated. For example, in the block trial experiment, a sinusoid of the same frequency as the stimulus is used as the model and then the Pearson correlation coefficient, r, is calculated for the time series of each voxel (Bandettini et al., 1993). The result is an image composed of r-values illustrated as the activation map shown in Figure 3. The high r-values indicate tissue that has responded in a sinusoidal fashion to the stimulus. Such images, also called maps of statistical parameters, are referred to as activation maps.

There are an increasing number of statistical tools being applied to fMRI data sets to extract the task-related activation and create the activation maps. Although the general steps remain similar - motion reduction, noise filtering, calculation of a statistical image, and smoothing and thresholding of the statistical image. There are many ways to accomplish these steps.

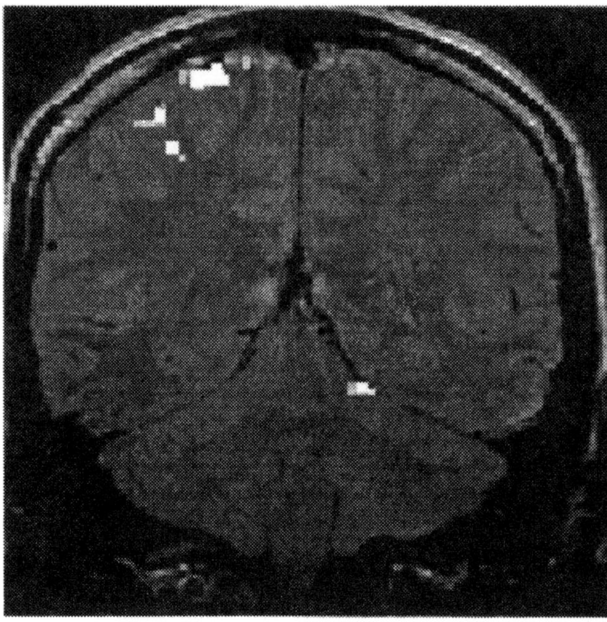

Figure 3. Finger tapping of the left hand using a block trial design. The radiological imaging convention is used - the right brain appears on the left side of the image as if the observer were looking directly at the subject. White indicates areas of activation which were overlaid on the anatomical fast-spin echo image. Note the degradation of spatial resolution (larger pixels) in the fMRI activation.

In principle, the activation maps should show only activation related to the task, but practically there are two major sources of artifactual activation in fMRI data. The first is motion, task-related head motion and physiological motion caused by respiration and cardiac pulsation. The second is activation seen in the large vessels draining the activated cortex as described above. The first correction, for head motion can be accomplished with an image registration algorithm (Woods et al., 1998a; Woods, Grafton, Watson, Sicotte & Mazziotta, 1998b). There are also a number of ways to reduce the physiological motion (Kim & Ugurbil, 1997; Sychra, Bandettini, Bhattacharya & Lin, 1994).

Techniques that have been applied include applications of the general linear statistical model including subtraction, correlation, t-test, analysis of covariance, and cluster analysis (Bandettini et al., 1993; Buchel & Friston, 1998; Bullmore et al., 1999;

Descombes, Kruggel & von Cramon, 1998; Frank, Buxton & Wong, 1998; Friston, Frith, Frackowiak & Turner, 1995a; Friston, Holmes, Poline, Price & Frith, 1996b; Friston et al., 1994; Fukuyama, 1999; Lange, 1996; Mayhew et al., 1998; Poline, Worsley, Evans & Friston, 1997; Rabe-Hesketh, Bullmore & Brammer, 1997; Turner et al., 1998; Zarahn et al., 1997). Alternative techniques such as fuzzy clustering, and wavelet analysis have also been applied (Baumgartner, Scarth, Teichtmeister, Somorjai & Moser, 1997; Brammer, 1998; Golay et al., 1998; Ruttimann et al., 1998; Wood & Johnson, 1999). The two most commonly used software packages are Statistical Parametric Mapping (SPM) from the Wellcome Cognitive Neurosciences Laboratory (URL: www.fil.ion.ucl.ac.uk/spm; Friston, 1997; Friston et al., 1998a; Friston, Frith, Fletcher, Liddle & Frackowiak, 1996a; Friston et al., 1996b; Friston et al., 1995b; Friston et al., 1994; Friston, Williams, Howard, Frackowiak & Turner, 1996c) and AFNI from the Medical College of Wisconsin, (URL: http://varda.biophysics.mcw.edu/~cox/afni; Cox & Hyde, 1997). Both of these freeware packages incorporate a general linear model for fMRI data analysis and include algorithms for motion correction, smoothing, and thresholding.

FMRI AND EYEBLINK CLASSICAL CONDITIONING DATA: ACQUISITION AND ANALYSES

The eyeblink classical conditioning data may be collected using either an MR compatible infrared motion-detection system (Lemieux & Glover, 1996) or an MR compatible opto-mechanical device (Ramnani, Toni, Josephs, Ashburner & Passingham, 1999). In our laboratory we have built and tested a new non-ferrous MRI-compatible eyeblink conditioning system. The device is shown schematically in Figure 4.

The experiments performed in the MRI scanner use a fiber optic waveguide to transmit the infrared light to and from the participant in the MRI scanner. The fiber optics are mounted to safety glasses to shine infrared light via fiber optic cables 1 cm in front of the cornea. Blink data from the detector are fed into the computer. The computer also controls the air puff which is delivered through a hole at the end of a plastic tube; the tube is also mounted to the safety glasses. The tone CS is delivered to the subject using an MRI-compatible Avotec Silent Scan communication system.

In our laboratory we use a spiral pulse sequence for data collection that has several advantages over echo-planar imaging (EPI) MR data collection (Glover & Lai, 1998; Lai & Glover, 1998)). Spiral scanning is less susceptible to the spatial warping introduced when collecting data around the interpeduncular fossa, the susceptibility artifact is present as a blur rather than spatial distortion. Spiral scanning is more robust against motion and flow artifacts than is EPI. Simulation results (Glover et al., 1996) demonstrated that spiral images were practically insensitive to flow artifacts up to linear velocities of 20 cm/s.

In our early pilot studies, functional MR time course images of the hippocampus and cerebellum were acquired in the coronal plane using 2D spiral MRI pulse. The imaging protocol used is summarized in Table 2. The 2D spiral pulse sequence acquires gradient-echoes with BOLD contrast. The 3D version of this sequence has

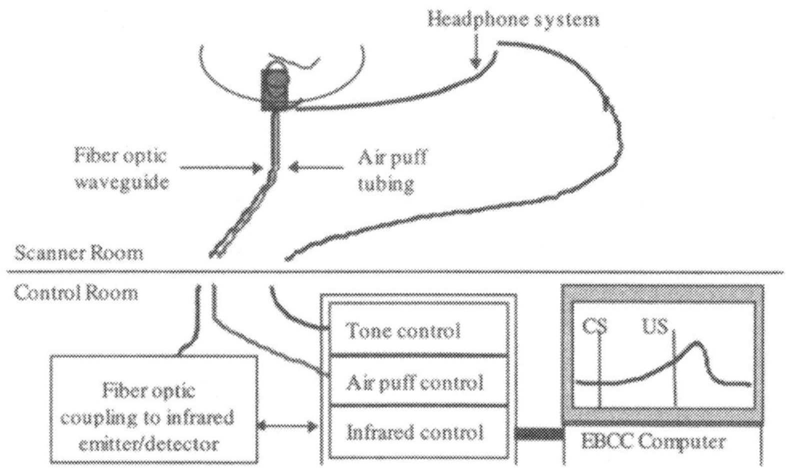

Figure 4. Schematic of the fMRI eyeblink classical conditioning system. A San Diego Instruments Eyeblink Conditioning System interfaced with a computer presents stimuli and records dependent blink responses. Eyeblink detection uses an infrared emitter (935 nm) and detector (Honeywell, Inc.).

some advantages over 2D spiral imaging. The advantages include reduced inflow effects and increased signal-to-noise ratio particularly in regions of the brain where large susceptibility interfaces exist such as the parietal and temporal lobes. However, the cerebellum is usually presented in coronal views and 3D coronal imaging results in wraparound artifact. The 3D data could also be taken in the axial plane and then reformatted into coronal images. This group's experience with 3D axial imaging has been that undesirable eyeblink motion appears in the cerebellar activation maps. Additionally, a study comparing motor task activation in 2D spiral, 3D spiral and EPI demonstrates no significant advantage of 3D over 2D spiral (Yang et al., 1998; Yang, Glover, Van Gelderen & Al, 1995).

Volumes collected during eyeblink classical conditioning are acquired in a plane perpendicular to the AC-PC plane (Talairach space) for post-acquisition inter-subject analysis. Pulse sequence parameters for fMRI data acquisition are: Single-shot 2D spiral with TR = 2000 ms, TE = 40 ms, flip angle = 50 deg., FOV = 240 mm, slice thickness = 5 mm, 12 oblique coronal slices, inplane resolution = 2.3 mm x 2.3 mm, scantime for each volume acquisition = 2 s. Fast-spin echo (FSE) images with T2 weighting are collected for anatomical localization. Surface and volume reconstruction may be performed on the 3D-SPGR T1-weighted images.

Table 2. Magnetic Resonance Imaging Protocol Parameters

Pulse Sequence	TR/TE	Resolution	Scan time
FSE: anatomy with good gray-white matter contrast	2000/68 ms	0.8 mm x 0.8 mm 5 mm slice	3 min.
2D-spiral: BOLD contrast 12 slices, 2s / scan	2000/40 ms	2.3 mm x 2.3 mm 5 mm slice	15 min.
3D-SPGR: T1-wtd. 60 slices,	27/9 ms	0.8 x 0.8 1.5 mm slice	4 mins.

The design for the behavioral data collection involves the use of the equipment described above to present the eyeblink conditioning stimuli to the participant in the MRI scanner. Before conditioning, the participant is scanned during a motor task (20 trials of a quick fist clench) to collect data for the fMRI impulse response function. Then the fMRI eyeblink conditioning experiment starts with the fMRI data acquisition triggered by the start of the conditioning procedure. The testing consists of the 500 ms, 1 kHz tone-CS and 100 ms, 3 psi corneal air puff-US stimuli in two 30 trial sequences. All the trials were paired CS-US presentations (US onset 400 ms after CS onset) with a random inter-trial interval of 16-20 s. This choice of inter-trial intervals reflects a compromise between the fMRI signal-to-noise ratio, which is optimal for intervals of 13-17 s, and the optimal interval for learning which is 20-30 s. The individual conditioning results are used to separate trials by response: CR, UR or alpha response.

Parameters for event-related fMRI include the duration of the stimulus, t, the number of trials, N, and the inter-trial period, T. The parameters T and t were optimized by simulating the signal expected for various stimulus paradigms by convolving the stimulus with the hemodynamic impulse response function as in Equation 1. We performed this optimization assuming a Poisson distribution ((Friston et al., 1994)), calculating an effective (normalized) signal-to-noise ratio (SNR) from

$$SNR = \text{sqrt}\{ N / (T * \text{power spectral density}(w))\} \quad \text{Eq.3}$$

N = number of trials averaged together for a single condition,
$g_c(w)$ = (which is dependent on t) is the intensity spectrum of the response,
w = frequency,
T = inter-trial interval.

A value of 8 s was assumed for the quantity λ (Friston et al., 1994) in the Poisson distribution used to model the hemodynamic response function. The fMRI signal-to-noise ratio depends on the stimulus duration, the interval between stimulus presentation, and the number of trials. Although the eyeblink conditioning behavioral data indicate that data should not be collected with inter-trial intervals (ITIs) shorter than 16 seconds, this calculation demonstrates that there will not be significant reduction in signal-to-noise ratio for trials with ITIs between 16 and 20 seconds.

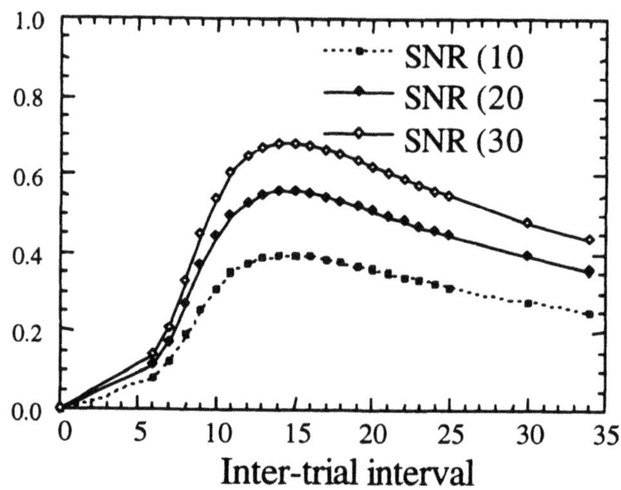

Figure 5. Plots of the signal-to-noise ratio (SNR) for 10, 20, and 30 single trials as the inter-trial interval is varied between 6 s and 35 s. A stimulus was presented at the start of the trial for 1 second.

Pilot data have been collected with inter-trial intervals varying between 16-20 s. After collection the data are processed according to the following description. Raw image data are reconstructed using a 2D fast Fourier transform including two corrections: a navigator correction to reduce susceptiblity artifacts and a distortion correction to reduce artifact due to magnetic field inhomogeneities (Glover & Lai, 1998). A volumetric motion compensation method (Woods et al., 1998a) is utilized to remove spatially coherent signal changes via the application of a partial correlation method to each slice in time.

One simple way to inspect the data after reconstruction and motion-correction is to choose a region-of-interest and then plot the time course (the signal from that region as a function of time). The signal changes are typically only 2-4% so averaging together the signals from the same type of trials is performed to improve the signal-to-noise ratio. This type of averaging over multiple time courses is called time-locked averaging.

Figure 6 shows a region of interest in Larsell's HVI, the region of the cerebellum believed to be involved in conditioning during eyeblink classical conditioning. Figure 7 shows the time-locked average of the signal over 7 CR trials. The activation appears to be typical for a single-trial response.

To create activation maps for the single-trial data, the hemodynamic fMRI impulse response function must be extracted from the data. The peak fitting routine models the response as a Poisson function and performs a least-square-fit to extract the width parameter lamba, λ and the time, t_0, of the peak response. The Poisson function results from this procedure can be used as the estimate of each individual's fMRI impulse response function. Then to create the reference function, the stimulus, represented as a series of delta functions, is convolved with fMRI impulse response function. Then that reference function can be correlated to the time course from each pixel to search for regions of the brain that responded to the stimulus.

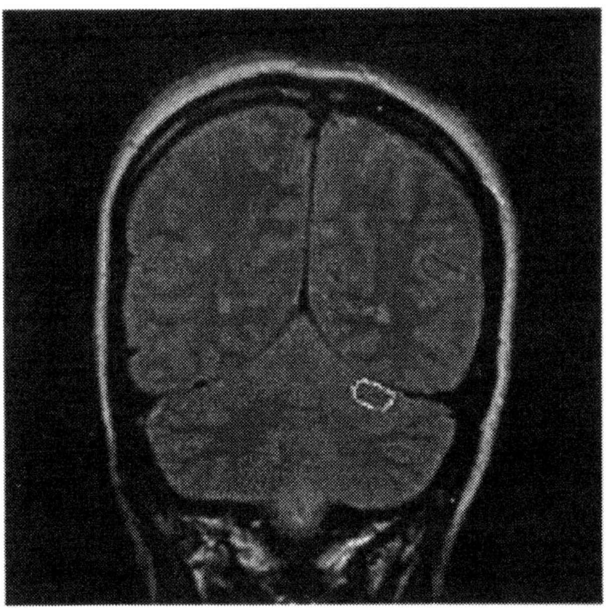

Figure 6. Fast spin-echo image showing the region in Larsell's HVI for which the time course is displayed in Figure 7. The region-of-interest is outlined in white.

After calculation of the correlation coefficient, r, for each pixel the resulting activation maps are spatially smoothed using a 3-by-3 pixel sigma (standard deviation) filter. The number of degrees of freedom, N, can be calculated from the smoothness of the data following Friston and then z-score maps can be calculated using Fisher's transformation. The final step is overlaying the activation maps on the FSE images for localization and interpretation of the results.

In the case of subject populations other than young adults, a challenge for the fMRI technique may come from the strong possibility that the measurements may require some additional sensitivity. For example, in the case of older adult subjects, recent work using photic stimulation detected decreased fMRI signal changes in older

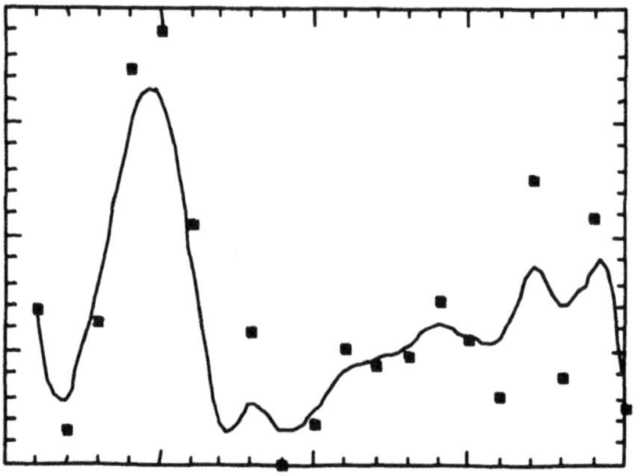

Figure 7. Representative time course for a time-locked average signal from single-trial eyeblink classical conditioning in the cerebellar lobule designated as Larsell's HVI. The seven trials that were averaged together were CR trials.

subjects (2.5 +/- 1.0% in the older subjects versus 4.0 +/- 1.6% in the younger, p = 0.01) (Ross et al., 1997). Smaller areas of activation have also been seen in older subjects when compared to younger subjects. We expect that the use of each individual's unique hemodynamic response function will improve our sensitivity.

SUMMARY AND CONCLUSIONS

The imaging technique of fMRI has a number of advantages over other brain imaging techniques that results in physiological images of the best possible spatial and temporal resolution. This imaging technique coupled with the precision possible from the large data base on the neural basis of eyeblink classical conditioning make studies of fMRI and eyeblink classical conditioning potentially significant. The neural basis of human associative learning may be imaged as it progresses in various structures in the brain.

In this chapter we have presented fMRI methodology as it applies to eyeblink classical conditioning along with some preliminary data collection with young adults using the delay procedure. In our laboratory and in the Wellcome Department of Cognitive Neurology at the Institute of Neurology in London (Ramnani et al., 1999), localized activation in cerebellar cortex ipsilateral to the conditioned eye has been identified in trials with CRs in young adults. Our data collected with fMRI has striking similarities to electrophysiological recordings in hippocampus and cerebellum in rabbits during the performance of CRs and URs (Lemieux & Woodruff-Pak, 1999).

Although we see great potential for the application of fMRI to eyeblink classical conditioning, it is evident from our discussion that the technique is complex and not without obstacles and problems. For example, motion artifact and weaker signal intensity in populations of interest such as children, older adults, and neurological patients challenge us to refine and improve our techniques. We feel that such effort is worthwhile as it may enable us to sample the rich variety of human subjects that will allow us to understand better the neurobiological basis of associative learning.

REFERENCES

Aine, C.J. (1995). A conceptual overview and critique of functional neuroimaging techniques in humans: I. MRI/FMRI and PET. *Critical Reviews in Neurobiology, 9(2-3)*, 229-309.

Anderson, B.J., & Steinmetz, J.E. (1994). Cerebellar and brainstem circuits involved in classical eyeblink conditioning. *Review of Neuroscience, 5*, 251-273.

Bandettini, P.A., Jesmanowicz, A., Wong, E.C., & Hyde, J.S. (1993). Processing strategies for time-course data sets in functional MRI of the human brain. *Magnetic Resonance in Medicine, 30(2)*, 161-173.

Bandettini, P.A., Wong, E.C., Hinks, R.S., Tikofsky, R.S., & Hyde, J.S. (1992). Time course EPI of human brain function during task activation. *Magnetic Resonance in Medicine, 25(2)*, 390-397.

Bandettini, P.A., Wong, E.C., Jesmanowicz, A., Hinks, R.S., & Hyde, J.S. (1994). Spin-echo and gradient-echo EPI of human brain activation using BOLD contrast: a comparative study at 1.5 T. *NMR in Biomedicine 7(1-2)*, 12-20.

Baumgartner, R., Scarth, G., Teichtmeister, C., Somorjai, R., & Moser, E. (1997). Fuzzy clustering of gradient-echo functional MRI in the human visual cortex. Part I: reproducibility. *Journal of Magnetic Resonance Imaging, 7(6)*, 1094-1101.

Berger, T.W., & Thompson, R. F. (1978) Identification of pyramidal cells as the critical elements in hippocampal neuronal plasticity during learning. *Proceedings of the National Academy of Sciences (USA), 75*, 1572-1576.

Blaxton, T.A., Zeffiro, T.A., Gabrieli, J.D.E., Bookheimer, S.Y., Carrillo, M.C., Theodore, W.H., & Disterhoft, J.F. (1996). Functional mapping of human learning: A positron-emission tomography study of eyeblink conditioning. *Journal of Neuroscience, 16*, 4032-4040.

Brammer, M.J. (1998). Multidimensional wavelet analysis of functional magnetic resonance images. *Human Brain Mapping, 6(5-6)*, 378-382.

Buckner, R.L. (1998). Event-related fMRI and the hemodynamic response. *Human Brain Mapping, 6(5-6)*, 373-377.

Buxton, R.B., Wong, E.C., & Frank, L.R. (1998). Dynamics of blood flow and oxygenation changes during brain activation: the balloon model. *Magnetic Resonance in Medicine, 39(6)*, 855-864.

Corkin, S. (1998). Functional MRI for studying episodic memory in aging and Alzheimer's disease. *Geriatrics, 53 Supplement 1*, S13-15.

Chen, L., Bao, S., Lockard, J.M., Kim, J.J., & Thompson, R.F. (1996). Impaired classical eyeblink conditioning in cerebellar lesioned and Purkinje cell degeneration (pcd) mutant mice. *The Journal of Neuroscience, 16*, 2829-2838.

Clark, R.E. & Squire, L.R. (1998). Classical conditioning and brain systems: The role of awareness. *Science, 280*, 77-81.

Clark, R.E., & Squire, L.R. (1999). Human eyeblink classical conditioning: Effects of manipulating awareness of the stimulus contingencies. *Psychological Science, 10*, 14-18.

Cox, R.W., & Hyde, J.S. (1997). Software tools for analysis and visualization of FMRI Data. *NMR in Biomedicine, 10*, 171-178.

Daum, I., & Schugens, M.M. (1996). On the cerebellum and classical conditioning. *Current Directions in Psychological Science, 5*, 58-61.

Detre, J.A., Zhang, W., Roberts, D.A., Silva, A.C., Williams, D.S., Grandis, D.J., Koretsky, A.P., & Leigh, J. S. (1994). Tissue specific perfusion imaging using arterial spin labeling. *NMR in Biomedicine, 7(1-2)*, 75-82.

Duyn, J.H., Yang, Y., Frank, J.A., Mattay, V.S., & Hou, L. (1996). Functional magnetic resonance neuroimaging data acquisition techniques. *Neuroimage, 4(3 Pt 3)*, S76-83.

Edelmann, R.R., Siewert, B., Darby, D.G., Thangaraj, V., Nobre, A.C., Mesulam, M.M., & Warach, S. (1994). Qualitative mapping of cerebral blood flow and functional localization with echo-planar MR imaging and signal targeting with alternating radio-frequency. *Radiology, 192(5)*, 513-520.

Fox, P.T., & Woldorff, M.G. (1994). Integrating human brain maps. *Current Opinion in Neurobiology, 4(2)*, 151-156.
Friston, K.J. (1997). Testing for anatomically specified regional effects. *Human Brain Mapping, 5(2)*, 133-136.
Friston, K.J., Fletcher, P., Josephs, O., Holmes, A., Rugg, M.D., & Turner, R. (1998a). Event-related fMRI: Characterizing differential responses. *Neuroimage, 7(1)*, 30-40.
Friston, K.J., Frith, C.D., Fletcher, P., Liddle, P.F., & Frackowiak, R.S. (1996a). Functional topography: Multidimensional scaling and functional connectivity in the brain. *Cerebral Cortex, 6(2)*, 156-164.
Friston, K.J., Frith, C.D., Liddle, P.F., & Frackowiak, R.S. (1991). Comparing functional (PET) images: The assessment of significant change. *Journal of Cerebral Blood Flow Metabolism, 11(4)*, 690-699.
Friston, K.J., Holmes, A., Poline, J.B., Price, C.J., & Frith, C.D. (1996b). Detecting Activations in PET and fMRI: *Levels of Inference and Power.* , *4(3)*, 223-235.
Friston, K.J., Holmes, A.P., Poline, J.B., Grasby, P J., Williams, S.C., Frackowiak, R.S., & Turner, R. (1995). Analysis of fMRI time-series revisited [see comments]. *Neuroimage, 2(1)*, 45-53.
Friston, K.J., Jezzard, P., & Turner, R. (1994). Analysis of Functional MRI Time Series. *Human Brain Mapping, 1*, 153-171.
Friston, K.J., Josephs, O., Rees, G., & Turner, R. (1998b). Nonlinear event-related responses in fMRI. *Magnetic Resonance in Medicine, 39(1)*, 41-52.
Friston, K.J., Williams, S., Howard, R., Frackowiak, R.S., & Turner, R. (1996c). Movement-related effects in fMRI time-series. *Magnetic Resonance in Medicine, 35(3)*, 346-355.
Glover, G.H. (1999). Deconvolution of impulse response in event-related BOLD fMRI. *Neuroimage, 9(4)*, 416-429.
Glover, G.H., & Lai, S. (1998). Self-navigated spiral fMRI: interleaved versus single-shot. *Magnetic Resonance in Medicine, 39(3)*, 361-368.
Glover, G.H., Lemieux, S.K., & Drangova, M. (1996). Decomposition of inflow and blood oxygenation level-dependent (BOLD) effects with dual-echo spiral gradient-recalled echo. *Magnetic Resonance in Medicine, 35*, 299-308.
Golay, X., Kollias, S., Stoll, G., Meier, D., Valavanis, A., & Boesiger, P. (1998). A new correlation-based fuzzy logic clustering algorithm for fMRI. *Magnetic Resonance in Medicine, 40(2)*, 249-260.
Green, J.T. & Woodruff-Pak, D.S. (in press). Eyeblink classical conditioning: Hippocampal formation is for neutral stimulus associations as cerebellum is for association-response. *Psychological Bulletin.*
Hajnal, J.V., Bydder, G.M., & Young, I.R. (1995). fMRI: Does correlation imply activation? *NMR in Biomedicine, 8(3)*, 97-100.
Hajnal, J.V., Collins, A.G., White, S.J., Pennock, J.M., Oatridge, A., Baudouin, C J., Young, I.R., & Bydder, G.M. (1993). Imaging of human brain activity at 0.15 T using fluid attenuated inversion recovery (FLAIR) pulse sequences. *Magnetic Resonance in Medicine, 30(5)*, 650-653.
Hlustik, P., Noll, D.C., & Small, S.L. (1998). Suppression of vascular artifacts in functional magnetic resonance imaging using MR angiograms. *Neuroimage, 7*, 224-231.
Hu, X., & Kim, S.-G. (1993). A new T2*-weighting technqiue for magnetic resonance imaging. *Magnetic Resonance in Medicine, 30*, 512-517.
Jack, C.R., Jr., Lee, C.C., & Riederer, S.J. (1995). Functional brain imaging with a standard 1.5-T magnetic resonance imaging system. *Academic Radiology, 2(10)*, 916-923.
Jueptner, M., & Weiller, C. (1995). Does measurement of regional cerebral blood flow reflect synaptic activity? - implication for PET and fMRI. *Neuroimage, 2*(148-156).
Kiebel, S.J., Ashburner, J., Poline, J.B., & Friston, K.J. (1997). MRI and PET coregistration--a cross validation of statistical parametric mapping and automated image registration. *Neuroimage, 5*(4 Pt 1), 271-279.
Kim, S.G. (1995). Quantification of relative cerebral blood flow change by flow-sensitive alternating inversion recovery (FAIR) technique: Application to functional mapping. *Magnetic Resonance in Medicine, 34(3)*, 293-301.
Kim, S.G., & Ugurbil, K. (1997). Functional magnetic resonance imaging of the human brain. *Journal of Neuroscience Methods, 74(2)*, 229-243.
Kwong, K.K. (1995). Functional magnetic resonance imaging with echo planar imaging. *Magnetic Resonance Quarterly, 11(1)*, 1-20.
Kwong KK, B.J., Chester D.A, et al. (1992). Dynamic magnetic resonance imaging of human brain activity during primary sensory stimulation. *Proceedings of the. National Academy of. Science., 89*, 5675-5679.
La Bar, K.S., & Disterhoft, J.F. (1998). Conditioning, awareness, and the hippocampus. *Hippocampus,*

8, 620-626.
Lai, S., & Glover, G.H. (1998). Three-dimensional spiral fMRI technique: a comparison with 2D spiral acquisition. *Magnetic Resonance in Medicine, 39(1)*, 68-78.
Lavond, D.G., Kim, J.J., & Thompson, R.F. (1993). Mammalian brain substrates of aversive classical conditioning. *Annual Review of Psychology, 44*, 317-342.
Lemieux, S.K., & Woodruff-Pak, D.S. (1999). An event-related functional MRI study of eyeblink classical conditioning in young adults. *Society for Neuroscience Abstracts, 25.*
Li, Y.-T., Woodruff-Pak, D.S., & Trojanowski, J.Q. (1994). Amyloid plaques in cerebellar cortex and the integrity of Purkinje cell dendrites. *Neurobiology of Aging, 15*, 1-9.
Logan, C.G., & Grafton, S.T. (1995). Functional anatomy of human eyeblink conditioning determined with regional cerebral glucose metabolism and positron-emission tomography. *Proceedings of the National Academy of Sciences (USA), 92*, 7500-7504.
Molchan, S.E., Sunderland, T., McIntosh, A.R., Herscovitch, P., & Schreurs, B.G. (1994). A functional anatomical study of associative learning in humans. *Proceedings of the National Academy of Science, (USA), 91*, 8122-8126.
Mayhew, J., Hu, D., Zheng, Y., Askew, S., Hou, Y., Berwick, J., Coffey, P.J., & Brown, N. (1998). An evaluation of linear model analysis techniques for processing images of microcirculation activity. *Neuroimage, 7(1)*, 49-71.
Menon, R.S., Gati, J.S., Goodyear, B.G., Luknowsky, D.C., & Thomas, C.G. (1998). Spatial and temporal resolution of functional magnetic resonance imaging. *Biochemistry and Cell Biology, 76(2-3)*, 560-571.
Moseley, M.E., & Glover, G.H. (1995). Functional MR imaging. Capabilities and limitations. *Neuroimaging Clinic North America, 5(2)*, 161-191.
Noll, D.C., Cohen, J.D., Meyer, C.H., & Schneider, W. (1995). Spiral k-space imaging of cortical activation. *Journal of Magnetic Resonance Imaging, 5*, 49-56.
Ogawa, S., Menon, R.S., Tank, D.W., Kim, S.G., Merkle, H., Ellermann, J.M., & Ugurbil, K. (1993). Functional brain mapping by blood oxygenation level-dependent contrast magnetic resonance imaging. A comparison of signal characteristics with a biophysical model. *Biophysical Journal, 64(3)*, 803-812.
Ramnani, N., Toni, I., Josephs, O., Ashburner, J., & Passingham, R.E. (1999). Learning-related plasticity during human classical eyeblink conditioning: Whole-brin, event-related fMRI. *NeuroImage, 9*, S980.
Rao, S.M., Binder, J.R., Hammeke, T.A., Bandettini, P.A., Bobholz, J.A., Frost, J.A., Myklebust, B.M., Jacobson, R D., & Hyde, J.S. (1995). Somatotopic mapping of the human primary motor cortex with functional magnetic resonance imaging [see comments]. *Neurology, 45(5)*, 919-924.
Rosen, B.R., Buckner, R.L., & Dale, A.M. (1998). Event-related functional MRI: Past, present, and future. *Proceedings of National Academy of Sciences (U S A), 95(3)*, 773-780.
Ross, M.H., Yurgelun-Todd, D.A., Renshaw, P F., Maas, L.C., Mendelson, J.H., Mello, N.K., Cohen, B.M., & Levin, J.M. (1997). Age-related reduction in functional MRI response to photic stimulation. *Neurology, 48(1)*, 173-176.
Ruttimann, U.E., Unser, M., Rawlings, R.R., Rio, D., Ramsey, N.F., Mattay, V.S., Hommer, D.W., Frank, J.A., & Weinberger, D.R. (1998). Statistical analysis of functional MRI data in the wavelet domain. *IEEE Transactions in Medical Imaging, 17(2)*, 142-154.
Sears, L.L., Finn, P.R., & Steinmetz, J.E. (1994). Abnormal classical eyeblink conditioning in autism. *Journal of Autism and Developmental Disorders, 24*, 737-751.
Siewert, B., Bly, B.M., Schlaug, G., Darby, D.G., Thangaraj, V., Warach, S., & Edelman, R.R. (1996). Comparison of the BOLD- and EPISTAR-technique for functional brain imaging by using signal detection theory. *Magnetic Resonance in Medicine, 36(2)*, 249-255.
Small, S.A., Perera, G.M., DeLaPaz, R., Mayeux, R., & Stern, Y. (1999). Differential regional dysfunction of the hippocampal formation among elderly with memory decline and Alzheimer's disease. *Annals of Neurology, 45(4)*, 466-472.
Solomon, P.R., Levine, E., Bein, T., & Pendlebury, W.W. (1991). Disruption of classical conditioning in patients with Alzheimer's disease. *Neurobiology of Aging, 12*, 283-287.
Steinmetz, J.E. (1996). The brain substrates of classical eyeblink conditioning in rabbits. In J. R. Bloedel, T. J. Ebner, & S. P. Wise (Eds.), *The Acquisition of Motor Behavior in Vertebrates* (pp. 89-114). MIT Press.
Steinmetz, J.E., Lavond, D.G., Ivkovich, D., Logan, C.G., & Thompson, R.F. (1992). Disruption of classical eyelid conditioning after cerebellar lesions: Damage to a memory trace system or a simple performance deficit? *Journal of Neuroscience, 12*, 4403-4426.
Steinmetz, J.E., & Thompson, R.F. (1991). Brain substrates of aversive classical conditioning. In J.

Madden IV, (Ed.), *Neurobiology of Learning, Emotion, and Affect* (pp. 97-120). New York: Raven Press.

Sychra, J.J., Bandettini, P.A., Bhattacharya, N., & Lin, Q. (1994). Synthetic images by subspace transforms. I. Principal components images and related filters. *Medical Physiology, 21(2)*, 193-201.

Turner, R., Howseman, A., Rees, G.E., Josephs, O., & Friston, K. (1998). Functional magnetic resonance imaging of the human brain: data acquisition and analysis. *Experimental Brain Research, 123(1-2)*, 5-12.

Thompson, R.F. (1986). The neurobiology of learning and memory. *Science, 233*, 941-947.

Thompson, R.F. & Krupa, D.J. (1994). Organization of memory traces in the mammalian brain. *Annual Review of Neuroscience, 17*, 519-549.

Timmann, D., Kolb, F.P., Baier, C., Rijntjes, M., Muller, S.P., Diener, H.C., & Weiller, C. (1996). Cerebellar activation during classical conditioning of the human flexion reflex: A PET study. *NeuroReport, 7*, 2056-2060.

Vazquez, A.L., & Noll, D.C. (1998). Nonlinear aspects of the BOLD response in functional MRI. *Neuroimage, 7(2)*, 108-118.

Weisskoff, R.M. (1995). Functional MRI: are we all moving towards artifactual conclusions? Or fMRI fact or fancy? *NMR in Biomedicine, 8(3)*, 101-103.

Welsh, J.P., & Harvey, J.A. (1989). Cerebellar lesions and the nictitating membrane reflex: Performance deficits of the conditioned and unconditioned response. *Journal of Neuroscience, 9*, 299-311.

White, I.M., Miller, D.P., White, W., Dike, G. L., Rebec, G.V., & Steinmetz, J.E. (1994). Neuronal activity in rabbit neostriatum during classical eyelid conditioning. *Experimental Brain Research, 99*, 179-190.

Wong, E.C., Buxton, R.B., & Frank, L.R. (1998). Quantitative imaging of perfusion using a single subtraction (QUIPSS and QUIPSS II). *Magnetic Resonance in Medicine, 39(5)*, 702-708.

Wong, E.C., Buxton, R.B., & Frank, L.R. (1999). Quantitative perfusion imaging using arterial spin labeling. *Neuroimaging Clinic North America, 9(2)*, 333-342.

Wood, J.C., & Johnson, K.M. (1999). Wavelet packet denoising of magnetic resonance images: importance of Rician noise at low SNR. *Magnetic Resonance in Medicine, 41(3)*, 631-635.

Woods, R.P., Grafton, S.T., Holmes, C.J., Cherry, S.R., & Mazziotta, J.C. (1998a). Automated image registration: I. General methods and intrasubject, intramodality validation. *Journal of Computer Assisted Tomography, 22(1)*, 139-152.

Woods, R.P., Grafton, S.T., Watson, J.D., Sicotte, N.L., & Mazziotta, J.C. (1998b). Automated image registration: II. Intersubject validation of linear and nonlinear models. *Journal of Computer Assisted Tomography, 22(1)*, 153-165.

Woodruff-Pak, D.S. (1997). Classical conditioning. In J.D. Schmahmann (Ed.), *The Cerebellum and Cognition* (pp. 341-366), San Diego: Academic Press.

Woodruff-Pak, D.S., Cronholm, J.F., & Sheffield, J.B. (1990). Purkinje cell number related to rate of eyeblink classical conditioning. *NeuroReport, 1*, 165-168.

Woodruff-Pak, D.S., Finkbiner, R.G., & Katz, I.R. (1989). A model system demonstrating parallels in animal and human aging: Extension to Alzheimer's disease. In Meyer, Simpkins & Yamamoto, Eds. *Novel Approaches to the Treatment of Alzheimer's Disease* (pp. 355-371). New York: Plenum.

Woodruff-Pak, D.S., Finkbiner, R.G., & Sasse, D.K. (1990). Eyeblink conditioning discriminates Alzheimer's patients from non-demented aged. *NeuroReport, 1*, 45-48.

Woodruff-Pak, D.S., & Papka, M. (1996). Huntington's disease and eyeblink classical conditioning: Normal learning but abnormal timing. *Journal of the International Neuropsychological Society, 2*, 323-334.

Woodruff-Pak, D.S., Papka, M., Romano, S., & Li, Y.-T. (1996). Eyeblink classical conditioning in Alzheimer's disease and cerebrovascular dementia. *Neurobiology of Aging. 17*, 505-512.

Woodruff-Pak, D.S., & Trojanowski, J.Q. (1996). The older rabbit as an animal model: Implications for Alzheimer's disease. *Neurobiology of Aging. 17*, 283-290.

Yang, Y., Glover, G.H., van Gelderen, P., Patel, A.C., Mattay, V.S., Frank, J.A., & Duyn, J.H. (1998). A comparison of fast MR scan techniques for cerebral activation studies at 1.5 tesla. *Magnetic Resonance in Medicine, 39*(Jan), 61-67.

Yang, Y., Glover, G.H., van Gelderen, P., & al, e. (1995). A comparison of functional magnetic resonance imaging using. *Magnetic Resonance in Medicine, 33*, 656-662.

Yang, Y., Glover, G.H., van Gelderen, P., Mattay, V.S., Santha, A.K., Sexton, R.H., Ramsey, N.F., Moonen, C.T., Weinberger, D.R., Frank, J.A., & Duyn, J.H. (1996). Fast 3D functional magnetic resonance imaging at 1.5 T with spiral acquisition. *Magnetic Resonance in Medicine, 36(4)*, 620-626.

Yang, Y., Wen, H., Mattay, V.S., Balaban, R.S., Frank, J.A., & Duyn, J.H. (1999). Comparison of 3D

BOLD functional MRI with spiral acquisition at 1.5 and 4.0 T. *Neuroimage, 9(4)*, 446-451.

Yamashita, H. (1993). Perceptual-motor learning in amnesic patients with medial temporal lobe lesions. *Perceptual and Motor Skills, 77,* 1311-1314.

Zarahn, E., Aguirre, G.K., & D'Esposito, M. (1997). Empirical analyses of BOLD fMRI statistics. I. Spatially unsmoothed data collected under null-hypothesis conditions. *Neuroimage, 5(3)*, 179-197.

5 DUAL-TASK AND REPEATED MEASURES DESIGNS: UTILITY IN ASSESSING TIMING AND NEURAL FUNCTIONS IN EYEBLINK CONDITIONING

John T. Green
Temple University

Richard B. Ivry
University of California-Berkeley

Diana S. Woodruff-Pak
Temple University

INTRODUCTION

Eyeblink classical conditioning has proven to be an extremely important paradigm for studying the neural substrates of learning and memory. The well-controlled delivery of stimuli and simple behavioral response measures make it ideal for testing with both humans and non-human species. Lesion and neurophysiological studies have led to the delineation of virtually the entire neural circuit required for eyeblink classical conditioning in rabbits, with the critical component being the cerebellum (see Steinmetz, 1996, for a review). This work has been complemented by neuropsychological (Daum et al., 1993; Lye, O'Boyle, Ramsden & Shady, 1988; Solomon, Stowe & Pendelbury 1989; Topka, Walls-Sole, Massaquoi & Hallett, 1993; Woodruff-Pak, Papka & Ivry, 1996) and imaging (Blaxton et al., 1996; Logan & Grafton, 1995; Molchan, Sunderland, McIntosh, Herscovitch & Schreurs, 1994; Schreurs et al., 1997) studies with humans, with the evidence suggesting that the neural substrates required for eyeblink classical conditioning are very similar across a range of species (see Woodruff-Pak, 1997, for a review).

It is important to consider why the cerebellum is central to eyeblink classical conditioning. Extensive effort has been devoted to identifying the neural pathways involved in representing the conditioned stimulus (CS) and unconditioned stimulus (US), emphasizing the convergence of these inputs in the deep cerebellar nuclei and cerebellar cortex. This convergence is essential for the formation of CS-US associations. A second important contribution of the cerebellum to eyeblink conditioning centers on the temporal processing capabilities of this structure. In well-trained subjects, the timing of the CR is exquisite, occurring just prior to the US, regardless of the CS-US interval. In this chapter, we focus on the temporal characteristics of eyeblink conditioning and how the requisite timing may be mediated by the cerebellum.

THE NEURAL SUBSTRATES OF EYEBLINK CLASSICAL CONDITIONING

The role of the cerebellum in eyeblink classical conditioning was first discovered in the early 1980s by Richard Thompson and his colleagues in a series of lesion and recording studies in rabbits (Lavond, Hembree & Thompson, 1985; Lincoln, McCormick & Thompson, 1982; McCormick, Clark, Lavond & Thompson, 1982; McCormick et al., 1981; McCormick & Thompson, 1984a, 1984b) and subsequently corroborated by other laboratories (e.g., Berthier & Moore, 1986, 1990; Yeo, Hardiman & Glickstein, 1985a). Virtually the entire circuit for eyeblink classical conditioning using the delay paradigm with a tone CS and an air puff US has been delineated (Thompson, 1986, 1990). Briefly, the tone CS projects bilaterally to pontine nuclei, from which mossy fibers innervate the cerebellar cortex and deep nuclei. The air puff US projects to the contralateral inferior olive in the medulla, which sends climbing fiber projections to the contralateral cerebellum (ipsilateral to the eye that receives the air puff). The association between the tone CS and air puff US can occur at two loci within the cerebellum. One critical locus is the ipsilateral interpositus nucleus (globose nucleus in humans) of the cerebellum, as shown by the fact that lesions here produce a permanent loss of the CR in trained animals as well as prevent acquisition in naive animals (Steinmetz et al., 1992). A second point of association is the cerebellar cortex. As discussed later in the chapter, the cerebellar cortex appears to be critical for shaping various aspects of the topography of the CR, such as amplitude and timing.

Support for the critical involvement of the cerebellum in learning of CRs also comes from studies of patients with cerebellar lesions (Daum et al., 1993; Lye et al., 1988; Solomon et al., 1989; Topka et al., 1993; Woodruff-Pak et al., 1996). Patients with lesions in the cerebellum are severely impaired in the acquisition of CRs in the delay paradigm. In addition, CR latencies on CS-alone trials of the few responses emitted by these patients tend to be abnormally long compared to those produced by age-matched controls (Topka et al., 1993).

The neural substrates of eyeblink conditioning in humans have also been studied using positron emission tomography (Blaxton et al., 1996; Logan & Grafton, 1995; Molchan et al., 1994; Schreurs et al., 1997). At present, this imaging work has not provided a consistent picture, although metabolic changes within the cerebellum were observed in all of the reported work. Schreurs and colleagues (Molchan et al., 1994; Schreurs et al., 1997) reported a decrease in blood flow in bilateral cerebellar cortex during conditioning. In contrast, Blaxton et al. (1996) reported both increases and decreases in blood flow in bilateral cerebellum and Logan and Grafton (1995) reported an increase in glucose uptake in bilateral cerebellum. These divergent results may, at least in part, be explained by differences in the testing procedures and methods of analysis. While a condition in which the CS and US were unpaired was used as the control in all of the studies, the time between administration of the control and experimental conditions varied. Moreover, the studies differed in terms of the inclusion of participants who failed to exhibit strong evidence of learning. Furthermore, across the studies, subjects were scanned at different phases during acquisition. Finally, Blaxton et al., Molchan et al., and Schreurs et al. measured cerebral blood flow changes while Logan and Grafton measured cerebral glucose metabolism.

DUAL-TASK STUDIES OF EYEBLINK CONDITIONING IN HUMANS

The study of the neural substrates of eyeblink classical conditioning in neurologically healthy humans has also been pursued in behavioral studies. We have used dual-task studies and repeated-measures designs to seek converging sources of evidence regarding the critical role of the cerebellum in eyeblink classical conditioning. These studies are consistent with the hypotheses that the cerebellum is not only critical for the formation of the association between the CS and US, but it is also essential for the precise timing of the CRs.

The use of dual-task designs has a long history within psychology (see Pashler, 1994 for a review). Decrements in performance when people perform two concurrent tasks have traditionally been explained by cognitive psychologists in one of two ways: (1) there is a limited amount of processing capacity that must be shared between tasks or (2) a common process is shared by the two tasks and concurrent use of this process produces interference. From a cognitive neuroscience perspective, Hypothesis 2 would imply that the shared process involves a common neural structure. One could then design a study to compare dual-task performance under two conditions: (1) conditions in which the tasks are hypothesized to involve a common neural system; (2) conditions in which the tasks are hypothesized to involve separable neural systems. By the dual-task logic, interference should only be obtained in the former condition (Green & Woodruff-Pak, 1997; Kinsbourne & Hicks, 1978; Kinsbourne & Hiscock, 1983; Papka, Ivry & Woodruff-Pak, 1995).

Papka et al. (1995) conducted a dual-task study to test the hypothesis that timed-interval tapping and eyeblink classical conditioning are dependent upon a shared cerebellar substrate. Eyeblink conditioning was assessed with a 400-ms delay paradigm using a tone CS and an air puff US. Concurrent with conditioning, separate groups of subjects were tested on a timed-interval tapping task, an explicit memory recognition task, a choice reaction-time task, or, for a baseline control, watching a silent video. In the timed-interval tapping task, subjects viewed red LEDs presented at a rate of 550-ms and were instructed to tap in synchrony with this stimulus. After 12 flashes of the LEDs, the lights stopped flashing and the subject's task was to continue tapping at the same pace until the end of the trial (31 unpaced taps). The mean inter-tap interval during the unpaced portion of tapping served as the primary dependent measure of interest. In previous work, patients with cerebellar lesions had been found to be impaired on an auditory version of this task, exhibiting increased variability in the timing of the inter-tap intervals (Franz, Ivry & Helmuth, 1996; Ivry & Keele, 1989; Ivry, Keele & Diener, 1988; Woodruff-Pak, et al. 1996).

Papka et al. (1995) reported selective interference between eyeblink conditioning and timed-interval tapping. Subjects in this group exhibited a reduction in the percentage of CRs compared to those tested in the control, video-watching condition. In contrast, subjects in the recognition memory and choice reaction-time conditions showed conditioning levels comparable to the control group (Figure 1).

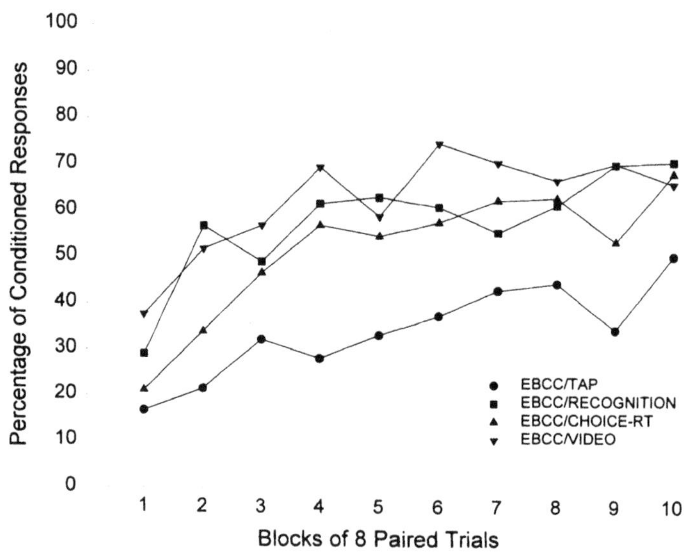

Figure 1. Mean percentage of conditioned responses across 10 blocks of eight paired conditioned stimulus-unconditioned stimulus eyeblink classical conditioning trials. (From "Selective disruption of eyeblink classical conditioning by concurrent tapping," by M. Papka, R.B. Ivry, and D.S. Woodruff-Pak, 1995, *Neuroreport, 6,* p. 1495. Copyright 1995 by Rapid Communications of Oxford Ltd. Reprinted with permission.)

The investigators' interpretation was that simultaneous timed-interval tapping interfered with eyeblink classical conditioning because both tasks rely on a common cerebellar substrate. It is important to note that timed-interval tapping and eyeblink classical conditioning do not interfere with each other simply because they are both motor tasks. Neither the choice reaction time task in Papka et al., (1995) nor a rotary pursuit task in which subjects must track a spinning target (Green & Woodruff-Pak, 1997), interfered with simultaneous eyeblink classical conditioning.

The conclusion that dual-task interference between eyeblink classical conditioning and timed-interval tapping are related to shared processing demands on the cerebellum is supported by several correlational findings obtained in our laboratory. First, temporal variability measured from the timed-interval tapping task accounts for a significant percentage of the variance in eyeblink conditioning observed across 150 subjects ranging in age from 20 to 89 years (Woodruff-Pak & Jaeger, 1998). That is, subjects who were most variable on the tapping task also tended to show the poorest levels of eyeblink conditioning. Second, when a group of patients with cerebellar lesions were tested on both tasks, the patients exhibited increased variability on the tapping task as well as significantly fewer CRs than control participants (Woodruff-Pak et al., 1996). Third, there was a significant correlation between tapping variability and percentage of CRs among the 14 normal control subjects in the previous study.

These results are in accord with the hypothesis that successful performances on these two tasks are dependent on the integrity of the cerebellum. We hypothesize that the commonality reflects the fact that precise timing is essential for both tasks, and it is the cerebellum that provides the requisite temporal representation (see Ivry, 1997). Timed-interval tapping requires an internal timing mechanism to maintain a constant tapping rate once the external pacing signal is eliminated. Eyeblink conditioning requires precise timing in order for the organism to learn the temporal relationship between the CS and US, and thus produce the anticipatory CR at the appropriate post-CS onset delay. The operation of the cerebellar timing system is taxed when the person is required to perform the two tasks concurrently.

TIMING IN EYEBLINK CLASSICAL CONDITIONING

If eyeblink conditioning requires the cerebellum for the precise timing of CRs, the next logical question to ask is, what form does this precise timing take? For example, how precise is "precise" timing? If we wish to localize a cerebellar timing system required for eyeblink classical conditioning, quantification of the precision of timing in eyeblink classical conditioning is critical. Following such a specification, we can make a finer-grained analysis of how damage to specific areas of the cerebellum disrupt CR timing. Specification of the precision of any perceptual system, from vision and hearing, to duration perception, can be aided by psychophysics. One of the goals of a psychophysical approach is to specify quantitative relationships between physical stimuli and an observer's perception of those stimuli. The applicability of Weber's law to timing in eyeblink classical conditioning may be seen as a first step towards specifying the precision of CR timing across the range of conditionable CS-US intervals.

Timing and Weber's law

A central concern in psychophysics is to determine the smallest difference between two stimuli that can be perceived. A basic method to identify difference thresholds is to have subjects compare two stimuli along a particular dimension. For duration discrimination, a standard stimulus of fixed duration may be presented on each trial and compared to a stimulus of variable duration that is either shorter or longer than the standard. While there are many variants to this approach, a widely-adopted method is to determine the values for the variable stimulus that are categorized as "longer than the standard stimulus" on 75% of the trials (upper threshold) and on 25% of the trials (lower threshold). The upper and lower thresholds bound an interval of uncertainty, where comparison stimulus values appear more or less equal to the standard. Dividing the interval of uncertainty in half yields the difference threshold, or the amount that the comparison stimulus must differ from the standard stimulus in order to be detected at a criterion level of performance (Figure 2) (see Engen, 1971).

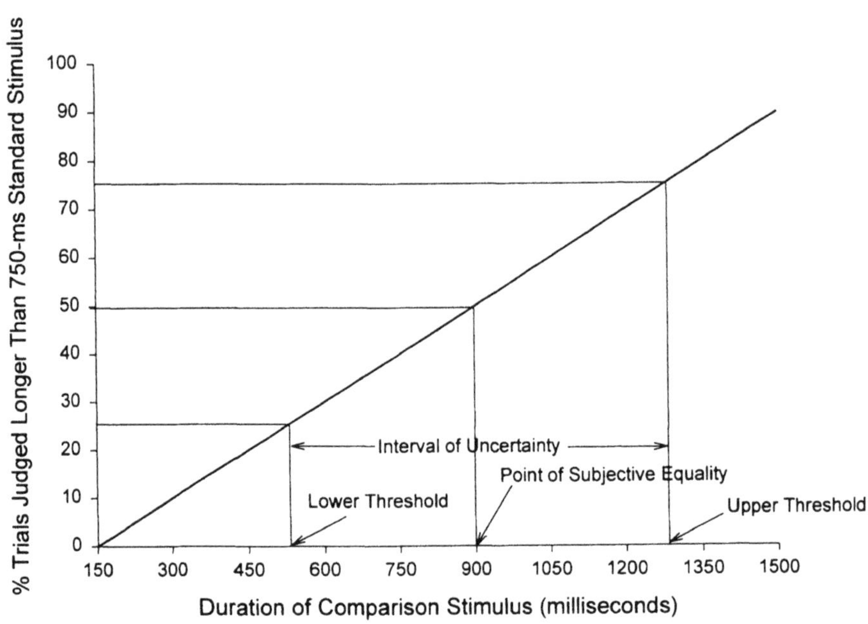

Figure 2. Calculation of difference thresholds for determining the Weber fraction in a temporal discrimination task.

The difference threshold is not absolute: It varies as a function of the magnitude of the standard stimulus. For example, the difference threshold for a standard stimulus of 1 s is considerably smaller than that for a standard stimulus of 100 s. Moreover, the dependency of the difference threshold to the magnitude of the standard is a function of the perceived magnitude of the standard. The perceived magnitude is measured as a point of subjective equality, a value that, in the time domain, would correspond to the point at which the stimulus is equally likely to be judged "shorter" or "longer" than the standard.

Across a variety of stimulus dimensions, it has been observed that the ratio relating the difference threshold to the point of subjective equality is constant (at least within a restricted range), a relationship known as Weber's law. The classic form of Weber's law can be written as:

$$k = \text{difference threshold} / \text{point of subjective equality} \quad (1)$$

where k, the Weber fraction, is a constant. Thus, for duration discrimination, the longer the duration, the larger the difference threshold. Equation 1 can also be written as:

$$k = \text{standard deviation} / \text{mean} \quad (2)$$

Equation 2 is particularly useful with classic psychophysical methods that use only a judgment of "equal" (such as the method of adjustment) between the comparison stimulus and the standard stimulus. The difference threshold can be transformed into a standard deviation score by making certain assumptions about the distribution describing a perceptual process such as the representation of duration.

In duration perception, variability tends to increase as a constant proportion of mean response time, yielding a constant Weber fraction. This is a temporal form of Weber's law (Allan, 1979; Gallistel, 1990; Gibbon, 1977; Killeen & Weiss, 1987). However, for very short durations (those under 100-200 ms), the Weber fraction tends to increase (Getty, 1975). In order to account for the increase in the Weber fraction at intervals under about 200-ms, Getty (1975) proposed a generalized form of Weber's law:

$$k = (\text{standard deviation} - c) / \text{mean} \quad (3)$$

where c is a constant assumed to reflect sensory noise unrelated to duration perception. Since eyeblink classical conditioning involves relatively short intervals, a determination of whether CR latencies obey Weber's law requires the use of Equation 3. An estimate of the value of c in Equation 3 can be made using a repeated-measures design in which each subject is tested at multiple intervals.

Slope analysis

Equation 3 provides a form of Weber's law that can be applied to tasks that use short durations, such as eyeblink classical conditioning. Determination of the value of the constant in Equation 3 can be made through the use of linear regression, or what Ivry and Hazeltine (1995; also Ivry & Corcos, 1993) referred to as slope analysis for measuring temporal and non-temporal sources of noise in tasks requiring precise timing. For this slope analysis, difference thresholds from at least three different intervals are required. These values are used to evaluate the generalized form of Weber's law (Equation 3) with the regression equation,

$$\text{standard deviation} = k * \text{mean} + c \quad (4)$$

where k (the slope) is assumed to represent variability (i.e., noise) due to timing processes and c (the intercept) is assumed to represent variability due to non-timing processes, such as sensorimotor transmission. If the intercept is subtracted from observed variability, one is left with only timing variability. A comparison between two tasks can then be performed, using the slope values to compare timing variability and the intercept values to compare non-temporal variability. The slope analysis can provide a method for specifying the effects of brain lesions on particular tasks: If a lesion increases the intercept but not the slope of the linear regression, then the lesion is affecting non-temporal sources of variability. If a lesion increases the slope, then the lesion is specifically affecting processes related to the representation of temporal information.

Wearden and McShane (1988) tested an interval production task in humans using intervals ranging from 500 ms to 1300 ms. Subjects were instructed to produce a particular target interval. Each subject was given 100 trials at each of six target intervals. Wearden and McShane carried out a linear regression conforming to Equation 4 on the averaged data and found a mean slope (i.e., generalized Weber fraction) of 0.12 and a mean intercept of about 20 ms. Ivry and Hazeltine (1995, Experiment 2) performed a similar experiment with intervals ranging from 325 ms to 550 ms. Over this range, they reported a mean slope of 0.05 and a mean intercept of 5.9 ms, values that reflect considerably more accurate performance than in the Wearden and McShane study. In another experiment in Ivry and Hazeltine (Experiment 1), timing was more precise when 30 intervals for a given duration were produced in a continuous sequence. Here the mean slope was 0.03, although there was an increase in the intercept to 12.7 ms. Ivry and Hazeltine suggested that the shallower slope in repetitive tapping was due to formation of a more accurate temporal representation. Thus, the slope analysis provides a method to evaluate whether particular manipulations are influencing temporal or non-temporal processes.

We applied the logic of slope analysis to eyeblink classical conditioning with the intention of comparing timing in eyeblink classical conditioning to timing in repetitive tapping (Green, Ivry & Woodruff-Pak, 1999). As discussed above, we have shown that repetitive tapping during eyeblink classical conditioning will disrupt the development of CRs (Papka et al., 1995). The reason for this disruption is hypothesized to be that both tasks engage the cerebellum. This led to the hypothesis that the cerebellum instantiates an internal timing system engaged in both repetitive tapping and eyeblink classical conditioning. Using the slope analysis approach, it becomes possible to compare performance on these two tasks, focusing on the sources of variability assumed to reflect the shared process, the cerebellar timing system. If both tasks engage the same timing system, we would expect them to show similar slopes (i.e., k in Equation 4).

We tested subjects at each of four different critical intervals: 325 ms, 400 ms, 475 ms, and 550 ms. At each interval, subjects received 100 trials of eyeblink classical conditioning and 24 trials of timed-interval tapping. One week separated testing at each interval. Slope analyses were conducted on each participants' CR latency data (both onset and peak CR latency) and inter-tap interval data using Equation 4. The slope for eyeblink classical conditioning, using either onset latency or peak latency as an index of timing, did not differ significantly from the slope for timed-interval tapping, suggesting they engaged a common timing system (Figure 3).

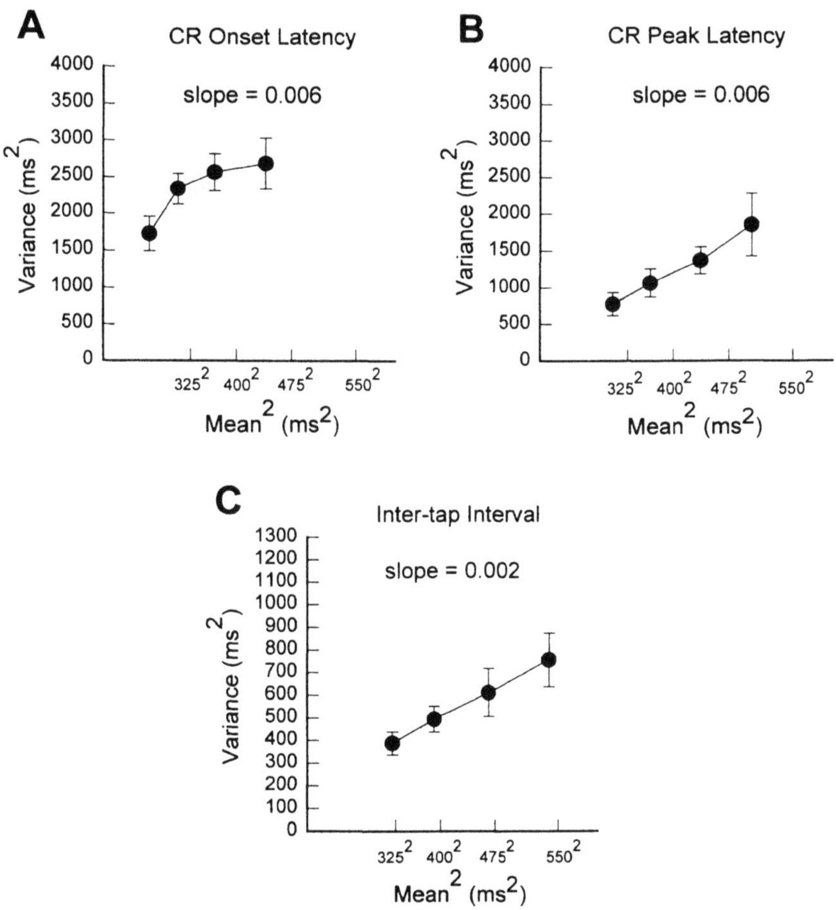

Figure 3. Variance of (a) conditioned response (CR) onset latency, (b) CR peak latency, and (c) inter-tap interval as a function of mean interval squared. Dashed lines represent linear regressions. Error bars show the standard error of the mean. (From "Timing in eyeblink classical conditioning and timed-interval tapping," by J.T. Green, R.B. Ivry, and D.S. Woodruff-Pak, 1999, *Psychological Science, 10*, p. 21. Copyright 1999 by American Psychological Society. Reprinted with permission.)

However, the mean slope for eyeblink classical conditioning (0.07) was somewhat steeper than the mean slope for repetitive tapping (0.04). There are at least two reasons for this difference. First, the conditioning data were obtained over the course of learning and thus timing is likely to be more variable than if performance had only been assessed under asymptotic conditions. Second, variability for the conditioning task is calculated over a series of trials with one observation (interval) produced on each trial. In contrast, variability on the tapping task is estimated by averaging across trials consisting of 30 intervals each. As noted above, Ivry and Hazeltine (1995) showed, the slope for temporal production is larger when only a single interval is produced on each trial compared to when a series of intervals are produced.

Repeated-measures designs in the study of timing in eyeblink conditioning

In well-trained subjects, the CR peaks just prior to US onset in eyeblink conditioning. This observation by itself would not be sufficient evidence that the learning process involves an explicit temporal representation of the CS-US interval. It is possible that the CR occurs prior to US onset because the CR is a delayed response elicited by the CS (similar to the reaction time observed with volitional movements), rather than a timed response in anticipation of the US. However, numerous studies have demonstrated that the CR onset and peak latencies vary as a function of the CS-US interval (Boneau, 1958; Burstein, 1965; Ebel & Prokasy, 1963; Prokasy, Ebel & Thompson, 1963), thus demonstrating the temporal properties of the learned representation. The focus in these studies has generally been on mean CR onset latency. Only Ebel and Prokasy (1963) reported the standard deviation of the response latencies. In Table 3 (p. 55), they reported means and standard deviations of onset latencies on CS-alone trials for groups tested at two different CS-US intervals (different combinations of 200-ms, 500-ms, or 800-ms). A slope analysis of these data (Equation 4) showed generalized Weber fractions that were relatively high (.31-.48), with the exception of the group shifted from a 500-ms to a 200-ms CS-US interval (.12). These generalized Weber fractions are much higher than we observed (Green et al., 1999). However, since they are calculated from CS-alone trials, they almost certainly include very long latency responses. We examined only responses within 200-ms of the US. In addition, the generalized Weber fractions calculated from Ebel and Prokasy are from pooled data whereas ours are calculated individually for each subject. Nevertheless, previous studies of eyeblink conditioning at multiple CS-US intervals clearly indicate that the CR is a timed response that occurs a short time before US onset, regardless of the CS-US interval. Future studies of CR timing would benefit from the slope analysis approach in which the precision of timing can be examined after controlling for non-timing factors.

THE NEURAL SUBSTRATES OF TIMING

As discussed briefly in the introductory section, the basic association between the tone CS and the corneal air puff US in eyeblink classical conditioning appears to be made in the deep (interpositus in rabbits and globose in humans) nucleus ipsilateral to the eye that receives the air puff US. This deep nucleus receive converging information about both the CS (via mossy fibers from pontine nuclei) and the US (via climbing fibers from the inferior olive). However, a second area of the cerebellum also receives converging CS and US information, specifically Larsell's hemispheric lobule VI (HVI) in the ansiform lobe of the cerebellar cortex. Numerous studies in rabbits have found that lesions of lobule HVI can affect the topography of CRs with only transient effects on the number of CRs (Harvey, Welsh, Yeo & Romano, 1993; Lavond & Steinmetz, 1989; Lavond, Steinmetz, Yokaitis & Thompson, 1987; Woodruff-Pak, Lavond, Logan, Steinmetz & Thompson, 1993; but see Yeo & Hardiman, 1992; Yeo, Hardiman & Glickstein, 1985b for a different view). More recently, Mauk and colleagues have demonstrated that lesions of a second region of cerebellar cortex, the anterior lobe, affect the timing of CRs without affecting CR acquisition (Garcia & Mauk, 1998; Perrett & Mauk, 1995; Perrett, Ruiz & Mauk, 1993).

Timing and the cerebellar cortex

Mauk and colleagues have examined changes in CR timing after lesions of cerebellar cortex. Perrett et al. (1993) tested rabbits using two different CSs (500 Hz and 8000 Hz tones), each of which was followed by an air puff US, but at a different CS-US interval. This form of a discrimination paradigm has been tested before in both humans (Kadlac & Grant, 1977; Kimble, Leonard & Perlmuter, 1968; Vandament, 1969) and rabbits (Hoehler & Leonard, 1976; Kehoe, Graham-Clarke & Schreurs, 1989; Kehoe, Horne & Horne, 1993; Mauk & Ruiz, 1992; Millenson, Kehoe & Gormezano, 1977) with the typical finding that subjects learn to emit a CR to each CS with a peak latency near the time of US onset. After learning the discrimination, Perrett et al. aspirated the anterior lobe of the cerebellar cortex in one group of rabbits. Rabbits given anterior cerebellar cortical lesions continued to emit CRs to both CSs but showed significantly shorter CR onset latencies and CR peak latencies (measured on CS-alone trials) than controls. CR latencies to the CS associated with a longer CS-US interval were similar to those observed following the CS associated with the shorter interval. While this might reflect a loss of discrimination, Perrett et al. argue that the deficit reflects a disruption of the timing of the CRs. In support of this hypothesis, they also report that rabbits trained in a 500 ms delay paradigm with a single CS also showed significantly shortened CR latencies after cerebellar cortical lesions.

One important piece of data neglected by Perrett et al. (1993) is the variability of latencies before and after lesions. As has been discussed throughout this chapter, the relationship of variability to mean response time (i.e., Weber's law) provides an index of the precision of timing. An increase in the Weber fraction would be expected after a lesion to a neural substrate involved in timing. It would be interesting to know whether the decrease in latency observed by Perrett et al. was accompanied by a change in variability. Inspection of Figures 2A and 2B (p. 1711) indicates a decrease in the mean but suggests little change in the variance of response latency. This would indicate an increase in the Weber fraction, which suggests that the precise timing of CRs was disrupted, as Perrett et al. hypothesized. The reason that it is important to account for response variability as well as mean response latency is that both may change in the same direction after a lesion, which would suggest that the precision of timing itself had not changed but, rather, that there was damage to sensorimotor processing of the CS and the CR. Perrett et al. suggested that damage to the anterior lobe of the cerebellum removed Purkinje cell inhibition from the interpositus nucleus. Normally, Purkinje cells would inhibit the interpositus from generating a response until just before US onset. In the case of an animal with a lesioned anterior lobe, the interpositus generates an immediate response to CS onset.

Although Perrett et al. (1993) suggested that the anterior lobe of the cerebellar cortex is the key locus of a cerebellar timing system engaged in eyeblink classical conditioning, other data suggest at least some involvement of the rest of the cerebellar cortex in CR timing. We reanalyzed peak latency data from Woodruff-Pak et al. (1993) and found that rabbits trained in the 250-ms delay paradigm and subsequently lesioned in the posterior lobe (ansiform and paramedian lobules) of cerebellar cortex showed a higher simple Weber fraction even after 5 sessions of post-lesion training when compared to pre-lesion performance (Figure 4).

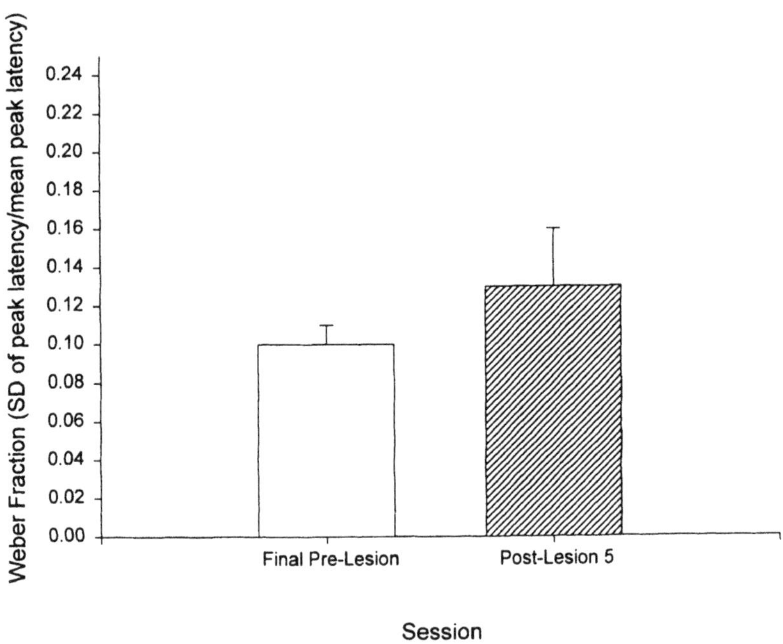

Figure 4. Simple Weber fraction (standard deviation/mean) for conditioned response peak latency immediately before and 5 days after cerebellar cortical lesions.

An increase in CR timing variability, at least between subjects, is also evident from inspection of Harvey et al.'s data (1993) (Table 1, p. 1632). Harvey et al. lesioned only the ansiform lobule in rabbits. Of course, since only one CS-US interval was tested in Woodruff-Pak et al.'s and Harvey et al.'s studies, it cannot be known for certain whether the simple Weber fractions increased after cerebellar cortical lesions due to a disruption of a timing or a non-timing system. Finally, disconnection of cerebellar cortex from the interpositus nucleus via localized infusions of picrotoxin near interpositus nucleus appears to increase CR latency variability (Figure 1d, p. 474) while revealing the short-latency CR observed by Perrett et al. (Garcia & Mauk, 1998). This suggests that other areas of cerebellar cortex besides just the anterior lobe may contribute to CR timing. Keele and Ivry (1990) suggested that the entire lateral cerebellum is critical for precise timing in many tasks. For example, lateral cerebellar lesions in humans disrupt the precise timing of taps in timed-interval tapping (Ivry, Keele & Diener, 1988).

The combined data from these studies of eyeblink classical conditioning and cerebellar cortical lesions suggests the need for a repeated-measures design in assessing timing in eyeblink classical conditioning. The use of a repeated-measures design would allow a slope analysis of CR latency data. A slope analysis would disentangle issues of changes in non-timing systems versus changes in timing systems caused by various lesions. Currently, it is not entirely clear where the CR timing system is located, although it seems very likely that some region of cerebellar cortex is involved.

Timing and the basal ganglia: Eyeblink conditioning

While most of the research on timing and eyeblink conditioning has focused on the cerebellum, there is also some evidence that damage to the basal ganglia may disrupt the precise timing of CRs. Woodruff-Pak and Papka (1996) tested patients with Huntington's disease, a degenerative disease in which the primary pathology involves severe atrophy of the striatum, the primary input structure of the basal ganglia. The simple Weber fraction for CR peak latency was larger for patients with Huntington's Disease compared to age-matched control subjects, indicating a disruption in timing (Figure 5).

This result occurred in the absence of deficits in the acquisition of CRs. Daum, Schugens, Breitenstein, Topka, and Spieker (1996) examined eyeblink conditioning in patients with Parkinson's disease, another degenerative basal ganglia disorder. Whereas they reported normal or even supra-normal conditioning in both medicated and unmedicated Parkinson's disease patients, they did not report whether the onset and peak latencies of CRs were normal or abnormal.

A few studies have used rabbits to examine the role of the basal ganglia in eyeblink classical conditioning. Lesions of the caudate nucleus slowed acquisition of CRs (Powell, Mankowski & Buchanan, 1978). Unfortunately, data on CR latencies were not reported in this study. Unit recordings during eyeblink classical conditioning showed that the basal ganglia formed a model of the CR (White et al., 1994). This CR model was similar to the neural model of the interpositus nucleus of the cerebellum during eyeblink classical conditioning. The main difference between the basal ganglia CR model and the interpositus nucleus CR model was that the basal ganglia model occurred only 10-ms to 50-ms before the behavioral CR, whereas the interpositus model occurs 30-ms to 60-ms before the behavioral CR (Steinmetz, 1996). White et al. suggested that the basal ganglia may receive CR-related information from the cerebellum. Basal ganglia are likely not involved in initiating CRs but may be involved in modulating CRs in some way. However, injections of haloperidol, a drug that decreases levels of dopamine in the basal ganglia, did not change CR onset latencies as assessed on CS-alone trials (Sears & Steinmetz, 1990).

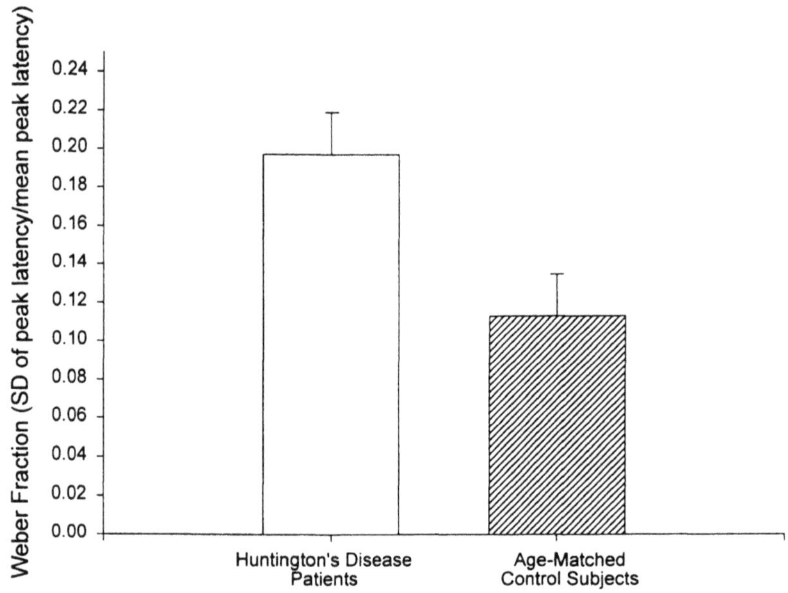

Figure 5. Simple Weber fraction (standard deviation/mean) for conditioned response peak latency for Huntington's Disease patients and age-matched control subjects.

At present, there are insufficient data to justify strong conclusions regarding the functional contribution of the basal ganglia to eyeblink conditioning. The results of Woodruff-Pak and Papka (1996) with Huntington's patients raise the possibility that the basal ganglia, perhaps in concert with the cerebellum, contribute to the timing of the CR. However, it is also possible that the observed reductions in CR latency may reflect generic changes in responsiveness, especially to meaningful stimuli.

Timing and the basal ganglia: The peak procedure

Although data are scant regarding basal ganglia involvement in timing in eyeblink classical conditioning, there is reason to think that the basal ganglia are involved in other tasks that require precise timing. One such task is the peak procedure task. This operant conditioning procedure is a discrete-trials version of a fixed-interval schedule in which the onset of a signal marks the beginning of the interval (Catania, 1970; Roberts, 1981). The first bar press after the criterion interval has elapsed since signal onset is rewarded with food. However, the peak procedure differs from the typical signaled bar pressing task in that, on some percentage of trials, no reinforcer is delivered. On these "empty" trials, the signal is lengthened (doubled or tripled) so that signal offset does not elicit responses. These empty trials allow the experimenter to assess the animal's memory of the time of reinforcer delivery without interference from reinforcer delivery itself. After sufficient training, bar pressing rate is found to peak at about the time a reinforcer would be expected.

The peak procedure is similar to eyeblink classical conditioning in that each trial begins with the presentation of an initially neutral stimulus, such as a tone, that is predictive of a second stimulus. The second stimulus, the air puff, evokes a reflexive response in classical conditioning; in the peak procedure, the second stimulus is the reinforcer, the food that becomes available after a fixed amount of time has elapsed. Thus in both tasks, the second stimulus is time-locked to the first stimulus and adaptive behavior requires that the animal learn this temporal relationship. However, there are some important differences between the two tasks. First, the time scales over which the tasks are run differ by an order of magnitude. Eyeblink classical conditioning is usually tested on intervals on the order of milliseconds and learning is severely attenuated with intervals longer than 1-2 s. The intervals used in the peak procedure usually range from 10 s to 40 s. Second, eyeblink conditioning requires that the animal make a conditioned response in order to avoid an aversive stimulus. The peak procedure reinforces an appetitive behavior. This may be an important distinction regarding cerebellar involvement. The cerebellum may not be engaged in timing tasks that reinforce an appetitive behavior (Steinmetz, Logue & Miller, 1993).

The peak procedure has spawned a rich psychological literature over the past two decades, delineating quantitative models of the performance of rats across a variety of manipulations. These models postulate specific component processes associated with the temporal, attentional, memory, and decision requirements of this task. Lesion and pharmacological studies have been used to link these hypothetical processes to particular neural systems. This work has focused on the contribution of the basal ganglia to timing processes (Gibbon et al., 1997; Meck, 1996), with lesions of this structure disrupting the timing and drug manipulations that influence dopamine levels producing systematic changes in the time at which the animals expect reinforcement. Importantly, when variability has been assessed, it appears that basal ganglia dysfunction leads to an increase in the Weber fraction (Gibbon et al., 1997).

Recently, the peak procedure has been adapted for testing in humans (Malapani et al., 1998; Rakitin et al., 1998). In this version of the peak procedure, subjects pressed the space bar of a computer keyboard as many times as needed to place a response at exactly the length of a target interval. Three target intervals were tested: 8, 12, and 21-sec. The variability of college-aged subjects' response functions increased as a constant proportion of increases in the target interval, demonstrating the Weber's law property of timing (Rakitin et al., 1998). Older subjects showed an increase in both the standard deviation of response time and the mean of response time but their data also conformed to the Weber's law property of timing. The researchers suggested that this was due to an increase in the noise of peripheral (i.e., non-timing) processes with age but no change in the timing system itself. In contrast, Parkinson's patients off their medication showed violations of the Weber's law property, suggesting that the basal ganglia are important for timing in the peak procedure in humans as well as rats (Malapani et al., 1998).

Further investigations with both humans and non-human mammals will be important for directly comparing the contributions of the cerebellum and basal ganglia in the representation of temporal information. Analytic tools such as that offered by the slope analysis should prove helpful in identifying different sources of variability. As noted above, the intervals used in the peak procedure and eyeblink classical conditioning are quite different. It is possible that the basal ganglia are involved in tasks extending over many seconds whereas the cerebellum is only involved in tasks involving intervals on the order of milliseconds (Ivry, 1996). The fact that Weber's law holds across different intervals raises the possibility that a common timing system is involved over these different ranges. On the other hand, the fact that Weber's law holds across many stimulus dimensions suggests that it reflects general principles associated with noisy biological processes.

Neural models of timing

What are the mechanisms by which precise CR timing is generated? At a psychological level, Sutton and Barto (1981) proposed the first information-processing model of classical conditioning that included an account of CR topography. Sutton and Barto hypothesized that the onset of a CS causes an "eligibility" trace to become active for a brief period in an adaptive element. The adaptive element represents a location of CS and US convergence. The onset of a US excites the adaptive element and causes a response. If the US excites the adaptive element while an eligibility trace is active, the CS that activated that eligibility trace becomes more strongly connected to the adaptive element. Eventually, the CS is able to excite the adaptive element and cause a response before the US is delivered.

One unrealistic assumption of the Sutton and Barto (1981) model is that CS onset instantaneously activates an eligibility trace in the adaptive element. Moore et al. (1986) added to the basic Sutton and Barto model a second trace, which they termed the "input" trace. The CS input trace begins 70-ms after CS onset and activates the eligibility trace 30-ms after input trace onset. These dual traces activated directly and indirectly by a CS yield a more realistic learning curve. Grossberg and Schmajuk (1989) introduced a different model in which the CS essentially activates a population (i.e., a spectrum) of input traces, and the trace most strongly active at US onset is strengthened.

In the last 10 years, theorists have moved towards grounding these theories in neural networks that are constrained by what is known about the relevant brain circuitry. Several groups of researchers have proposed neural network models of eyeblink classical conditioning that attempt to account for the precise timing of CRs using cerebellar circuitry known to be involved in eyeblink classical conditioning

(Buonomano & Mauk, 1994; Fiala, Grossberg & Bullock, 1996; Moore, Desmond & Berthier, 1989). These models suggest several ways in which CR timing may be mediated by the cerebellum at a cellular level.

Briefly, cerebellar cortex is composed of three separate cellular layers (Burt, 1993). The outermost layer is composed of stellate and basket cells; the middle layer contains Purkinje cell bodies, and the inner layer is composed of an enormous number of granule cells and a smaller number of Golgi cells. Below the cerebellar cortex are the deep nuclei. Inhibitory axons from Purkinje cells project to the deep nuclei. One of the deep nuclei, the interpositus nucleus in rabbits and the globose nucleus in humans, is critical for eyeblink classical conditioning. The interpositus/globose nucleus projects contralaterally to the red nucleus and to the ventrolateral nucleus of the thalamus, both areas outside of the cerebellum. In all of the current models, the neural instantiation for the precise timing of CRs centers on synaptic plasticity at the Purkinje cells, modifying the inhibitory signals these neurons provide to the interpositus/globose nucleus. In essence, the cerebellar cortex is hypothesized to shape the CR so that it occurs at the right point in time. Different schemes have been proposed for the implementation of this temporal representation.

Moore et al. (1989) suggested a neural network model of eyeblink classical conditioning in which the CS is fed through a string of neuronal elements associated with pontine nuclei that each project to a granule cell in cerebellar cortex. Thus, granule cells digitize CS duration into discrete chunks of time, one per neuronal element. Each granule cell projects to both a Purkinje cell and a Golgi cell. Purkinje cells are assumed to be adaptive elements that mediate changes in the CS-US connection strength and generate the network output. Golgi cells represent the time since CS onset. Golgi cells connected to each granule cell inhibit that cell until the US is delivered, at which time the granule cell inhibits a connected Purkinje cell. The granule cell input to the Purkinje cells will result in disinhibition of the interpositus/globose cells and allow a response to be generated. Granule cells that are active at the time of US onset are strengthened. The next time a CS is delivered, this granule cell will be more likely to inhibit its connected Purkinje cells so that a response is generated at the appropriate point in time. Recently, a feedback circuit involving the red nucleus and a brain stem nucleus has been added to the basic model in order to account for findings from more complex classical conditioning paradigms (Moore, Choi & Brunzell, 1998). However, the basic timing features remain the same (Figure 6).

Buonomano and Mauk (1994) took a different approach and suggested that a population vector of granule cell activity encodes the CS duration. In their model, a mossy fiber input pattern activated by a particular CS activates a set of granule cells. This set of granule cells will activate in turn, a unique set of Golgi cells, which can inhibit the granule cells via negative feedback. The same set of granule cells also inhibits a unique set of Purkinje cells. As in Moore et al.'s (1989) model, particular CS-US intervals are stored by changing the strength of connections between granule cells and Purkinje cells.

Finally, Fiala et al. (1996) proposed that intracellular cascades in Purkinje cells encode CS duration. Fiala et al.'s model is a neural instantiation of Grossberg and

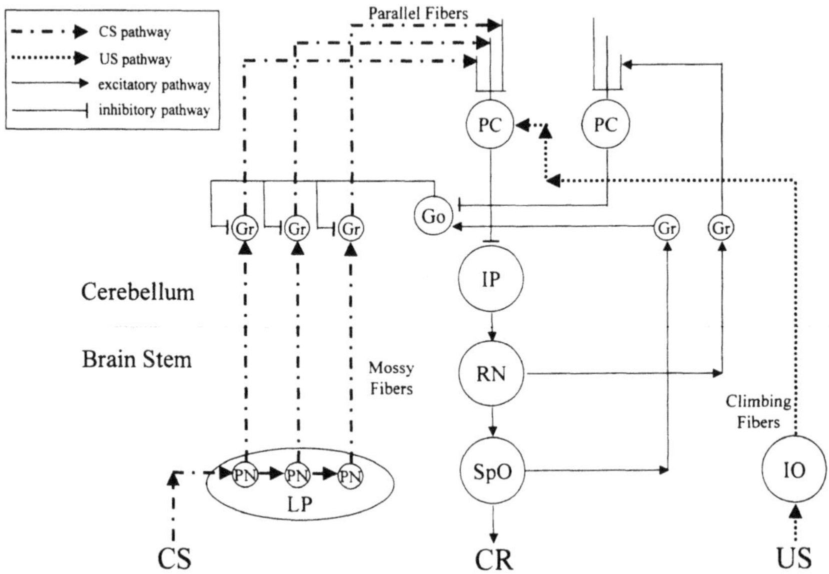

Figure 6. Moore et al.'s (1989) proposed neural instantiation of an artificial neural network model of timing in eyeblink classical conditioning. Abbreviations: Purkinje cell (PC); granule cell (Gr), interpositus nucleus (IP); red nucleus (RN); spinal trigeminal nucleus (SpO); pontine nucleus (PN); lateral pons (LP); inferior olive (IO). *Note:* only those pathways involved in CR timing are shown.

Schmajuk's (1989) spectral timing model. The spectrum of input traces in Grossberg and Schmajuk is instantiated as a cascade of second messenger systems coupled to metabotropic glutamate receptors on Purkinje cells. Purkinje cells whose intracellular response time approximates the CS-US interval decrease simple spike firing at US onset, which disinhibits interpositus/globose nucleus cells that generate the CR.

While these models differ in substantial ways, an essential feature of all of them is their capability to represent temporal information in an explicit and continuous manner. Such mechanisms are required to sustain a representation of the CS so that it can be associated with a US that can occur at arbitrary points in time. These models underscore an essential feature of eyeblink classical conditioning. It is not sufficient to simply associate the two stimulus events. The organism must also be able to extract and represent the interval between the stimuli in order to learn in an adaptive manner.

SUMMARY AND CONCLUSIONS

Dual-task designs and repeated-measures designs are useful in the study of eyeblink classical conditioning. Dual-task designs can be used to determine whether two tasks share a common neural substrate. As shown by Papka et al. (1995), two tasks that had independently been linked to the cerebellum, repetitive tapping and eyeblink classical conditioning, were found to interact, whereas other motor and memory tasks did not (e.g., Green & Woodruff-Pak, 1997). This suggests that timed-interval tapping and eyeblink classical conditioning share a common neural substrate in the cerebellum, a commonality hypothesized to reflect the fact that both tasks require precise timing.

Repeated-measures designs allow a more fine-grained examination of timing. One such method, the slope analysis (Ivry & Corcos, 1993; Ivry & Hazeltine, 1995) is useful for examining different sources of variability that affect performance on temporal processing tasks. Temporal variability generally increases as a constant proportion of mean response time, a form of Weber's law. However, some portion of the total variability in such tasks is due to noise in systems that are not time dependent, and these sources will be constant across a range of intervals. At very short intervals, this non-timing variability contributes disproportionately to observed variability in the timing of responses. Slope analysis allows a subtraction of non-timing variability (i.e., the intercept of a linear regression) from timing variability (i.e., the slope of a linear regression). The application of the slope method to eyeblink classical conditioning provided new evidence of a common source of temporal variability for eyeblink conditioning and timed interval tapping (Green et al., 1999).

Future studies of timing in eyeblink classical conditioning would benefit from similar analyses. For example, lesions of a putative timing system should cause an increase in the slope of the function relating standard deviation to mean CR latency, while lesions that affect other systems should cause an increase in the intercept but no change in the slope. In this way, we can move beyond cataloging whether a particular neural structure is associated with eyeblink conditioning, and ask how that structure contributes to this task. Given the precise neuroanatomical and neurophysiological data on eyeblink classical conditioning, such studies with a model task such as eyeblink classical conditioning may help us to determine how the brain computes time.

REFERENCES

Berthier, N.E., & Moore, J.W. (1986). Cerebellar Purkinje cell activity related to the classically conditioned nictitating membrane response. *Experimental Brain Research, 63*, 341-350.

Berthier, N.E., & Moore, J.W. (1990). Activity of deep cerebellar nuclear cells during classical conditioning of nictitating membrane extension in rabbits. *Experimental Brain Research, 83*, 44-54.

Blaxton, T.A., Zeffiro, T.A., Gabrieli, J.D.E., Bookheimer, S.Y., Carrillo, M.C., Theodore, W. H., & Disterhoft, J.F. (1996). Functional mapping of human learning: A positron-emission tomography study of eyeblink conditioning. *Journal of Neuroscience, 16*, 4032-4040.

Boneau, C.A. (1958). The interstimulus interval and the latency of the conditioned eyelid response. *Journal of Experimental Psychology, 56*, 464-471.

Burstein, K.R. (1965). Effect of UCS intensity upon the acquisition of conditioned responses acquired under a lengthened interstimulus interval. *Journal of Experimental Psychology, 70*, 147-150.

Burt, A.M. (1993). *Textbook of Neuroanatomy*. Philadelphia, PA: Saunders.

Catania, A.C. (1970). Reinforcement schedules and psychophysical judgments. In W. N. Schoenfeld (Ed.), *The Theory of Reinforcement Schedules (pp. 1-42)*. New York: Appleton-Century-Crofts.

Daum, I., Schugens, M.M., Ackermann, H., Lutzenberger, W., Dichgans, J., & Birbaumer, N. (1993). Classical conditioning after cerebellar lesions in humans. *Behavioral Neuroscience, 107*, 748-756.

Daum, I., Schugens, M.M., Breitenstein, C., Topka, H., & Spieker, S. (1996). Classical eyeblink conditioning in Parkinson's Disease. *Movement Disorders, 11*, 639-646.

Ebel, H.C., & Prokasy, W.F. (1963). Classical eyelid conditioning as a function of sustained and shifted interstimulus intervals. *Journal of Experimental Psychology, 65*, 52-58.

Engen, T. (1971). Psychophysics: I. Discrimination and detection. In J. W. Kling & L. A. Riggs (Eds.), *Woodworth & Schlosberg's Experimental Psychology (3rd edition) (pp. 11-46)*. New York: Holt, Rinehart and Winston.

Fiala, J.C., Grossberg, S., & Bullock, D. (1996). Metabotropic glutamate receptor activation in cerebellar Purkinje cells as substrate for adaptive timing of the classically conditioned eye-blink response. *Journal of Neuroscience, 16*, 3760-3774.

Garcia, K.S., & Mauk, M.D. (1998). Pharmacological analysis of cerebellar contributions to the timing and expression of conditioned eyelid responses. *Neuropharmacology, 37*, 471-480.

Getty, D. (1975). Discrimination of short temporal intervals: A comparison of two models. *Perception & Psychophysics, 18*, 1-8.

Gibbon, J. (1977). Scalar expectancy theory and Weber's law in animal timing. *Psychological Review, 84*, 279-325.

Gibbon, J., Malapani, C., Dale, C.L., & Gallistel, C.R. (1997). Toward a neurobiology of temporal cognition: Advances and challenges. *Current Opinion in Neurobiology, 7*, 170-184.

Green, J.T., & Woodruff-Pak, D.S. (1997). Concurrent eyeblink classical conditioning and rotary pursuit performance: Implications for independent nondeclarative memory systems. *Neuropsychology, 11*, 474-487.

Green, J.T., Ivry, R.B., & Woodruff-Pak, D.S. (1999). Timing in eyeblink classical conditioning and timed-interval tapping. *Psychological Science, 10*, 20-24.

Harvey, J.A., Welsh, J.P., Yeo, C.H., & Romano, A.G. (1993). Recoverable and nonrecoverable deficits in conditioned responses after cerebellar cortical lesions. *Journal of Neuroscience, 13*, 1624-1635.

Hoehler, F.K., & Leonard, D.W. (1976). Double responding in classical nictitating membrane conditioning with single-CS dual-ISI training. *Pavlovian Journal of Biological Science, 11*, 180-190.

Homzie, M.J. (1967). Performance in classical eyelid conditioning as a function of the lengthening of the CS-UCS interval. *Psychonomic Science, 7*, 211-212.

Ivry, R.B. (1996). The representation of temporal information in perception and motor control. *Current Opinion in Neurobiology, 6*, 851-857.

Ivry, R.B. (1997). Cerebellar timing systems. *International Review of Neurobiology, 41*, 555-573.

Ivry, R.B., & Corcos, D.M. (1993). Slicing the variability pie: Component analysis of coordination and motor dysfunction. In K.M. Newell, & Corcos, D.M. (Eds.), *Variability and Motor Control (pp. 415-447)*. Champaign, IL: Human Kinetics.

Ivry, R.B., & Hazeltine, R.E. (1995). Perception and production of temporal intervals across a range of durations: Evidence for a common timing mechanism. *Journal of Experimental Psychology: Human Perception and Performance, 21*, 3-18.

Ivry, R.B., & Keele, S.W. (1989). Timing functions of the cerebellum. *Journal of Cognitive Neuroscience, 1*, 136-152.

Ivry, R.B., Keele, S.W., & Diener, H.C. (1988). Dissociation of the lateral and medial cerebellum in movement timing and movement execution. *Experimental Brain Research, 73*, 167-180.

Kadlac, J.A., & Grant, D.A. (1977). Eyelid response topography in differential interstimulus interval conditioning. *Journal of Experimental Psychology: Human Learning and Memory, 3*, 345-355.

Kehoe, E.J., Graham-Clarke, P., & Schreurs, B.G. (1989). Temporal patterns of the rabbit's nictitating membrane response to compound and component stimuli under mixed CS-US intervals. *Behavioral Neuroscience, 103*, 283-295.

Kehoe, E.J., Horne, P.S., & Horne, A.J. (1993). Discrimination learning using different CS-US intervals in classical conditioning of the rabbit's nictitating membrane response. *Psychobiology, 21*, 277-285.

Keele, S.W., & Ivry, R. (1990). Does the cerebellum provide a common computation for diverse tasks? *Annals of the New York Academy of Sciences, 608*, 179-211.

Kimble, G.A., Leonard, III, T.B., & Perlmuter, L.C. (1968). Effects of interstimulus interval and discrimination learning in eyelid conditioning using between- and within-Ss designs. *Journal of Experimental Psychology, 77*, 652-660.

Kinsbourne, M., & Hicks, R.E. (1978). Functional cerebral space: A model for overflow, transfer, and interference effects in human performance: A tutorial review. In J. Requin (Ed.), *Attention and Performance VII (pp. 345-362).* Hillsdale, NJ: Erlbaum.

Kinsbourne, M., & Hiscock, M. (1983). Asymmetries of dual-task performance. In J. B. Hellige (Ed.), *Cerebral hemisphere asymmetry: Method, theory, and application (pp. 255-334).* New York: Praeger.

Lavond, D.G., Hembree, T.L., & Thompson, R.F. (1985). Effects of kainic acid lesions of the cerebellar interpositus nucleus on eyelid conditioning in the rabbit. *Brain Research, 326,* 179-182.

Lavond, D.G., & Steinmetz, J.E. (1989). Acquisition of classical conditioning without cerebellar cortex. *Behavioural Brain Research, 33,* 113-164.

Lavond, D.G., Steinmetz, J.E., Yokaitis, M.H., & Thompson, R.F. (1987). Reacquisition of classical conditioning after removal of cerebellar cortex. *Experimental Brain Research, 67,* 569-593.

Lincoln, J.S., McCormick, D.A., & Thompson, R.F. (1982). Ipsilateral cerebellar lesions prevent learning of the classically conditioned nictitating membrane/eyelid response. *Brain Research, 242,* 190-193.

Logan, C.G., & Grafton, S.T. (1995). Functional anatomy of human eyeblink conditioning determined with regional cerebral glucose metabolism and positron-emission tomography. *Proceedings of the National Academy of Sciences, (USA), 92,* 7500-7504.

Lye, R.H., O'Boyle, D.J., Ramsden, R.T., & Schady, W. (1988). Effects of a unilateral cerebellar lesion on the acquisition of eye-blink conditioning in man. *Journal of Physiology, 403,* 58P.

Malapani, C., Rakitin, B., Levy, R., Meck, W.H., Deweer, B., Dubois, B., & Gibbon, J. (1998). Coupled temporal memories in Parkinson's disease: A dopamine-related dysfunction. *Journal of Cognitive Neuroscience, 10,* 316-331.

Mauk, M.D., & Ruiz, B.P. (1992). Learning-dependent timing of Pavlovian eyelid responses: Differential conditioning using multiple interstimulus intervals. *Behavioral Neuroscience, 106,* 666-681.

McAllister, W.R. (1953). The effect on eyelid conditioning of shifting the CS-US interval. *Journal of Experimental Psychology, 45,* 423-428.

McCormick, D.A., Lavond, D.G., Clark, G.A., Kettner, R.E., Rising, C.E., & Thompson, R.F. (1981). The engram found? Role of the cerebellum in classical conditioning of nictitating membrane and eyelid responses. *Bulletin of the Psychonomic Society, 18,* 103-105.

McCormick, D.A., & Thompson, R.F. (1984a). Cerebellum: Essential involvement in the classically conditioned eyelid response. *Science, 223,* 296-299.

McCormick, D.A., & Thompson, R.F. (1984b). Neuronal responses of the rabbit cerebellum during acquisition and performance of a classically conditioned nictitating membrane-eyelid response. *Journal of Neuroscience, 4,* 2811-2822.

Millenson, J.R., Kehoe, E.J., & Gormezano, I. (1977). Classical conditioning of the rabbit's nictitating membrane response under fixed and mixed CS-US intervals. *Learning and Motivation, 8,* 351-366.

Molchan, S.E., Sunderland, T., McIntosh, A.R., Herscovitch, P., & Schreurs, B.G. (1994). A functional anatomical study of associative learning in humans. *Proceedings of the National Academy of Sciences, (USA), 91,* 8122-8126.

Moore, J.W., Choi, J-S., & Brunzell, D.H. (1998). Predictive timing under temporal uncertainty: The time derivative model of the conditioned response. In D.A. Rosenbaum & C.E. Collyer (Eds.), *Timing of Behavior: Neural, Psychological, and Computational Perspectives (pp. 3-34).* Cambridge: MIT Press.

Moore, J.W., Desmond, J.E., & Berthier, N.E. (1989). Adaptively timed conditioned responses and the cerebellum: A neural network approach. *Biological Cybernetics, 62,* 17-28.

Moore, J.W., Desmond, J.E., Berthier, N.E., Blazis, D.E.J., Sutton, R.S., & Barto, A.G. (1986). Simulation of the classically conditioned nictitating membrane response by a neuron-like adaptive element: Response topography, neuronal firing, and interstimulus intervals. *Behavioural Brain Research, 21,* 143-154.

Papka, M., Ivry, R.B., & Woodruff-Pak, D.S. (1995). Selective disruption of eyeblink classical conditioning by concurrent tapping. *Neuroreport, 6,* 1493-1497.

Pashler, H. (1994). Dual-task interference in simple tasks: Data and theory. *Psychological Bulletin, 116,* 220-244.

Perrett, S.P., & Mauk, M.D. (1995). Extinction of conditioned eyelid responses requires the anterior lobe

of cerebellar cortex. *Journal of Neuroscience, 15*, 2074-2080.
Perrett, S.P., Ruiz, B.P., & Mauk, M.D. (1993). Cerebellar cortex lesions disrupt learning-dependent timing of conditioned eyelid responses. *Journal of Neuroscience, 13*, 1708-1718.
Powell, D.A., Mankowski, D., & Buchanan, S. (1978). Concomitant heart rate and corneoretinal potential conditioning in the rabbit (*Oryctolagus cuniculus*): Effects of caudate lesions. *Physiology & Behavior, 20*, 143-150.
Prokasy, W.F., Ebel, H.C., & Thompson, D.D. (1963). Response shaping at long interstimulus intervals in classical eyelid conditioning. *Journal of Experimental Psychology, 66*, 138-141.
Rakitin, B.C., Gibbon, J. , Penney, T.B., Malapani, C., Hinton, S.C., & Meck, W.H. (1998). Scalar expectancy theory and peak-interval timing in humans. *Journal of Experimental Psychology: Animal Behavior Processes, 24*, 15-33.
Roberts, S. (1981). Isolation of an internal clock. *Journal of Experimental Psychology: Animal Behavior Processes, 7*, 242-268.
Schreurs, B.G., McIntosh, A.R., Bahro, M., Hersocovitch, P., Sunderland, T., & Molchan, S.E. (1997). Lateralization and behavioral correlation of changes in regional cerebral blood flow with classical conditioning of the human eyeblink response. *Journal of Neurophysiology, 77*, 2153-2163.
Sears, L.L., & Steinmetz, J.E. (1990). Haloperidol impairs classically conditioned nictitating membrane responses and conditioning-related cerebellar interpositus activity in rabbits. *Pharmacology, Biochemistry, & Behavior, 36*, 821-830.
Solomon, P.R., Stowe, G.T., & Pendlebury, W.W. (1989). Disrupted eyelid conditioning in a patient with damage to cerebellar afferents. *Behavioral Neuroscience, 103*, 898-902.
Steinmetz, J.E. (1996). The brain substrates of classical eyeblink conditioning in rabbits. In J.R. Bloedel, T.J. Ebner, & S.P. Wise (Eds.), *The acquisition of motor behavior in vertebrates (pp. 89-114)*. Cambridge: MIT Press.
Steinmetz, J.E., Lavond, D.G., Ivkovich, D., Logan, C.G., & Thompson, R.F. (1992). Disruption of classical eyelid conditioning after cerebellar lesions: Damage to a memory trace system or a simple performance deficit? *Journal of Neuroscience, 12*, 4403-4426.
Steinmetz, J.E., Logue, S.F., & Miller, D.P. (1993). Using signaled barpressing tasks to study the neural substrates of appetitive and aversive learning in rats: Behavioral manipulations and cerebellar lesions. *Behavioral Neuroscience, 107*, 941-954.
Sutton, R.S., & Barto, A.G. (1981). Toward a modern theory of adaptive networks: Expectation and prediction. *Psychological Review, 88*, 135-170.
Thompson, R.F. (1986). The neurobiology of learning and memory. *Science, 233*, 941-947.
Thompson, R.F. (1990). Neural mechanisms of classical conditioning in mammals. *Philosophical Transactions of the Royal Society of London B, 329*, 161-170.
Topka, H., Valls-Sole, J., Massaquoi, S.G., & Hallett, M. (1993). Deficit in classical conditioning in patients with cerebellar degeneration. *Brain, 116*, 961-969.
Vandament, W.E. (1969). Response latency as a function of interstimulus interval in conditioned eyelid discrimination. *Journal of Experimental Psychology, 82*, 561-565.
White, I.M., Miller, D.P., White, W., Dike, G.L., Rebec, G.V., & Steinmetz, J.E. (1994). Neuronal activity in rabbit neostriatum during classical eyelid conditioning. *Experimental Brain Research, 99*, 179-190.
Wing, A.M., & Kristofferson, A.B. (1973). Response delays and the timing of discrete motor responses. *Perception & Psychophysics, 14*, 5-12.
Woodruff-Pak, D.S. (1997). Evidence for the role of the cerebellum in classical conditioning in humans. *International Review of Neurobiology, 41*, 385-410.
Woodruff-Pak, D.S., & Jaeger, M. (1998). Predictors of eyeblink classical conditioning over the adult age span. *Psychology and Aging, 13*, 193-205.
Woodruff-Pak, D.S., Lavond, D.G., Logan, C.G., Steinmetz, J.E., & Thompson, R.F. (1993). Cerebellar cortical lesions and reacquisition in classical conditioning of the nictitating membrane response in rabbits. *Brain Research, 608*, 67-77.
Woodruff-Pak, D.S., & Papka, M. (1996). Huntington's disease and eyeblink classical conditioning: Normal learning but abnormal timing. *Journal of the International Neuropsychological Society, 2*, 323-334.

Woodruff-Pak, D.S., Papka, M., & Ivry, R.B. (1996). Cerebellar involvement in eyeblink classical conditioning in humans. *Neuropsychology, 10,* 443-458.

Yeo. C.H., & Hardiman, M.J. (1992). Cerebellar cortex and eyeblink conditioning: A reexamination. *Experimental Brain Research, 88,* 623-638.

Yeo, C.H., Hardiman, M.J., & Glickstein, M. (1985a). Classical conditioning of the nictitating membrane response of the rabbit. I. Lesions of the cerebellar nuclei. *Experimental Brain Research, 60,* 87-98.

Yeo, C.H., Hardiman, M.J., & Glickstein, M. (1985b). Classical conditioning of the nictitating membrane response of the rabbit. II. Lesions of the cerebellar cortex. *Experimental Brain Research, 60,* 99-113.

6 USING EYEBLINK CONDITIONING TO ASSESS NEUROCOGNITIVE DEVELOPMENT IN HUMAN INFANTS

Dragana Ivkovich
Duke University, US EPA

Carol O. Eckerman
Duke University

Norman A. Krasnegor
NICHD

Mark E. Stanton
Duke University, US EPA

INTRODUCTION

Classical eyeblink conditioning has become a successful paradigm for studying both cognitive and neural processes underlying learning and memory in several species, including humans. Over 50 years of research has generated a wealth of knowledge about the behavioral properties and parametric laws of eyeblink conditioning in adult organisms (e.g., Gormezano, Kehoe & Marshall 1983; Kimble & Pennypacker, 1963; Spence, 1953). In addition, recent advances in clinical and basic neurosciences suggest that similar neural mechanisms subserve eyeblink conditioning in both humans and animal models (e.g., Daum et al., 1993; Lavond, Kim & Thompson, 1993; Woodruff-Pak, Logan & Thompson 1990). Eyeblink conditioning can be studied throughout human development, from infancy to old age; and animal models for studying the neural substrates of these life-span changes have been developed (Solomon & Pendlebury, 1988; Stanton & Freeman, 1994; Woodruff-Pak & Thompson, 1988). As a result of these advances, eyeblink conditioning could become a powerful tool for studying the developmental psychobiology of learning and memory in the human.

One of the many advantages of eyeblink conditioning for developmental studies is that it is a simple technique applicable across a broad range of ages and abilities. The variety of conditioning paradigms also provide a way of specifically studying the development of cognitive processes (e.g. association, short-term memory, attention, inhibitory learning) and their underlying neural substrates (e.g. cerebellum, hippocampus, forebrain) in human infants. Further, to the extent that developmental changes in young infants' eyeblink conditioning behavior may reflect postnatal maturational changes in brain development, developmental studies of eyeblink conditioning may lead us toward a better understanding of neurobehavioral developmental disorders (Stanton & Freeman, 1994).

Despite this potential, relatively few studies on the development of eyeblink conditioning exist for human infants and young children (e.g., Little, Lipsitt & Rovee-Collier, 1984; Fitzgerald & Brackbill, 1976; Ohlrich & Ross, 1968). Successful conditioning has been reported, but relatively little work has been conducted that fully exploits the advantages of studying the development of eyeblink conditioning phenomena in human infancy.

In this chapter we describe in some detail the procedures that we have developed, as well as the conditioning parameters and paradigms chosen for our initial studies of acquisition of eyeblink conditioning in infants. These procedures have been used successfully with 4- and 5-month-old human infants in our laboratory, the Infant Learning Project at Duke University. Our primary goal has been to establish delay eyeblink conditioning procedures that could (1) be adapted for use over a broad age range, (2) be used with infants varying in likely central nervous system damage; and (3) enable comparisons with developing animals (see Stanton & Freeman, 1994). We also will present findings from two experiments in which we used the procedures described to begin to address the developmental course of delay eyeblink conditioning in human infants.

PROCEDURES FOR EYEBLINK CONDITIONING HUMAN INFANTS

In developing procedures that would yield effective conditioning in young infants and form the basis for a programmatic series of developmental studies, a variety of issues were considered. How would the conditioning stimuli, an audible tone and a corneal air puff, be delivered? How long would the infant be awake and cooperative? How might we entertain the infant to maintain alertness and reduce mobility, without physically restricting the baby's movements, since restraint often results in increased fussy behavior and discontent (Sternberg & Campos, 1990)? Most importantly, how would we measure infant eyeblink behavior and assess learning?

General Methods

Maintaining Infant State

Of primary importance in developing a protocol to use with young infants around 4 to 5 months of age, was the need to maintain the cooperation of the infant for about 30-45 minutes -- from the time of arrival at the laboratory to the end of the conditioning session, which itself lasted about 15 minutes. We developed specific procedures aimed at maintaining the infant's state.

The goal was to maintain a quiet alert state for the duration of the conditioning session. The length of time that an infant was attentive and cooperative appeared to increase when the infant was prepared for conditioning in one room and then conditioned in another. The change in context by moving between rooms was often beneficial for keeping the infant alert because 10-20 minutes had already transpired in the first room while parents were briefed on procedures, given time to ask questions, and asked to sign consent forms. At this time parents were also encouraged to feed the infant before conditioning preparations began. The final step was to prepare the infant by putting on a special headband that would enable stimulus delivery to the eye and applying EMG electrodes which would record eyeblink activity during the conditioning session.

Once in the room where conditioning was to take place, infants were entertained with a variety of objects. A standardized visual display of brightly colored objects was presented on a table positioned about 75 cm in front of the infant. The display included marionettes, mobiles, and stuffed animals (see Figure 1) that were held and gently moved by an experimenter according to a choreographed routine. A fixed sequence of 7 items was used and each lasted about 3-4 minutes, or about 7 paired conditioning trials (see General Protocol and Apparatus). The display operator was able to see a trial counter that enabled her to know when to change items. Occasionally, however, some flexibility in the timing or order of the display items was

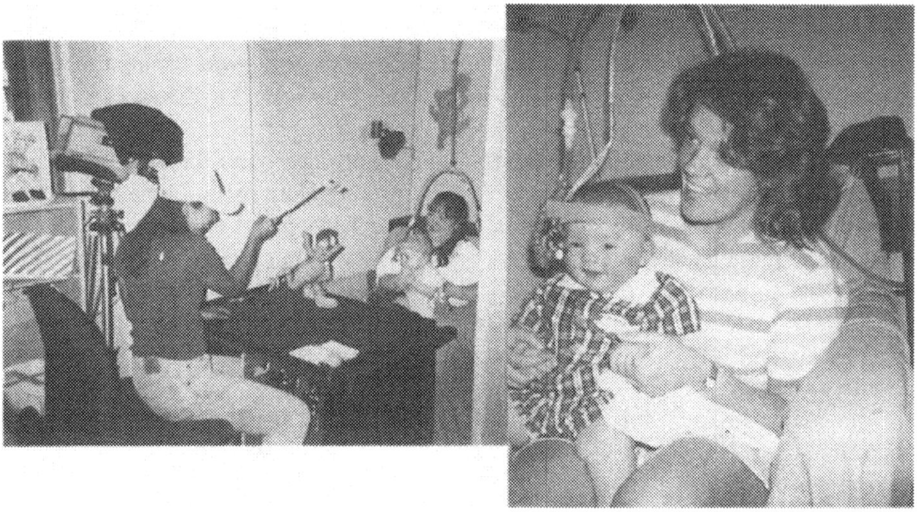

Figure 1. Photograph of the conditioning room showing an example of the visual display -- a marionette being manipulated to engage the infant subject. A video camera for recording the session is located to the left of the display operator. Suspended above the parent's head are extensions of the EMG recording wires and tubing for air puff delivery, so as to allow the subject some freedom of movement. Fabric-covered, sound-attenuating, and electrical-noise-reducing panels stand around the subject area.

effective in maintaining the attention of an infant who had become fussy. Also, we found that infants were much more cooperative when the display operator was visible, rather than hidden behind a curtain as with a puppet stage. The display operator was instructed not to hold the infant's gaze and not to interact with the infant by way of facial or auditory expressions, but to remain silent and maintain a steady pleasant face. In addition, background instrumental music ("Beauty and the Beast" from Walt Disney's animated picture) was played at low volume during the conditioning session. Completely silent surroundings are rather unusual for an awake infant and the music provided a small level of background auditory stimulation and prevented the room from becoming unusually silent, in order to reduce fussy behavior. Extraneous sound was attenuated by a 6-foot high three-sided panel, lined with acoustic foam, that was placed around the chair where parent and infant were seated. This panel also blocked the view of the rest of the room, where a second investigator quietly monitored the equipment used for running and recording the session. As such, the panel was valuable in limiting additional distractions that might turn away the attention of the infant or parent from the visual display and conditioning situation.

Another important part of maintaining the infant for the duration of the conditioning procedures involved parental cooperation. The mother-infant dyad is critical to an infant's state. We found that by placing a mirror at the parent's eye level, about 3 feet to the front and right of where parent and infant were seated, the parent was able to monitor the infant's general state as well as reactions to the stimuli and visual display. This served two important functions. First, since the infant was facing away from the parent this was effective in preventing parents from turning the infant around or trying to glimpse the infant's face, which only served to distract the infant and interfered with video recording. Occasionally, the parent and infant used the mirror to interact with each other briefly -- a comforting feature for both infant and parent. Second, parents were instructed to support the infant in a sitting position and to help occupy the infants' hands should they try to displace the air tube or headband, but not to immobilize the infant. By using the mirror, parents were able to effectively monitor their infant's movements and prevent potentially disruptive grappling and reaching. It was stressed that the parents should not completely immobilize the infants' arms for extended periods of time, since restraint can elicit anger and fussiness in infants.

The many small details of maintaining the infant's state for the duration of conditioning evolved through some trial and error, and through a great deal of practice in comfortably fitting the headband on the infant and giving ideal instructions to parents for seating and maintaining the infant during the session. Our goal was for infants to complete a criterion number of trials. This criterion was 30 tone-air puff trials for paired sessions and 30 tone-alone trials for unpaired sessions. There was a clear investigator practice effect involved in reducing attrition rates from our first experiment to the second. In the first experiment, 61.5% of the infants who visited the laboratory did not yield reliable data because they either failed to achieve the criterion number of trials or there were technical/ procedural difficulties during data collection. About 70% of the attrition was accounted for by failure to complete the criterion number of trials during one conditioning session. Only 30% of the attrition was due to technical or procedural difficulties which arose as a result of the nature of developing new conditioning procedures. In contrast, only 48.6% of the subjects in the second experiment did not meet inclusion criteria. Half of these infants were excluded because they failed to complete the criterion number of trials. This is even more impressive given that all subjects were required to participate in two conditioning sessions and had to meet the criterion on two separate occasions. Because we carefully controlled the amount of time between the two visits (7 $\pm$ 1 day), the other half of the subjects were lost due to rescheduling conflicts which arose when there was an illness in the family or some other uncontrollable factor. Technical and procedural difficulties were practically eliminated in the second experiment; there were only three such instances. Chi-square analyses confirmed that there was no selective attrition based on gender, age, or conditioning procedures in either study. During the past few months of conducting conditioning studies with five-month-old full-term and very-prematurely-born infants, our attrition rate has dropped even further. During this time, only 26.7% of the infants who visited our lab did not meet criteria to be included in recent studies. This is significant improvement, especially since infants are now required to provide usable data for three or four sessions. As we saw in Experiment 2, half of the time exclusions are still due to the failure to complete a criterion number of trials and half of the time they are due to rescheduling conflicts. Thus, discounting the issue of rescheduling, attrition rates have dropped from 61% to 24% to 13% over the course of our studies. Despite the many concerns that need to be addressed when working with infants, some attention to detail and practice can dramatically improve attrition rates.

General Protocol and Apparatus

During preparations, a specially crafted soft headband (mentioned earlier) was secured by Velcro across the infant's forehead and around the head to support a flexible plastic tube (made of LOC-LINE coolant hose segments) which delivered the air puff US to the subject's right eye. In addition, three adhesive gel-electrodes (Silver Sircuit resting EKG Electrodes, Kendall-LTP, Chicopee, MA), cut into 1/4" wide strips (1" long), were applied to the corner of the right eye (recording electrode), the right temple (differential electrode), and the back of the neck (ground) to collect electromyographic (EMG) records of eyeblinks during the conditioning session. These positions were determined to be optimal to reduce artifact recording from the infant's natural body movements. The recording electrode was vertically centered as close to the corner of the eye as possible without impeding the eyeblink. The differential electrode was placed, close to horizontal, on the temple so as to avoid cheek and jaw muscles that produce large movement artifacts. The ground electrode was placed between the neck and shoulder just under the infant's clothing.

In the conditioning room, then, connectors on the headband were attached to the tube that would deliver the air puff and to the computer for on-line recording of EMG. Infants sat on a parent's lap facing the table on which the visual display described earlier was presented. During the conditioning session, infants experienced presentations of a tone conditioned stimulus (CS; 1kHz, 80 dB) and air puff unconditional stimulus (US; approximately 1/20 lb/in^2). Above the head, about 18 inches to either side, were two small 7-Ohm speakers directed to the infant's ear level for delivery of the tone CS. The air puff US was generated by an audio speaker that acted as a bellows device and ejected a momentary pulse of air. This air puff device was especially designed for use with infants. It was incapable of producing harmful air pressures or a continuous stream of air stimulation. This device was used in place of a pressurized air tank and regulator-valve system commonly used in eyeblink conditioning studies. A custom-built eyeblink conditioning system (U.S. E.P.A, Health Effects Research Laboratory, Research Triangle Park, NC) controlled presentation of the stimuli. The EMG record was first amplified close to the source of the signal using an in-line field-effect transistor (FET, Radio Shack, Model# 2N3819; see Brakel, Babb, Mahnke & Verzeano, 1971). This reduced cable-movement artifact and improved the signal-to-noise ratio as the signal was transmitted over 6 feet to a pre-amplifier (Grass Instruments, Model # P511; amplification=20 x 1000; ½ amp. lo frequency = 30 Hz; ½ amp. hi frequency = 1 kHz). The signal was then integrated on-line, and amplified 1.4 times by a custom-built integrator/amplifier (U.S. E.P.A.) for subsequent analysis. The acoustic panels encompassing the subject area were also lined with copper mesh, thereby creating a partial Faraday cage that was grounded to reduce electrical noise which sometimes caused interference with the EMG signal.

Two video cameras, one placed about 1 m to the front and right of the infant and a second focused on a signal box, yielded a continuous video record (by way of a split-screen generator) of the infant's head and of the signal box. On the signal box were a trial counter and LED lights indicating when the tone and air puff stimuli were on (see Figure 2, top). These lights were later used in coding eyeblink behavior. The person operating the visual display for the infant also monitored the video camera, adjusting its position as necessary to maintain a clear view of the infant's right eye during the conditioning session.

Paired Conditioning Sessions. In order to assess acquisition of eyeblink conditioning in human infants, we began by using the delay procedure, in which the CS and US overlap in time and coterminate. A 750-ms tone was presented such that the last 100 ms overlapped and coterminated with a gentle puff of air to the right eye. This arrangement produced an inter-stimulus or delay interval of 650 ms between CS and US onset (Figure 2, bottom). The inter-trial interval (ITI) varied from 8-16 s (average = 12 s). Every 6th trial in a block of 10, as well as trials 1 and 2 at the start of the session, was an air puff-alone trial to test the unconditioned reflex (UR). Every tenth trial was a tone-alone trial to test for eyeblink conditioned responses (CRs). If, over time, infants learned to associate the occurrence of the tone with the air puff, we expected to see anticipatory CRs either occurring after the tone but prior to the air puff on paired trials, or in response to the tone when it was presented alone. A maximum of 50 trials was presented (about 15-20 minutes), but the session was terminated earlier if the infant became overly fussy.

Unpaired Conditioning Sessions. To control for the possibility of changes in blinking to the tone CS that might result from non-associative aspects of stimulus exposure, it was necessary to include separate groups of infants who experienced unpaired conditioning sessions. During these sessions, there was no associative contingency between the tone and air puff. Subjects experienced the same 43 tones and 45 puffs as used for paired conditioning, but the stimuli were presented explicitly unpaired, 4-8 s apart (average = 6 s) in a manner that matched the paired condition for stimulus density. The criteria for terminating a session were the same as those for paired sessions.

Eyeblink Coding

Two records of eyeblink behavior were collected: video and EMG. Videotapes were coded by two independent observers. The video was coded frame-by-frame to determine whether or not a blink of the right eye occurred during a given trial and when during the trial the blink occurred. Standard speed video cameras record at 60 Hz so that 1 frame captures about 16.7 ms of real time. CRs were defined as blinks that started within 21 frames (350 ms) prior to onset of the air puff. Unconditioned responses (URs) were blinks that started within the 15 frames (250 ms) after onset of the air puff. On tone-alone trials, any response within the combined CR and UR periods was considered a CR. Blinks occurring in the 300 ms period immediately following tone onset were coded as alpha or startle responses (SR). Responses during this period were distinguished from CRs and considered to be either reflexive reactions to the tone or voluntary eyeblink responses which are often observed in adult human eyeblink conditioning (see Figure 2, bottom). Trials in which the subject's right eye was out of view were excluded (< 10%). The percentage of agreement between observers was 98% for both experiments presented in this chapter. All videos were independently coded by two observers and then compared on a trial-by-trial basis. Agreement was defined as both coders concurring (1) that an eyeblink had occurred, (2) whether or not it was a CR, and (3) that the CR started and peaked about the same time ($\pm$ 2 frames agreement). Both observers recoded the few trials for which there was disagreement. As a result of recoding, most differences were resolved; the remaining trials without agreement were marked as missing data and excluded from further analyses.

Obtaining reliable EMG records was more problematic than obtaining reliable video records of eyeblink behavior. EMG recordings were sometimes sensitive to facial and head movements and showed large inter-subject variability in signal-to-noise ratio. Nevertheless, they were usable for about 83% of the sessions. The CR acquisition data presented below relied primarily on video codings; EMG was used, whenever possible, to examine response properties which could not be quantified by video. For sessions with usable EMG, UR amplitudes were obtained as a measure of US efficacy and used to compare groups of subjects for somatosensory responsiveness to the US. For trials on which video analysis confirmed the occurrence of a UR (excluding trials with a CR), UR amplitudes were averaged across subjects for each session and conditioning group. In addition, when video confirmation of a response was used, EMG could be used to assess response latency within 2.5 ms; however, frame-by-frame video analysis also yielded latency information within 16.7 ms resolution, which is adequate for most behavioral purposes (see Additional Analyses of Interest).

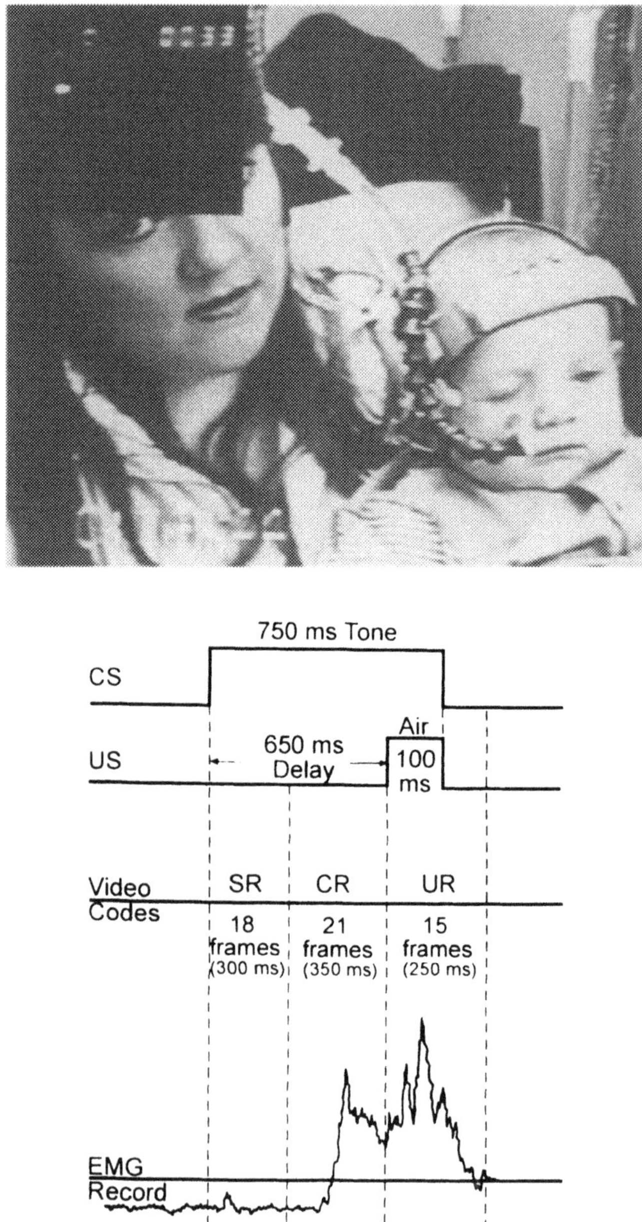

Figure 2. Top: A two-camera system is used to capture (1) a close-up of the infant's face and (2) a signal box (upper left corner) indicating the trial number and the presence or absence of the conditioning stimuli. Bottom: The conditioning paradigm (lines 1 and 2), partitioning of a trial into SR, CR, and UR periods for video analysis (line 3), and a sample EMG tracing of a CR (line 4). Abbreviations: conditioned stimulus (CS), unconditioned stimulus (US), startle response (SR), conditioned response (CR), unconditioned response (UR), electromyography (EMG).

Acquisition Measures and Data Analysis

Our primary measure of acquisition was the percentage of CRs. For analysis purposes, trials were reblocked into sets of six trials, all of one type, for five successive blocks per session (total of 30 trials). For paired conditioning sessions, the percentage of CRs was obtained for blocks of six paired trials; for unpaired sessions, the percentage of CRs was obtained for blocks of six tone-alone trials, with trials sampled to correspond in sequence with the tones on paired trials during paired sessions. Blocks containing less than four codable trials were excluded and subjects with missing blocks were excluded from further analyses. These data were plotted to produce learning curves and analyzed using between-groups repeated measures ANOVAs across sessions and blocks. Post-hoc Newman-Keuls comparisons were made as needed. All statistics reported below were significant using two-tailed values with $p < .05$ unless otherwise noted. Mean percentage CR values are reported together with the standard error of the mean (SEM).

The number of trials-to-criterion (TTC), another acquisition measure which reflects the rate of learning, was determined for each session. The learning criterion was set at three CRs out of six consecutive trials on paired trials or tone-alone trials, for paired and unpaired sessions respectively. The six-trial block was advanced trial-by-trial until the criterion was obtained and the final trial in the sequence was noted. Subjects who did not reach criterion during a given session, were assigned a score of 40 (the maximum number of trials + 10). The 50% criterion level (3/6) was chosen because it was more than two standard deviations above the spontaneous CR rate of unpaired controls (9.1% $\pm$ 19.9 SD). The spontaneous CR rate for unpaired controls was based on data combined across Experiments 1 and 2, across age, and across blocks within a session because none of these factors yielded statistical differences.

Two Empirical Studies

Experiment 1

There were two major goals in Experiment 1. The first was to establish delay eyeblink conditioning procedures that could be readily used with four- and five-month-old human infants. The second goal was to assess whether longitudinal designs could be used when conditioning sessions at earlier ages failed to produce evidence of clear conditioning. Are there carry-over effects from earlier conditioning experiences to later ones even when evidence of conditioning is nonexistent or weak at the earlier age?

In this first experiment, infants were given one session of either paired or unpaired conditioning at four months of age to assess acquisition at this age. About half of the infants from each group returned one month later, at five months of age, for a second session. This time all subjects received paired conditioning. An additional group of naive five-month-olds who received their first paired conditioning session at that age was compared to the returning five-month-olds. Comparisons across these three groups at five months of age enabled us to assess whether there were longitudinal carry-over effects in the groups that received prior conditioning at four months of age.

Subjects and Design. Data are presented for fifty-seven infants (31 males and 26 females) who visited our laboratory for the first time at either four or five months of age (n = 35 and 22, respectively). Participant families were recruited by mail from local county birth records. About 19% of the families indicated interest in our study by returning a reply card, and 49% of these agreed to participate when subsequently contacted by phone. The resulting subjects were primarily from non-Hispanic white families (88%) in which both parents had completed four or more years of college (87%).

Four-month-olds were randomly assigned to one of two conditioning groups: paired (n = 16, mean age = 127 days, range: 116-136) or unpaired (n = 19, mean age = 122 days, range: 110-140). Of these, seven paired and eight unpaired subjects returned for a second conditioning session at five months of age. Subjects were asked to participate in a second session when they had completed a criterion number of trials during the first session and yielded reliable EMG records. The mean interval between sessions was 32 days (range: 27-42). All subjects received paired conditioning during the second session. An additional group of naive five-month-olds (n = 22, mean age = 152 days, range = 141-172) was seen for the first time at five months and received one paired conditioning session.

Conditioning within one session at four months of age. The percentage of CRs across five blocks of trials was compared between groups of four-month-old infants who received paired versus unpaired conditioning. Infants receiving paired tone-air puff trials showed some conditioning relative to unpaired controls (Block x Group: $F_{4,132}$ = 3.41, $p < .05$). Newman-Keuls analysis revealed that there was a significant increase in the percentage of CRs between Block 1 (0.0% $\pm$ 0.0 SEM) and Block 5 (30.0% $\pm$ 8.0 SEM) for the paired group, but not the unpaired group (5.4% $\pm$ 2.3 vs. 10.2% $\pm$ 5.1). This increase was small, however, and levels of conditioning for individuals in the paired group on Block 5 varied widely (0% to 83% CRs). There were no differences in UR amplitudes between the groups (paired = 3.6 $\pm$ 0.4 arbitrary EMG units; unpaired = 3.4 $\pm$ 0.5) which could account for the observed differences in CR percentage.

Conditioning at five months as a function of prior conditioning experience. At five months of age, three groups of infants were compared across five blocks of paired conditioning. Infants who received either paired or unpaired conditioning one month earlier were compared to infants who were conditioned for the first time at five months (see Figure 3, Session 2). A 3 x 5 (Group x Block) repeated measures ANOVA yielded a significant main effect of block ($F_{4,136}$ = 10.51, $p < .01$) but no main effect of group or Group x Block interaction. Thus, all groups demonstrated some learning at five months. An ANOVA of UR amplitudes did not reveal a significant difference between the three groups (paired = 3.3 $\pm$ 1.2 arbitrary EMG units; unpaired = 3.51 $\pm$ 0.3; naive 5 month = 3.19 $\pm$ 0.5).

To further examine what appeared to be slower conditioning in the group with no previous conditioning experience (naive five month), another ANOVA was performed only on the first two conditioning blocks. This revealed a significant Group x Block interaction ($F_{1,34}$ = 6.24, $p < .01$). Newman-Keuls comparisons indicated there was a significant increase in percent CRs from Block 1 to 2 for the groups with previous paired ($p < .001$) and unpaired ($p < .001$) conditioning, but not for the Naive five-month-olds. Thus, during Session 2, infants with prior conditioning experience, whether paired or unpaired, demonstrated learning sooner than infants who received paired conditioning for the first time.

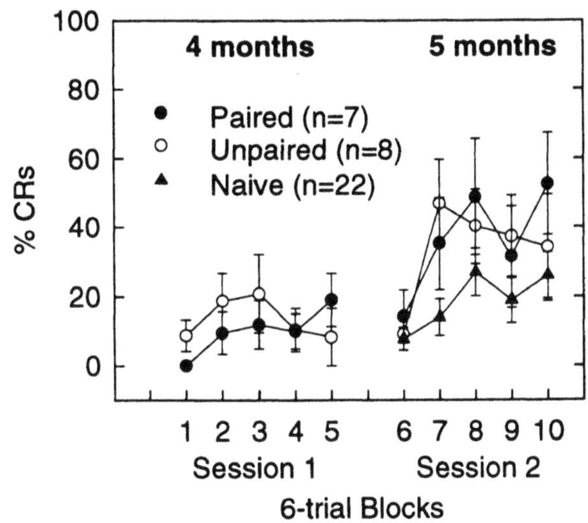

Figure 3. Mean (± SEM) percentage of conditioned responses (CRs) as a function of trial block and session. Data are presented for four-month-old infants, who underwent either paired or unpaired conditioning, and then returned at five months for paired conditioning. Also presented are data from naïve five-month-old infants who only received one paired conditioning session.

<u>Comparisons between four and five month conditioning sessions.</u> Both longitudinal and cross-sectional comparisons were performed for infants conditioned at four and five months of age. For the longitudinal comparison, the two subsets of infants (seven paired and eight unpaired) who were first seen at four months and returned at five months for a paired conditioning session were compared (see Figure 3). These two groups did not differ, but both performed significantly better during Session 2. A 2 x 2 x 5 (Group x Session x Block) repeated measures ANOVA revealed a main effect of session ($F_{1,13} = 12.26$, $p < .01$) and block ($F_{4,52} = 6.12$, $p < .01$), and a marginally significant Session x Block interaction ($F_{4,52} = 2.32$, $p = .07$). A 2 x 2 (Group x Session) ANOVA performed on UR amplitudes did not yield significant effects of group or session which could account for the differences observed for the percentage of CRs.

In a cross-sectional comparison between naive four- and naive five-month-olds, during their first session of paired conditioning (see Figure 3- paired group in Session 1 vs. naive group in Session 2), infants at both ages demonstrated some increase in percent CRs , but five-month-olds did not condition better than four-month-olds. The

2 x 5 (Group x Block) repeated measures ANOVA revealed a significant main effect of block ($F_{4,144} = 12.28$, $p < .01$), but no main effect or interaction involving group.

Comparisons based on the trials-to-criterion measure. The rate of learning during the first conditioning session for infants at four months of age is presented in Figure 4A using the TTC measure. An independent t-test between groups revealed that there was no significant difference between paired or unpaired groups (30 ± 3 trials vs. 34 ± 3, t (33) = 0.99). Since the means for each group were between the maximum number of trials (30) and the maximum value assigned to non-criterion subjects (40), this indicates that a significant level of CR responding was not achieved by either group. Also, there was no difference between infants who received paired conditioning for the first time at four or five months of age (paired, Session 1: 30 ± 3 vs. naïve 5 month, Session 1: 31 ± 3; t (36) = -0.09).

TTC data for subjects with two conditioning sessions are presented in Figure 4B. A 2 x 2 (Group x Session) repeated measures ANOVA revealed that there was no difference in TTC between infants who received paired conditioning on visit 1 and infants who received unpaired conditioning on visit 1. However, there was a significant session effect ($F_{1,13} = 13.31$, $p < .01$). Subjects reached the 3/6 criterion sooner during the second session than during the first session (20 ± 5 trials vs. 33 ± 4, respectively). These TTC data were consistent with the percentage CR data and suggested that there was some residual effect of prior conditioning experience that was maintained over the one-month interval between sessions.

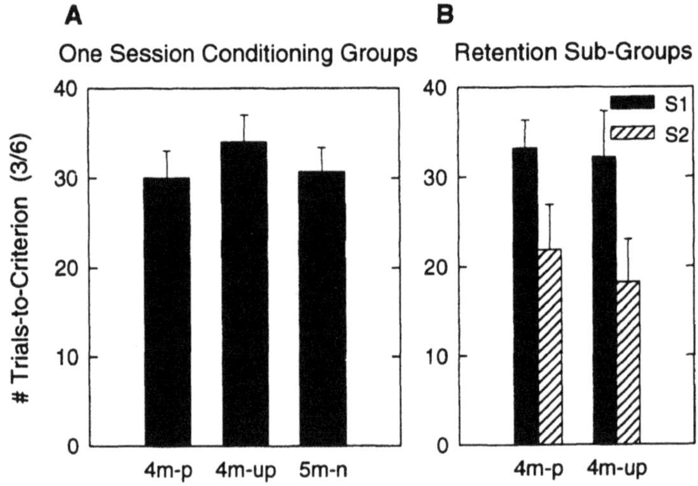

Figure 4. Mean (± SEM) trials-to criterion presented as a function of conditioning group, age, and session for: (A) naïve four-month-olds (4m) who received one session of either paired (p) or unpaired (up) conditioning compared to naïve five-month-olds who received one paired session (5m-n) and (B) the sub-group of four-month-olds who received either paired (4m-p) or unpaired (4m-up) conditioning during Session 1 (S1) and then received paired conditioning during Session 2 (S2) one month later.

In summary, Experiment 1 showed only weak evidence of conditioning in either four- or five-month-olds given only one session of paired conditioning. In contrast, five-month-old infants benefited from their previous experience with either paired or unpaired conditioning at four months of age. This carry-over effect indicates that cross-sectional studies should be used when the goal is to identify developmental changes in conditioning performance. It also suggests that some nonassociative aspect of the testing situation during the first session can facilitate performance during the second session.

Experiment 2

In this experiment we pursued a multiple-session design using a shorter interval (one week) between sessions in separate groups of four- and five-month-olds. We also added groups of five-month-olds to examine the possible non-associative effects of unpaired stimulus experience and familiarity with the testing environment on subsequent eyeblink conditioning. This enabled us to determine (1) whether experience with tones and air puffs facilitated subsequent acquisition even when there was no associative contingency during the first session or (2) whether familiarity with the training environment or context *per se* was sufficient to produce facilitation. CR percentage data from this study have been published (Ivkovich, Collins, Eckerman, Krasnegor & Stanton, 1999) and are reviewed here. In addition, we include here trials-to-criterion (TTC) data as well as additional analyses on CR latency and amplitude measures, the convergence of video and EMG data, and UR amplitude as a predictor of individual conditionability.

Subjects and Design. Subjects were recruited to participate in two conditioning sessions, 6-8 days apart, at either four- or five-months of age (± 10 days). Recruitment procedures were the same as in Experiment 1. Data are presented here for the 57 infants who reached the criterion number of trials (see Maintaining Infant State) during both sessions. Four- and five-month-olds were randomly assigned to one of two groups that received two identical conditioning sessions, paired (n = 21) or unpaired (n = 21). Other five-month-olds were assigned to one of two exposure control groups which received different experiences during the first session, either unpaired conditioning (CS/US-exposure; n = 7) or exposure to the conditioning situation without any CS or US presentations (context-exposure; n = 8), and then received paired training 6-8 days later. During their first session, infants in the context-exposure group were prepared for the conditioning session, the air puff delivery tube was put in place in front of the eye, and they viewed the object display for the same amount of time as the average conditioning session (about 15 minutes) while video and EMG recordings were collected.

Conditioning at four and five months of age. The percentage of CRs was compared, across five blocks and two sessions, for paired and unpaired groups at each age (see Figure 5). In contrast to Experiment 1, there was no increase in CRs for the paired group during the first training session as compared to the unpaired group. However, at each age, a substantial increase in the percentage of CRs emerged during the second session for the paired group only. The percentage of CRs reached asymptote around 80% for five-month-olds, as compared to 60% for four-month-olds, but this difference was not statistically significant. As in the previous experiment, one paired conditioning session was insufficient to produce reliable conditioned responding, but two sessions yielded robust conditioning.

Conditioning at five months as a function of prior experience. When the percentage of CRs during Session 2 was compared for all the five-month groups (paired, CS/US exposure, and context-exposure), there was now a difference, not seen

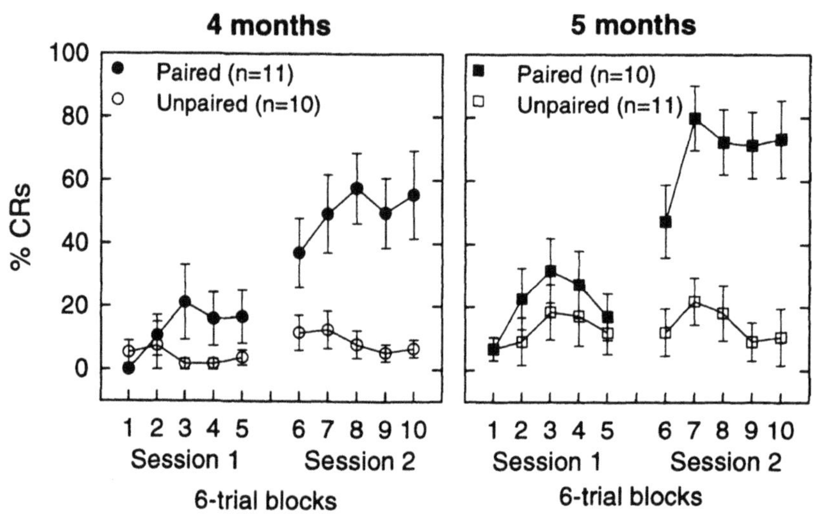

Figure 5. Mean (± SEM) percentage of conditioned responses (CRs) as a function of trial block and training session, for cross-sectional samples of four-month-old (left) and five-month-old (right) infants who received two sessions of either paired or unpaired conditioning, one-week apart.

in Experiment 1, between the paired and CS/US-exposure groups (see Figure 6, Session 2). The paired group, which was undergoing its second session of paired conditioning, produced a significantly higher percentage of CRs relative to the two groups that were experiencing paired training for the first time, and which did not differ from one another. In fact, the paired group started at around 50% CRs within the first block of the second session, significantly higher than the 10% CRs for the other two groups. Comparisons of the last block of the first session and the first block of the second session showed a significant increase in the percentage of CRs for the paired group only. This suggests that there was retention of learning from the first to the second paired training session that was produced only by prior paired training, even though an analysis of the first session did not reveal any significant acquisition.

Comparisons based on the trials-to-criterion measure. Separate analyses comparing paired and unpaired groups at four and five months of age in terms of the TTC measure were consistent with the CR percentage analysis. A 2 x 2 (Group x Session) repeated measures ANOVA at each age revealed that subjects achieved the criterion of 3/6 CRs much faster during the second session than during the first (main effect of session at four month: $F_{1,19} = 19.6$, $p < .001$; five month: $F_{1,19} = 15.7$, $p < .001$), and this change was greater for paired than unpaired groups (Group x Session interaction at four month: $F_{1,19} = 4.6$, $p < .05$; five month: $F_{1,19} = 8.4$, $p < .01$). These data are presented in Figure 7 (left panel).

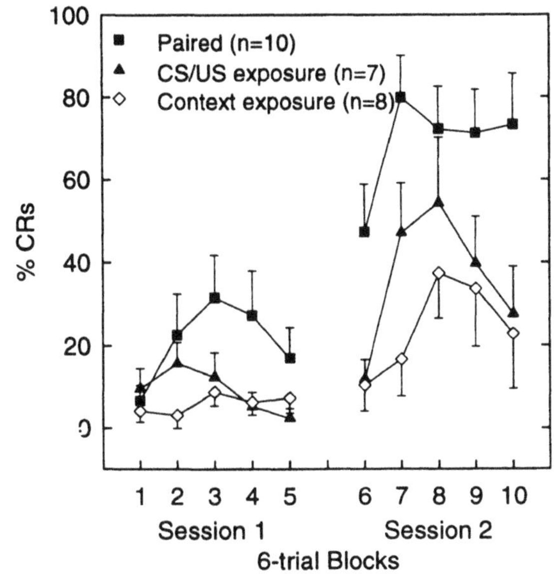

Figure 6. Mean (± SEM) percentage of conditioned responses (CRs) as a function of trial block and session, for three groups of five-month-olds. These groups underwent different experiences during Session 1 but all received paired training during Session 2.

There was a small difference between TTC and CR percentage measures when Session 2 data were examined for the three five-month-old groups (see Figure 7, right panel). As with the percentage of CRs, a three-way ANOVA between the groups on Session 2 revealed a significant main effect of group ($F_{2,22} = 4.87$, $p < .05$). However, in contrast to the CR percentage data, the paired group (TTC = 10 ± 3) was not significantly different from the CS/US-exposure group (TTC = 18 ± 6). Consistent with the CR percentage results, the paired group was significantly different from the context-exposure group (TTC= 30 ± 5), and the CS/US-exposure and context-exposure groups did not significantly differ from one another. These TTC findings reflect the intermediate position of the CS/US-exposure group, such that unpaired CS/US exposure appeared to produce some facilitation of paired conditioning, but not as much as prior experience with paired conditioning. The TTC for the exposure groups during Session 2 was not significantly different from that for the paired group during Session 1 (TTC = 29 ± 5).

In summary, the results of Experiment 2 indicate, once again, that one conditioning

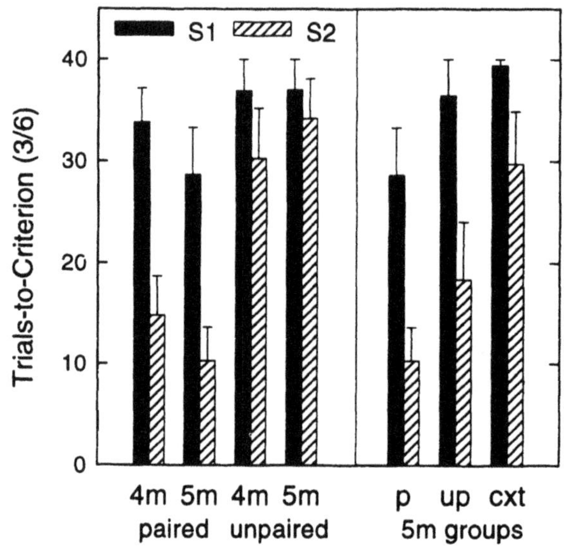

Figure 7. Mean (± SEM) trials-to criterion presented as a function of age, conditioning group, and session. Left: Data for paired and unpaired groups at four and five months of age for each of two sessions. Right: Data for five-month-olds who received different conditioning experiences during Session 1 and paired conditioning during Session 2. Abbreviations: four-month-olds (4m), five-month-olds (5m), Session 1(S1), Session 2 (S2), paired (p), unpaired CS/US-exposure (up), context-exposure (cxt).

session was insufficient to yield reliable conditioning. However, infants given two paired conditioning sessions, a week apart, at either four- or five-months of age produced robust and consistent eyeblink CRs during the second session. At five months of age, the benefits of a multiple-session design appear to be associative in nature even though significant conditioning was not observed during the first session. An interesting graded effect was produced by the three different initial conditioning experiences. Familiarity with the environment/context had no effect on later paired conditioning. Unpaired stimulus exposure which may have either reduced the novelty or increased the salience of the testing stimuli, produced a moderate effect and slightly improved subsequent paired conditioning. Prior experience with paired conditioning produced the largest facilitory effect on subsequent paired conditioning.

Additional Analyses of Interest

A few additional analyses deserve to be addressed as they are an important part of the methodological development we have pursued with these infant studies. First, we examined whether there were other measures of eyeblink behavior, such as CR latency and amplitude, which could be obtained from the present data. Second, we addressed the issue of whether there was convergence between EMG and video codings of infant eyeblink behavior. Third, we performed a simple correlation to assess whether or not US efficacy could predict the conditionability of individual infants.

CR latency and amplitude during paired conditioning. Since there were no significant differences in our primary learning measures (CR percentage and TTC) between the four- and five-month-old paired groups in Experiment 2, these groups were combined ($n = 21$) for an analysis of CR latency and amplitude. The resulting data are plotted in Figure 8 in comparison to CR percentage (Figure 8A) for the combined group. For latency, we used the frame-by-frame video measure of when an eyeblink occurred. We determined the beginning of a conditioned eyeblink (onset latency) and full eye closure (peak latency) by counting the number of video frames from that point to the time the US was delivered. Since we know that one video frame has a time-resolution of 16.7 ms, we were able to calculate onset and peak latency by multiplying the number of frames by this factor. Onset and peak latency, respectively, changed significantly across the two conditioning sessions ($F_{1,19} = 33.59$ and 29.79, $p < .001$) and five blocks ($F_{4,76} = 8.23$ and 6.47, $p < .001$), and the Session x Block interaction was significant ($F_{4,76} = 3.45$ and 4.49, $p < .05$). CRs were produced progressively earlier (see Figure 8B) and in greater anticipation of the air puff as learning proceeded, thus resulting in eyeblinks that adaptively peaked around the time of air puff onset.

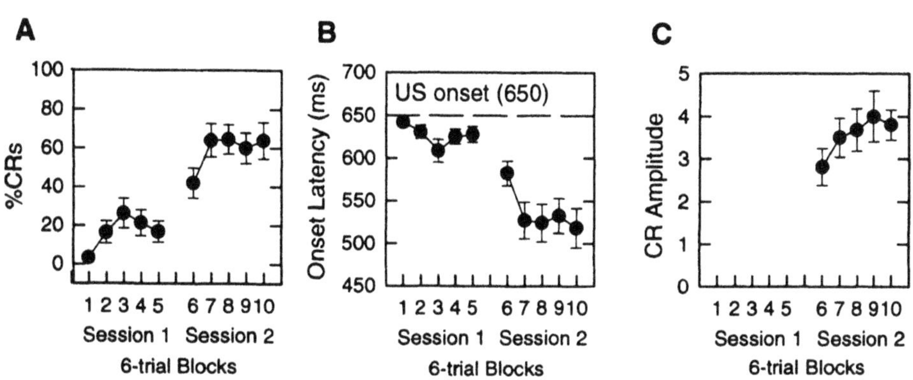

Figure 8. Combined data for four- and five-month-old paired groups from Experiment 2 as a function of trial block and session. (A) Mean (± SEM) percentage of conditioned responses (CRs). (B) Mean (± SEM) latency from tone onset to the onset of a conditioned response. Onset of the unconditioned stimulus (US) is 650 ms after onset of the conditioned stimulus. (C) Mean (± SEM) conditioned response (CR) amplitude in arbitrary EMG units for subjects with at least 20 CRs in Session 2.

For CR amplitude, we used EMG records on trials where there was agreement between the video and EMG codings as to the occurrence of a CR, and obtained a session average of CR amplitude for each subject. Because of the individual variability in the numbers of CRs for each subject, and the fact that there were few CRs for any subject during their first conditioning session, CR amplitudes were analyzed for subjects with at least 20 CRs during the second session (n = 10). CR amplitude increased significantly across blocks during Session 2 ($F_{4,36} = 3.34, p < .05$; Figure 8C). CR amplitude may prove to be valuable in future studies comparing different risk populations as a way of distinguishing the quality of a CR. Together, CR latency and amplitude data show that we can obtain further data on acquisition processes using other measures of eyeblink behavior. The adaptiveness or size of the response may be especially useful in making comparisons between risk groups.

Video versus EMG records of eyeblink behavior. Determining the convergence between video and EMG in our studies was important since animal and adult human studies have typically used EMG, whereas we found that video codings more reliably yielded usable data than our present EMG recording techniques. For example, for the 57 subjects in Experiment 2, video was usable for 100% of the cases, whereas EMG was usable for 75.4% of these same subjects.

To analyze video and EMG convergence, we again used the four- and five-month paired groups from Experiment 2. When both EMG and video data from the second conditioning session were usable (n = 17), they were compared on a trial-by-trial basis for the detection of CRs. We counted how often the video and EMG codings agreed that a CR had occurred, or that no CR had occurred. When there was disagreement, we used the video as our reliable measure and counted how often the EMG missed a CR or falsely detected a CR. The two measurement techniques concurred 73.6 ± 6.3% regarding whether a CR occurred. This agreement was not very high and reflects the difficulties with our current EMG technique. Disagreements between EMG and video were due to false detection of CRs slightly more often (57.8%) than missed CRs (42.2%).

Despite the difficulties with EMG recording, however, when both EMG and video data were usable, the two measurement techniques concurred 95.4 ± 1.4% regarding CR onset latency to within 50 ms (average difference = 38.2 ± 9.3 ms). This suggests that both measurement techniques are evaluating the same response and that frame-by-frame video coding can provide timing data in the absence of other recording techniques. It also suggests, however, that a combination of video and EMG codings can provide a more complete profile of the eyeblink CR in young infants by enabling the selection of valid EMG trials for measures such as CR amplitude, mentioned earlier, that are not obtainable by video.

US efficacy as a predictor of conditionability. Using the combined four- and five-month-old paired groups from Experiment 2 again, we examined the possible correlation between UR amplitude and TTC. The purpose of this correlation was to see if the effectiveness of the US during Session 1, as measured by response (UR) amplitude, produced an effect on the rate of conditioning, as measured by a single TTC value over two sessions. We did not manipulate US intensity. Instead, all subjects were conditioned using the same air puff and we used the UR amplitude as a measure of the subject's perceived value of the air puff stimulus or their sensitivity to the air puff stimulus.

The average UR amplitude for each subject was based on a sample of 10 codable trials from Session 1, when EMG data were available (86% of the subjects, $n = 18$). The 10 trials consisted of all the codable air-alone trials (maximum 7) dispersed throughout a paired session, plus the first few available, codable, non-CR paired trials, until data were obtained from a total of 10 trials. UR amplitude averaged 3.2 arbitrary EMG units ($\pm$ 0.4) and ranged from 0.09 to 6.75 for individuals. The TTC value was the number of paired trials, over two sessions (maximum 30 trials each session), until a criterion of 3 CRs out of 6 consecutive trials was achieved. TTC values ranged from 8 to 80 trials, where those infants who did not reach criterion in the 60 paired trials analyzed were assigned a value of 80. The average TTC in this sample was 32.0 $\pm$ 4.2 trials, indicating that several subjects did not reach criterion within the first 30 conditioning trials, but did so early in the second session. There was no correlation between UR amplitude and TTC. Differences in UR amplitude were not predictive of an infant's conditionability. There was enough range in the measures being correlated, however, to suggest that it was valid to perform such an analysis. This result does not mean, however, that manipulations of US intensity would not yield differences in conditioning rates.

Most infants in our studies were very responsive to the air puff and responded with eyeblinks that were robust in size and frequency. The average percentage of URs was 92.8% $\pm$ 3.9, although individual percentages ranged from 50-100%. In fact the two subjects who produced only 50% URs also had some of the lowest UR amplitudes, but this was not predictive of subsequent conditioning. Although it appears that the air puff was insufficient to elicit a somatosensory response in a few infants, we made significant efforts to ensure that the stimulus was being delivered properly. The lack of correlation may be due to the large variability in conditioning during infancy or to the nature of surface EMG recordings which have more intra- and inter-subject signal variability than other types of recording measures. Surface EMG recordings are sensitive to varying skin types and environmental conditions (e.g., temperature, humidity). There is also the added factor of difficulty in optimally placing the primary electrode close to the infant's eye and limiting the involvement of other facial muscle groups when the infant has a small face, pudgy face, or receded eyes. Also, there may have been some small variations in the initial positioning of the air puff delivery tube for individual subjects as well as some variation over the course of a session as a result of the infant's movements. Despite some variability in positioning the EMG electrodes and the air puff delivery tube, our data for the percentage of URs (a video measure) and UR amplitude (an EMG measure) confirm that the air puff delivered was effective in eliciting eyeblinks for most subjects. Nevertheless, the amplitude of the reflexive eyeblink response was not predictive of learning in our studies with infants.

SUMMARY AND CONCLUSIONS

Implications for Design and Methodology

The data collected in these studies have several implications for how we should approach infant studies of eyeblink conditioning, both from design and methodological perspectives. The major design implications emerge from the findings that (1) infants benefit from multiple conditioning sessions and (2) it is important to take into consideration all prior conditioning experience when assessing outcome. In addition, our data demonstrate that there are a number of learning and performance measures that can describe infant acquisition processes. It remains to be determined, however, which of these will be most useful in describing potential differences between infants who vary in biological risk or are conditioned using different behavioral paradigms. Finally, our data suggest that it is advantageous to use both video and EMG recording techniques to best describe infant eyeblink behavior.

Our data clearly indicate that, although infants do not demonstrate learning during a single conditioning session, learning emerges during a second conditioning session. This is the case for both four-and five-month-old infants. The increase in age, from four to five months, was not enough to yield an improvement in conditioning that could eliminate the need for a second session. Consequently, the importance of the multiple-session design is in the carry-over effects from one session to the next and not in the subject's age. Given that we have demonstrated carry-over effects over as long as one-month, it appears that cross-sectional designs are more appropriate than longitudinal designs when looking for the onset of specific learning and memory processes during development. These findings suggest that even when no clear learning is observed in an infant at a young age, we cannot consider that same infant to be a naive participant in later similar studies. It follows that when studying developmental changes in eyeblink conditioning over a range of infant ages we must carefully document all previous conditioning experiences as they may become influential factors in subsequent performance.

The measures we used to assess learning, percentage of CRs and TTC, yielded similar results with regard to major groups differences. This is important because it suggests that either measure can effectively represent infant acquisition rates. The advantage of the CR percentage data is the ability to produce learning curves to describe group acquisition trends. On the other hand, the single value obtained for TTC, could be a useful outcome measure for studying individual differences. In addition, it is possible that CR percentage and TTC may not capture the nature of differences between groups but that the differences lie in other measures. For this reason, it is important that the procedures described here also enable us to obtain measures of UR percentage and amplitude as well as CR latency and amplitude.

The other important consideration that emerged from our examination of various measures was the importance of basing our analyses on combined video and EMG codings. Since, for us, video records were more reliable than EMG records, it was encouraging to find that in the absence of EMG, frame-by-frame video coding can provide timing data, such as was demonstrated with CR latency. Alternatively, although CR and UR amplitude measures cannot be obtained by video, video can be used to help select EMG records for such measurements. Together, video and EMG can provide a more complete and reliable profile of the eyeblink conditioning behavior in young infants than is possible with either technique alone.

Developmental Phenomena of Eyeblink Conditioning

In addition to the design and methodological lessons learned from the two experiments in this chapter, the findings also have revealed three intriguing developmental phenomena. First, there appears to be unexpressed learning, during a single conditioning session at these ages, which produces carry-over effects to subsequent conditioning sessions. Second, in the context of other existing studies of infant eyeblink conditioning, there is evidence for postnatal development of eyeblink conditioning. Finally, there is a clear lack of inhibition following pre-exposure to unpaired stimuli, contrary to results from adult studies.

Our studies yielded robust conditioning when infants were given two sessions of paired training. It appears that unexpressed learning can take place during initial conditioning and become manifest after a retention interval. The positive transfer across sessions occurs even under conditions that produce little conditioning during the first session. We have demonstrated carry-over effects across sessions over one-week and one-month intervals. In Experiment 2 (one-week interval) we showed that the major carry-over effect is associative, resulting from paired conditioning which influences later conditioning, rather than a nonassociative effect due to factors such as exposure to the context or exposure per se to the conditioning stimuli. A similar result has been observed in developing rats (Stanton, Fox & Carter, 1998). These findings suggest that the distinction between acquisition versus expression of learning may be important in developmental studies of Pavlovian conditioning and underscores the value of the three-group design we employed with the five-month-olds in Experiment 2 for addressing this issue.

Our data also suggest, in three ways, that there is postnatal development of eyeblink conditioning. First, the levels of conditioning observed in Experiment 2 were higher than those previously reported for younger human infants given similar amounts of training (Lintz, Fitzgerald & Brackbill, 1967; Little, Lipsitt & Rovee-Collier, 1984) but lower than those commonly observed in human adults who reach conditioning levels of 60-80% CRs in less than 50 trials (Solomon & Pendlebury, 1988). Within our studies there also appeared to be a trend toward improvement in the final percentage of CRs from four to five months for infants given two paired conditioning sessions (Experiment 2). Second, although we do not know what ISI is optimal for delay conditioning for the four-five-month-olds in our study, the fact that the 650 ms ISI we chose yielded faster conditioning than was observed by Little et al. (1984) using a 500 ms ISI suggests that the poor efficacy of conventional ISIs for infant eyeblink conditioning may not generalize beyond the first month or two of development. Although it is difficult to compare across studies, due to procedural differences, the pattern of findings that emerges is not inconsistent with the suggestion that delay eyeblink conditioning in human subjects develops gradually but substantially during the first five months of life. Third, comparing our data with earlier studies also suggests that there may be postnatal development of retention. In Experiment 2, infants demonstrated a statistically significant increase in percent CRs from the end of Session 1 to the beginning of retention testing during Session 2. The increase we observed over a one-week retention interval was from about 20% CRs to 40% (four-month-olds) or 50% (five-month-olds) on the first block of the second paired session.

This was larger than the retention effect reported by Little et al. (1984) over a 10 day period in human infants, starting around 20 days of age. In fact, although the 20-day-olds in Little's study showed perfect retention in that they ended the first session and began the second session at 20% CRs, the 30-day-olds in that study did not demonstrate retention. Instead, these infants demonstrated "savings", a drop in CR percentage over the retention interval but rapid acquisition during the second session that was facilitated relative to the first session. Since our infants appeared to demonstrate retention which produced immediate facilitation within the first block of the second conditioning session, this raises the possibility that long-term retention of eyeblink conditioning also continues to improve during the first five months of age.

Postnatal development of retention also may explain the differences between Experiments 1 and 2 in the effects of unpaired pre-exposure on subsequent paired conditioning. In Experiment 1, infants who received unpaired-followed-by-paired conditioning demonstrated facilitated conditioning during the second session which was just as robust as that of the paired-paired group, whereas in Experiment 2 unpaired pre-exposure had less of a facilitatory affect on later paired conditioning. In both experiments, paired conditioning occurred at five months of age. However, in Experiment 1, initial unpaired conditioning took place around four months of age and there was a one-month retention interval whereas, in Experiment 2, unpaired training occurred at five months of age and there was a 6-8 day retention interval. Either variable could be important and it remains to be seen whether the differences seen here were due simply to differences in retention interval or to the postnatal development of inhibitory or memory processes.

The results of unpaired pre-exposure are noteworthy for yet another reason. They reveal a behavioral phenomenon that may be unique to the young developing organism. In adult subjects, pre-exposure to unpaired presentations of the CS and US *impairs* subsequent performance during paired conditioning, a phenomenon attributed to conditioned inhibition (Rescorla, 1967) or learned irrelevance (Mackintosh, 1974). There was no evidence for such an impairment in the present study or in a similar study involving infant rodents (Stanton et al., 1998). Infant mammals may not be able to learn that the CS and US are negatively correlated during unpaired training in the way that adults seem to do. According to one theoretical account of such learning (Rescorla, 1972), infants may not show this effect because of differences in contextual or configural processing. By this account, contextual stimuli compete with the CS for associative strength during unpaired pre-exposure in a manner that retards conditioning to the CS during subsequent paired conditioning. Failure to process context would eliminate this inhibitory effect of unpaired pre-exposure. Interestingly, temporal cortical structures appear to be involved in contextual processing (Penick & Solomon, 1991) and temporal damage eliminates the learned irrelevance effect (Allen & Gluck, 1997). The failure to observe learned irrelevance in infant rats (Stanton et al., 1998) and humans (Experiment 2) may reflect immaturity of temporal cortical brain structures (Nicolle, Barry, Veronesi & Stanton, 1989; Rudy, 1992).

In summary, these findings have established effective eyeblink conditioning procedures in four-five month-old human infants. As a result, we have begun to describe the development of delay eyeblink conditioning during infancy. The two studies reported here also have helped identify unique developmental phenomenon, including: (1) unexpressed learning, (2) postnatal development and (3) lack of inhibition following pre-exposure to unpaired stimuli.

REFERENCES

Allen, M.T., & Gluck, M.A. (1997). Learned irrelevance pre-exposure inhibits acquisition of the classically conditioned rabbit eyeblink response. *Society for Neuroscience Abstracts, 23,* 785.

Brakel, S., Babb, T, Mahnke, J., & Veranzo, M. (1971). Brief communication: A compact amplifier for extracellular recording. *Psychology and Behavior, 6,* 731-733.

Daum, I., Schugens, M.M., Ackerman, H., Lutzenberger, W., Dichgans, J., & Birbaumer, N. (1993). Classical conditioning after cerebellar lesions in humans. *Behavioral Neuroscience, 107,* (5), 748-756.

Fitzgerald, H.E., & Brackbill, Y. (1976). Classical conditioning in infancy: Development and constraints. *Psychological Bulletin, 83,* 353-376.

Gormezano, I., Kehoe, E.J., & Marshall, B.S. (1983). Twenty years of classical conditioning research with the rabbit. *Progress in Psychobiology and Physiological Psychology, 10,* 197-275.

Ivkovich, D., Collins, K.L., Eckerman, C.O., Krasnegor, N.A., & Stanton, M.E. (1999). Classical delay eyeblink conditioning in 4- and 5-month-old human infants. *Psychological Science 10* (1), 4-8.

Kimble, G.A. & Pennypacker, H.S., (1963). Eyelid conditioning in young and aged subjects. *The Journal of General Psychology, 103,* 283-289.

Lavond, D.G., Kim, J.J., & Thompson, R.F. (1993). Mammalian substrates of aversive classical conditioning. *Annual Review of Psychology, 44,* 317-342.

Lintz, L.M., Fitzgerald, M.E., & Brackbill, Y. (1967). Conditioning the eyeblink response to sound in infants. *Psychonomic Science, 7,* 405-406.

Little, A.H., Lipsitt, L.P., & Rovee-Collier, C. (1984). Classical Conditioning and Retention of the Infant's Eyelid Response: Effects of Age and Interstimulus Interval. *Journal of Experimental Child Psychology, 37,* 512-524.

Mackintosh, N.J. (1974). *The Psychology of Animal Learning.* New York: Academic Press.

Nicolle, M.M., Barry, C.C., Veronesi, B., & Stanton, M.E. (1989). Fornix transections disrupt the ontogeny of latent inhibition in the rat. *Psychobiology, 17,* 349-357.

Ohlrich, E.S., & Ross, L.E. (1968). Acquisition and differential conditioning of the eyelid response in normal and retarded children. *Journal of Experimental Child Psychology, 6,* 181-193.

Penick, S. & Solomon, P.R. (1991). Hippocampus, context, and conditioning. *Behavioral Neuroscience, 105,* 611-617.

Rescorla, R.A. (1967). Pavlovian conditioning and its proper control procedures. *Psychological Review, 74,* 71-80.

Rescorla, R.A. (1972). Informational variables in Pavlovian conditioning. In G.H. Bower (Ed.), *The Psychology of Learning and Motivation, Volume 6,* (pp. 1-46). Orlando, FL: Academic Press.

Rudy, J.W. (1992). Development of learning: From elemental to configural associative networks. In C. Rovee-Collier, & L.P. Lipsett (Eds.), *Advances in Infancy Research, Volume, 7,* (pp. 247-289). Norwood, N.J.: Ablex.

Solomon, P.R., & Pendlebury, W.W. (1988). A model systems approach to age-related memory disorders. *Neurotoxicology, 9,* 443-462.

Spence, K.W. (1953). Learning and performance in eyelid conditioning as a function of the intensity of the UCS. *Journal of Experimental Psychology, 45,* 57-63.

Stanton, M.E., & Freeman, J.H., Jr. (1994). Eyeblink conditioning in the infant rat: An animal model of learning in developmental neurotoxicology. *Environmental Health Perspectives, 102,* (Supplement 2), 131-139.

Stanton, M.E., Fox, G.D., & Carter, C.S. (1998). Ontogeny of the conditioned eyeblink response in rats: Acquisition or expression? *Neuropharmacology, 37,* 623-632.

Sternberg, C.R., & Campos, J.J. (1990). The development of anger expressions in infancy. In N.L. Stein & B. Leventhal (Eds.), *Psychological and Biological Approaches to Emotion,* (pp. 247-282). Hillsdale, N.J.: Lawrence Erlbaum Associates, Inc.

Woodruff-Pak, D.S., & Thompson, R.F. (1988). Cerebellar correlates of classical conditioning across the life span. In P.B. Baltes, D.M. Featherman, & R.M. Lerner (Eds.), *Life-span Development and Behavior, Volume 9,* (pp.1-37). Hillsdale, NJ: Lawrence Erlbaum Associates.

Woodruff-Pak, D.S., Logan, C.G., & Thompson, R.F. (1990). Neurobiological substrates of classical conditioning across the life span. In A. Diamond (Ed.), *The Development and Neural Bases of Higher Cognitive Functions: Annals of the New York Academy of Sciences, Volume 608*, (pp. 150-178). New York: The New York Academy of Sciences.

ACKNOWLEDGMENTS

We would like to thank K. L. Collins, E. Frederick, L. Giulino, A. Haggerty, J. Lee, B. Tao, C. Westlake, L. Willer, and M Wiley for their assistance with this work and B. Goldman for sharing with us her experience in infant eyeblink conditioning. Support for this research was provided in part by U.S. Environmental Protection Agency Cooperative Agreement No. CR-820-430 and Social and Behavioral Sciences Research Grant No. 12-FY96-0511 from the March of Dimes Birth Defects Foundation to C. O. Eckerman and by National Institute of Mental Health Postdoctoral Fellowship No. MH11729 to D. Ivkovich. This manuscript has been reviewed by the National Health and Environmental Effects Research Laboratory, U.S.E.P.A., and approved for publication. Mention of trade names or commercial products does not constitute endorsement or recommendation for use.

7 CLASSICAL EYEBLINK CONDITIONING IN NORMAL AND AUTISTIC CHILDREN

Lonnie L. Sears
University of Louisville

Joseph E. Steinmetz
Indiana University

INTRODUCTION

Classical eyeblink conditioning research with infants and children has a history dating back to the 1930s (Wenger, 1936) paralleling its use with adults (Hilgard, 1931). Despite this shared history the number of adult studies far exceeds that of studies applying eyeblink conditioning to questions of childhood development. Ross (1966) reviewed eyeblink conditioning research and, at that time, counted approximately 150 adult studies in the literature compared to only 3 studies of children. This ratio of child to adult studies has not changed a great deal since the 1960s, likely for two reasons. First, including development as an additional parameter in an eyeblink conditioning study increases the complexity of the research design and analysis. Second, and probably most significant, eyeblink conditioning in infants and children can create additional difficulties in experimental procedures such as in recording behavioral responses, presenting conditioning stimuli, and in maintaining the cooperation of a youthful subject. Fortunately, many of these difficulties have been addressed in research with the infant (Little, Lipsitt & Rovee-Collier, 1984) and with the child (Ross, 1966) yielding a number of studies identifying normal developmental patterns in eyeblink conditioning. These studies raise intriguing questions regarding the neurodevelopment of associative learning and also provide a framework for the study of developmental disabilities, such as in autism, which is described later in this chapter.

EXPERIMENTAL PROCEDURES FOR INFANTS AND CHILDREN

Classical eyeblink conditioning in infants and children often requires modification of procedures used with adults. One consideration in infants is positioning and alertness for stimulus presentation. Newborns are usually conditioned while supine (Little et al., 1984) while older infants have been conditioned sitting in a parent's lap (Ivkovich, Collins, Eckerman, Krasnegor & Stanton, 1999). Rather than a predetermined intertrial interval, which is often used with the adult, infant conditioning requires that trials be presented when the infant is alert. Gaining the necessary cooperation of infants for conditioning can be difficult. The study by Ivkovich et al. (1999), for example, completed conditioning on 57 infants but 64 infants were unable to complete conditioning trials. For both infants and children some means of maintaining attention is needed such as displaying brightly colored objects and toys (Ivkovich et al., 1999) or using silent movies (Ross, 1966).

Another challenge for conditioning can be stimulus presentation and response recording. Presentation of a mild air puff across the infant's eye requires a means of safely and comfortably securing a nozzle for delivery of the air puff on the infant's head, which is possible with the use of a soft band secured with Velcro (Ivkovich et al., 1999). Some researchers have also attached a photocell assembly to the headband to record eyeblinks (Little et al., 1984) while another study measured eyeblinks from videotape due to difficulties in identifying eyeblinks with EMG (Ivkovich et al., 1999).

In young children a standard conditioning apparatus similar to the adult can be used where headgear holds in place a nozzle for air puff delivery and also a device for recording the eyeblink. This type of apparatus has been used for conditioning children as young as 3 years of age with developmental disabilities (Ross, 1966).

Several eyeblink recording methods have been used. Electrodes have been placed on the head to record eyeblinks in children while the air puff was delivered through a nozzle attached to headphones (Sears, Finn & Steinmetz, 1994). The eyeblink has also been recorded in children by attaching a thread to the arm of a potentiometer and taping it to the eyelid (Ross, 1966). The tone conditioned stimulus (CS) in studies with young children has been delivered with headphones (Sears et al., 1994) or speakers (Ross, 1966). Infant studies require the use of speakers for tone delivery (Ivkovich et al., 1999). The more recent use of eyeglasses capable of recording eyeblinks with an infrared photobeam may be particularly applicable to studies with young children because of the simplicity and minimal invasiveness provided by this technology.

NEURODEVELOPMENTAL ASPECTS OF EYEBLINK CONDITIONING

Although eyeblink conditioning has been adapted for use in infants and children, the developmental aspects of the conditioned response (CR) have not been systematically studied using either a cross-sectional or longitudinal approach. To appreciate the developmental changes in normal children, however, two bodies of literature can be reviewed. One focus of research has been the study of conditioning in infants to address questions of normal infant learning capabilities and brain function (Lipsitt, 1990). The second research area providing normative information is the study of classical eyeblink conditioning in children with mental retardation (Ross, 1966). Since non-disabled children were included in several studies of mental retardation, age-related changes in conditioning during normal development can be identified. Although more research is needed, studies of infants and children indicate that normal development involves age-related changes in the associative learning capacity, optimal interstimulus interval (ISI), and the ability to condition using complex stimuli. These changes in the conditioned eyeblink response correspond with development of the cerebellum and hippocampus, areas of the brain that are involved in this type of associative learning.

Developmental Trends in Associative Learning

Studies of eyeblink conditioning in infants and children indicate that dramatic changes in associative learning occur in the first six months of life, a time paralleling significant postnatal development of the cerebellum. The changes in conditioning seen in infancy and early childhood likely reflect enhanced cerebellar involvement in early motor learning which is necessary for the acquisition of increasingly complex sensorimotor behaviors (Altman & Bayer, 1997). The involvement of the cerebellum in this early motor learning appears to be in place at birth based on studies of eyeblink conditioning in the newborn.

Newborn Conditioning

Wenger (1936) applied the eyelid conditioning paradigm used by Hilgard (1931) to the study of infants hypothesizing that classical conditioning would not be possible due to immature cerebral cortical function (which was at the time thought to be a possible neural substrate for conditioning). In contrast to expectations Wenger reported that, in newborns, a neutral tactile vibration CS could be paired with a light unconditioned stimulus (US) to produce a 69% CR level after 124 paired trials (over multiple sessions with a 3000 msec ISI). Since unpaired presentations produced only 29% eyelid responses in three additional subjects, Wenger concluded that conditioning, although unstable, is present in the newborn.

Although this initial study had methodological concerns including a small sample size, a more recent study supported the observation that eyeblink conditioning is possible in the newborn. Little et al. (1984) found that 10-day-old infants can be conditioned to a level of 28% CRs after 50 paired trials with a tone CS and air puff US (ISI = 1500 msec). Interestingly, the 10-day old infants did not show retention of the response at a follow-up session while 20- and 30- day old infants demonstrated retention from the previous session. Retention of the eyeblink response appears to develop later than the ability to acquire the eyeblink response and may be present in 20-day-old infants.

In mature human and nonhuman subjects the ability to form the CS – US association in eyeblink conditioning requires an intact cerebellum (Topka, Valls-Sole, Massaquoi & Hallett, 1993; McCormick & Thompson, 1984). The effect of cerebellar lesions on conditioning in infants and children has not been studied. Evidence from studies in the infant rat, however, indicates that the cerebellum is also essential for eyeblink conditioning in the immature organism based on studies of lesion effects (Freeman, Clark & Stanton, 1995). Further evidence of the involvement of the cerebellum in early conditioning is provided by studies of gene knockout mice. The Purkinje cell degeneration (pcd) mouse, for example, has a loss of Purkinje cells during development and is impaired in classical eyeblink conditioning (Chen et al., 1996). This finding indicates a close correspondence of cerebellar development and associative learning and also demonstrates that cerebellar abnormalities occurring early in development can disrupt eyeblink conditioning.

Support for the involvement of the cerebellum in newborn eyeblink conditioning is also provided by evidence that the essential eyeblink circuitry is functional at birth. In a study of brain metabolism using positron emission tomography (PET), Chugani, Phelps, and Mazziotta (1987) reported that, in human infants, the cerebellar metabolic rate was closer to adult metabolic values than any other brain region, suggesting relatively advanced neural development at birth. At full-term birth, the cellular structure of the human cerebellum resembles that of the rat near postnatal Day 19 (Bayer, Altman, Russo & Zhang, 1993), an age when eyeblink conditioning develops in the rat (Stanton, Freeman & Skelton, 1992). By postnatal Day 19 in the rat, Purkinje cells and neurons of the deep nuclei have migrated (Altman, 1972) and stimulation of mossy and climbing fibers evoke Purkinje cell spikes (Puro & Woodward, 1977a; 1977b). Further evidence that cerebellar eyeblink circuitry is functional in the human newborn is also provided by evidence of a functional cerebellar efferent system (Cholley, Wassef, Arsenio-Nunes, Brehier & Sotelo, 1989) which is part of the CR pathway (Chapman, Steinmetz, Sears & Thompson, 1990).

Infancy to Early Childhood

Between infancy and early childhood the acquisition rate for the conditioned eyeblink response dramatically increases. In apparently the only study of conditioning across this age span Rendle-Short (1961) reported that "ease of conditioning" increased from 6-month-old to 4-year-old children. The results of that study, however, are difficult to interpret due to methodological concerns, such as the subjective use of an anticipatory response for a CR. Several studies that have evaluated conditioning in either 1-month-old, 5-month-old or 4 year old children can be compared, however, to support the observation of Rendle-Short. In contrast to a 28% CR level reported in 1-month-old newborns (Little et al., 1984), 5-month old infants demonstrate conditioning levels near 80% per block using a similar number of trials (Ivkovich et al., 1999). By 5 months of age the conditioning rate appears to be similar to that seen in adults (Woodruff-Pak & Thompson, 1988). Adult levels of conditioning are also apparent in early childhood. While the optimal interstimulus interval for 4- to 6-year-old children is longer than for the adult (see discussion below), Werden and Ross (1972) reported asymptotic conditioning levels near 70% per block for this age. Children six and seven years of age also show virtually identical acquisition rates (Ohlrich & Ross, 1968) to that seen in adults. Based on these cross-study comparisons the associative learning capacity in late infancy and early childhood is enhanced, relative to the newborn, paralleling the development of more complex sensorimotor behaviors that are required for the infant's adaptation to his or her environment (Herschkowitz, Kagan & Zilles, 1997).

The ability of children in late infancy and early childhood to approach the conditioning levels seen in the adult suggests that maturation of the cerebellum between the newborn and late infant stages enhances associative learning. While in aging changes in Purkinje cell numbers relate to conditioning level in rabbits

(Woodruff-Pak, Cronholm & Sheffield, 1990) changes in Purkinje cell numbers are not involved in improved conditioning during early childhood since generation of Purkinje cells occurs in the prenatal period (Altman, 1972). Rather, the improved conditioning in early childhood corresponds to postnatal alterations in the granular layer of the cerebellum. Changes in the granular layer may be associated with improved conditioning since these changes are associated with increased parallel fiber - Purkinje cell synaptogenesis (Altman & Bayer, 1997) which is thought to be part of the CS pathway for conditioning (Thompson et al., 1997). In the human cerebellum neuronal migration in the internal granular layer continues until two years of age, which is also near the time the external granular layer disappears, suggesting that maturation of parallel fiber - Purkinje cell contacts continues postnatally till the age of two years. At this age the cellular organization of the cerebellum resembles the adult (Gadsdon & Emery, 1976). Maturational changes due to synaptogenesis and neuronal outgrowth during infancy and early childhood are also supported by receptor binding studies in humans. Marked postnatal increases in receptor binding are observed in several neurotransmitter systems including GABA (Brooks-Kayal, 1993) and glutamate (Johnson, Perry, Ince, Shaw & Perry, 1993). Both neurotransmitters appear to be involved in eyeblink conditioning (Thompson et al., 1997).

Effects of the CS - US Interval on Conditioning

The interval between CS and US onset affects the acquisition of the CR. In adults, an ISI of between 350 to 900 msec is optimal for eyeblink conditioning (Kimble, 1947; Finkbiner & Woodruff-Pak, 1991). A 500 to 800 msec ISI is also within an optimal range for children based on the similarity in CR acquisition between children this age and young adults (Braun & Geiselhart, 1959; Ohlrich & Ross, 1968; Werden & Ross, 1972). A shift in the optimal ISI for conditioning appears to occur from infancy into early childhood. Little et al. (1984) compared eyeblink conditioning in 10 to 30 day old infants using different ISIs and found that 1500 msec was an optimal ISI across all ages. Based on these limited parametric studies there appears to be a shortening of the optimal ISI from infancy into early childhood when the optimal ISI for learning appears is similar to the adult. The superior conditioning in infants using a relatively longer ISI parallels findings from studies of classical conditioning in rats (Caldwell & Werboff, 1962). Interestingly, a longer ISI may also be optimal for elderly subjects (Woodruff-Pak & Thompson, 1988).

The shortening of the optimal ISI from infancy through childhood may relate to maturational changes in the cerebellum. One possibility is that changes in the optimal ISI are a result of improved ability to make temporal discriminations, which may involve the CS pathway including parallel fiber – Purkinje cell connections (Perrett, Ruiz & Mauk, 1993). The CS pathway appears to be late developing compared to other elements of the eyeblink circuitry (as previously described). Based on the close relationship of the formation of the granular layer and parallel fiber – Purkinje cell synaptogenesis (Altman & Bayer, 1997), the CS pathway may continue maturational changes up to two years of age in the human. Thus the refinement of the cerebellar cortex may relate to a shortening of the optimal ISI in these early years. Changes in the optimal ISI occurring up to eight years of age may also relate to findings from structural MRI studies (Caviness, Kennedy, Richelme, Rademacher & Filipek, 1996) and functional studies of cerebellar metabolism with PET (Chugani et al., 1987). Both structural and functional brain imaging studies of the cerebellum indicate that progressive developmental events, such as formation of synapses and dendritic processes, are occurring up to the ages of seven to nine years paralleling the apparent shift in the optimal ISI toward the adult form. These later developmental events may further enhance the ability of the cerebellar cortical areas to make finer temporal discriminations.

Stimuli Complexity and Conditioning

Research on eyeblink conditioning in children indicates that development of the learned response is affected by the complexity of the conditioning stimuli. Trace conditioning, for example, is a more complex task than delay conditioning since termination of the CS prior to US onset requires the subject to "remember" the CS trace. The stimulus trace needed for trace conditioning appears to make the task more difficult for infants and children. Infants perform more poorly on trace conditioning across a range of interstimulus intervals and display short latency responses relative to delay conditioning (Lipsitt, 1990). Werden and Ross (1972) compared 4- to 6-year-old children to college students and found that only the children had a performance decrement in trace conditioning compared to delay.

Children also have poorer performance in discrimination reversal compared to adults. Ohlrich and Ross (1968) found that normally developing 6- to 7-year-old children display differential conditioning when either a low or high frequency tone is presented with one tone signaling the US (the CS+) while the other tone is a CS- indicating that no US follows the tone. Unlike college students, however, the children were unable to reverse the CS discrimination and respond to the previous CS-. Based on these limited studies in infants and children it appears that the acquisition of trace conditioning and discrimination reversal is another example of an underlying developmental process in this type of associative learning. Age-related changes in the ability for trace conditioning and reversal learning may relate to development of the limbic system, which is occurring into adulthood.

The hippocampus appears to be involved in conditioning when using complex stimuli such as in trace conditioning and discrimination reversal. Lesions involving the hippocampus disrupt trace conditioning in rabbits (Solomon, VanderSchaaf, Thompson & Weisz, 1986) and humans (Clark & Squire, 1998). Similarly, hippocampal lesions impair discrimination reversal learning in rabbits (Orr & Berger, 1985) and humans (Daum, Channon, Polkey & Gray, 1991). The most notable changes in the hippocampus that are occurring from middle childhood into adolescence involve myelination of corticolimbic pathways. In humans, myelination of the perforant pathway doubles between the first and second decade of life (Benes, 1994). The perforant pathway projects from entorhinal cortex to the dentate gyrus and appears to be important in hippocampal plasticity as demonstrated in studies of long-term potentiation (LTP). Of potential relevance is the finding that induction of hippocampal

LTP in rabbits enhances conditioning (Berger, 1984) supporting a role for this pathway in modulating the eyeblink response. Maturation of this pathway and other corticolimbic pathways during late childhood and early adolescence could enhance the ability of the hippocampus to facilitate eyeblink conditioning in trace conditioning and discrimination reversal.

APPLICATION TO AUTISM

Autism is a developmental disorder characterized by severe impairments in communication and social relating and by ritualistic and repetitive patterns of behavior (American Psychiatric Association, 1990). The abnormalities in brain development underlying autism are not known but a variety of research evidence suggests that multiple primary deficits may be involved in the disorder, including abnormalities in the cerebellum and hippocampus (Goodman, 1989; Minshew, Goldstein & Siegel, 1997; Rutter, 1988). Given the evidence for cerebellar and limbic involvement in development of the CR, classical eyeblink conditioning provides a measure of functional cerebellar neuropathology in autism. This paradigm is particularly useful for studying autism since a single behavioral response can be used to evaluate learning across a wide age range despite severe language impairments.

Neuropathology in Autism

Cerebellar abnormalities have been identified in histoanatomic and brain imaging studies in autism. Bauman, Filipek, and Kemper (1997) reported findings from post-mortem studies of nine autistic brains. Cerebellar pathology was observed in every brain. Most notable was a marked reduction in Purkinje cell numbers in cerebellar hemispheres, especially in posterolateral regions. A variable reduction in granule cell numbers in the hemispheres was also noted. No abnormalities were observed in the vermis of any of the brains. Age-related cerebellar abnormalities were suggested based on observations of the deep nuclei. In the younger brains cells in the deep nuclei tended to be enlarged but comparable in number to controls. In contrast the deep nuclei of the older brains were reported to have small, pale neurons that were reduced in numbers compared to controls. Other laboratories have also identified post-mortem cerebellar abnormalities in persons with autism (Bailey et al., 1998; Ritvo et al., 1986; Williams, Hauser, Purpura, Delong & Swisher, 1980).

Brain imaging studies using MRI and PET also provide evidence of cerebellar abnormalities in autism. Although one MRI study indicated that persons with autism had a reduced area of vermal lobules VI and VII (Courchesne, Townsend & Saitoh, 1994), a later study suggested that when subjects with autism were compared to IQ-matched controls there were no differences in area of the vermis although the total cerebellum appeared enlarged in autism (Piven, Saliba, Bailey & Arndt, 1997). Functional cerebellar abnormalities have been identified with PET by Chugani et al. (1997) who reported increased serotonin synthesis in the dentate nuclei of children with autism.

Two laboratories have reported histoanatomic studies of the hippocampus in autism. Bauman and Kemper (1985) first reported an increased cell density in the hippocampus and related limbic areas. Later studies suggested smaller cell bodies in area CA4 in two autistic brains and increased dendritic branching across all areas of the hippocampus (Raymond, Bauman & Kemper, 1989). A recent study of the hippocampus in five autistic brains, however, found no difference in neuronal density in any area of the hippocampus (Bailey et al, 1998). Involvement of the limbic system in autism has also been suggested based on observations of the effects of early lesions on behavioral development (Bachevalier & Merjanian, 1994).

A Study of Eyeblink Conditioning in Autism

Based on the consistent histoanatomic evidence of cerebellar pathology in autism the authors completed a study of classical eyeblink conditioning (Sears et al., 1994). Subjects for the study were 11 persons with autism (age range = 7 to 22) and 11 age-, gender-, and IQ- comparable controls. Delay conditioning occurred over two sessions and involved 135 tone CS and air puff US paired trials (ISI = 350 msec) followed by 60 unpaired trials to evaluate extinction of the response.

Acquisition and Extinction Rate

Subjects with autism acquired the CR faster than controls based on a comparison of the number of trials needed to reach a learning criterion of nine CRs on 10 consecutive trials (Figure 1). The autism group reached learning criterion in an average of 34.5 trials in contrast to controls who required an average of 56.1 trials. Subjects with autism also displayed a faster extinction rate of the learned response (Figure 1). The acquisition and extinction rates were associated with age in normal controls with older subjects displaying faster conditioning and extinction of the response. The Pearson correlation of age and acquisition rate (measured as trials to criterion) for controls was -.62 ($p < .01$) while the correlation of extinction rate (measured as decrease in CR amplitude) and age was .83 ($p < .001$). In subjects with autism, however, age did not correlate with acquisition or extinction rate suggesting differences in the development of the conditioned eyeblink response in persons with autism.

Response Timing and Amplitude

Although subjects with autism displayed rapid acquisition of the learned response the CRs were poorly timed. Across conditioning trials the autism group displayed peak eyeblink latencies that were significantly shorter than controls by an average of about 50 ms (Figure 2). While controls displayed peak eyeblinks near the US onset after reaching asymptotic levels of responding, subjects with autism displayed "double-peaked" responses where an early CR occurred followed by eye opening and then

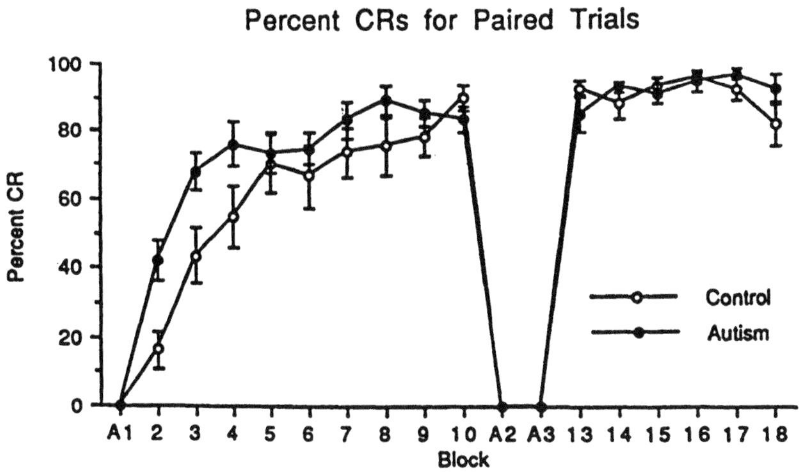

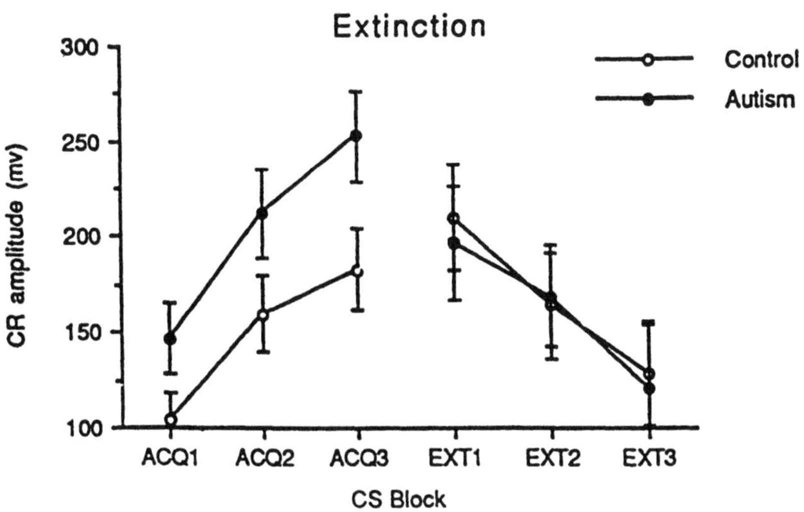

Figure 1. (Upper) Mean percent CRs across acquisition blocks for autism and control groups. "A" represents a block of air puff alone trials. Subjects with autism conditioned faster than controls (Lower) CR amplitude across acquisition and extinction trials. Each block represents mean CR amplitude averaged across five CS alone trials for acquisition (ACQ) or extinction (EXT). Subjects with autism had a larger decline in CR amplitude for extinction trials. (From "Abnormal classical eye-blink conditioning in autism," by L.L. Sears, P.R. Finn, and J.E. Steinmetz, 1994, *Journal of Autism and Developmental Disorders, 6*, p. 741 and 744. Copyright 1994 by Plenum Puslishing Corporation. Reprinted with permission).

closure with US presentation. An additional finding when evaluating group differences was that subjects with autism had larger amplitude CRs.

Nonassociative Factors

Measures assessing nonassociative factors that may produce eyeblink response differences between groups were also evaluated. There were no group differences in UR latency or UR amplitude suggesting that group differences were not due to problems with performance of the eyeblink response. No differences in the number of spontaneous blinks or alpha responses were observed suggesting that these types of responses did not produce group differences in CRs due to a misclassification of eyeblink responses. Differences in autism appeared to be due to learning-related factors, therefore, rather than nonassociative or performance-related factors.

Implications for Autism

Results of this initial study indicated that persons with autism display conditioning abnormalities characterized by facilitated acquisition and extinction of a short latency, high amplitude CR. Across the age span covered in this study it also appeared that the relationship of age and CR acquisition was altered in autism. Further studies are needed to replicate this finding. Results of this study, however, lead to several testable hypotheses regarding the neurodevelopment of associative learning in autism.

Facilitated Conditioning and the Olivocerebellar Pathway

The finding of facilitated conditioning in autism may be counterintuitive based on the evidence of cerebellar abnormalities in the disorder. The rapid acquisition of the poorly-timed CR, however, may not be "better" but may suggest deviant interactions of various neural systems involved in learning (i.e., normally, the acquisition and extinction of this task must be considered against the background of ongoing activity in the motor system). While persons with autism learned and extinguished the response at a more rapid rate, they had an abnormal "topography" of the executed response. Control subjects eventually produced an eyeblink that was maximal at US onset (as reported in many previous studies) while subjects with autism had a blink with an early peak thus producing a less "efficient" response, i.e., the persons with autism began opening their eyes before the air puff onset.

Eyeblink studies in gene knockout mice may provide a clue to the abnormal conditioning seen in autism. These mutant mice preparations are a result of inactivation or "knockout" of specific genes that lead to alterations in cerebellar development and function. With these mice the effects of subtle developmental abnormalities on eyeblink conditioning can be evaluated to learn more about the involvement of the cerebellum in the neurodevelopment of associative learning. Several of these gene knockout mice display impaired eyeblink conditioning. For

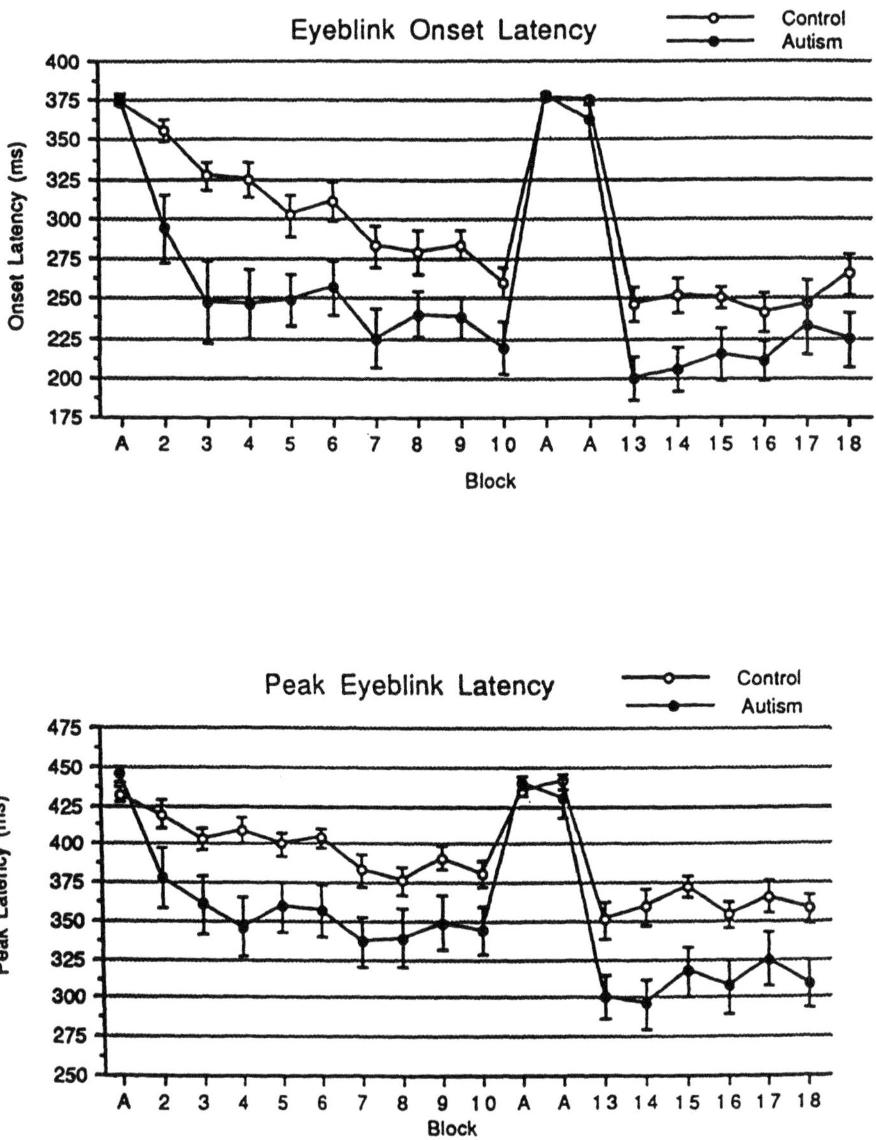

Figure 2. Mean CR onset and peak latencies across acquisition blocks. "A" refers to blocks of trials of air puff US alone trials. Subjects with autism had a significantly shorter CR onset and peak latencies than controls. (From "Abnormal classical eyeblink conditioning in autism," by L.L. Sears, P.R. Finn, and J.E. Steinmetz, 1994, *Journal of Autism and Developmental Disorders, 6*, p. 743. Copyright 1994 by Plenum Puslishing Corporation. Reprinted with permission).

example, pcd mice lose Purkinje cells during the postnatal period and are severely impaired in acquisition of the CR (Chen, Bao, Lockard, Kim & Thompson, 1996). The CRs that are observed in pcd mice tend to be short latency eyeblinks. Gene knockout mice that are deficient in cerebellar long-term depression (LTD) also display impaired conditioning (Aiba et al., 1994; Shibuki et al., 1996) as do mice lacking brain-derived neurotrophic factor (Bao, Chen, Qiao, Knusel & Thompson, 1998). Of potential relevance for autism is the protein kinase C - gamma isoform (PKCg) gene knockout mouse. This mouse retains multiple climbing fiber innervation of Purkinje cells rather than the typical single climbing fiber innervation seen in the adult mouse. Chen et al. (1995) reported that these mice rapidly acquired the conditioned eyeblink response and displayed high amplitude CRs. The conditioning pattern of PKCg deficient mice indicates that abnormalities in cerebellar development could produce facilitated conditioning as seen in autism (which was also characterized by rapid acquisition of high amplitude CRs).

Abnormalities in the olivocerebellar system have been hypothesized based on the cerebellar abnormalities observed in post-mortem autism studies (Bauman et al., 1997). In autism there appear to be normal cell numbers in the inferior olive and dentate nuclei but a reduced number of Purkinje cells (40% to 60% loss). The reduction in Purkinje cells in autism, as hypothesized by Bauman et al. may be associated with abnormal connectivity in the olivocerebellar system. This model suggests that climbing fibers develop primary (rather than collateral) connections with the deep nuclei leading to an abnormal increase in deep nuclei innervation by climbing fibers rather than the typical pattern of olivocerebellar connectivity (Altman & Bayer, 1997). The normal cell numbers in the inferior olive and dentate and reduced Purkinje cells may, based on this model, lead to hyperexcitability in the deep nuclei, a site of plasticity in eyeblink conditioning. Based on this model the abnormal olivocerebellar connectivity in autism and in the PKCg knockout mouse may lead to facilitated conditioning due to an enhancement of the climbing fiber "teaching input" which is thought to be involved in cerebellar motor learning (Albus, 1971; Marr, 1969).

Other Mechanisms of Facilitated Conditioning

The possibility that facilitated conditioning in autism represents abnormal olivocerebellar connectivity does not rule out other mechanisms for facilitated conditioning. Facilitated learning in rabbits has been observed when pontine stimulation is used as the CS possibly due to increased activation of the CS pathway (Steinmetz et al., 1986). In autism hyperexcitability in the CS pathway may be one reason for facilitated conditioning just as increased activation facilitates conditioning in rabbits. Several arguments suggest this is not the case. First, since facilitated extinction of the response is also seen in autism, the enhanced CS pathway model is less likely since a "supranormal" CS may be expected to continue evoking a CR when normally the ability of the CS to recruit a neuronal response is in decline. In contrast, an enhanced US teaching pathway may facilitate the learning that the CS signals no US. A second argument against the possibility that the CS pathway is hyperexcitable in autism is that there were no differences in the number of alpha responses in autism during conditioning. Alpha responses are short latency (i.e. onset less than 80 msec) orienting responses to the tone CS. If the tone presented "supranormal" activation of the auditory pathway it is likely that the number of alpha responses would be increased. Finally, it is unlikely that increased activity in the auditory CS pathway facilitated conditioning based on studies of brainstem evoked responses in persons with autism. A number of studies of auditory evoked responses indicate that persons with autism, matched by age and IQ to controls, have normal brainstem responses to tones (Minshew, Goldstein & Siegel, 1997).

Another possibility is that hippocampal abnormalities in autism are associated with facilitated conditioning. Berger (1984) demonstrated that conditioning could be enhanced by establishing long-term potentiation (LTP) in the hippocampus prior to conditioning. Thus, limbic system abnormalities in autism may involve an enhanced capacity for LTP, although it is more likely that hippocampal abnormalities would have no effect. While the capacity for LTP in autism cannot be tested it appears more likely that hippocampal abnormalities would either have no effect on conditioning rate, based on studies of hippocampal lesions (Solomon & Moore, 1975), or would impair conditioning based on the effects of disrupted hippocampal activity during conditioning (Solomon, Solomon, VanderSchaaf & Perry, 1983).

Age Differences in Conditioning

Acquisition and extinction rates were correlated with age in the control group (age range 6 to 23 years) but not in the autism group (age range = 7 to 23 years). The differences in the relationship of age and acquisition rate between groups suggest developmental differences in eyeblink conditioning in persons with autism. In normally-developing children, the significant correlation of acquisition rate and age was due to slower conditioning in the younger age range. The differential effects of age on conditioning rate did not account for facilitated conditioning in autism, however, since differences between groups were significant with age as a covariate.

The altered relationship of age to conditioning in subjects with autism may be explained by the observations of olivocerebellar abnormalities described by Bauman et al. (1997). In that study the Purkinje cell loss in the hemispheres was apparent across all ages but the relationship of Purkinje to deep nuclei cell numbers changed with age. In the brains of young children with autism the deep nuclei had appropriate numbers of enlarged cells. In older persons with autism, however, the post-mortem findings suggested reduced cell size and number. Since the relationship of Purkinje and deep nuclei cell number may have an effect on excitability, the decrease in neurons in the deep may reduce the CS-evoked cerebellar activity in autism. As a result, in younger subjects with autism, the increased deep nuclei excitability may yield an enhanced learning of a short-latency CR while in older subjects the conditioning rate is more similar to controls because of reduction in excitability secondary to an altered Purkinje cell - deep nuclei connectivity.

The Cerebellum and Autistic Behavior

To our knowledge there are no other studies of eyeblink conditioning in autism. Studies have reported eyeblink conditioning in other developmental disorders, however, and persons with autism appear to have a unique learning profile. In contrast to autism, adults with Down syndrome or Fragile X syndrome (chromosomal disorders associated with mental retardation) do not display facilitated conditioning (Woodruff-Pak, Papka & Simon, 1994), although in Fragile X syndrome short-latency CRs are observed (D.S. Woodruff-Pak, personal communication). The possibility that facilitated conditioning in autism may be unique among developmental disorders is also suggested by early studies that found normal or impaired patterns (depending on the ISI) of delay conditioning in persons with mental retardation of unknown or unspecified etiology (Cromwell, Palk & Folshee, 1961; Franks & Franks, 1962; Ohlrich & Ross, 1968). These results suggest that facilitated conditioning is not a feature of other developmental disorders despite the possibility that these disorders also involve cerebellar pathology (Schaefer et al., 1996). Further comparison of the patterns of cerebellar pathology in other developmental disorders with that seen in autism may help identify the effects of regional abnormalities in cerebellar development on associative learning.

The unique pattern of facilitated conditioning in autism suggests that eyeblink conditioning differences in autism may reflect cerebellar involvement in the behavioral manifestations of the disorder rather than being a nonspecific finding associated with developmental disorders in general. The mechanism by which the cerebellum may be involved in autistic behaviors, however, is uncertain. Recent evidence regarding cerebellar involvement in nonmotor function indicates that cerebellar abnormalities could disrupt a variety of processes that are abnormal in autism.

Leiner, Leiner, and Dow (1986) proposed that the cerebellum may play a similar role in nonmotor functions as has been described in motor skills. Based on lesion and brain imaging studies, the cerebellum has been hypothesized to be involved in nonmotor functions such as language (Molinari, Leggio & Silveri, 1997), affective expression (Schmahmann & Sherman, 1997), executive function (Hallett & Grafman, 1997), attention shifting (Akshoomoff & Courchesne, 1992) and timing (Ivry & Keele, 1989). Deficits in these areas are relevant since many of these functions have been identified as abnormal in autism. Deficits in language areas and affective expression are part of the diagnostic criteria for autism (American Psychiatric Association, 1994) while impaired executive function and attention control are associated neuropsychological features of the disorder (Ozonoff, 1997). The alteration in normal cerebellar and forebrain interactions that may produce these abnormalities, however, is not understood. Classical eyeblink conditioning may provide a paradigm that can be used to identify disrupted interactions among learning systems in the brain of persons with autism.

Evaluating Distributed Brain Processes in Autism

The varied symptoms and neurological abnormalities that have been reported in autism may be a result of multiple primary deficits and distributed information processing abnormalities (Rutter, 1988; Goodman, 1989; Minshew et al., 1997; Sears et al., 1999). There is evidence, for example, that social deficits in autism may result from developmental abnormalities involving the limbic system (Bachevalier & Merjanian, 1994). Another site of neuropathology in autism may be the caudate nuclei which appear to be enlarged in autism and associated with ritualistic and repetitive (but not social or communicative) behaviors, based on the correlation of severity of ritualistic behavior and caudate volume (Sears et al., 1999). The evidence that multiple brain abnormalities may underlie different aspects of autistic behavior indicates that cerebellar abnormalities in autism may be a component of altered cerebellar – forebrain interactions. The pattern of facilitated delay conditioning observed in autism suggests that cerebellar abnormalities have the potential to disrupt forebrain function in a manner similar to that observed during conditioning when cerebellar function is altered.

Cerebellar – Hippocampal Interactions in Associative Learning

Whereas the essential circuitry for eyeblink conditioning involves the brainstem and cerebellum, the involvement of the hippocampus in trace and reversal conditioning (described earlier) represents an interaction of two learning and memory systems. While the cerebellum appears to be the site of associative learning for the CR, the hippocampus is involved in modulating the response such as when formation of a memory trace is required for trace conditioning. The involvement of the hippocampus in trace conditioning may represent a declarative memory function (Clark & Squire, 1998). Studies in the rabbit demonstrate that the normal hippocampal plasticity observed during associative learning can be disrupted by lesions of the cerebellum (Sears & Steinmetz, 1990) The hippocampus may require input from the cerebellum related to features of the CR. The hippocampus, in turn, modulates cerebellar processing of the CS – US relationship allowing for the CR to be adapted under certain conditions, such as when complex stimuli are used for conditioning or when a nonoptimal ISI is used. Thus, the cerebellum and hippocampus interact to produce the most adaptively-timed CR, based on the context created by the parameters used for the conditioning stimuli (Sears & Steinmetz, 1990).

In the case of autism, facilitated conditioning as a result of cerebellar abnormalities provides for efficient learning of the response. The heightened cerebellar plasticity, however, may be maladaptive if the ability of the hippocampus to modulate the response according to contextual information is disrupted. This model predicts that by altering conditioning parameters the normal modulation of the CR by the hippocampus is impaired in autism. This finding would suggest that abnormal cerebellar – hippocampal interactions underlie impaired associative learning in autism which may also generalize to other types of behavior and learning systems. Although trace conditioning has not been tested in autism, for example, the impairments in declarative memory (Minshew et al., 1997) may be associated with trace conditioning abnormalities that have been observed in other disorders with memory impairments (Clark & Squire, 1997).

Cerebellar Interactions with Other Brain Areas

Applying classical eyeblink conditioning to the study of multiple brain abnormalities in autism can also provide a framework for understanding patterns of strengths and weaknesses in autism. For example, while discrete motor learning is facilitated in autism (based on delay eyeblink conditioning), the ability to coordinate motor movements for more complex tasks is impaired suggesting abnormal cerebrocerebellar interactions involving motor control (Minshew et al., 1997). The cerebellum has also been proposed to be part of a phonological processing loop (Desmond, Gabrieli, Wagner, Ginier & Glover, 1997), which is a strength in autism in contrast to the impairments in reading comprehension (Minshew et al., 1997). The discrepancy in these skills may indicate that the normal interactions of brain regions involved in reading are altered in autism. Understanding abnormal cerebellar – hippocampal interactions in autism, through the use of the classical eyeblink conditioning paradigm, may demonstrate mechanisms whereby facilitated cerebellar function disrupts interactions with these and other brain systems relevant to understanding the strengths and deficits in autism.

Symptom Variability in Autism

Understanding autism from the context of abnormalities in a distributed processing system involving the cerebellum may also be useful for explaining the variability within the disorder. Variability in intelligence, for example, occurs in autism, ranging from severe mental retardation to above average functioning (American Psychiatric Association, 1994). There is also variability in language function, visual-perceptual skills, social skills, and motor coordination (Wing, 1997). The variability within the disorder may relate to the degree of abnormality in cerebellar function in conjunction with the variability in disrupted function in other brain areas such as the hippocampus. To test these hypotheses the relationship of eyeblink conditioning and autistic symptoms can be evaluated using a variety of conditioning parameters and subjects with autism who have a wide range of behaviors typical of the variability observed in the disorder.

SUMMARY AND CONCLUSIONS

Studies of classical eyeblink conditioning in normally developing infants and children demonstrate that the capacity for associative learning is present at birth and develops throughout childhood. Developmental changes also occur in the optimal ISI for conditioning and in the ability to condition using complex stimulus presentations, such as in trace conditioning and discrimination reversal. The presence of eyeblink conditioning in the newborn and subsequent development of the response corresponds to maturation of the cerebellum and hippocampus. In autism, a developmental disorder with subtle cerebellar abnormalities, eyeblink conditioning is abnormal. Persons with autism display facilitated conditioning of a short-latency eyeblink response. The observation that gene knockout mice display a similar profile of facilitated conditioning and short latency CRs suggest that there may be olivocerebellar abnormalities in autism. These cerebellar abnormalities may account for some of the behavioral manifestations of autism through deviant cerebellar - forebrain interactions. Further studies of eyeblink conditioning in persons with autism are needed to replicate the findings from delay conditioning and to evaluate learning patterns with manipulations of the conditioning parameters. These types of studies will contribute to our understanding of the behavioral effects of altered cerebellar and forebrain function in autism.

REFERENCES

Aiba, A., Kano, M., Chen, C., Stanton, M.E., Fox, G.D., Herrup, K., Zwingman, T.A., & Tonegawa, S. (1994). Deficient cerebellar long-term depression and impaired motor learning in mGluR1 mutant mice. *Cell, 79*, 377-388.

Akshoomoff, N.A., & Courchesne, E. (1992). A new role for the cerebellum in cognitive operations. *Behavioral Neuroscience, 106*, 731-738.

Albus, J.S. (1971). A theory of cerebellar function. *Mathematical Biosciences, 10*, 25-61.

Altman, J. (1972). Postnatal development of the cerebellar cortex in the rat. II. Phases in the maturation of Purkinje cells and of the molecular layer. *Journal of Comparative Neurology, 145*, 399-463.

Altman, J., & Bayer, S.A. (1997). *Development of the Cerebellar System in Relation to its Evolution, Structure, and Functions.* New York: CRC Press Inc.

American Psychiatric Association. (1994). *Diagnostic and statistical manual of mental disorders (4th ed.).* Washington DC: APA.

Bachevalier, J. & Merjanian, P. (1994). Contribution of medial temporal lobe structures in infantile autism: A neurobehavioral study in primates. In M. Bauman (Ed.), *Neurobiology of Autism.* Baltimore: John Hopkins Press.

Bailey, A., Luthert P., Dean, A., Harding, B., Janota, I., Montgomery, M., Rutter, M., & Lantos, P. (1998). A clinicopathological study of autism. *Brain, 121*, 101-117.

Bao, S., Chen, L., Qiao, X., Knusel, B., & Thompson, R.F. (1998). Impaired eye-blink conditioning in waggler, a mutant mouse with cerebellar BDNF deficiency. *Learning and Memory, 5*, 355-364.

Bauman, M.L., Filipek, P.A., & Kemper, T.L. (1997). Early infantile autism. In J.D. Schmahmann (Ed.), *The Cerebellum and Cognition.* San Diego: Academic Press.

Bauman, M.L. & Kemper, T.L. (1985). Histoanatomic observations of the brain in early infantile autism. *Neurology, 35*, 866-874.

Bayer, S.A., Altman, J., Russo, R.J., & Zhang, X. (1993). Timetables of neurogenesis in the human brain based on experimentally determined patterns in the rat. *Neurotoxicology, 14*, 83-144.

Berger, T.W. (1984). Long-term potentiation of hippocampal synaptic transmission affects rate of behavioral learning. *Science, 224*, 627-630.

Braun, H.W., & Geiselhart, R. (1959). Age differences in the acquisition and extinction of the conditioned eyelid response. Journal of Experimental Psychology, 57, 386-388.

Brooks-Kayal, A.R., & Pritchett, D.B. (1993). Developmental changes in human g-aminobutyric $acid_A$ receptor subunit composition. *Annals of Neurology, 34*, 687-693.

Caldwell, D.F., & Werboff, J. (1962). Classical conditioning in newborn rats. *Science, 136*, 1118-1119.

Caviness, V.S., Jr., Kennedy, D.N., Richelme, C., Rademacher, J., & Filipek, P.A. (1996). The human brain age 7-11 years: A volumetric analysis based on magnetic resonance images. *Cerebral Cortex, 6*, 726-736.

Chapman, P.F., Steinmetz, J.E., Sears, L.L., & Thompson, R.F. (1990). Effects of lidocaine injection in the interpositus nucleus and red nucleus on conditioned behavioral and neuronal responses. *Brain Research, 537*, 140-156.

Chen, L., Bao, S., Lockard, J.M., Kim, J.J., & Thompson, R.F. (1996). Impaired classical eyeblink conditioning in cerebellar-lesioned and Purkinje cell degeneration (pcd) mice. *The Journal of Neuroscience, 16*, 2829-2838.

Chen, C., Kano, M., Abeliovich, A., Chen, L., Bao, S., Kim, J.J., Hashimoto, K., Thompson, R.F., &

Tonegawa, S. (1995). Impaired motor coordination correlates with persistent multiple climbing fiber innervation in PKCg mutant mice. *Cell, 83*, 1233-1242.

Cholley, B., Wassef, M., Arsenio-Nunes, L., Brehier, A., & Sotelo, C. (1989). Proximal trajectory of the brachium conjunctivum in rat fetuses and its early association with the parabrachial nucleus. A study combining in vitro HRP anterograde axonal tracing and immunocytochemistry. *Developmental Brain Research, 45*, 185-202.

Chugani, H.T., Phelps, M.E., & Mazziotta, J.C. (1987). Positron emission tomography study of human brain functional development. *Annals of Neurology, 22*, 487-497.

Chugani, D.C., Muzik, O., Rothermel, R., Behen, M., Chakraborty, P., Mangner, T., da Silva, E.A., & Chugani, H.T. (1997). Altered serotonin synthesis in the dentatothalamocortical pathway in autistic boys. *Annals of Neurology, 42*, 666-669.

Clark, R.E. & Squire, L.R. (1998). Classical conditioning and brain systems: The role of awareness. *Science, 280*, 77-81.

Courchesne, E., Townsend, J., & Saitoh, O. (1994). The brain in infantile autism. *Neurology, 44*, 214-223.

Cromwell, R.L., Palk, B.E., & Foshee, J.G. (1961). Studies in activity level: V. The relationships among eyelid conditioning, intelligence, activity level, and age. *American Journal of Mental Deficiency, 65*, 744-748.

Desmond, J.E., Gabrieli, J.D.E., Wagner, A.D., Ginier, B.L., & Glover, G.H. (1997). Lobular patterns of cerebellar activation in verbal working-memory and finger-tapping tasks as revealed by functional MRI. *The Journal of Neuroscience, 17*, 9675-9685.

Daum, I., Channon, S., Polkey, C.E., & Gray, J.A. (1991). Classical conditioning after temporal lobe lesions in man: Impairment in conditioned discrimination. *Behavioral Neuroscience, 105*, 396-408.

Finkbiner, R.G, Woodruff-Pak, D. S. (1991). Classical eyeblink conditioning in adulthood: Effects of age and interstimulus interval on acquisition in the trace paradigm. *Psychology & Aging, 6*, 109-117.

Franks, V., & Franks, C. (1962). Conditionability in defectives and in normals related to intelligence and organic deficit: The application of a learning theory model to a study of the learning process in mental defectives. In B. Richards (Ed.), *Proceedings of the London Conference on the Scientific Study of Mental Deficiency* (1960). Dagenham, England: May and Baker.

Freeman, J.H., Jr., Carter, C.S., & Stanton, M.E. (1995). Early cerebellar lesions impair eyeblink conditioning in developing rats: Differential effects of unilateral lesions on postnatal day 10 or 20. *Behavioral Neuroscience, 109*, 893-902.

Gadsdon, D.R., & Emery, J.L. (1976). Some quantitative morphological aspects of post-natal human cerebellar growth. *Journal of the Neurological Sciences, 29*, 137-148.

Goodman, R. (1989). Infantile autism: A syndrome of multiple primary deficits? *Journal of Autism and Developmental Disorders, 3*, 409-424.

Hallett, M. & Grafman, J. (1997). Executive function and motor skill learning. In J.D. Schmahmann (Ed.), *The Cerebellum and Cgnition*. San Diego: Academic Press.

Herschkowitz, N., Kagan, J., & Zilles, K. 1997). Neurobiological bases of behavioral development in the first year. *Neuropediatrics, 28*, 296-306.

Hilgard, E.R. 1931). Conditioned eyelid reactions to a light stimulus based on the reflex with to sound. *Psychological Monographs, 41*, 1-50.

Ivkovich, D., Collins, K.L., Eckerman, C.O., Krasnegor, N.A., & Stanton, M.E. (1999). Classical delay eyeblink conditioning in 4- and 5- month-old human infants. *Psychological Science, 10*, 4-8.

Johnson, M., Perry, E.K., Ince, P.G., Shaw, P.J., & Perry, R.H. (1993). Autoradiographic comparison of the distribution of [^{3}H]MK801 and [^{3}H]CNQX in the human cerebellum during development and aging. *Brain Research, 615*, 259-266.

Kimble, G.A. (1947). Conditioning as a function of the time between conditioned and unconditioned stimuli. *Journal of Experimental Psychology, 37*, 1-15.

Leiner, H.C., Leiner, A.L., & Dow, R.S. (1986). Does the cerebellum contribute to mental skills? *Behavioral Neuroscience, 103*, 998-1008.

Little, A.H., Lipsitt, L.P., & Rovee-Collier, C. (1984). Classical conditioning and retention of the infant's eyelid response: Effects of age and interstimulus interval. *Journal of Experimental Child Psychology, 37*, 512-524.

Lipsitt, L.P. (1990). Learning processes in the human newborn: Sensitization, habituation, and classical conditioning. *Annals of the New York Academy of Sciences, 608*, 113-127.

Marr, D. (1969). A theory of cerebellar cortex. *Journal of Physiology, 202*, 437-470.

McCormick, D., Steinmetz, J.E. & Thompson, R.F. (1985). Lesions of the inferior olivary complex cause extinction of the classically conditioned eyeblink response. *Brain Research, 359*, 120-130.

McCormick, D., & Thompson, R.F. (1984). Cerebellum: Essential involvement in the classically conditioned eyelid response. *Science, 223*, 296-299.
Minshew, N.J., Goldstein, G., & Siegel, D.J. (1997). Neuropsychologic functioning in autism: Profile of a complex information processing disorder. *Journal of the International Neuropsychological Society, 3*, 303-316.
Molinari, M., Leggio, M.G., & Silveri, M.C. (1997). Verbal fluency and agrammatism. In J.D. Schmahmann (Ed.), *The Cerebellum and Cognition*. San Diego: Academic Press.
Ohlrich, E., & Ross, L. (1968). Acquisition and differential conditioning of the eyelid response in normal and retarded children. *Journal of Experimental Child Psychology, 6*, 181-193.
Orr, W.B., & Berger, T.W. (1985). Hippocampectomy disrupts the topography of conditioned nictitating membrane responses during reversal learning. *Journal of Comparative and Physiological Psychology, 99*, 35-45.
Ozonoff, S. (1997). Causal mechanisms of autism: Unifying perspectives from an information-processing framework. In D.J. Cohen and F.R. Volmkar (Eds.), *Handbook of Autism and Pervasive Developmental Disorders* (2nd ed.). New York: John Wiley & Sons Inc.
Perrett, S.P., Ruiz, B.P., & Mauk, M.D. (1993). Cerebellar cortex lesions disrupt learning-dependent timing of the conditioned eyelid responses. *The Journal of Neuroscience, 13*, 1708-1718.
Piven, J., Saliba, K., Bailey, J., & Arndt, S. (1997). An MRI study of autism: The cerebellum revisited. *Neurology, 49*, 546-551.
Puro, D.G., & Woodward, D.J. (1977a). Maturation of evoked mossy fiber input to rat cerebellar Purkinje cells. *Experimental Brain Research, 28*, 427-441.
Puro, D.G., & Woodward, D.J. (1977b). Maturation of evoked climbing fiber input to rat cerebellar cells. *Experimental Brain Research, 28*, 85-100.
Raymond, G., Bauman, M., & Kemper, T. (1989). The hippocampus in autism. *Annals of Neurology, 26*, 483-484.
Rendle-Short, J. (1961). The puff test. *Archives of Diseases of Childhood, 36*, 50-57.
Ritvo, E.R., Freeman, B.J., Scheibel, A.B., Duong, T., Robinson, H., Guthrie, D., & Ritvo, A. (1986). Lower Purkinje cell counts in the cerebella of four autistic subjects: Initial findings of the UCLA-NSAC autopsy research report. *American Journal of Psychiatry, 146*, 862-866.
Ross, L.E. (1966). Classical conditioning and discrimination learning research with the mentally retarded. In N.R. Ellis (Ed.), *International Review of Research in Mental Retardation (Vol. 1)*. New York: Academic Press.
Rutter, M. (1988). Biological basis of autism: Implications for intervention. In F.J. Menolascino & J.A. Stark (Eds.), *Preventive and Curative Intervention in Mental Retardation*. Baltimore: Brookes.
Schaefer, G.B., Thompson, J.N., Bodensteiner, J.B., McConnell, J.H., Kimberling, W.J., Gay, C.T., Dutton, W.D., Hutchings, D.C., & Gray, S.B. (1996). Hypoplasia of cerebellar vermis in neurogenic syndromes. *Annals of Neurology, 39*, 382-384.
Schmahmann, J.D. & Sherman, J.C. (1997). Cerebellar cognitive affective syndrome. In J.D. Schmahmann (Ed.), *The Cerebellum and Cognition*. San Diego: Academic Press.
Sears, L.L., Finn, P.R., & Steinmetz, J.E. (1994). Abnormal classical eye-blink conditioning in autism. *Journal of Autism and Developmental Disorder, 24*, 737-751.
Sears, L.L. & Steinmetz, J.E. (1990). Acquisition of classically conditioned-related activity in the hippocampus is affected by lesions of the cerebellar interpositus nucleus. *Behavioral Neuroscience, 104*, 681-692.
Sears, L.L., Vest, C., Mohamed, S., Bailey, J., Ranson, B.J., & Piven, J. (1999). An MRI study of the basal ganglia in autism. *Progress in Neuro-Psychopharmacology and Biological Psychiatry, 23*, 613-624.
Shibuki, K., Gomi, H., Chen, L., Bao, S., Kim, J.J., Wakatsuki, H., Fujisaki, T., Fujimoto, K., Katoh, A., Ikeda, T., Chen, C., Thompson, R.F., & Itohara, S. (1996). Deficient cerebellar long-term depression, impaired eyeblink conditioning, and normal motor coordination in GFAP mutant mice. *Neuron, 16*, 587-599.
Solomon, P.R. & Moore, J.W. (1975). Latent inhibition and stimulus generalization of the classically conditioned nictitating membrane response in rabbits following dorsal hippocampal ablations. *Journal of Comparative Physiological Psychology, 69*, 1192-1203.
Solomon, P.R., Solomon, S.D., VanderSchaaf, E.R., & Perry, H.E. (1983). Altered activity in the hippocampus is more detrimental to classical conditioning than removing the structure. *Science, 220*, 329-331.
Solomon, P.R., VanderSchaaf, E. R., Thompson, R.F., & Weisz, D.J. (1986). Hippocampus and trace conditioning of the rabbit's classically conditioned nictitating membrane response. *Behavioral*

Neuroscience, 100, 729-744.
Stanton, M.E., Freeman, J.H., Jr., & Skelton, R.W. (1992). Eyeblink conditioning in the developing rat. *Behavioral Neuroscience, 106,* 657-665.
Steinmetz, J.E., Logan, C.G., Rosen, D.J., Thompson, J.K., Lavond, D.G., & Thompson, R.F. (1987). Initial localization of the acoustic conditioned stimulus projection system to the cerebellum essential for classical eyeblink conditioning. *Proceedings of the National Academy of Sciences (USA), 84,* 3531-3535.
Steinmetz, J.E., Rosen, D.J., Chapman, P.F., Lavond, D.G., & Thompson, R.F. (1986). Classical conditioning of the rabbit eyelid response with a mossy fiber stimulation CS. I. Pontine nuclei and middle cerebellar peduncle stimulation. *Behavioral Neuroscience, 100,* 871-880.
Thompson, R.F., Bao, S., Chen, L., Cipriano, B.D., Grethe, J.S., Kim, J.J., Thomspon, J.K., Tracy, J.A., Weninger, M.S., & Krupa, D.J. (1997). Associative learning. In J.D. Schmahmann (Ed.), *The Cerebellum and Cognition.* San Diego: Academic Press.
Topka, H., Valls-Sole, J., Massaquoi, S.G., & Hallet, M. (1993). Deficit in classical conditioning in patients with cerebellar degeneration. *Brain, 116,* 961-969.
Wenger, M.A. (1936). An investigation of conditioned responses in human infants. *University of Iowa Studies in Child Welfare, 12,* 8-90.
Werden, D., & Ross, L. (1972). A comparison of the trace and delay classical conditioning performance of normal children. *Journal of Experimental Child Psychology, 14,* 126-132.
Williams, R.S., Hauser, S.L., Purpura, D.P., Delong, G.R., & Swisher, C.N. (1980). Autism and mental retardation: Neuropathologic studies performed in four retarded persons with autistic behavior. *Archives of Neurology, 37,* 749-753.
Wing, L. (1997). Syndromes of autism and atypical development. In D.J. Cohen and F.R. Volkmar (Eds.), *Handbook of Autism and Pervasive Developmental Disorders* (2nd ed.). New York: John Wiley & Sons, Inc.
Woodruff-Pak, D.S., Cronholm, J.F., & Sheffield, J.B. (1990). Purkinje cell number related to rate of eyeblink classical conditioning. *Neuroreport, 1,* 165-168.
Woodruff-Pak, D.S., Papka, M., & Simon, E. (1994). Eyeblink classical conditioning in Down's syndrome, Fragile X syndrome, and normal adults over and under age 35. *Neuropsychology, 8,* 14-24.
Woodruff-Pak, D.S., & Thompson, R.F. (1988). Cerebellar correlates of classical conditioning across the life span. In P.B. Baltes, D.M. Feathermore, & R.M. Lerner (Eds.), *Life-span Development and Behavior.* Hillsdale NJ: Elseiver Press.

8 HUMAN EYEBLINK CLASSICAL CONDITONING IN NORMAL AGING AND ALZHEIMER'S DISEASE

Diana S. Woodruff-Pak
Temple University

INTRODUCTION

At both neurobiological and behavioral levels, eyeblink classical conditioning is likely the best characterized among all associative learning paradigms. Initially, the neural circuitry was identified in rabbits, and more recently comparable circuitry has been identified in mice, rats, cats, and monkeys. One of the contributions of our laboratory has been to demonstrate in studies of patients with various neurological lesions and in normal adults with behavioral manipulations, that the neural circuitry supporting eyeblink conditioning is similar in humans and other mammals. We have also identified parallels in normal aging and eyeblink conditioning among several mammalian species.

Three aims of this chapter with regard to normal aging are to: (1) point out that simple eyeblink classical conditioning is a form of nondeclarative (implicit) learning and memory that *does* show age-related impairment; (2) document the age-related impairment in the various procedures of the eyeblink classical conditioning paradigm; and (3) consider causes for the age-related impairment.

Aims addressing eyeblink classical conditioning and dementing diseases associated with aging are to: (1) discuss why simple eyeblink classical conditioning has a high sensitivity for Alzheimer's disease (AD); (2) consider the potential of simple eyeblink conditioning in the early detection of AD; and (3) examine the success of eyeblink classical conditioning in the differential diagnosis of neurodegerative diseases expressed in advancing age.

SEPARATE NONDECLARATIVE LEARNING AND MEMORY CIRCUITS AND DIFFERENT AGE FUNCTIONS

Qualities that characterize nondeclarative learning and memory include: (a) the medial-temporal lobe circuitry that is essential for declarative memory processes is not critical; (b) learning can occur in the absence of awareness; (c) retrieval is relatively inflexible – it requires the same modality and similar contexts. Nondeclarative memory consists of multiple, dissociable processes, including repetition priming, motor skill learning, non-associative learning, and simple classical conditioning (Squire, 1992). For some years neuropsychological evidence has accumulated that nondeclarative memory systems are separable.

A classical approach in human neuropsychology is to examine cognitive performance in patients with localized brain lesions or neurodegenerative diseases that characteristically affect certain brain regions. For example, Alzheimer's disease (AD) is considered a cortical dementing disease because it results in degeneration of the cerebral cortex - in particular in the frontal, parietal, and temporal lobes. The first signs of this disease appear in the medial-temporal lobe region that is essential for declarative memory. Huntington's disease (HD) on the other hand first affects subcortical structures - the basal ganglia. Eventually HD affects the cerebral cortex - especially in the frontal cortical region called motor cortex. Parkinson's disease (PD) depletes the substantia nigra dopamine system, primarily impairing function of the basal ganglia. Comparisons of patients with AD, HD, and PD on cognitive tasks can provide insights about the brain substrates of the tasks.

The "gold-standard" in neuropsychology is the double dissociation - the result that Patient Group 1 (for example, patients with dense amnesia) with lesions in Region 1 (in our example, medial-temporal lobes) is impaired on Task A (in our example, delayed recall) but not Task B (e.g. timed-interval finger tapping), whereas Patient Group 2 (for example, patients with ataxia) with lesions in Region 2 (for these patients it would be lesions in the cerebellum) is impaired on Task B (timed-interval finger tapping) but not on Task A (delayed recall). These results indicate that Region 1 is necessary for the cognitive processes involved in Task A but not Task B, and Region 2 is necessary for the cognitive processes involved in Task B but not Task A. In our example, the medial-temporal lobes are necessary for delayed recall but not for timed-interval finger tapping, whereas the cerebellum is necessary for timed-interval finger tapping but not delayed recall.

Heindel, Salmon, Shults, Walicke, and Butters (1989) compared patients with AD, HD, and PD on two nondeclarative tasks, rotary pursuit and repetition priming. There was a double dissociation with the AD and HD groups. Patients with AD and presumed diffuse lesions in frontal, temporal, and parietal cortex were impaired on repetition priming (word-stem completion) but not on rotary pursuit, whereas patients with HD and presumed lesions in motor cortex and basal ganglia were impaired on rotary pursuit and not repetition priming. Patients with PD and presumed impairment limited to basal ganglia who were not demented performed normally on both rotary pursuit and repetition priming.

Data collected in our laboratory with 120 young adult participants in dual-task conditions indicate that eyeblink classical conditioning and repetition priming (word-stem completion) produce no cross-task interference and are thus likely subserved by separate brain memory systems (Green, Small, Downey-Lamb & Woodruff-Pak, in press). Two groups of participants' performances on eyeblink conditioning were virtually identical when one group was performing a word-stem completion priming task simultaneously with eyeblink conditioning and the other group was watching a silent video with eyeblink conditioning. A stronger test of the separability of these two nondeclarative forms of learning and memory was carried out by Downey-Lamb (1999) as part of her doctoral dissertation when she tested older adults in dual-task conditions of word-stem completion (see Figure 1).

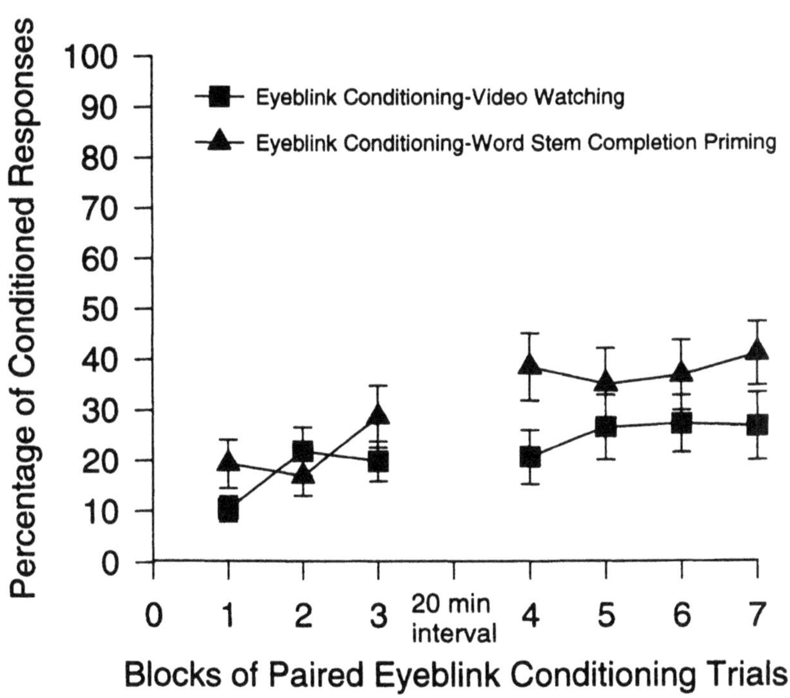

Figure 1. Dual-task (eyeblink conditioning and word-stem completion priming) versus single task (eyeblink conditioning and watching a silent video) performance of eyeblink classical conditioning in older adults ranging in age for 60 to 90 years. There were 20 older adults in each group (Downey-Lamb, 1999).

The fact that older adults tend to perform more poorly as the complexity of the task is increased is interpreted as an indicator of limited processing resources. The perspective of a diminution of processing capacity in older adulthood is longstanding (e.g., Birren, 1964; Welford, 1958), and contemporary research addressing issues such as aging and working memory continue to reinforce this position (e.g., Esposito, Kirby, Van Horn, Ellmore & Berman, 1999; Guerrier, Manivannan & Nair, 1999; Small, Stern, Tang & Mayeux, 1999). From the perspective that older adults have a diminished processing capacity, it follows that older adults might be impaired in the dual-task performance of word-stem completion priming and eyeblink classical conditioning even though younger adults are not impaired in this dual-task situation. Thus, a strong test of the separability of nondeclarative tasks is to examine this dual-task performance in older adults. Testing 20 older adults in the age-range of 60 to 90 years in the dual-task of priming and conditioning and 20 older adults on priming and conditioning as single tasks, Downey-Lamb (1999) found no differences in the performance of eyeblink conditioning. Performance on word-stem completion was also similar in the single-task and dual-task conditions.

We have also provided some evidence for the lack of interference between eyeblink conditioning and rotary pursuit (Green & Woodruff-Pak, 1997). One-hundred undergraduate students of a mean age of 22 years participated in one of five conditions: Group 1 performed a dual task consisting of paired CS and US eyeblink classical condition and rotary pursuit; Group 2 performed a dual task consisting of explicitly unpaired CS and US eyeblink conditioning and rotary pursuit; Group 3 performed paired CS and US eyeblink conditioning while watching a silent video; Group 4 performed explicitly unpaired CS and US eyeblink conditioning while watching a silent video; Group 5 performed rotary pursuit alone. Participants performing rotary pursuit and conditioning acquired CRs about as well as participants conditioned while watching a silent video. Rotary pursuit performance was not affected in the dual-task condition, either. Both in the paired and unpaired conditions, the UR amplitude was less in the dual-task condition, and we interpreted this result to indicate that eye movement and illumination differences required for rotary pursuit likely reduced UR amplitude.

Different nondeclarative tasks such as repetition priming, motor skill learning, and eyeblink classical conditioning are subserved by brain memory systems that are separate and remote from one another. The cerebellum is essential for all procedures in eyeblink classical conditioning such as delay, trace, discrimination, and discrimination reversal. However, motor skill learning relies primarily on motor cortex (e.g., Grafton et al., 1992) and visual repetition priming requires occipital cortex (Gabrieli et al., 1995). When a priming task requires production as well as perception (as in the case of word-stem completion priming) the frontal cortex is necessary (Gabrieli et al., in press).

Cognitive psychologists have amassed a large literature on priming, and this form of nondeclarative memory is frequently represented as characterizing implicit or nondeclarative memory systems. Based on these studies of priming, a common assumption was held in the psychology of aging that nondeclarative forms of learning and memory were relatively spared in old age (e.g., Graf, 1990; Light & La Voie, 1993). It is the case that age differences in repetition priming are small. Large sample sizes are required to demonstrate a significant age difference in repetition priming because the effect size is small. In the case of word-stem completion priming, the age difference in performance may result from the well-documented deficit in frontal lobe function associated with normal aging (Winocur, Moscovitch & Stuss, 1996).

In addition to testing older adults in dual-task performance of eyeblink classical conditioning and word-stem completion priming, Downey-Lamb (1999) tested dual-task performance of word-stem completion priming and sequential finger tapping in young and older adults. Moscovitch (1994) provided some evidence that sequential tapping engages the prefrontal cortex, and Winocur et al. (1996) suggested a role for prefrontal cortex in word-stem completion priming. Downey-Lamb (1999) supported these predictions in young and older adults by demonstrating that combining sequential tapping and word-stem completion as a dual-task impaired performance in both tasks compared to single-task performance. In young adults, sequential tapping and eyeblink conditioning as a dual task impaired eyeblink conditioning (but not tapping) suggesting cerebellar involvement in the sequential finger tapping task. Papka, Ivry, and Woodruff-Pak (1996) reported a similar result for a finger tapping task known to engage the cerebellum, timed-interval tapping.

Aging affects the different brain substrates of the various nondeclarative tasks differently, making it likely that behavior would show different age functions on the different nondeclarative measures. Perceptual priming shows little effect of aging (Winocur et al., 1996), whereas word-stem completion priming shows a small effect of age. Age differences in motor skill learning are only apparent in about half of the studies of age and motor skill learning. In two forms of nondeclarative learning and memory there is relative stability with age. However, in a third nondeclarative form, simple eyeblink classical conditioning, large age differences are evident (see Figure 2).

Age differences in simple eyeblink classical conditioning have been documented for decades (Braun & Geiselhart, 1959; Kimble & Pennypacker, 1963; Solyom & Barik, 1965). Investigators who first reported adult age effects in eyeblink conditioning compared young and older adults in the delay procedure. The main and striking result was the relative inability of the older adults to acquire CRs. The result somewhat unexpected because classical conditioning was considered a fundamental and relatively simple form of learning.

Eyeblink Classical Conditioning and Awareness

One of the defining qualities of nondeclarative learning and memory is the fact that it can occur without awareness (see Chapter 11, this volume for a thorough elaboration of this issue). One line of support for the nondeclarative quality of simple classical conditioning (as well as repetition priming and rotary pursuit) comes from studies of amnesic patients who lack awareness of previous training sessions (see Chapter 10, this volume). Patients with amnesia do not remember previous sessions, and they typically have lesions in the medial-temporal lobes. Thus, tasks that rely on nondeclarative brain memory systems should be acquired normally by amnesic patients, whereas tasks that require declarative memory should be impaired.

As described in Chapter 10, a number of studies have examined simple eyeblink classical conditioning in amnesic patients with medial-temporal lobe lesions. Amnesics' acquisition of eyeblink conditioning in the simple delay procedure in which the conditioned stimulus (CS) and unconditioned stimulus (US) overlap is normal or near-normal. Acquisition of rotary pursuit has been found to be normal in amnesic patients with lesions in the medial-temporal lobes (Brooks & Baddeley, 1976; Corkin, 1968; Heindel, Butters & Salmon, 1988; Yamashita, 1993) as has repetition priming (Cermak, Talbot, Chandler & Wolbarst, 1985; Graf, Squire & Mandler, 1984; Jacoby & Witherspoon, 1982; Warrington & Weiskrantz, 1968; 1970).

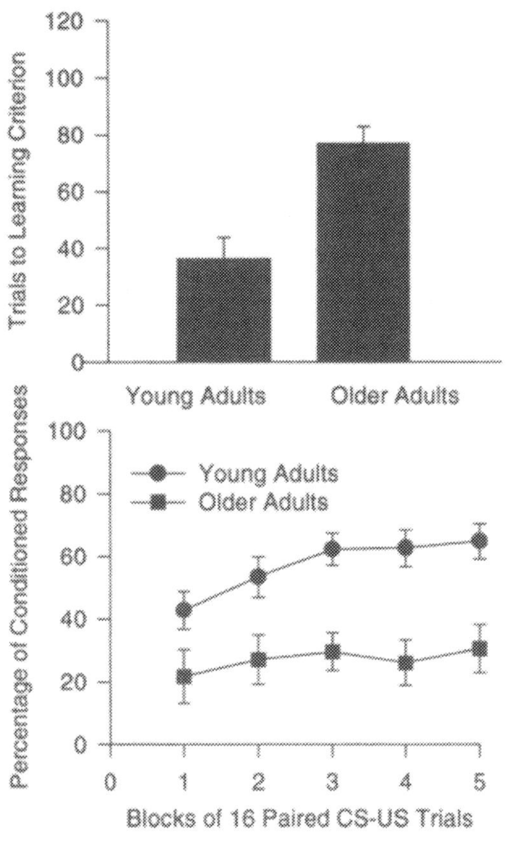

Figure 2. Top: Trials to a learning criterion of eight CRs in nine consecutive trials in 20 young adults aged 17-29 years and 20 older adults aged 63-80 years. Bottom: Percentage of CRs for 5 blocks of 16 paired tone and corneal air puff trials for the same adults. Error bars are standard error of the mean. (Data from Woodruff-Pak & Finkbiner, 1995a, 1995b).

Eyeblink classical conditioning is nondeclarative because learning occurs in the absence of awareness. In the case of amnesic participants, they acquire conditioned responses (CRs) but cannot remember that they have been tested. For example, although he was tested for 14 sessions in the delay procedure and attained a learning criterion of eight CRs in nine consecutive trials, H.M. did not recall previous conditioning sessions. In each session, H.M. reported that he had not worn the conditioning apparatus before. At the beginning of each session we would ask H.M. if he remembered the headband we had put on his head, and we would show it to him. His response was always, "No, I don't." H.M. had no recollection of the experimenters, apparatus, instructions, or procedure and responded to each session as if it were novel to him (Woodruff-Pak, 1993).

Using the delay procedure, investigators have documented for many decades that there is little relationship between normal participants' reported awareness and conditioning performance (e.g., Grant, 1973; Hilgard & Humphreys, 1938; Kimble, 1962; Papka, Ivry & Woodruff-Pak, 1997). Even when participants were informed of task procedures and CS-US contingencies prior to conditioning, performance was not necessarily better than that of naive subjects (McAllister & McAllister, 1958). Indeed, declarative instructions have actually been shown to interfere with conditioning (e.g., Cole, 1939; Hilgard & Marquis, 1940; Razran, 1955). As described by Clark and Squire in Chapter 11 of this volume, awareness becomes critical for conditioning in more complex classical conditioning procedures.

Dual Task Evidence on Conditioning and Awareness

When participants are performing two tasks simultaneously, they can condition well even when they are unaware that they are performing eyeblink classical conditioning (Papka, Ivry & Woodruff-Pak, 1995). Dual-task performance was assessed in 140 adults during eyeblink classical conditioning and a secondary task (timed-interval tapping, recognition memory, choice reaction time, or video viewing); only secondary task instructions were given. Four groups received paired eyeblink conditioning stimulus presentation in the delay procedure and three groups received explicitly unpaired conditioning stimuli. Although they focused on the secondary task and were not told about the conditioning task, participants acquired CRs at high normal levels. Post-session interviews probed participants' awareness of eyeblink conditioning stimulus contingencies and production of CRs (Papka, Ivry & Woodruff-Pak, 1997). Reported awareness of paired conditioning stimulus contingencies and CR production were not related to actual eyeblink classical conditioning performance. Furthermore, 27% of the participants receiving explicitly unpaired stimuli reported a stimulus contingency when none existed. The dissociation between awareness and performance provides additional support for the categorization of simple eyeblink classical conditioning as a form of nondeclarative learning.

Questionnaire Evidence on Awareness and Aging

Post-conditioning interviews of subjects tested in the delay procedure suggest that even when subjects display knowledge of the relationship between the CS and the US (e.g., report that the CS always came on before the US), their perceived awareness of responding and actual responding are not consistent. When we compared post-conditioning interviews of 40 young versus 40 older adults, questionnaire responses indicated greater awareness of CS-US contingencies in young adults and more awareness that they were blinking to the tone (producing CRs; Woodruff-Pak & Finkbiner, 1995b). Young adults who were better conditioners had greater insight. Nevertheless, among many participants who produced a high percentage of CRs, there was a lack of insight about their performance. Many of the high conditioning (over 50% CRs) subjects said that they *never* blinked to the tone. Of the 14 older subjects producing more than 50% CRs, over 35% stated that they never produced a CR (blinked to the tone). About the same percentage (37%) of high conditioning young adults stated that they never blinked to the tone.

Even when subjects are producing CRs and are aware that they are blinking to the tone, it is not clear that they have complete insight into what they are doing. A 73-year-old man who produced 59% CRs said, "It's funny -- I'm blinking at the tone." (Woodruff-Pak & Finkbiner, 1995b, p. 123). He recognized that he was responding to the tone CS, but he did not have a clear insight into why he was doing that. It was funny, or puzzling to him that he was blinking to the tone.

Whereas some participants who conditioned well had insight about blinking to the tone CS, many high performing participants had no insight whatsoever into their performance. This result indicates that insight is not essential for conditioning to occur. We are reluctant to use the relationship between insight and performance in simple eyeblink conditioning to suggest an explanation for age differences in conditioning. Older adults condition more poorly and have less awareness of the CS-US contingency and less insight about their blinks. However, it is likely that their lower levels of CR production gave them less opportunity to develop insight rather than their lower insight resulted in lower CR production.

AGE DIFFERENCES IN EYEBLINK CLASSICAL CONDITIONING IN HUMANS

Classical conditioning had its origin in Russia in the laboratory of Ivan Pavlov, and it was also Russian scientists Gakkel and Zinina who first discovered the age-related impairment in human eyeblink classical conditioning in the mid-1950s (reported in Jones, 1959). This observation of a large effect of age on eyeblink classical conditioning has been replicated and extended in many laboratories.

Age Differences in the Delay Eyeblink Conditioning Procedure

When data on eyeblink classical conditioning were collected over the entire adult age span instead of just with young and older adults, it became apparent that the age differences appeared as early as middle age. Using the delay eyeblink conditioning procedure with a 400 ms interval between a tone CS and corneal air puff US in 124 adults ranging in age from 18-83 years, we found that age differences in acquisition in eyeblink conditioning emerged in the age-decade of the 40s (Woodruff-Pak & Thompson, 1988). These results were independently replicated using the same 400 ms delay procedure by Solomon, Pomerleau, Bennett, James, and Morse (1989). Durkin, Prescott, Furchgott, Cantor, & Powell (1993) reported age differences in both eyeblink and heart-rate classical conditioning in a sample of young, middle aged, and older adults.

The samples reported in studies of eyeblink conditioning and normal aging published before the mid-1990s had few participants beyond the age of 75 years. It was unclear whether the age-related deficit increased with each age-decade after the 40s or whether it plateaued. To address this issue, eyeblink conditioning in the 400 ms delay procedure was assessed in 190 participants over the age range of 20-89 years, with 150 trained in the paired condition and 40 trained in the explicitly unpaired control condition (Woodruff-Pak & Jaeger, 1998). There was a statistically significant effect of age. Analysis of polynomial contrasts indicated a significant linear and a significant quadratic trend. Age differences showed a plateau after early adulthood with no significant differences in percentage of CRs between age groups in the 40s through the 80s. The correlation between percentage of CRs and age was -0.51 ($p < 0.001$). The percentage of CRs was significantly lower relatively early in adulthood with no additional significant deficit after the decade of the 40s.

Is there a CS-US Interval in the Delay Procedure that Eliminates the Effect of Normal Aging?

The 400 ms CS-US interval appears optimal for young participants, but large age effects may occur because this interval is too short for older participants. The processes of aging that result in impaired conditioning at shorter CS-US intervals in middle aged and older adults have yet to be clearly identified. However, when given a long enough CS-US interval, performance in older adults equals that of younger adults (see Figure 3).

Acquisition in the 400 and 750 ms delay eyeblink conditioning procedure was tested in 40 young and 40 older adult participants (Woodruff-Pak & Finkbiner, 1995a), and these participants all returned 24 hours later for a second conditioning session and retention testing (Woodruff-Pak & Finkbiner, 1995b). Eyeblink conditioning was performed by one-half of the participants using a 400 ms stimulus interval and one-half using a 750 ms interval. There were large age differences in performance on both CS-US intervals in both daily sessions, and performance did not improve in Session 2. Providing older adults with one additional training session on eyeblink conditioning did not result in significant improvement in their performance. A CS-US interval of 750 ms was not long enough to equate the performance of young and older adults.

Solomon, Blanchard, Levine, Valezquez, and Groccia-Ellison (1991) compared college-aged and older adult (61-86 years) participants in the delay procedure at CS-

US intervals of 400, 650, and 900 ms. There were significant age differences at the 400-ms CS-US interval, but age differences were not statistically significant at the 650- and 900-ms intervals. This result is seemingly in conflict with the results of Woodruff-Pak & Finkbiner (1995a) who reported significant age differences in the 750 ms delay procedure. Solomon et al. (1991) compared groups of 20 participants in young and old age groups on three intervals. After reporting a significant main effect of age and a significant age by interval interaction, they stated that post hoc comparisons indicated that only the age difference at 400 ms was significant. Post hoc tests are extremely conservative, and although the magnitude of the age differences were smaller at the 650 and 900 ms intervals than at the 400 ms interval, the differences were still relatively large. In fact, the data in the Woodruff-Pak and Finkbiner (1995a) study are quite comparable with data in the Solomon et al. (1991) study. However, using post hoc tests, Solomon et al. concluded that there were no significant age effects in the 650 and 900 ms delay procedures. Woodruff-Pak and Finkbiner (1995a, 1995b) found that the effect of age was robust in the 750 ms delay procedure when the statistical comparisons were direct rather than post hoc.

A major aim of a subsequent study was to determine for eyeblink classical conditioning in the delay procedure whether there is an optimal interval between the CS and US for middle-aged and older adults when associative learning is equal to that in the young (Woodruff-Pak, Jaeger, Gorman, & Wesnes, 1999). Normal adults in the young, middle-age, and older adult age range were conditioned at three CS-US intervals: 500, 1000, and 1500 ms. On the basis of pilot data, we predicted that there would be no significant age differences at CS-US intervals of 1000 and 1500 ms, but that young participants would outperform older participants at the 500 ms CS-US interval.

A total of 144 young, middle-aged, and older adults were tested on eyeblink classical conditioning at CS-US intervals of 500, 1000, or 1500 ms. From our previous studies, we knew that middle-aged and older adults were impaired at a 400 ms CS-US interval. Here we observed that the addition of 100 ms to the CS-US interval enabled equal conditioning in middle-aged and young adults. Thus, in the delay procedure with a 500 ms CS-US interval, there were no age differences between groups of subjects of a mean age of 21 and 48 years. At a 1000 ms CS-US interval, older adults (mean age of 75 years) remained significantly impaired compared to young and middle-aged adults. It was only at the 1500 ms CS-US interval that conditioning was equal for the three age groups.

Comparing eyeblink conditioning in young, middle-aged, and older adults in the 400 ms delay procedure in which we have collected most of our data and the 500, 1000, and 1500 ms intervals, the following pattern emerges. At the 400 ms interval, middle-aged and older adults produce significantly fewer CRs than do young adults, but middle-aged adults perform as well as young adults in the 500 ms delay procedure. Older adults are significantly poorer at acquiring CRs until there is 1500 ms between the CS and the US as shown in Figure 3.

Possible Causes of Age Differences in Delay Eyeblink Classical Conditioning

In searching for mechanisms to account for the age-related differences in eyeblink classical conditioning, it is important to examine all possible sources of differences. For example, the intensity of the CS and US affect the rate of conditioning. Age differences in hearing acuity and corneal sensitivity are potential sources making the older adults impaired. These effects are sensory. Thus, if these differences in sensitivity could account for the age difference in acquisition of CRs, the age-related deficit would not involve associative learning.

Non-Associative Factors Related to Age Differences in Eyeblink Conditioning

Controls for peripheral factors such as hearing, corneal sensitivity, motor aspects of the response, sensitization, and habituation were carried out by Durkin et al., (1993), Solomon et al., (1989), Woodruff-Pak and Thompson (1988), and Woodruff-Pak and Jaeger (1998). None of these investigators found evidence that such peripheral factors could account for the large age-related effects on conditioning in the delay procedure.

One age-related effect that is not related to associative learning is the age difference we observed in UR amplitude. In some (but not all) of our studies of age and eyeblink classical conditioning, older adults had significantly lower UR amplitudes (e.g., Woodruff-Pak & Jaeger, 1998). With the magnitude of the blink response being less, we were concerned that this factor might affect the production of CRs. The magnitude of the UR depends in part upon the size of the eye. To calibrate our equipment to measure the amplitude of the UR, we measured the distance between the top and bottom eyelid. We suspected that the age effect in UR amplitude was related at least in part to age differences in eye size as the size of the eye affects the magnitude of the blink. Analysis of variance was used to compare eye size (vertical height in mm from the top eyelid to the bottom eyelid) by decade. Age differences in eye size were almost significant, with older adults having smaller eye sizes. To control for the contribution of UR amplitude and eye size on the variance in the percentage of CRs, UR amplitude and eye size were used as co-variates in an analysis of co-variance comparing seven age groups on percentage of CRs. With the effects of UR amplitude and eye size held constant, the effect of age was still significant. Smaller eye sizes and other factors associated with smaller UR amplitude in older adults cannot account for all of the variance associated with age differences in associative learning.

Central Associative Learning-Related Causes of Age Differences in Eyeblink Conditioning

In rabbits, we found highly significant correlations between the number of Purkinje cells in cerebellar cortex and the rate of conditioning in three different samples (Woodruff-Pak, Cronholm & Scheffeld, 1990; Woodruff-Pak & Trojanowski, 1996). The fewer Purkinje cells a rabbit had, the longer it took to acquire CRs. In autopsy studies of human cerebellum, the existing data suggest that cerebellar Purkinje cell loss begins early in adulthood (Hall, Miller & Corsellis, 1975). Relatively few tasks are available to test cognitive abilities that clearly involve the cerebellum. Two tasks that measure individual variability in cerebellar function are eyeblink classical conditioning and timed-interval tapping. These measures show differences as a function of age and indicate that age-related effects in the cerebellum may affect cognitive performance in older adults. Indeed, age differences in eyeblink conditioning occur in middle age at a time when Purkinje cell loss becomes evident.

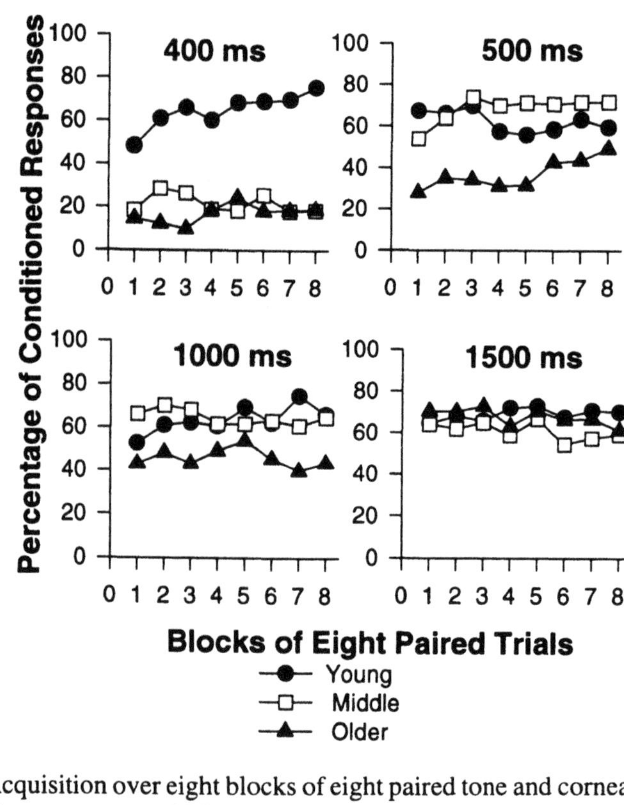

Figure 3. Acquisition over eight blocks of eight paired tone and corneal air puff trials as assessed by percentage of CRs in three age groups (young, middle aged, and older) at conditioned stimulus (CS)-unconditioned stimulus (US) intervals of 400, 500, 1000, and 1500 ms (Data from Woodruff-Pak & Jaeger, 1998; Woodruff-Pak, Jaeger, Gorman & Wesnes, 1999).

Although it is not possible to visualize Purkinje cells in cerebellar cortex with neuroimaging techniques, anatomic magnetic resonance imaging (MRI) scans of cerebellum are useful in estimating cerebellar cortical volume. Because Purkinje cells are the largest and most elaborated cells in cerebellar cortex, age-related differences in cerebellar volume likely reflect Purkinje cell loss. Three published MRI studies reported a decrease in cerebellar volume with age (Luft et al., 1998; Raz, Torres, Spencer, White & Acker, 1992; Raz et al., 1998). Anatomical MRI data on young and older adults in our laboratory are consistent with these results (Figure 4).

Normal aging is associated with changes in posture and gait (Simoneau & Leibowitz, 1996) that likely reflect the contribution of the cerebellum to normal aging of motor function. Less recognized in the research literature in gerontology is the potential of cerebellar function to affect cognition in aging. One of the most vigorous areas of current research in behavioral neuroscience involves the putative role of the cerebellum in cognition (Schmahmann, 1997). It has become well-known in clinical neurology and neuroscience that the cerebellum is essential for the coordination of movement, but less attention has been directed to observations that date back almost as long that cognitive and behavioral impairment may occur in association with cerebellar lesions (Dow & Moruzzi, 1958; Schmahmann, 1991, 1996). Whereas the earlier suggestions that there may be a cerebellar contribution to nonmotor function were largely dismissed as merely a reflection of co-existing disease in the cerebral cortex, more recent data collected independently in a number of laboratories and clinics converge in identifying a role in cognition for the cerebellum. In the domain of associative learning, we propose that age-related impairment in eyeblink classical conditioning is associated with the documented loss in cerebellar volume that is likely a reflection of Purkinje cell loss.

Age Differences in Acquisition in the Trace Conditioning Procedure

In the trace classical conditioning procedure, the CS turns off, a blank period ensues, and then the US turns on. There is no overlap between the CS and US, and the intervening blank period between CS and US is called the "trace." Pavlov designed this procedure to incorporate the requirement that a memory trace be formed by the organism between the CS and US. For normal human participants, there is evidence that performance in the delay and trace procedures is comparable because the CS-US interval is the variable that affects performance (Finkbiner & Woodruff-Pak, 1991; Ross & Ross, 1971). However, there is mounting evidence that the essential neural substrates for the trace procedure (when the trace interval is sufficiently long) include the medial-temporal lobes and the cerebellum, whereas the essential neural substrates for the delay procedure include only the cerebellum (see Chapters 9, 10, and 11 in this volume).

Using both 900 and 1800 ms intervals in the trace conditioning procedure, Finkbiner and Woodruff-Pak (1991) reported significant age differences in acquisition. Older adults aged 64-81 years produced significantly fewer CRs even in these long CS-US intervals. At the 1800 ms trace interval, the sample included a middle-aged group as well as young and older adults, and all participants were tested for three consecutive daily sessions. The first two sessions each contained 90 paired presentations of a 400 ms tone CS, a 1400 ms trace period, and a 100 ms corneal air puff US. The third session included 18 presentations in the 1800 ms trace procedure

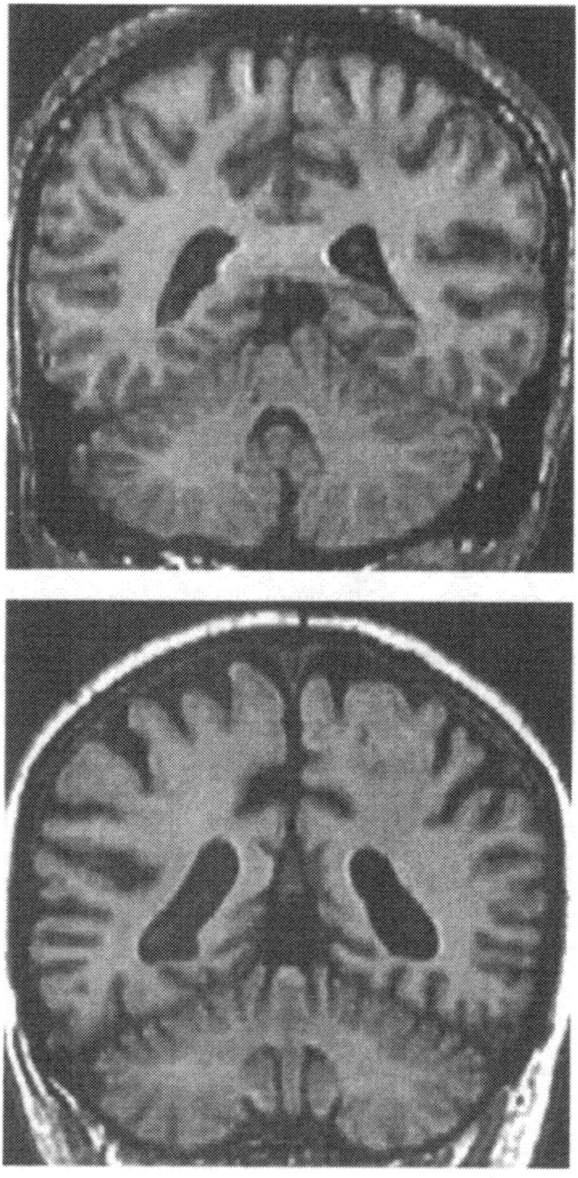

Figure 4. MRI of a coronal view of the cerebral cortex and cerebellum of a young male (20 years; TOP) and of an older male (79 years; BOTTOM). Shrinkage in the older cerebellum is evident as deep sulcal grooves in cerebellar cortex. (Woodruff-Pak and Lemieux, unpublished data. Supported by a grant from the Harry Stern Family Foundation).

identical to the two previous sessions, and 90 presentations of the CS alone to test extinction. Middle-age participants performed as well as young adults, indicating that extending the CS-US interval eliminated the conditioning difference between young and middle-aged adults observed at the 400 ms CS-US interval.

Reliable age-differences were observed in the overall levels of acquisition and extinction of CRs attained by the three age groups. The lack of age by training block interactions for any of the analyses indicate that it was the asymptotic level of performance, not the rate of learning that differentiated the older age group from the young and middle-aged cohorts. Middle-aged and younger subjects demonstrated nearly identical performance on most measures of learning. On the other hand, older subjects aged 64 to 81 years were clearly at a disadvantage on this trace conditioning task involving long CS-US intervals.

Several aspects of this study of the effects of aging in the long trace procedure indicated a lack of continuity between the typical findings in studies of aging using the short delay procedure. The fact that subjects ranging in age from 39 to 52 with a mean age of 45 years conditioned as well as 20 year-olds using the 1800 ms trace procedure is problematic if we wish to draw parallels between trace and delay methods. As mentioned previously, in the 400 ms delay eyeblink classical conditioning procedure age-differences in conditioning appear by the age-decade of the 40s and become exacerbated in individuals in their 50s. In the long trace procedure, subjects in their 40s and early 50s conditioned in a manner similar to subjects twenty years of age. Because this result of improved conditioning in middle age with extension of the CS-US interval to 500 ms was observed in the delay procedure (Woodruff-Pak et al., 1999), we can assume that it is CS-US interval rather than the trace procedure that impairs conditioning in middle-aged adults.

The long CS-US trace conditioning procedure represents a more difficult task for rabbits than does the short CS-US delay procedure. However, the reverse may be true for humans. Longer CS-US intervals apparently give middle-aged subjects more time for responding to a CS. The finding of Ross and Ross (1971) that trace and delay methods produce similar conditioning when the CS-US intervals are equivalent suggest that it is the length of the CS-US interval rather than trace/delay differences per se that are responsible for the different results with the two procedures in middle-aged humans.

The fact that the hippocampus becomes essential when the trace interval exceeds a critical interval in rabbits (Moyer, Dayo & Disterhoft, 1990) and humans (Clark & Squire, 1998) may explain why older adults but not middle-aged adults are impaired at the 1800 ms trace interval. It may be that cerebellar Purkinje loss impairs eyeblink classical conditioning in the delay procedure with shorter CS-US intervals, whereas age-related impairment in the hippocampus may impair conditioning at long trace intervals. There is some evidence that Purkinje cells are lost beginning early in middle age, but the hippocampus is relatively preserved until late life. Thus, it is only in older adults that we see the impairment in the long trace procedure that is hippocampally dependent. Additional discussion of these important issues on the role of the hippocampus in human eyeblink classical conditioning is presented in Chapter 10 by McGlinchey-Berroth and in Chapter 11 by Clark and Squire in this volume.

Aging and Complex Conditioning Procedures

One of the facts that becomes clear when carrying out an overview of eyeblink classical conditioning and aging is that complex conditioning procedures have seldom been used to test young, let alone older adults. Whereas discrimination and discrimination reversal procedures have been tested in amnesic patients (see Chapter 10 in this volume), we could not find published investigations focused directly on these forms of conditioning in normal aging. A recent exception is the work of Clark and Squire (1998, 1999, Chapter 11 in this volume) who used older adult subjects as control participants for their older amnesic subjects. Clark and Squire (1998, 1999) combined a discrimination procedure with a trace procedure and observed that in their group of normal older subjects, conditioning depended on whether subjects were aware of the CS-US contingencies. Previously, it was pointed out that there are statistically significant age differences in awareness in eyeblink conditioning experiments in the delay procedure (Woodruff-Pak & Finkbiner, 1995b). Awareness is not related to magnitude of conditioning (e.g., Papka et al., 1997), and we concluded that age differences in awareness could not account for the age differences in acquisition of CRs in the delay procedure. In the long trace conditioning procedure, in which awareness may be essential for acquisition, age differences in awareness may be a critical factor.

Aging, Retention, and Eyeblink Classical Conditioning

To test retention in eyeblink conditioning, more than one session of testing is involved. In a nondeclarative task, retrieval is relatively inflexible – requiring the same modality and similar contexts. Retention must be tested in the same manner as acquisition with the presentation of paired CS and US trial, but then relearning is confounded with retention. A means to test "pure" retention is to present the CS alone. However, CS-alone presentation also results in extinction. To address this problem, a typical strategy is to use a relatively small number of CS-alone trials and then use paired CS-US trials. In this manner retention and relearning are assessed.

A five-year retention study of young, middle-aged, and older adults was carried out by Solomon et al. (1998). The participants were 39 individuals who had been tested in the 400 ms delay eyeblink conditioning procedure previously and who returned to be tested five years later. At the time of the retest, the age range was 23-31 years for the young, 45-52 years for the middle-aged, and 69-78 years for the older adults. Participants experienced 20 CS-alone trials to test retention and 70 paired CS-US trials to test relearning. After a 5-year interval, young participants still showed good retention (45% CRs). Middle-aged adults showed reduced retention (28% CRs), and older adults showed little or no retention (less than 5% CRs). The ability to reacquire CRs also showed a decline with age. The investigators concluded that retention of CRs lasts over long time periods, but it is age dependent. Retention and relearning in older adults was quite poor when compared with the performance of young adults.

Relearning in elderly adults in the 400 ms delay procedure was tested at annual intervals over a three-year period by Ferrante and Woodruff-Pak (1995). The ages of the healthy subjects ranged from 69 to 94 years, with a mean age of 83.2 years at the time of the one-year follow-up study. Striking stability was observed in individual acquisition rates. Those individuals who conditioned well at the first test period also conditioned well in the follow-up sessions, and poor conditioners continued to condition poorly.

The subjects for this longitudinal study were selected from a group that had been the non-demented control subjects for an eyeblink classical conditioning study of adults diagnosed with probable AD (Woodruff-Pak, Finkbiner & Sasse, 1990). An unanticipated result of a longitudinal follow-up of healthy elderly adults who were good (>25% CRs) or poor conditioners (<25% CRs) was that most of the poor conditioners became demented or died within three years of initial eyeblink conditioning testing. We had predicted that eyeblink classical conditioning would be impaired in AD beyond the impairment observed in normal aging, but we did not expect that eyeblink conditioning might detect AD early, before declarative memory impairment was measurable. We have continued to explore the potential of eyeblink conditioning in the 400 ms delay procedure for the early identification of individuals at risk for AD.

EYEBLINK CLASSICAL CONDITIONING AND ALZHEIMER'S DISEASE

The human research on Alzheimer's disease (AD) and other neurodegenerative diseases was undertaken on the basis of hypotheses derived from the animal model – classical conditioning of the nictitating membrane (NM) response in rabbits. One of the strengths of this kind of an approach with a parallel animal model is that we can test neurobiological treatments such as drugs and trophic agents in the animal model and perfect them for use in humans.

With animal studies it had been demonstrated that pyramidal neurons in the hippocampus are activated during classical conditioning of the NM/eyeblink response, and that the septo-hippocampal cholinergic system plays a modulatory role during conditioning (Berger, Berry & Thompson, 1986). Although the hippocampus is not essential for acquisition in the delay classical conditioning procedure, disruption or facilitation of the hippocampus affects the rate of conditioning. In rabbits, disruption of muscarinic cholinergic receptors with scopolamine injections impairs acquisition of CRs, and this disruption occurs only when the hippocampus is intact (e.g., Solomon, Solomon, Vander Schaaf & Perry, 1983).

Activity recorded in the CA1 region of the hippocampus forms a predictive "model" of the amplitude-time course of the learned behavioral response. Firing to the tone-CS and corneal air puff-US occurs only under conditions where the stimuli are paired and produce behavioral learning (Berger, Alger & Thompson, 1976). When the CS and US are presented independently in the explicitly unpaired procedure, there is no hippocampal response to the tones or air puffs. The hippocampal modeling of the behavioral CR and UR is generated largely by hippocampal pyramidal neurons in the CA1 and CA3 fields (Berger, Rinaldi, Weisz & Thompson, 1983). In neuropathological studies of human brains, West, Coleman, Flood, and Troncoso (1994) identified pyramidal cells in the CA1 field of hippocampus as the cells selectively lost in AD.

It is our working hypothesis that selective loss of hippocampal pyramidal cells and disruption of the septo-hippocampal cholinergic system impairs acquisition of eyeblink classical conditioning in AD beyond the impairment observed in normal aging. We initially based the prediction of severe disruption of eyeblink classical conditioning in AD patients on data collected with the rabbit model system. More recently, West and colleagues (1994) reported selective loss of hippocampal pyramidal cells; the very cells in rabbits that fire just before the behavioral CR and UR are produced.

Based on the results with the animal model, we hypothesized that patients with a diagnosis of probable AD would be impaired in eyeblink conditioning beyond the deficit due to normal aging (Woodruff-Pak, Finkbiner & Katz, 1989). The hypothesis that eyeblink conditioning would be severely impaired in AD was confirmed and replicated (e.g., Woodruff-Pak, Finkbiner & Sasse, 1990; Woodruff-Pak, Papka, Romano & Li, 1996) and independently replicated (Solomon, Levine, Bein & Pendlebury, 1991).

Adults with Down's syndrome develop AD neuropathology around the age of 35 years, and we demonstrated in 22 adults over the age of 35 years with Down's syndrome that eyeblink classical conditioning in the 400 ms delay procedure was comparable to conditioning in elderly patients with AD (Woodruff-Pak, Papka & Simon, 1994). Control subjects for the older adults with Down's syndrome were age-matched adults with Fragile X syndrome, also caused by an abnormal chromosome. Adults over the age of 35 years with Fragile X syndrome conditioned like normal older adults.

Neurological Test Performance in Elderly Good and Poor Conditioners

Additional assessment of the 17 good and poor conditioners over the next two years involved administration of an extensive battery of neuropsychological tests to measure cognitive functioning (Downey-Lamb & Woodruff-Pak, 1999). Neuropsychological assessment included tests of memory, attention, executive function, language, and visuospatial/visuoconstructional abilities, capacities that are known to deteriorate in AD. Our aim was to determine if older adults who conditioned poorly had cognitive impairment indicative of AD two years later.

We were pleased that 100% of the 17 elderly subjects agreed to participate in the follow-up testing. Two years after the eyeblink conditioning test, all eight older adults who produced more than 25% CRs remained cognitively normal. Poor eyeblink conditioners were impaired in the cognitive domains affected by AD: Memory, executive function, visuospatial ability, attention, and language. The impairment of poor conditioners in executive function (Word Fluency) and visuospatial ability (Clock Drawing) are illustrated in Figure 5. Most of the poor conditioners were impaired in several cognitive domains and were at risk for dementia, and one was actually diagnosed with probable AD six months after neuropsychological testing for this study. Another poor conditioner demonstrated serious deficits but had not been diagnosed with AD three years after the eyeblink conditioning test. A third poor conditioner died five months after completing the study.

Eyeblink Classical Conditioning and Other Neurodegenerative Diseases

Because it is possible that any form of brain damage might impair eyeblink classical conditioning, the following research is discussed to demonstrate that lesions affecting eyeblink conditioning in humans are specific to the neural circuitry involved in this learning and identified in rabbits. Comparison of eyeblink classical conditioning in several neurodegenerative diseases or chromosomal abnormalities is presented in Figure 6. In both rabbits and humans, the cerebellum is essential for acquisition and retention of the conditioned eyeblink response. The hippocampus plays a modulatory role in acquisition in that manipulations of the hippocampal cholinergic system can alter the rate of learning.

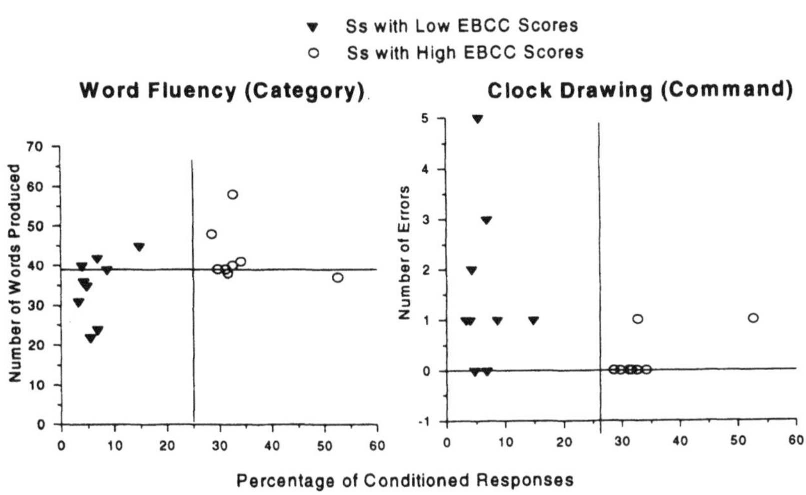

Figure 5. Performance of 17 older adults (mean age of 79.2 years) with good and poor eyeblink conditioning performance on neuropsychological tests of Word Fluency and Clock Drawing. Poor conditioners were unable to generate as many words in a category and made more errors in drawing a clock (Downey-Lamb & Woodruff-Pak, 1999).

Cerebrovascular Dementia

If eyeblink classical conditioning discriminates probable AD because of hippocampal disruption and cell loss in the CA1 hippocampal region, it is important to examine performance on this test in patients who exhibit behavioral dementia that is not caused by AD. In the case of cerebrovascular dementia (CVD; multi-infarct dementia or progressive subcortical vascular encephalopathy) as defined by Brun et al. (1990), there is not a predictable pattern of lesions. Infarcts can occur in many places in the brain. Thus, we anticipated that patients with CVD would be impaired beyond normal aging levels on eyeblink classical conditioning when their infarcts involved the cerebellar circuitry documented for this form of associative learning. We predicted a wider range of eyeblink conditioning performance in patients with CVD, with some conditioning like normal age-matched subjects when lesions were in cortical regions not including the cerebellar or medial-temporal lobe circuitry. The greater range of performance could be measured as greater variability in scores. On the other hand, all probable AD patients should be impaired because of the involvement of the hippocampal cholinergic system.

Forty-eight patients diagnosed with probable AD and 23 patients with CVD were tested in the 400 ms delay eyeblink classical conditioning procedure and compared to healthy, age-matched control subjects (Woodruff-Pak et al., 1996). Variability in the percentage of CRs was significantly greater in CVD patients than in patients with probable AD. This result supported the hypothesis that probable AD patients are all poor performers on eyeblink conditioning due to the disruption of the hippocampal cholinergic function by the disease. CVD patients were more variable in their performance, presumably because brain lesions caused by the disease were not consistently located in the same region. CT scan and other clinical data available on the CVD patients did not clearly indicate the locus of lesions of many of the patients. Although we did not have complete documentation of the locus of lesions in all CVD patients, we did have identification of some lesions. For those CVD patients with documented lesions in the circuitry essential to eyeblink classical conditioning, there was impaired conditioning. Patients with documented lesions in brain regions not essential for eyeblink conditioning acquired CRs like normal control subjects.

There were several CVD patients among our sample of 23 who conditioned at a high normal level. Among the 48 probable AD patients in our study, only one conditioned at a relatively high normal level. Twenty-six percent of the CVD patients produced over 25% CRs, whereas only 10% of the probable AD patients produced over 25% CRs. Although eyeblink classical conditioning did not differentiate all probable AD patients from CVD patients, the six CVD patients producing more than 25% CRs might be considered to be without AD neuropathology. Patients clinically diagnosed with vascular dementia, when autopsied, are often (40% to 50% of the cases) found to have sufficient neurofibrillary tangles and neuritic or senile beta-amyloid plaques to meet the pathological criteria for AD (Burst, 1988; Khachaturian, 1985). In these living patients, it was not possible to examine brain neuropathology, but it may be that up to half of the CVD patients in our sample produced fewer than 25% CRs because they have AD neuropathology as well as CVD.

Huntington's Disease

Huntington's disease (HD) is a progressive degenerative neurological disease resulting in abnormalities of voluntary movement and dementia. The basal ganglia are grossly atrophied, and there is thinning and shrinkage of the cerebral cortex. The hippocampus and hippocampal cholinergic system, however, remain relatively intact, as does the cerebellum. Although the eyeblink reflex is hyposensitive in HD, we anticipated that this lack of excitability could be overcome with an air puff directed at the cornea. On the basis of what is known about the neural circuitry essential or normally involved in eyeblink classical conditioning, it seemed likely that the pattern of neurodegeneration in HD would not interfere with this form of associative learning. Thus, it was anticipated that patients with HD would condition relatively normally.

Performance of seven patients with HD was compared to age-matched, healthy participants using the 400 ms delay eyeblink classical conditioning procedure (Woodruff-Pak & Papka, 1996). There were no differences in production of CRs between HD patients and normal control subjects, but the timing of the CR was

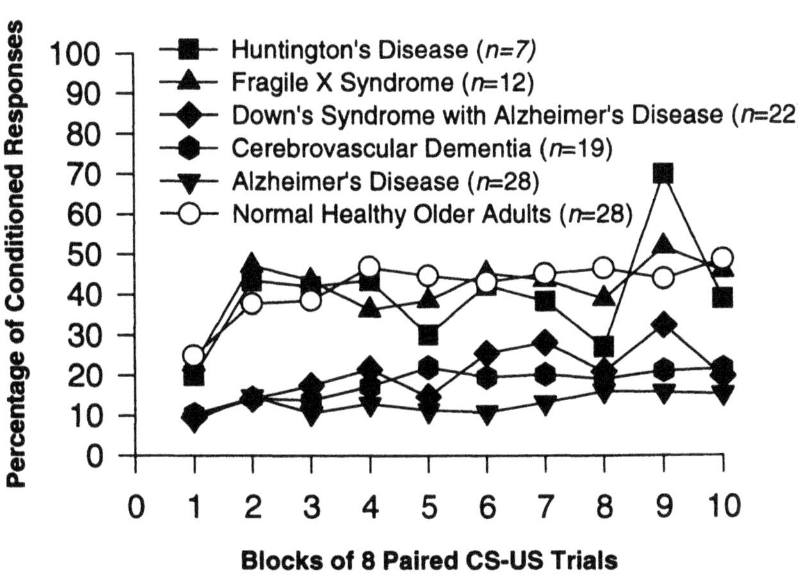

Figure 6. Percentage of conditioned responses over ten 8-trial blocks of paired tone and air puff presentations in five patient groups compared to a group of healthy older adults. The patients were diagnosed with Huntington's disease, Fragile X syndrome, Down's syndrome and Alzheimer's disease, or cerebrovascular dementia. Normal control subjects were age matched to patients with probable AD.

abnormal in HD. These results indicated that the ability to acquire CRs was normal in HD, but the striatum may have some role in optimizing the timing of the CR.

The neostriatum is not essential for eyeblink classical conditioning in rabbits, although lesions of the caudate nucleus (Powell, Mankowski & Buchanan, 1978) and disruption of neostriatal dopamine (Harvey & Gormezano, 1981; Kao & Powell, 1988; Sears & Steinmetz, 1990) impair acquisition. Extracellular recording of multiple- and single-unit responses in neostriatum of rabbits during eyeblink classical conditioning revealed conditioning-related patterns of neural firing. However, the neostriatal units related to the CR occurred too late to initiate the CR (White et al., 1994). The investigators suggested that the neostriatum may receive CR-related information from other structures such as the cerebellum that are critical for the optimal timing of the CR.

Parkinson's Disease

It was anticipated that Parkinson's disease (PD) patients, like HD patients, would perform normally on eyeblink classical conditioning because the cerebellum is not lesioned in PD, and the hippocampus is also relatively spared in non-demented PD patients. The only evidence that might lead to a prediction of impairment in eyeblink conditioning in PD was reported by Kao and Powell (1988) who lesioned the substantia nigra in rabbits and observed retarded acquisition of CRs. The mechanism by which substantia nigra lesions affected conditioning in rabbits may have been pharmacological. Dopaminergic mechanisms may modulate blink reflex excitability (Basso, Strecker & Evinger, 1993; Evinger et al., 1993). Parkinson's disease, which involves neuron loss in the substantia nigra and reduction of striatal dopamine, may affect blink rate and the blink reflex. Blink rate was significantly lower in unmedicated PD patients, but it was normal in HD patients (Karson, Burns, LeWitt, Foster & Newman, 1984). A number of studies have demonstrated that the blink reflex is abnormal in PD patients (e.g., Matsumoto et al., 1992) Thus, if eyeblink conditioning in patients with PD was poor, it might be due to dopaminergic effects impairing eyeblinks. This effect would be independent of the neural circuitry involved in the learned or conditioned eyeblink response.

Daum, Schugens, Breitenstein, Topka, and Spieker (1996) did not observe an abnormal blink to a corneal air puff in 10 medicated and nine unmedicated patients with idiopathic PD. Rather, the UR was intact. Across 60 acquisition trials in a delay procedure with a 720 ms CS-US interval, both medicated and unmedicated PD patients showed significant acquisition that was comparable or even superior to acquisition in healthy, age-matched subjects. Sommer, Grafman, Clark, and Hallett (in press) reported normal acquisition in 11 medicated PD patients tested in the 400 ms delay procedure using a weak shock to the skin over the supraorbital nerve as the US. In a subset of patients tested in the trace conditioning procedure, acquisition was similar in PD patients and normal control subjects. PD patients in these two studies did not show signs of dementia. These results of normal acquisition of CRs in patients with PD indicate that degeneration of nigrostriatal pathways does not impair eyeblink classical conditioning.

Eyeblink Classical Conditioning as a Neuropsychological Test

There is a practical advantage to eyeblink classical conditioning in terms of its application to patients. Many neuropsychological tests require a fairly high level of cognitive functioning and fail to differentiate among types of dementia. The tests are beyond the capacity of the patients, and they all perform at floor levels. In addition, patients may leave the testing situation more depressed than when they entered because they have been reminded once again about their failing abilities. This is not the case with eyeblink classical conditioning. *Here we have a test that is so simple, a rabbit can do it!* Eyeblink classical conditioning poses no threat to subjects' self esteem. Indeed, one of our major problems is alleviating boredom with the task. We show subjects silent movies to entertain them and maintain their attention.

SUMMARY AND CONCLUSIONS

Eyeblink classical conditioning is a useful model system for the study of the neurobiology of learning, memory, and aging which also has application to dementia. Parallel age differences in conditioning in the short-delay procedure appear in middle age in rabbits and humans that may be caused at least in part by loss of cerebellar Purkinje cells. It is only when the CS-US interval is extended to 1500 ms that the age differences in delay eyeblink classical conditioning disappear. The smaller body of evidence on the effects of normal aging in the trace, discrimination, and other complex classical conditioning procedures also suggests age-related impairment.

Eyeblink classical conditioning has relevance to AD because of the involvement of the hippocampal cholinergic system. AD profoundly affects the hippocampal cholinergic system, and our observation that Alzheimer's patients condition poorly or not at all may be related to the abnormally functioning hippocampus and loss of hippocampal CA1 pyramidal cells. Alzheimer's patients and patients with Down's syndrome and AD consistently perform poorly in eyeblink conditioning, but patients with dementia diagnosed as cerebrovascular dementia are not consistently poor conditioners. We suspect that CVD patients condition poorly only when some of the circuitry involved in classical conditioning has been affected. Patients with HD, PD, and Fragile X syndrome condition as well as normal age-matched adults. Eyeblink conditioning may be useful in differential diagnosis in dementia and also in detecting AD early in its onset. Because eyeblink conditioning is simple, non-threatening, and non-invasive, it may become a useful addition to test batteries designed to differentiate normal aging from dementia and AD from other types of dementia. Eyeblink conditioning may also detect AD early, before declarative memory impairment is evident.

REFERENCES

Basso, , M.A., Strecker, R.E., & Evinger, C. (1993). Midbrain 6-hydroxydopamine lesions modulate blink reflex excitability. *Experimental Brain Research, 94*, 88-96.

Berger, T.W., Alger, B., & Thompson, R.F. (1976). Neuronal substrate of classical conditioning in the hippocampus. *Science, 192*, 483-485.

Berger, T.W., Berry, S.D., & Thompson, R.F. (1986). Role of the hippocampus in classical conditioning of aversive and appetitive behaviors. In R.L. Isaacson & K.H. Pribram (Eds.), *The Hippocampus (pp. 203-239)*. New York: Plenum Press.

Berger, T.W., Rinaldi, P.C., Weisz, D.J., & Thompson, R.F. (1983). Single-unit analysis of different hippocampal cell types during classical conditioning of rabbit nictitating membrane response. *Journal of Neurophysiology, 50*, 1197-1219.

Birren, J.E. (1964). *The Psychology of Aging*. Englewood Cliffs, NJ: Prentice Hall.

Braun, H.W., & Geiselhart, R. (1959). Age differences in the acquisition and extinction of the conditioned eyelid response. *Journal of Experimental Psychology, 57*, 386-388.

Brooks, D.N., & Baddeley, A.D. (1976). What can amnesic patients learn? *Neuropsychologia, 14*, 111-122.

Brun, A., Gustafson, L., Risberg, J., Hagberg, B., Johansson, A., Thulin, A.K., & Englund, E. (1990). Clinico-pathological correlates in dementia: A neuropathological, neuropsychiatric, neurophysiological, and psychometric study. In M. Bergener & S.I. Finkel (Eds.), *Clinical and Scientific Psychogeriatrics (Volume 2, pp. 1-28)*. New York: Springer.

Burst, J.C.M. (1988). Vascular dementia is overdiagnosed. *Archives of Neurology, 45*, 799-801.

Cermak, L.S., Talbot, N., Chandler, K., & Wolbarst, L.R. (1985). The perceptual priming phenomenon in amnesia. *Neuropsychologia, 23*, 615-622.

Clark, R.E., & Squire, L.R. (1998). Classical conditioning and brain systems: The role of awareness. *Science, 280*, 77-81.

Clark, R.E., & Squire, L R. (1999). Human eyeblink classical conditioning: Effects of manipulating awareness of the stimulus contingencies. *Psychological Science, 10*, 14-18.

Cole, L.E. (1939). A comparison of the factors of practice and knowledge of experimental procedure in conditioning the eyelid response of human subjects. *Journal of General Psychology, 20*, 349-373.

Corkin, S. (1968). Acquisition of motor skill after bilateral medial temporal-lobe excision. *Neuropsychologia, 6*, 255-265.

Daum, I., Schugens, M.M. , Breitenstein, C., Topka, H., & Spieker, S. (1996). Classical eyeblink conditioning in Parkinson's disease. *Movement Disorders, 11*, 639-646.

Dow, R.S. & Moruzzi, G. (1958). *The Physiology and Pathology of the Cerebellum*. Minneapolis: University of Minnesota Press.

Downey-Lamb, M.M. (1999). Dual task performance in younger and older adults: Evidence for brain structures engaged during nondeclarative tasks. Unpublished doctoral dissertation, Temple University.

Downey-Lamb, M.M., & Woodruff-Pak, D.S. (1999). Early detection of cognitive deficits using eyeblink classical conditioning. *Alzheimer's Reports, 2*, 37-44.

Durkin, M., Prescott, L., Furchtgott, E., Cantor, J., & Powell, D.A. (1993). Concomitant eyeblink and heart rate classical conditioning in young, middle-aged, and elderly human subjects. *Psychology and Aging, 8*, 571-581.

Esposito, G., Kirkby, B.S., Van Horn, J.D., Ellmore, T.M., & Berman, K.F. (1999). Context-dependent, neural system-specific neurophysiological concomitants of ageing: Mapping PET correlates during cognitive activation. *Brain, 122*, 963-979.

Evinger, C., Basso, M.A., Manning, K.A., Sibony, P.A., Pellegrini, J.J., & Horn, A.K.E. (1993). A role for the basal ganglia in nicotinic modulation of the blink reflex. *Experimental Brain Research, 92*, 507-515.

Ferrante, L.S., & Woodruff-Pak, D.S. (1995). Longitudinal investigation of eyeblink classical conditioning in the old-old. *Journal of Gerontology: Psychological Science, 50B*, P42-50.

Finkbiner, R.G., & Woodruff-Pak, D.S. (1991). Classical eyeblink conditioning in adulthood: Effects of age and interstimulus interval on acquisition in the trace paradigm. *Psychology and Aging, 6*, 109-

117.
Gabrieli, J.D.E., Fleischman, D.A., Keane, M.M., Raminger, S., Rinaldi, J., Morrell, F., & Wilson, R. (1995). Double dissociation between memory systems underlying explicit and implicit memory in the human brain. *Psychological Science, 6*, 76-82.
Gabrieli, J.D.E., Vaidya, C.J., Stone, M., Francis, W.S., Thompson-Schill, S.L., Fleischman, D.A., Tinklenberg, J.R., Yesavage, J.A., & Wilson, R. S. (in press). Convergent behavioral and neuropsychological evidence for a distinction between identification and production forms of repetition priming. *Journal of Experimental Psychology: General.*
Graf, P. (1990). Life-span changes in implicit and explicit memory. *Bulletin of the Psychonomic Society, 28*, 353-358.
Graf., P., Squire, L.R., & Mandler, G. (1984). The information that amnesic patients do not forget. *Journal of Experimental Psychology: Learning, Memory, and Cognition, 10*, 164-178.
Grafton, S.T., Mazziotta, J.C., Presty, S., Friston, K.J., Frackowiak, R.S. J., & Phelps, M.E. (1992). Functional anatomy of human procedural learning determined with regional cerebral blood flow and PET. *Journal of Neuroscience, 12*, 2542-2548.
Grant, D.A. (1973). Cognitive factors in eyelid conditioning. *Psychophysiology, 10*, 75-81.
Green, J.T., & Woodruff-Pak, D.S. (1997). Concurrent eyeblink classical conditioning and rotary pursuit performance: Implications for independent nondeclarative systems. *Neuropsychology, 11*, 474-487.
Guerrier. J.H., Manivannan, P., & Nair, S.N. (1999). The role of working memory, field dependence, visual search, and reaction time in the left turn performance of older female drivers. *Applications in Ergonomics, 2*, 109-119.
Hall, T.C., Miller, K.H., & Corsellis, J.A.N. (1975). Variations in the human Purkinje cell population according to age and sex. *Neuropathology and Applied Neurobiology, 1*, 267-292.
Harvey, J.A., & Gormezano, I. (1981). Effects of haloperidol and pimozide on classical conditioning of the rabbit nictitating membrane response. *Journal of Pharmacology and Experimental Therapy, 218*, 712-719.
Heindel, W.C., Butters, N., & Salmon, D.P. (1988). Impaired learning of a motor skill in patients with Huntington's Disease. *Behavioral Neuroscience, 102*, 141-147.
Heindel, W.C., Salmon, D.P., Shults, C.W., Walicke, P.A., & Butters, N. (1989). Neuropsychological evidence for multiple implicit memory systems: A comparison of Alzheimer's, Huntington's, and Parkinson's disease patients. *Journal of Neuroscience, 9*, 582-587.
Hilgard, E.R., & Humphreys, L.G. (1938). The effect of supporting and antagonistic voluntary instructions on conditioned discrimination. *Journal of Experimental Psychology, 22*, 291-304.
Hilgard, E.R., & Marquis, D.G. (1940). *Conditioning and Learning*. New York: Appleton-Century.
Jacoby, L.L., & Witherspoon, D. (1982). Remembering without awareness. *Canadian Journal of Psychology, 36*, 300-324.
Jones, H.E. (1959). Intelligence and problem-solving. In J. E. Birren (Ed.), *Handbook of Aging and the Individual (pp. 700-783)*. Chicago: University of Chicago Press.
Kao, K.-T., & Powell, D.A. (1988). Lesions of the substantia nigra retard Pavlovian eye-blink but not heart rate conditioning in the rabbit. *Behavioral Neuroscience, 102*, 515-525.
Karson, C.N., Burns, S., LeWitt, P.A., Foster, N.L., & Newman, R.P. (1984). Blink rates and disorders of movement. *Neurology, 34*, 677-678.
Khachaturian, Z.S. (1985). Diagnosis of Alzheimer's disease. *Archives of Neurology, 42*,1097-1105.
Kimble, G.A. (1962). Classical conditioning and the problem of awareness. *Journal of Personality, 30*, 27-45.
Kimble, G.A., & Pennypacker, H.S. (1963). Eyelid conditioning in young and aged subjects. *Journal of Genetic Psychology, 103*, 283-289.
Light, L.L., & La Voie, D. (1993). Direct and indirect measures of memory in old age. In P. Graf & M.E.J. Masson (Eds.), *Implicit Memory (pp. 207-230)*. Hillsdale, NJ: Erlbaum.
Luft, A.R., Skalej, M., Welte, D., Kolb, R., Burk, K., Schulz, J.B., Klockgether, T., & Voigt, K. (1998). A new semiautomated, three-dimensional technique allowing precise quantification of total and regional cerebellar volume using MRI. *Magnetic Resonance in Medicine, 40*, 143-151.
Matsumoto, H., Noro, H., Kaneshige, Y., Chiba, S., Miyano, N., Motoi, Y., & Yanada, Y. (1992). A correlation study between blink reflex habituation and clinical state in patients with Parkinson's disease. *Journal of the Neurological Sciences, 107*, 155-159.

McAllister, W.R., & McAllister, D.E. (1958). Effect of knowledge of conditioning upon eyelid conditioning. *Journal of Experimental Psychology, 25*, 579-583.

Moyer, J.R., Deyo, R.A., & Disterhoft, J.F. (1990). Hippocampectomy disrupts trace eye-blink conditioning in rabbits. *Behavioral Neuroscience, 104*, 243-252.

Papka, M., Ivry, R.B., & Woodruff-Pak, D.S. (1995). Selective disruption of eyeblink classical conditioning by concurrent tapping. *NeuroReport, 6*, 1493-1497.

Papka, M., Ivry, R.B., & Woodruff-Pak, D.S. (1997). Eyeblink classical conditioning and awareness revisited: Results of a dual-task study. *Psychological Science, 8*, 404-408.

Powell, D.A., Mankowski, D., & Buchanan, S. (1978). Concomitant heart rate and corneoretinal potential conditioning in the rabbit (*Oryctolagus cuniculus*): Effects of caudate lesions. *Physiology and Behavior, 20*, 143-150.

Raz, N., Torres, I.J., Spencer, W.D., White, K., & Acker, J.D. (1992). Age-related regional differences in cerebellar vermis observed *in vivo*. *Archives of Neurology, 49*, 412-416.

Raz, N., Dupuis, J.H., Briggs, S.D., McGavran, C., & Acker, J.D. (1998). Differential effects of age and sex on the cerebellar hemispheres and the vermis: A prospective MR study. *American Journal of Neuroradiology, 19*, 65-71.

Razran, G. (1955). A direct laboratory comparison of Pavlovian conditioning and traditional associative learning. *Journal of Abnormal Social Psychology, 51*, 649-652.

Ross, S.M., & Ross, L.E. (1971). Comparison of trace and delay classical conditioning as a function of interstimulus interval. *Journal of Experimental Psychology, 91*, 165-167.

Schmahmann, J.D. (1991). An emerging concept: The cerebellar contribution to higher function. *Archives of Neurology, 48*, 1178-1187, and *49*, 1230.

Schmahmann, J.D. (1996). From movement to thought: Anatomic substrates of the cerebellar contribution to cognitive processing. *Human Brain Mapping, 4*, 174-198.

Schmahmann, J.D. (1997). *The Cerebellum and Cognition. International Review of Neurobiology, Volume 41*. New York: Academic Press.

Sears, L.L., & Steinmetz, J.E. (1990). Haloperidol impairs classically conditioned nictitating membrane responses and conditioning-related cerebellar interpositus nucleus activity in rabbits. *Pharmacology, Biochemistry and Behavior, 36*, 821-830.

Simoneau, G.G. & Leibowitz, H.W. (1996). Posture, gait, and falls. In J. E. Birren & K. W. Schaie (Eds.), *Handbook of the Psychology of Aging (4th ed.)*, 204-235. San Diego: Academic Press.

Small, S.A., Stern, Y., Tang, M., & Mayeux, R. (1999). Selective decline in memory function among healthy elderly. *Neurology, 52*,1392-1396.

Solomon, P.R., Blanchard, S., Levine, E., Velazquez, E., & Groccia-Ellison, M. (1991). Attenuation of age-related conditioning deficits in humans by extension of the interstimulus interval. *Psychology and Aging, 6*, 36-42.

Solomon, P.R., Flynn, D., Mirak, J., Brett, M., Coslov, N., & Groccia, M. (1998). Five-year retention of the classically conditioned eyeblink response in young adult, middle-age, and older humans. *Psychology and Aging. 13*, 186-192.

Solomon, P.R., Levine, E., Bein, T., & Pendlebury, W.W. (1991). Disruption of classical conditioning in patients with Alzheimer's disease. *Neurobiology of Aging, 12*, 283-287.

Solomon, P.R., Pomerleau, D. Bennett, L., James, J., & Morse, D.L. (1989). Acquisition of the classically conditioned eyeblink response in humans over the lifespan. *Psychology and Aging, 4*, 34-41.

Solomon, P.R., Solomon, S.D., Vander Schaaf, E., & Perry, H.E. (1983). Altered activity in the hippocampus is more detrimental to classical conditioning than removing the structure. *Science, 220*, 329-331.

Solyom, L., & Barik, H.C. (1965). Conditioning in senescence and senility. *Journal of Gerontology, 20*, 483-488.

Sommer, M., Grafman, J., Clark, K., & Hallett, M. (in press). Learning in Parkinson's disease: Eyeblink-conditioning, declarative learning and procedural learning. *Journal of Neurology, Neurosurgery, and Psychiatry*.

Squire, L.R. (1992). Memory and the hippocampus: A synthesis from findings with rats, monkeys, and humans. *Psychological Review, 99*, 195-231.

Warrington, E.K., & Weiskrantz, L. (1968). New method of testing long-term retention with special reference to amnesic patients. *Nature, 217*, 972-974.

Warrington, E.K., & Weiskrantz, L. (1970). Amnesic syndrome: Consolidation or retrieval? *Nature, 228*, 628-630.

Welford, A.T. (1958). *Ageing and Human Skill.* London: Oxford University Press.

West, M.J., Coleman, P.D., Flood, D.G., & Troncoso, J.C. (1994). Differences in the pattern of hippocampal neuronal loss in normal aging and Alzheimer's disease. *Lancet, 344*, 769-772.

White, I. M., Miller, D.P., White, W., Dike, G.L., Rebec, G.V., & Steinmetz, J.E. (1994). Neuronal activity in rabbit neostriatum during classical eyelid conditioning. *Experimental Brain Research, 99*, 179-190.

Winocur, G., Moscovitch, M., & Stuss, D.T. (1996). Explicit and implicit memory in the elderly: Evidence for double dissociation involving medial temporal- and frontal-lobe functions. *Neuropsychology, 10*, 57-65.

Woodruff-Pak, D.S. (1993). Eyeblink classical conditioning in H.M.: Delay and trace paradigms. *Behavioral Neuroscience, 107*, 911-925.

Woodruff-Pak, D.S., Cronholm, J.F., & Sheffield, J.B. (1990). Purkinje cell number related to rate of eyeblink classical conditioning. *NeuroReport, 1*, 165-168.

Woodruff-Pak, D.S., & Finkbiner, R.G. (1995a). Larger nondeclarative than declarative deficits in learning and memory in human aging. *Psychology and Aging, 10*, 416-426.

Woodruff-Pak, D.S., & Finkbiner, R.G. (1995b). One-day retention of eyeblink classical conditioning and verbal free recall in young and older adults. *Aging and Cognition, 2*, 108-127.

Woodruff-Pak, D.S., Finkbiner, R.G., & Katz, I.R. (1989). A model system demonstrating parallels in animal and human aging: Extension to Alzheimer's disease. In Meyer, Simpkins & Yamamoto, Eds. *Novel Approaches to the Treatment of Alzheimer's Disease (pp. 355-371).* New York: Plenum.

Woodruff-Pak, D.S., Finkbiner, R.G., & Sasse, D.K. (1990). Eyeblink conditioning discriminates Alzheimer's patients from non-demented aged. *NeuroReport, 1*, 45-48.

Woodruff-Pak, D.S., & Papka, M. (1996). Huntington's disease and eyeblink classical conditioning: Normal learning but abnormal timing. *Journal of the International Neuropsychological Society, 2*, 323-334.

Woodruff-Pak, D.S., Papka, M., Romano, S., & Li, Y.-T. (1996). Eyeblink classical conditioning in Alzheimer's disease and cerebrovascular dementia. *Neurobiology of Aging. 17*, 505-512.

Woodruff-Pak, D.S., Papka, M., & Simon, E.W. (1994). Eyeblink classical conditioning in Down's Syndrome, Fragile X Syndrome, and normal adults over and under age 35. *Neuropsychology, 8*, 14-24.

Woodruff-Pak, D.S., Romano, S.J., & Hinchliffe, R.M. (1996). Detection of Alzheimer's disease with eyeblink classical conditioning and the pupil dilation response. *Alzheimer's Research, 2*, 173-180.

Woodruff-Pak, D.S., & Thompson, R.F. (1988). Classical conditioning of the eyeblink response in the delay paradigm in adults aged 18-83 years. *Psychology and Aging, 3*, 219-229.

Woodruff-Pak, D.S., & Jaeger, M. (1998). Predictors of eyeblink classical conditioning over the adult age span. *Psychology and Aging, 13*, 193-205.

Woodruff-Pak, D.S., Jaeger, M., Gorman, C., & Wesnes, K.A. (1999). Relationships among age, CS-US interval, and neuropsychological test performance. *Neuropsychology, 13*, 90-102.

Woodruff-Pak, D.S., & Thompson, R.F. (1988). Classical conditioning of the eyelid response in the delay paradigm in adults aged 18-83 years. *Psychology and Aging, 3*, 219-229.

Woodruff-Pak, D.S., & Trojanowski, J.Q. (1996). The older rabbit as an animal model: Implications for Alzheimer's disease. *Neurobiology of Aging. 17*, 283-290.

Yamashita, H. (1993). Perceptual-motor learning in amnesic patients with medial temporal lobe lesions. *Perceptual and Motor Skills, 77*, 1311-1314.

9 EYEBLINK CONDITIONING IN NEUROLOGICAL PATIENTS WITH MOTOR IMPAIRMENTS

Markus M. Schugens
Ruhr-University of Bochum

Helge R. Topka
University of Tübingen, Germany

Irene Daum
Ruhr-University of Bochum

INTRODUCTION

Classical conditioning of the eyeblink response has been used in experimental psychology research with human subjects for many decades, but interest in its application to the assessment of memory and learning in brain-damaged patients emerged only recently and dates back to the late 1970s. At this stage, theoretical and empirical evidence for the similarity of the rules underlying eyeblink conditioning in animals and in humans was well established (Moore & Gormezano, 1977), and knowledge about its neuronal circuitry was accumulating in the animal literature (Thompson et al., 1976).

In many species, including human subjects, eyeblink conditioning typically involves the pairing of an acoustic conditioned stimulus (CS) with a corneal air puff unconditioned stimulus (US) in a delay procedure, i.e. the US follows the CS after a fixed time interval (400-800 ms) and both stimuli coterminate. The reflex unconditioned eyeblink response (UR) in humans later occurs as a conditioned response (CR) before US onset. The respective responses in rabbits have two components, an eyeblink together with a sweep of the nictitating membrane (NM) across the eye.

Neurobiological research in rabbits had initially implicated the hippocampus in the mediation of eyeblink conditioning because of significant correlations between the firing rates of hippocampal pyramidal cells and the development of behavioral learning (Thompson et al., 1980). Early neuropsychological investigations also centered on the study of amnesic patients. The case reports indicated that hippocampal damage in humans did not impair eyeblink conditioning (Weiskrantz & Warrington, 1979; Daum, Channon & Canavan, 1989); this finding was later replicated and extended in a number of group studies (for a review see Chapter 10 in this volume). Integrity of the hippocampal system was thus not necessary for the acquisition or - as recently reported - the long-term retention of eyeblink CRs over weeks and months (Schugens & Daum,

1999). Similar conclusions were reached by lesion studies in animals, and hippocampal firing is now thought to represent correlated rather than essential activity (see Thompson, 1991).

In the 1980s, findings derived from a range of different research techniques and strategies suggested that the cerebellum and related brainstem circuitry were critically involved in eyeblink conditioning. Electrophysiological activity in cerebellar structures was found to predict the development and the form of eyeblink CRs, and lesions to cerebellar cortex, nuclei or their major afferents abolished previously learned CRs and disrupted acquisition in naive animals when the air puff was directed to the ipsilesional eye (for a summary see Thompson, 1991). On the basis of these results, Thompson (1991) developed a model of the essential neuronal circuitry for eyeblink conditioning. This model entails the convergence of CS and US information in the cerebellum and the learning-related cerebellar influence on brainstem motor nuclei which control eyeblinks via efferent pathways. While there has been considerable controversy concerning the exact nature of the cerebellar involvement (e.g. Bloedel et al., 1991; Thompson & Krupa, 1994), it is generally agreed that cerebellar damage has a profound effect on eyeblink conditioning.

The review in this chapter concentrates on neuropsychological studies of patients with damage to the cerebellum and other brain systems involved in motor control. These data have made an important contribution to current concepts about the neuroanatomical basis of simple delay conditioning, and neuropsychology continues to contribute to the understanding of the neural correlates of more complex forms of learning and the organization of memory in the brain.

CONDITIONING STUDIES OF PATIENTS WITH DISORDERS OF MOTOR SYSTEMS

Damage to the Cerebellum and Brainstem Circuitry

Two single case studies provided initial support for the cerebellar hypothesis in human subjects. A severe acquisition deficit was observed in a patient with a right cerebellar hemisphere infarction when the air puff US was administered to the right eye (ipsilateral to the lesion) (Lye, O`Boyle, Ramsden & Schady, 1988). There was, however, rapid acquisition and strong conditioning when the US was directed to the contralesional eye. Subsequent shifts of the US to the eye ipsilateral to the cerebellar damage did not reliably evoke eyeblink CRs while testing of the contralesional eye continued to reveal good conditioning. Even though the eyeblink UR appeared to be normal in both eyes, irrespective of the side of air puff application, the authors pointed out that they could not rule out that nonassociative factors (motor or sensory deficits) affected conditioning performance. More detailed information on the nature of a possible interference by such factors was not given in the brief report.

A second case description confirmed that eyeblink conditioning is severely disrupted after damage to cerebellar circuitry. The report was based on a patient with an ischemic pontine lesion which also affected cerebellar afferents. Learning was characterized by a significantly lower CR frequency compared to controls and a lack of change in CR rates across training blocks (Solomon, Stowe & Pendlebury, 1989). There was thus no evidence of associative learning. It should be noted, however, that the exact nature of the lesion and in particular the extent of extra-cerebellar damage remained unclear.

As there is considerable interindividual variability with respect to overall CR frequency and with regard to learning rates across training in normal volunteers, group studies with well-matched clinical and control participants are of particular importance in conditioning studies. So far, three controlled group investigations have been published which described eyeblink CR acquisition in three independent samples of patients with cerebellar lesions.

The study by Topka and coworkers (1993) comprised five patients with pure cerebellar cortical atrophy, seven patients with combined cerebellar and brainstem damage (olivopontocerebellar atrophy, OPCA) and normal control subjects. The experimental procedure involved the pairing of a tone CS with a periorbital shock US; the CS preceded the US by a fixed interval of 400 ms. Eyelid movements were assessed on the basis of electromyographic activity from the orbicularis oculi muscle. The reflex blink to the shock US and measures of blink reflex excitability were normal, but the development of eyeblink CRs was severely impaired in both clinical groups. The conditioning deficit was partly attributed to inappropriate timing of the eyeblink CRs (Topka, Valls-Sole, Massaquo & Hallet, 1993).

The investigation by Daum and coworkers (1993) included only patients for which all available evidence (clinical and neuroradiological data) indicated that the damage was restricted to the cerebellum. Three patients suffered from unilateral cerebellar lesions (ischemic damage or tumor removal) and four patients suffered from degenerative cerebellar ataxia. The delay procedure involved a tone CS and a corneal air puff US with a fixed 720 ms interstimulus interval. In addition to eyelid movements (recorded by a photocell system), electrodermal activity and the electroencephalogram (EEG) were recorded during the course of acquisition. As a group, the patients with cerebellar lesions showed severe eyeblink conditioning impairments compared to a group of age- and IQ-matched control participants; their overall CR frequencies were very low, and there was no increase of CR rates across training blocks (see Figure 1).

The patients did not differ from controls on UR amplitude, measures of electrodermal conditioning, EEG measures of CS-US association or cognitive associative learning as indexed by verbal paired associates learning (Daum et al., 1993). Cerebellar lesions thus selectively disrupted classical conditioning of somatomotor responses without affecting concomitant associative learning in other response systems. A similar pattern of differential effects of cerebellar damage has been reported in animal studies (Lavond, Lincoln, McCormick & Thompson, 1984). Two further aspects of this study are noteworthy. There was considerable variability of conditioning performance within the group of cerebellar patients. Five of the patients did not appear to develop any CRs. The CR frequencies of two patients were, however, in the normal range and the CR rates decreased from acquisition to extinction (see Daum et al., 1993). One of these two patients had undergone surgery which had left the deep cerebellar nuclei intact, the other patient suffered from very mild clinical symptoms and slight cerebellar atrophy. It is possible that the cerebellar damage in these patients did not involve the areas critical for the mediation of eyeblink conditioning. The exact topography (and severity) of cerebellar dysfunction may thus affect the observed deficit at the behavioral level to a significant degree.

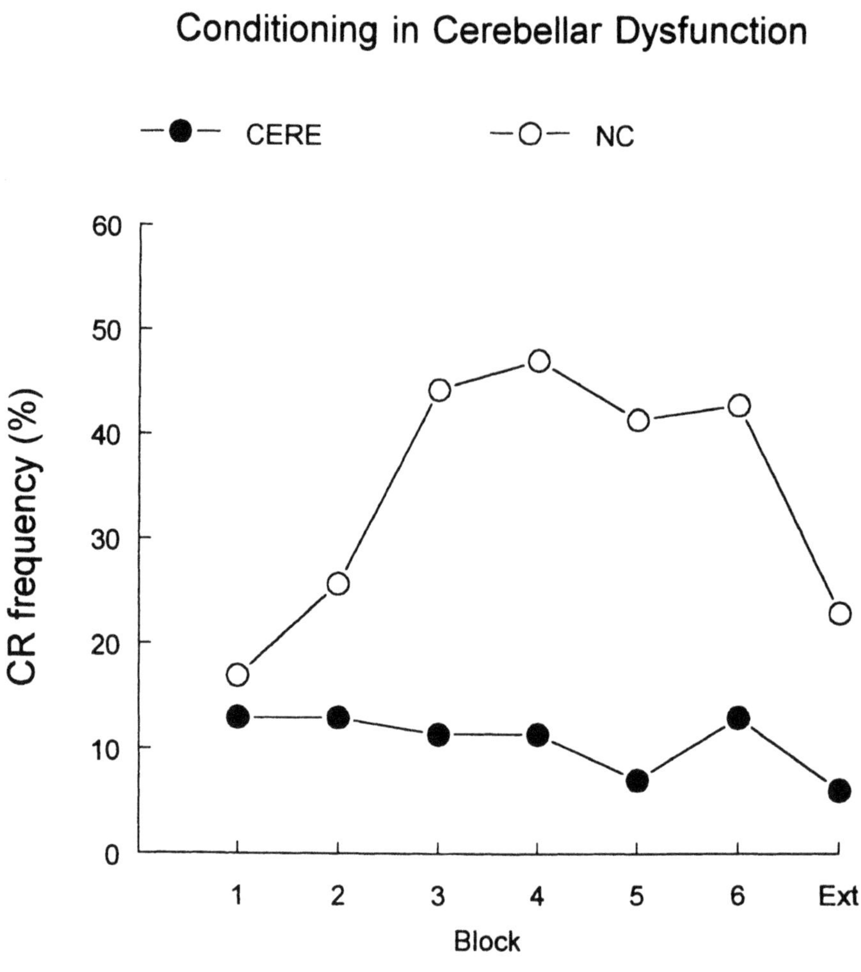

Figure 1. Development of CR frequency across acquisition and extinction in patients with cerebellar dysfunction (CERE) and control subjects (NC).

The second aspect relates to the question of the role of deficient timing of eyeblinks with respect to acquisition impairments. Cerebellar lesions may lead to impaired motor initiation, and late motor CRs may be masked by the UR (see Keele & Ivry, 1991). In the experimental procedure used in the Daum et al. (1993) study, 18 of the 60 acquisition trials were "tone-alone" trials, on which masking effects could not occur. For these trials, it was possible to separately analyze eyeblinks that satisfied conventional CR latency criteria (450 ms after CS onset up to US impact) and long-latency CRs (onset up to 1 s after CS offset). The patients with cerebellar lesions showed a number of long-latency CRs on the tone-alone trials, but a similar number of mis-timed CRs was observed in the control subjects, and the CR frequency group differences remained highly significant when the mis-timed CRs were added to the conventionally defined CRs. Deficient timing alone can thus not convincingly account for the eyeblink conditioning deficit observed in patients with cerebellar lesions (see Daum et al., 1993).

In a replication and extension of the two studies described so far, Woodruff-Pak, Papka and Ivry (1996) investigated eyeblink conditioning in seven patients with unilateral cerebellar lesions, seven patients with bilateral damage and 20 control subjects. The procedure involved a tone CS, air puff US and a 400 ms delay. The UR amplitude was intact in both clinical groups. The unilaterally lesioned patients showed significantly lower CR frequencies when the eye ipsilateral to the cerebellar damage was tested, while the CR rates were intact when acquisition was assessed by the blinks of the contralesional eye. These results clearly mirror the pattern reported for conditioning studies in animals (see Thompson & Krupa, 1994). The CR frequencies of the patients with bilateral cerebellar dysfunction were significantly lower than those of the control participants, but there were no differential effects for the right and the left eye. In the controls, the eyeblink CR rates correlated significantly with a clock measure from a timed-interval tapping task, and this correlation provides further support for a cerebellar involvement in the precise timing of the eyeblink CR (see Ivry, 1993; Woodruff-Pak et al., 1996). As in the earlier study by Daum et al. (1993), the cerebellar patients who demonstrated severe eyeblink CR acquisition deficits were not significantly impaired on cognitive associative learning as assessed by verbal paired associates learning (Woodruff-Pak et al., 1996). Their learning problems thus appeared to be specific to eyeblink conditioning.

In summary, there is now convincing evidence in support of the hypothesis that cerebellar integrity is necessary for normal eyeblink conditioning in human subjects. The evidence stems from neuropsychological studies which differed in patient samples, in the nature of the US (air puffs vs. shocks), the duration of the CS-US interval (400 ms vs. 720 ms) and the eyeblink measurement techniques (photocell system vs. EMG). Despite these procedural differences, the findings and conclusions were consistent across studies.

The observation that many patients with cerebellar lesions acquire a small number of eyeblink CRs and are therefore not completely unable to condition is difficult to interpret. It is likely that the critical structures in the human cerebellum are never completely damaged by ischemic lesions or neurodegenerative disease. The exact site and extent of cerebellar damage has to be considered, although the conventional neuroradiological data rarely allow detailed analyses in this regard. Inspection of individual differences in the clinical samples has so far revealed that lateral hemispheric lesions do not seem to interfere with eyeblink CR acquisition, and a small number of CRs can be produced when the deep nuclei are spared (Daum et al., 1993; Woodruff-Pak et al., 1996).

In summary, the data from patients with cerebellar lesions concur with the results from animal lesion studies in that cerebellar circuitry serves as the substrate for eyeblink conditioning.

Supportive Evidence for a Cerebellar Role in Conditioning

Several different research areas have provided supportive evidence for the hypothesis of an essential cerebellar role in human eyeblink conditioning (see Woodruff-Pak et al., 1996; Daum & Schugens, 1996). The first area relates to the pharmacological manipulation of cerebellar function in healthy humans and its effect on acquisition. The non-competitive NMDA antagonist memantine has a high receptor binding affinity to the cerebellum, and compared to other compounds such as ketamine, a relatively low affinity to forebrain structures, including the hippocampus (Porter & Greenamyre, 1995). A single dose of memantine was found to retard acquisition of eyeblink CRs in a double-blind placebo-controlled study in healthy volunteers, while memory for word lists or visual patterns as well as attention and verbal fluency were unaffected (Schugens et al., 1997). This performance pattern is consistent with regional variation in the receptor blocking effects of memantine and its particularly high affinity to cerebellar structures.

The second line of supportive evidence stems from neuroimaging data. A range of PET studies have consistently shown significant cerebellar activation changes during acquisition of eyeblink conditioning. These studies are reviewed by McIntosh and Schreurs (see Chapter 3, this volume) and will therefore not be further discussed in this chapter. Similarly, investigations from neurodevelopmental research have demonstrated an age-associated decline in conditioning which can be explained in terms of neuropathological changes in the human cerebellum accompanying the normal aging process; this literature and its relevance for the hypothesis of the cerebellar mediation of eyeblink conditioning is reviewed by Woodruff-Pak (see Chapter 8, this volume). Along similar lines, deviant eyeblink CR topography in autistic children may also be interpreted as evidence for an involvement of the cerebellum or cerebellar-hippocampal interactions in eyeblink conditioning; the latter hypothesis is based on findings of multiple dysfunctional brain systems in autism which involve both the cerebellum and the limbic system (see Chapter 7, this volume). Finally, the administration of dual-task procedures has revealed that experimental tasks with certain motor or timing requirements which tap into cerebellar function interfere with the acquisition when carried out during eyeblink conditioning while tasks that are primarily dependent upon other brain structures (e.g. hippocampus-dependent declarative memory tasks) have no disruptive effect (see Chapter 5, this volume). Taken together, the clinical studies of patients cerebellar dysfunction as well as investigations in healthy volunteers using different cognitive neuroscience approaches are consistent in their conclusion of a cerebellar involvement in eyeblink conditioning.

Damage to the Substantia Nigra and the Neostriatum

Recent neuroimaging studies in healthy human subjects have raised interest in the possible role of the striatum in acquisition of eyeblink conditioning though the exact nature of this involvement is unclear. Molchan and coworkers (1994) and Logan and Grafton (1995) observed learning-related activation changes not only in the cerebellum, but also in the striatum (as well as a number of other brain areas). The finding that the former study reported a decrease in striatal activation while the latter reported an increase might be explained by differences in the amount of learning at the time of scanning (see Woodruff-Pak & Papka, 1996).

Lesions to the substantia nigra were found to retard eyeblink CR acquisition in rabbits, while the concomitant conditioning of autonomic responses was unimpaired (Kao & Powell, 1986). Along similar lines, the pharmacological disruption of the dopaminergic system led to impaired acquisition (Harvey & Gormezano, 1981; Sears & Steinmetz, 1990). While these results would imply an essential involvement of the substantia nigra and the dopaminergic system in the underlying circuitry, detailed analyses of the correlations of neuronal activity in the caudate nucleus and the putamen suggested a modulatory role of the striatum (White et al., 1994). The striatum might influence the timing and the topography of eyeblink CRs via its projections to cerebellar-brainstem circuitry; the striatum might also serve to integrate eyeblink CRs with other ongoing motor activities (White et al., 1994).

As both the substantia nigra and the striatum are damaged in Parkinson`s disease (PD), the conditioning data of patients suffering from this neurological condition may shed some light on the possible involvement of the nigrastriatal system. The conditioning procedure completed by cerebellar patients (see Daum et al., 1993) was therefore studied in 10 medicated and nine unmedicated patients with idiopathic PD and matched control subjects (Daum, Schugens, Breitenstein, Topka & Spiekes, 1996). Both the medicated and unmedicated PD patients showed mild to moderate clinical symptoms, but the medicated patients had on average suffered from the disease for a longer period of time. Analogous to the study with cerebellar patients, electrodermal activity and the EEG were recorded in parallel with eyeblinks.

PD patients and controls did not differ with respect to UR amplitudes or subjective ratings of US intensity or blink rates. There were also no group differences for electrodermal CRs or event-related potential measures of stimulus association. While the learning rates across training blocks were comparable in all groups, the medicated PD patients showed significantly higher overall CR frequencies during both acquisition and extinction than the control subjects and therefore evidence of facilitation (see Figure 2; Daum et al., 1996). CR frequencies were also increased in the unmedicated patients during the early stage of acquisition in the first two training blocks.

Taken together, these results suggest that delay eyeblink conditioning is not impaired by degeneration of nigrostriatal pathways; autonomic associative learning and electrocortical measures of stimulus association are also unaffected. This pattern appears to contradict the animal literature which reported retarded eyeblink conditioning after substantia nigra lesions (Kao & Powell, 1986). The use of radiofrequency lesioning techniques suggests damage to both cell bodies and fibers of passage, and these more extensive lesions might have also damaged the structures involved in the blink reflex or the CR in addition to the substantia nigra (see Daum et al., 1996). The finding of intact eyeblink conditioning after nigrostriatal dysfunction in humans is consistent with the conclusion by White et al. (1994) suggesting that the striatum is not primarily involved in conditioning.

The observation of a facilitation of conditioning in PD patients was unexpected in light of the animal data, but can be explained in terms of the pathological changes in

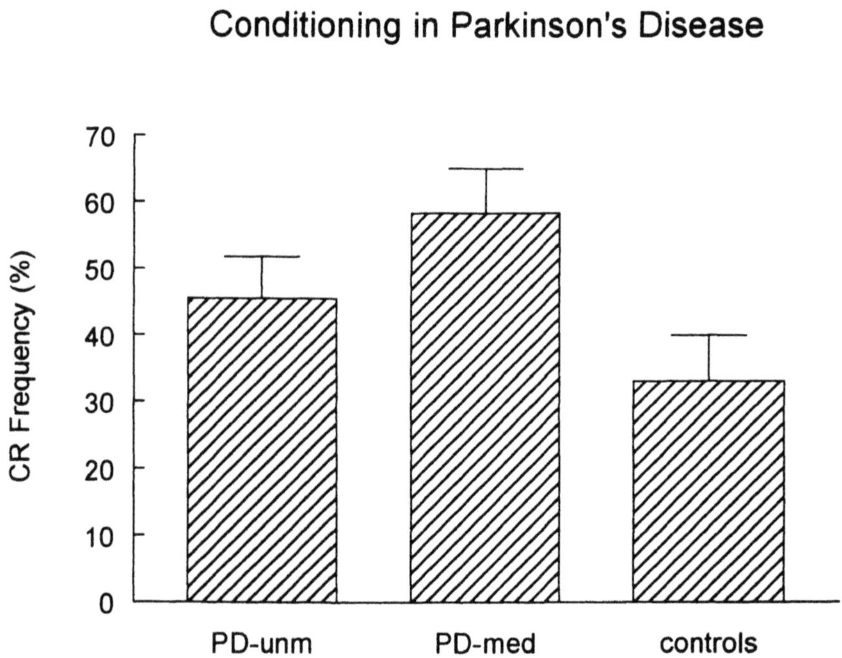

Figure 2. Mean CR frequency in unmedicated (PD-unm) and medicated Parkinson`s disease patients (PD-med) and control subjects

Parkinson`s disease outside the nigrostriatal system. These changes may affect the function of inhibitory brainstem interneurons subserving trigeminofacial reflexes (see Kimura, 1973). Enhanced excitability of reflex pathways might underlie the facilitation of eyeblink conditioning in PD (see Daum et al., 1996). The complex neuropathological changes in PD do not easily map onto the lesions used in experimental animal research and may not be functionally equivalent to the neuropharmacological manipulations of the dopaminergic system, e.g. induced by haloperidol which led to a delay in acquisition in rabbits (Sears & Steinmetz, 1990).

Huntington`s disease (HD) is a hereditary neurodegenerative disorder which mainly affects the striatum and the cerebral cortex. Atrophy of the caudate nucleus is common, and metabolic changes in the putamen and the globus pallidus may occur prior to clinical symptoms (Grafton, Mazziota, Pahl, George-Hyslop & Haines, 1990). Woodruff-Pak and Papka (1996) investigated delay conditioning in seven patients with HD and compared their learning data to those of healthy controls as well as a range of clinical comparison groups (patients with cerebellar damage, probable Alzheimer´s disease and patients with Down syndrome over the age of 35). The HD patients were in the early stages of the disease. Six patients did not show evidence of dementia, one patient scored in the mild dementia range. The HD patients did not differ from controls with respect to UR latency or amplitude, indicating that their blink reflexes were unimpaired. Significant learning across training blocks was observed in the HD patients, and the overall CR frequencies as well as the learning rates were comparable to the scores of the control subjects. The CR percentages of the HD patients were significantly higher than the CR rates of the other clinical groups (for details see Woodruff-Pak & Papka, 1996).

In summary, the learning data of the HD patients confirmed that the striatum is not essentially involved in the acquisition of eyeblink conditioning. More detailed analyses of the features of the CRs in the HD patients did, however, lend support to the hypothesis of a possible modulatory role. The CR peak latencies in the HD patients were significantly shorter than the corresponding latency scores in the control subjects. This finding suggests deficient CR timing, since the implementation of a CR is optimal when it peaks close to airpuff onset, so that the eye is closed at US impact. The CRs in the HD patients occurred about 40 ms early and were therefore not optimally timed to be adaptive (Woodruff-Pak & Papka, 1996). This observation supports the suggestion by White and coworkers (1994) who argued on the basis of electrophysiological recordings that striatal activity might be projected to the essential brainstem-cerebellar circuits underlying CR mediation. This striatal input might serve to optimize CR features such as latency or amplitude, and the disruption of striatal function in HD patients might interfere with this role (see Woodruff-Pak & Papka, 1996).

The neuropsychological studies discussed so far have centered on the role of the striatum in simple delay conditioning. More complex learning is assessed in latent inhibition procedures. The latent inhibition effect refers to the delay in acquisition which is observed if the paired CS-US presentation is preceded by a number of CS alone trials (Lubow & Gewirtz, 1994). The delay occurs because the organism had learned in the preexposure phase that the CS did not have any informational content. Eyeblink conditioning latent inhibition effects were demonstrated in animal research and shown to be reduced by hippocampal lesions (Solomon & Moore, 1975). More recent approaches relate the modulation of latent inhibition to the dopaminergic system. Dopamine agonists were consistently shown to reduce latent inhibition, whereas antagonists increase latent inhibition effects (Lubow & Gewirtz, 1994).

Consistent with the pharmacological studies, latent inhibition was found to be smaller in acute schizophrenics with evidence of abnormally high levels of dopaminergic activity (see Lubow & Gewirtz, 1994). Little is known about latent inhibition in patients with a dopamine deficiency, e.g. patients suffering from Parkinson's disease. As dopamine antagonists were found to increase latent inhibition in pharmacological studies, a similar pattern would be expected in PD. In order to explore this issue, PD patients and age-matched controls completed eyeblink conditioning under one of two conditions: a) the preexposure condition: 20 tone-alone trials, 60 tone-airpuff and 20 extinction trials or b) 60 tone-air puff and 20 extinction trials. Compared to the non-preexposed PD patients ($n = 14$), the overall CR frequency was significantly lower during acquisition and extinction in the preexposed PD group ($n = 14$), and the first CR tended to occur later. There were no differences between the controls with and without CS preexposure and thus no evidence of latent inhibition (though mild latent inhibition effects could be demonstrated using the same experimental procedure with subjects in the age decade of the 20s who were on average 30 years younger than the participants serving as controls for the PD patients). In summary, these data offer some support to the idea of a dopaminergic modulation of latent inhibition and also indicate the usefulness of more complex forms of eyeblink conditioning in the investigation of the neuronal basis of learning.

Dystonias

As both patients with cerebellar damage and patients with basal ganglia dysfunction show changes in acquisition or response parameters of conditioned eyeblinks, the question arises as to whether other motor disorders would also affect conditioning. Dystonia is characterized by involuntary muscle contractions which lead to repetitive movements or abnormal postures; typical examples of focal dystonias are torticollis or writer´s cramp which affect the muscles of the neck or hand and arm, respectively. The pathophysiology is so far not well understood, but there is evidence which links focal dystonias to dysfunction of the basal ganglia, particularly to damage of the putamen and the thalamus (see Topka & Dichgans, 1998).

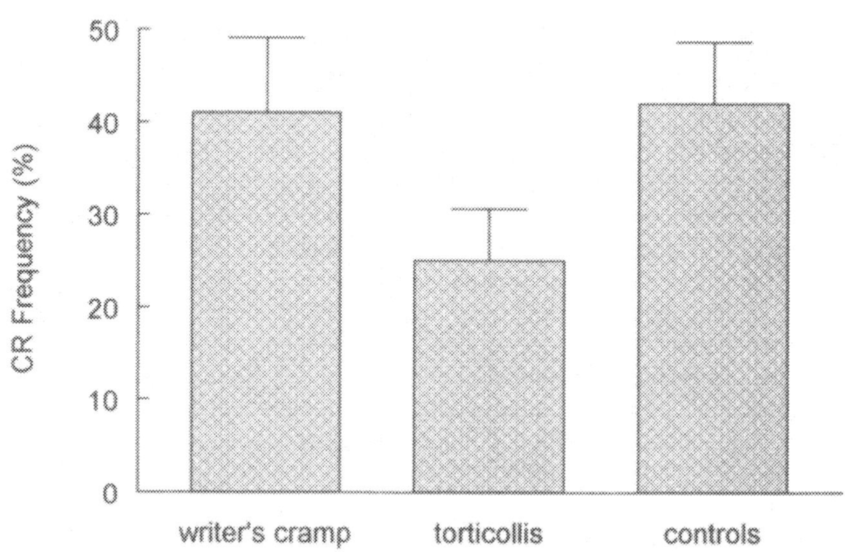

Figure 3. Mean CR frequency in patients with focal dystonias (writer's cramp and spasmodic torticollis) and control subjects.

In a recent study, delay eyeblink conditioning was examined in 14 patients with cervical dystonia (spasmodic torticollis) and 12 patients with writer`s cramp. Acquisition and extinction were compared to the learning curves of 14 age-matched control subjects (Topka, Künzer, Schugens & Daum, 1998). The three groups did not differ significantly on UR amplitude or subjective US intensity ratings. While the learning rates across acquisition (in terms of linear trends across blocks) and the decrease in CR frequency from acquisition to extinction were similar in all groups, the patients suffering from spasmodic torticollis showed significantly lower overall CR rates than the control subjects. The conditioning scores of patients with writer`s cramp were unimpaired (see Figure 3). The eyeblink conditioning deficit of the torticollis patients was not accompanied by problems in verbal paired associative learning; all groups achieved similar scores on this test.

The impairment observed in the torticollis patients is difficult to interpret within the framework of specific changes of motor systems in the brain, since the pathology in dystonias remains to be determined fully (see Topka & Dichgans, 1998). It is possible that a long history of cervical dystonia affects the adaptability of cerebellar-brainstem reflex circuitry and therefore the acquisition of eyeblink conditioning (see Topka et al., 1998). It is noteworthy that conditioning problems were not found in a form of dystonia which did not involve the head and neck. The differential learning pattern in spasmodic torticollis and writer`s cramp patients suggests that different types of focal dystonias might be associated with pathological or functional changes in different motor systems in the central nervous system.

IMPLICATIONS AND FURTHER DIRECTIONS

An important issue of future research into the relationship between motor systems and eyeblink conditioning in human subjects relates to neurodevelopmental questions. So far neuropsychological studies have focussed on patients with cerebellar or striatal damage acquired in adulthood. It remains to be determined whether normal cerebellar development is necessary for the (later) acquisition of eyeblink conditioning or whether other brain structures mediate learning in case of early cerebellar dysfunction. Findings in animals with early damage or impaired maturation mirror the results obtained with lesions in adulthood, indicating that normal cerebellar development is necessary for later learning (see Chapter 7 in this volume). In humans, little is known about the effects of developmental cerebellar malformations on memory and learning. The clinical symptoms associated with congenital or early malformations are characterized by very large interindividual variability and they range from severe ataxia and mental retardation to normal or unremarkable motor and cognitive abilities (see Daum & Ackermann, 1995). The changes in CR latency and topography in autistic children with probable cerebellar dysfunction indicate that eyeblink conditioning may be dependent upon normal cerebellar development. The finding that such CR deficits were more pronounced in younger compared to older autistic subjects further emphasize the importance of the study of developmental trends (see Chapter 7 in this volume). As there is some discussion concerning the extent und relevance of cerebellar damage in autism (e.g. Ciaranello & Ciaranello, 1995), studies with children with specific cerebellar developmental malformations documented by neurological and neuroradiological evidence would be very useful for further clarification of the role of cerebellar maturation and possible compensatory mechanisms.

A further research direction would involve the study of patients with hereditary degenerative diseases of the cerebellum. Recent advances in neurogenetics have resulted in the detailed description of different subgroups of patients with spinocerebellar ataxias which differ with respect to genetic abnormality, cerebellar pathology as well the extent of extracerebellar damage (Schöls et al., 1998). The comparative investigation of eyeblink conditioning in these clinical groups could help to further clarify the exact nature of the cerebellar role.

The interpretation of conditioning as an example of nondeclarative learning has led to insights into the organization of memory in the brain which are important for theoretical approaches, and the multiple memory systems view in particular (Squire, 1992). Double dissociations are rare in neuropsychological research. Patients with cerebellar damage showed severe eyeblink conditioning impairments on one hand, and normal declarative memory on the other hand (see Daum et al., 1993; Woodruff-Pak et al., 1996). Amnesic patients who completed the same conditioning procedure and the same memory tests acquired eyeblink CRs normally, while their delayed recall was severely impaired (Schugens & Daum, 1999). In addition, all cerebellar patients had acquired knowledge about relevant task features, while such knowledge was absent in the amnesics in post-experimental interviews. The double dissociation between two memory systems and two brain systems offers strong support to the distinction between declarative and nondeclarative memory (Squire, 1992).

The nondeclarative memory system is considered a collection of heterogeneous abilities, with different components being mediated by different neuroanatomical systems (Squire, 1992; Daum & Ackermann, 1997). The findings from eyeblink conditioning studies in neurological patients support this view. The cerebellar patients who showed conditioning impairments in the Daum et al. (1993) study did not differ from control subjects on a range of other nondeclarative or implicit memory tasks, such as word stem completion priming or perceptual and cognitive skill acquisition (Daum et al., 1993; Schugens, Ackermann & Daum, 1998). Along similar lines, the unmedicated PD patients who acquired eyeblink CRs normally (Daum et al., 1996), had problems in learning new cognitive and motor skills (e.g. Schugens, Breitenstein, Ackermann & Daum, 1999). The striatum and the cerebellum thus appear to mediate different components of nondeclarative memory.

In summary, eyeblink conditioning has served as a valuable tool in the investigation of brain-behavior relationships in human neuropsychology and will continue to make an important contribution to the neuropsychology of memory and learning.

REFERENCES

Bloedel, J.R., Bracha, V., Kelly, T.M., & Wu, J.Z. (1991). Substrates for motor learning: Does the cerebellum do it all? *Annals of the New York Academy of Science, 627*, 305-318.

Cianarello, A.L., & Cianarello, R.D. (1995). The neurobiology of infantile autism. *Annual Review of Neuroscience, 18*, 101-128.

Daum, I., & Ackermann, H. (1995). Cerebellar contributions to cognition. *Behavioural Brain Research, 67*, 201-210.

Daum, I., & Ackermann, H. (1997). Non-deklaratives Gedächtnis - Neuropsychologische Befunde und neuroanatomische Grundlagen. *Fortschritte der Neurologie, Psychiatrie, 65*, 122 -132.

Daum, I., Channon, S., & Canavan, A.G.M. (1989). Classical conditioning in patients with severe memory problems. *Journal of Neurology, Neurosurgery and Psychiatry, 52*, 47-51.

Daum, I., & Schugens, M.M. (1996). On the cerebellum and classical conditioning. *Current Directions in Psychological Science, 5*, 58-61.

Daum, I., Ackermann, H., Schugens, M.M., Reimold, C., Dichgans, J., & Birbaumer, N. (1993). The cerebellum and cognitive functions in humans. *Behavioral Neuroscience, 107*, 411-419.

Daum, I., Schugens, M.M., Ackermann, H., Lutzenberger, W., Dichgans, J., & Birbaumer, N. (1993). Classical conditioning after cerebellar lesions in humans. *Behavioral Neuroscience, 107*, 748-756.

Daum, I., Schugens, M.M., Breitenstein, C., Topka, H., & Spieker, S. (1996). Classical eyeblink conditioning in Parkinson's disease. *Movement Disorders, 11*, 639-646.

Grafton, S.T., Mazziotta, J.C., Pahl, J.J., George-Hyslop, S., & Haines, J.L. (1990). A comparison of neurological, metabolic, structural, and genetic evaluations in persons at risk for Huntington's disease. *Annals of Neurology, 28*, 614-621.

Harvey, J.A., & Gormezano, I. (1988). Effects of haloperidol and pimozide on classical conditioning of the rabbit nictitating membrane response. *Journal of Pharmacology and Experimental Therapy, 218*, 712-719.

Ivry, R.B. (1993). Cerebellar involvement in the explicit representation of temporal information. In P. Tallal, A. Galaburda, R.R. Linas & C. von Euler (Eds). *Temporal information processing in the nervous system: Special reference to dyslexia and dysphasia*. New York: *New York Academy of Sciences*.

Kao, K., & Powell, D.A. (1986). Lesions of substantia nigra retard Pavlovian somatomotor learning but do not affect autonomic conditioning. *Neuroscience Letters, 64*, 1-6.

Keele, S.W., & Ivry, R.B. (1991). Does the cerebellum provide a common computation for diverse tasks? A timing hypothesis. *Annals of the New York Academy of Sciences, 608*, 179-211.

Kimura, J. (1973). Disorders of interneurons in Parkinsonism - the orbicularis oculi reflex to paired stimuli. *Brain, 96*, 87-96.

Lavond, D.G., Lincoln, J.C., McCormick, D.A., & Thompson, R.F. (1984). Effect of bilateral lesions of the dentate and interpositus cerebellar nuclei on conditioning on heart rate and nictitating membrane eyelid responses in the rabbit. *Brain Research, 305*, 323-330.

Logan, C.G., & Grafton, S.T. (1995). Functional anatomy of human eyeblink conditioning determined with regional cerebral glucose metabolism and positron emission tomography. *Proceedings of the National Academy of Science (USA), 92*, 7500-7504.

Lubow, R.E., & Gewirtz, J.C. (1995). Latent inhibition in humans: Data, theory and implications for schizophrenia. *Psychological Bulletin, 117*, 87-103.

Lye, R.H., O'Boyle, D.J., Ramsden, R.T., & Schady, W. (1988). Effects of unilateral cerebellar lesion on the acquisition of eyeblink conditioning in man. *Journal of Physiology, 403*, 58.

Molchan, S.E., Sunderland, T., McIntosh, A.R., Herscovitch, P., & Schreurs, B.G. (1994). A functional anatomical study of associative learning in humans. *Proceedings of the National Academy of Science (USA), 91*, 8122-8126.

Moore, J.W., & Gormezano, I. (1997). Classical conditioning. In M.H. Marx & M.E. Bunch, (Eds.). *Fundamentals and applications of learning*. New York: MacMillan.

Porter, R.H., & Greenamyre, J.T. (1995). Regional variations in the pharmacology of NMDA receptor channel blockers: Implications for therapeutic potential. *Journal of Neurochemistry, 64*, 614-623.

Schöls, L., Krüger, R., Amoiridis, G., Przuntek, H., Epplen, J.T., & Riess, O. (1998). Spinocerebellar ataxia type 6: Genotype and phenotype in German kindreds. *Journal of Neurology, Neurosurgery and Psychiatry, 54*, 67-73.

Schugens, M.M., Ackermann, H., & Daum, I. (1999). Deklaratives und nondeklaratives Gedächtnis bei zerebellären Funktionsstörungen. In P. Calabrese, (Ed.). *Gedächtnis und Gedächtnisstörungen*. Lengerich: Pabst.

Schugens, M.M., Breitenstein, C., Ackermann, H., & Daum, I. (In press). Role of the striatum and the cerebellum in motor skill acquisition. *Behavioural Neurology.*

Schugens, M.M., Daum, I., Egerter, R., Schepelmann, K., Klockgether, T., & Löschmann, P.-A. (1997). The NMDA antagonist memantine impairs classical eyeblink conditioning in humans. *Neuroscience Letters, 224*, 57-60.

Schugens, M.M., & Daum, I. (1999). Long-term retention of eyeblink conditioning in amnesia. *NeuroReport, 10*, 149-152.

Sears, L.L., Finn, P.R., & Steinmetz, J.E. (1994). Abnormal classical eyeblink conditioning in autism. *Journal of Autism and Developmental Disorders, 24*, 737-751.

Sears, L.L., & Steinmetz, J.E. (1990). Haloperidol impairs classically conditioned nictitating membrane responses and conditioning-related cerebellar interpositus nucleus activity in rabbits. *Pharmacology, Biochemistry and Behavior, 36*, 821-830.

Solomon, P.R., & Moore, J.W. (1975). Latent inhibition and stimulus generalization of the classically conditioned nictitating membrane response in rabbits following dorsal hippocampal ablations. *Journal of Comparative and Physiological Psychology, 89*. 1192-1203.

Solomon, P.R., Stowe, G.T., & Pendlebury, W.W. (1989). Disrupted eyelid conditioning in a patient with damage to cerebellar afferents. *Behavioral Neuroscience, 103*, 898-902.

Squire, L.R. (1992). Memory and the hippocampus: A synthesis from findings with rats, monkeys, and humans. *Psychological Review, 99*, 195-231.

Thompson, R.F. (1991). Are memory traces localized or distibuted? *Neuropsychologia, 29*, 571-582.

Thompson, R.F., Berger, T.W., Berry, S.D., Hoehler, F.K., Kettner, R.E., & Weisz, D.J. (1980). Hippocampal substrate of classical conditioning. *Physiological Psychology, 8*, 262-279.

Thompson, R.F., Berger, T.W., Cegavske, C.F., Patterson, M.M., Roemer, R.A., Teyler, T.J., & Young, R.A. (1976). The search for the engram. *American Psychologist, 31*, 209-227.

Thompson, R.F., & Krupa, D.J. (1994). Organization of memory traces in the mammalian brain. *Annual Review of Neuroscience, 17*, 519-549.

Topka, H, & Dichgans, J. (1998). Dyskinesien. In T. Brandt, J. Dichgans & H.C. Diener, (Eds.). *Therapie und Verlauf neurologischer Erkrankungen*, Kohlhammer: Stuttgart.

Topka, H., Künzer, K., Schugens, M.M., & Daum, I. (1998). Classical conditioning of the eyeblink response in central nervous system disorders. In J. Valls-Sole & E. Tolosa, (Eds.). *Brainstem reflexes and functions*, Madrid, ENE Publishers.

Topka, H., Valls-Sole, J., Massaquoi, S.G., & Hallett, M. (1993). Deficit in classical conditioning in patients with cerebellar degeneration. *Brain, 116*, 961-969.

Weiskrantz, L., & Warrington, E.K. (1979). Conditioning in amnesic patients. *Neuropsychologia, 17*, 187-194.

White, I.M., Miller, D.P., White, W., Dike, G.L., Rebec, G.V., & Steinmetz, J.E. (1994). Neuronal activity in rabbit neostriatum during classical eyelid conditioning. *Experimental Brain Research, 99*, 179-190.

Woodruff-Pak, D.S., & Papka, M. (1996). Huntington's disease and eyeblink classical conditioning: Normal learning but abnormal timing. *Journal of the International Neuropsychological Society, 2*, 323-334.

Woodruff-Pak, D.S., Papka, M., & Ivry, R.B. (1996). Cerebellar involvement in eyeblink classical conditioning in humans. *Neuropsychology, 10*, 443-458.

ACKNOWLEDGMENT

The conditioning studies by our group which are described in this chapter were supported by the German Research Society (Da 259/4-1, 4-2).

10 EYEBLINK CLASSICAL CONDITIONING IN AMNESIA

Regina McGlinchey-Berroth
Brockton/West Roxbury Dept. VA Medical Center
Harvard Medical School
Boston University School of Medicine

INTRODUCTION

Understanding normal cognitive function through the study of individuals with brain damage is a principal goal of cognitive neuropsychology. Seminal works in the latter part of the 19th century by such eminent scholars as Broca, Wernicke, Hughlings Jackson, and others set the stage for what would become an entirely new and rapidly growing field within psychology focusing scientist's attention on untangling the mysteries of higher mental function in conjunction with revealing their underlying neural representation in the brain. The decades of the 1980s and 1990s have seen tremendous progress in identifying and localizing the neural substrates of classical associative learning in animals, primarily through the work of Richard Thompson and his colleagues. Much remains to be seen with regard to the extent to which their well-defined model maps onto human associative learning. A major difficulty is, of course, that is it impossible to obtain the fine level of control with regard to lesion localization and size in humans as is possible in animals; naturally occurring lesions do not always respect functional neuroanatomical boundaries. In humans, one must simply take what nature presents and understand that any residual behavior reflects the functioning of residual brain tissue that was unaffected by the lesion (or even compensatory mechanisms by other regions of the brain). Regardless of this inherent "messiness," however, it is encouraging that the data collected to date do suggest a high degree of correspondence between the two models. It is also intriguing that there appears to be some subtle and some not-so-subtle differences between the two models that may reflect important differences between humans and animals with regard to eyeblink classical conditioning.

In this chapter, I will review only a small portion of the research that has been conducted examining the neural underpinnings of eyeblink classical associative learning using patients with neurological disorders. While many such patients have provided relevant data and are reviewed elsewhere in this volume [e.g., Alzheimer's disease (Solomon, Brett, Groccia-Ellison & Oyler, 1995; Solomon, Levine, Bein & Pendlebury, 1991; Woodruff-Pak, Finkbiner & Sasse, 1990; Woodruff-Pak, Papka, Romano & Li, 1996b), vascular dementia (Woodruff-Pak et al., 1996b), Huntington's disease (Woodruff-Pak, 1996), frontal lobe lesions (Daum, Channon, Polkey & Gray, 1991), cerebellar lesions (Daum et al., 1993; Daum & Schugens, 1996; Lye, O'Boyle, Ramsden & Schady, 1988; Solomon, Stowe & Pendlebury, 1989; Topka, Valls-Sole, Massaquoi & Hallett, 1993; Woodruff-Pak, Papka & Ivry, 1996a, etc.], the focus here will be the study of individuals with a pure amnesic syndrome. I say pure because significant memory deficits can occur in the context of other motor, perceptual or cognitive deficits such as found in patients with Alzheimer's, Parkinson's, and Huntington's disease as well as vascular dementia, traumatic brain injury, and psychiatric illnesses such as depression. The amnesic syndrome of primary concern in this chapter is characterized by a significant impairment in new learning (i.e., anterograde amnesia), an inability to recall events prior to the onset of the precipitating illness (i.e., retrograde amnesia) *in the context of normal or near normal performance on tests of intelligence and immediate memory* (see Bauer, Tobias & Valenstein, 1993). While a relatively rare phenomenon, amnesia can be caused by damage to two different anatomical systems: either medial temporal lobe structures (etiologies include anoxia, encephalitis, status epilepticus, bilateral temporal lobectomy, tumor) or to damage to the diencephalon (i.e., mammillary bodies and thalamus; primary etiologies being Korsakoff's Syndrome or tumor).

As it turns out, the classical description of amnesia as outlined above is unrealistically simplistic. In fact, not all forms of new learning are impaired in amnesia and identifying islands of preserved learning has been the focus of much research. The dissociation between impaired memory and preserved memory seems to map well onto the dichotomous classification scheme outlined by Squire (1987). Declarative memory is concerned with the explicit retrieval of events or information and is severely disrupted in amnesia (e.g., Cohen & Squire, 1980; Graf & Schacter, 1985). Procedural memory is involved primarily in implicit tasks where learning is revealed by improvements in performance over the course of experience, without any direct reference to the learning experience. For example, amnesics can learn new perceptual, cognitive and motor skills, even though they are completely unable to recall the learning experience (e.g., Charness, Milberg & Alexander, 1988; Cohen & Squire, 1980; Gabrieli, Corkin, Mickel & Growdon, 1993; Milner, Corkin & Teuber, 1968). Additionally, amnesics show a normal benefit from a prior exposure of a stimulus or a normal repetition priming effect (e.g., Gabrieli, Keane, Zarella & Poldrack, 1997; Gabrieli, Milberg, Keane & Corkin, 1990; Hamann, Squire & Schacter, 1995; Keane, Gabrieli, Noland & McNealy, 1995; Musen & Squire, 1992; Schacter & Church, 1995; Warrington & Weiskrantz, 1968; Warrington & Weiskrantz, 1970). Lastly, eyeblink classical associative conditioning has been shown to be intact *under some experimental conditions and only in some types of amnesic patients.* Remarkably, both of these qualifications, the experimental conditions and the type of amnesic patient, appear to be predictable *a priori* based on the animal model developed by Thompson and his colleagues.

While the structures that Thompson and colleagues initially reported to be most implicated in associative learning are regions of the brainstem and midbrain, the cerebellum, hippocampal formation, and certain regions of the cerebral cortex (Thompson, 1986; Thompson et al., 1983), the primary focus of research has been on the cerebellum and hippocampus. Overwhelming evidence from the animal literature (rabbits) now indicates that only the cerebellum is both necessary and sufficient in the learning and memory of adaptive conditioned responses (CRs). For example, McCormick and colleagues (McCormick et al., 1981; McCormick & Thompson, 1984b) demonstrated that neuronal activity in localized regions of the cerebellar cortex and anterior lateral interpositus nucleus exhibit pattern changes in discharge frequency preceding the CR by approximately 60 ms. This activity was highly correlated with the amplitude and shape of the behavioral CR but not the unconditioned response (UR) and it increased over learning trials in close correlation with behavioral learning. Further, lesion studies have confirmed the cerebellum's essential role in basic associative learning. For example, it has been demonstrated that lesions of the lateral cerebellar cortex and nuclei, the lateral interpositus-medial dentate nuclear region, and the superior cerebellar peduncle permanently abolish the ipsilesional CR, while having no effect on the UR (Clark, McCormick, Lavond & Thompson, 1984; Lavond, Hembree & Thompson, 1985; Lavond, Lincoln, McCormick & Thompson, 1984; Lavond, McCormick, Clark, Holmes & Thompson, 1981; Lincoln, McCormick & Thompson, 1982; McCormick, Clark, Lavond & Thompson, 1982a; McCormick, Guyer & Thompson, 1982b; McCormick et al., 1981; McCormick & Thompson, 1984a; Steinmetz, Lavond, Ivkovich, Logan & Thompson, 1992; Thompson et al., 1983; Woodruff-Pak, Lavond & Thompson, 1985; Yeo, Hardiman & Glickstein, 1985).

In contrast, the hippocampus, while active during delay classical conditioning, is not essential since rabbits have been found to be unimpaired in delay eyeblink conditioning following hippocampal lesions (Akase, Alkon & Disterhoft, 1989; Berger & Orr, 1983; Schmaltz & Theios, 1972; Solomon & Moore, 1975). In fact, the hippocampus appears to be essential only in relatively more complex learning tasks. One such task is the trace conditioning task where there is a temporal separation between the conditioned stimulus (CS) and the unconditioned stimulus (US). For example, Solomon and colleagues (Solomon, Vander Schaaf, Norbe, Weisz & Thompson, 1986) reported that lesions of the hippocampus disrupt acquisition of the trace, but not the delay, nictitating membrane (NM) CR (but see James, Hardiman & Yeo, 1987; Port, Romano, Steinmetz, Mikhail & Patterson, 1986). Moyer, Deyo and Disterhoft (1990) found that acquisition could be totally eliminated with a 500 ms trace interval in rabbits who had undergone more complete hippocampectomies than those reported by Solomon et al. (1986). Interestingly, these investigators also found that when a CR did occur, it was of short-latency and nonadaptive. Other forms of higher-level associative learning that have been found to be dependent on the hippocampus include but are not limited to latent inhibition (Solomon & Moore, 1975), blocking (Solomon & Moore, 1975) and discrimination reversal but not simple discrimination (Berger & Orr, 1983; Orr & Berger, 1985).

The brief review above provides us with a basic outline in which to investigate eyeblink classical conditioning in individuals with amnesia. The animal literature suggests that whether or not amnesic individuals display intact or preserved eyeblink classical conditioning depends on lesion localization and conditioning paradigm. Below, I present the current literature regarding eyeblink conditioning in amnesia organized by paradigm. While this has the unfortunate consequence that some published works with multiple experiments are broken up into separate sections, it does provide a better conceptual understanding of the work that has been accomplished. In the first section, studies that have used a simple delay conditioning paradigm are presented. In these studies, there is only one CS that is consistently paired with a US and they coterminate. In the second section, studies that have used a simple trace conditioning paradigm are presented. Similarly to the delay paradigm, these studies have one CS that is consistently paired with a US but the CS and the US are temporally separated. In the third section we examine amnesic's conditioning performance on higher-level discrimination tasks. In these tasks, there are at least two CSs and only one predicts the US. Studies in this section have used both the delay and trace paradigm and investigate amnesic's ability to learn simple and conditional discriminations, their ability to reverse a previously learned discrimination and their ability to learn a temporal discrimination.

DELAY EYEBLINK CONDITIONING

Weiskrantz and Warrington were the first to ask the question of "whether conditioning using the classical paradigm is, in fact, possible in amnesic patients" (Weiskrantz & Warrington, 1979; p. 187). They evaluated the performance of two severely amnesic individuals. One, R.P., became amnesic due to probable encephalitis and was severely impaired for both verbal and nonverbal material. R.P. achieved a full-scale IQ on the Wechsler Adult Intelligence Scale of 116, higher than the average score of 100. The second individual, A.S., became amnesic due to alcoholic Korsakoff's Syndrome. Like R.P., A.S. was amnesic for both verbal and nonverbal material and performed above average on the WAIS, achieving a full-scale score of 123.

The CS consisted of both an auditory (3800 Hz, 35 dB tone) and visual (pilot lamp, 6 V, 014 A) stimulus. As this was really the first such eyeblink conditioning study with amnesics and the investigators were "blazing their own trail" as it were, the procedures differed somewhat between the two participants. For R.P., the CS was presented for 600 ms, whereas for A.S., it was presented for 800 ms; for both, the 200 ms US air puff coterminated with the CS. Also, for R.P., the conditioning session began immediately, whereas for A.S., there was a series of CS alone trials prior to the beginning of the paired presentation of the CS and US. The patients were tested on two successive days and were given blocks of extinction trials (tone alone) during each session. The conditioning sessions were recorded on videotape for purposes of tabulating the CRs "off-line". After realizing that the UR was masking the CR, Weiskrantz and Warrington included "probe" trials in which the CS was presented alone.

The percentage of trials on which a CR occurred indicated that by about trial 50, both patients were showing reliable conditioning, despite being completely unable to describe the test situation from memory. Additionally, retention of both patients appeared to be quite good (especially so for A.S.) both following 10 minute rest breaks and between the two testing sessions. It is noteworthy that the extinction data diverge somewhat for the two patients. R.P.'s extinction performance is somewhat variable showing a complete elimination of CRs during the first session on day two, but only slight decrements in CRs at the end of day one and the end of day two. A.S., in contrast, showed absolutely no decrement in CRs at the beginning of the last session on day one. Unfortunately, it is impossible to evaluate the normalcy of R.P's extinction performance due to the lack of a control group (a problem also for the evaluation of conditioning performance in general), but certainly it is safe to conclude that A.S. was impaired in extinction. Unfortunately, the authors do not comment on this possibility and one can only speculate whether this difference was related to etiology or the slight differences in procedures between the two patients. It is also noteworthy that A.S. showed acquisition at all given that the cause of amnesia was alcoholic Korsakoff's Syndrome. Radiological and postmortem studies of the neuropathology of alcoholism have indicated that prolonged use of alcohol leads to a pattern of brain damage characterized by brain shrinkage, including a reduction in the white matter (Harper & Krill, 1985) and cerebral gray matter (Jernigan et al., 1991), and most important to the current context, extensive cerebellar degeneration (Harper, 1982; Harper & Kril, 1990; Torvik, 1985; Torvik, Lindboe & Rodge, 1982). As I shall discuss below, there may be significant variability in the conditioning performance of Korsakoff's amnesics that may be related to the extent and precise topology of cerebellar atrophy.

Woodruff-Pak also examined simple delay eyeblink conditioning in amnesic individuals (Woodruff-Pak, 1993). The patients in this study included H.M. who became amnesic following bilateral removal of medial temporal lobe structures to control seizures. Notably, H.M. also had marked cerebellar atrophy in the vermis and hemispheres. A second amnesic suffered from herpes simplex encephalitis that produced medial temporal lesions and a loss of CA1 cells (the damage was assumed to be bilateral, although the left lesions were more pronounced on a computerized tomograpy (CT) scan). The performance of each patient was compared to a matched (with regard to age and education) control participant. The CS consisted of a 1000 Hz, 80-dB tone that was presented for 500 ms binaurally. The US was 100 ms air puff that followed tone onset by 400 ms. The participants viewed a silent movie during the conditioning sessions. H.M. was tested in the delay paradigm over the course of eight sessions of 90 trials each during which the CS was always paired with the US (H.M.'s control received seven sessions). A subsequent series of six sessions of 90 trials consisted of 80 paired CS-US trials and 10 CS alone trials (it should be mentioned that there were five sessions of trace conditioning that occurred five weeks after session eight). The encephalitic patient was tested in the delay paradigm for two sessions consisting of 90 trials.

As shown in Figure 1, H.M. was slow to acquire CRs during the initial eight sessions; he did not produce a normal percentage of CRs for his age until session six. During the second set of six sessions, H.M. produced enough CRs to remain within one standard deviation of the normal mean for his age range. H.M. also did not reach criterial learning until session six at which time he achieved eight CR's in nine consecutive trials. However, when considering only CS alone trials when there was a significantly longer period of time to produce a CR, (compare 400 ms on paired trials to 1200 ms on CS alone trials) H.M. achieved 60 percent CRs by session three. The encephalitic patient was also slow to acquire CRs in the delay paradigm relative to others of his/her age range during session one, but did achieve 44 percent CRs in session two, which was equivalent to the control subject for H.M. On CS alone trials, the encephalitic patient performed similarly to his/her matched control.

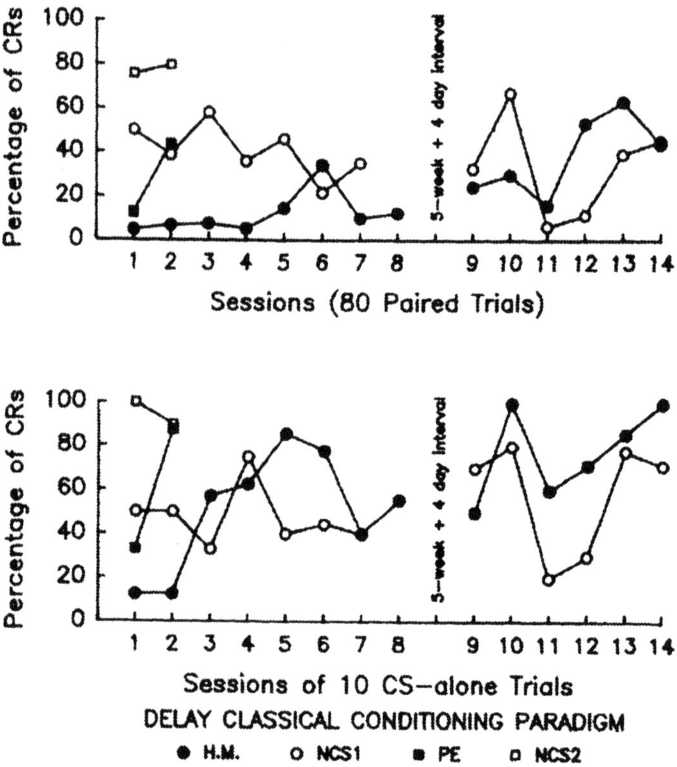

Figure 1. Percentage of conditioned responses in delay eyeblink conditioning from Woodruff-Pak (1993). Paired conditioned stimulus-unconditioned stimulus trials are presented in the top panel and unconditioned stimulus trials are in the bottom panel. (From "Eyeblink classical conditioning in H.M.: Delay and trace paradigms," by D.S. Woodruff-Pak, 1993, *Behavioral Neuroscience, 107*, p.911-925. Copyright 1993 by the American Psychological Association. Reprinted with permission.)

Based on the findings that H.M. was slow to acquire CRs during the CS-US paired trials, but was relatively unimpaired in the unpaired CS alone trials, Woodruff-Pak concluded that H.M. simply needed more time to respond (Corkin, 1968) and concluded that "his conditioning in the delay paradigm is relatively normal" (p. 922). It was suggested that the noted cerebellar atrophy might have increased the number of trials that it required H.M. to achieve criterial learning. This possibility is supported by research examining conditioning performance in other populations of patients with cerebellar atrophy (e.g, Topka et al., 1993). The encephalitic patient also performed within normal limits for acquisition. Interestingly, H.M. did not express any awareness of the training sessions, whereas the encephalitic patient (and the controls) was able to express the CS-US contingencies.

The findings from the Woodruff-Pak study are suggestive that delay eyeblink conditioning is intact in amnesia, as would be expected based on the animal literature. However, due to the cerebellar atrophy in H.M. and the relatively superior performance of the second control subject (which may have overestimated the encephalitic patient's relative impairment), it is difficult to judge the normalcy of the amnesic patient's performance. As such, we have also examined delay eyeblink classical conditioning in a larger group of amnesic individuals (Gabrieli et al., 1995). This study included seven amnesic participants and seven age, education and verbal IQ matched control subjects. Amnesia was caused by encephalitis (2 patients), anoxic episode (2), right posterior communicating artery aneurysm (1), status epilepticus (1) and closed head injury (1). All amnesics were significantly impaired on the Delay scale of the Wechsler Memory Scale-Revised (WMS-R) (Wechsler, 1987) and the Warrington Recognition Test (Warrington, 1984), but were found to be within normal limits on the attention scale of the WMS-R and full-scale IQ on the Wechsler Adult Intelligence Scale-Revised (WAIS-R).

The CS was an 85-dB 1 kHz tone of 850 ms duration delivered over headphones. The US was a 100 ms air puff delivered to the right eye that coterminated with the CS. Participants were tested in three conditions. During pseudoconditioning, the trials consisted of blocks of randomized, never paired tone (15 trials) or air puff (15 trials). During conditioning, the CS was always paired with the US (60 trials); there was a 750 ms interstimulus interval (ISI). During extinction, the CS was presented alone. As shown in Figure 2, the amnesics produced a similar percentage of CRs as the normal controls during each phase of the experiment. They showed similar base rates of CRs to tones during pseudoconditioning, similar levels of acquisition during the conditioning phase and a similar reduction of CRs during the extinction phase. It should also be noted that the interpretation of the data was not complicated by differences between groups with regard to UR latency or UR amplitude.

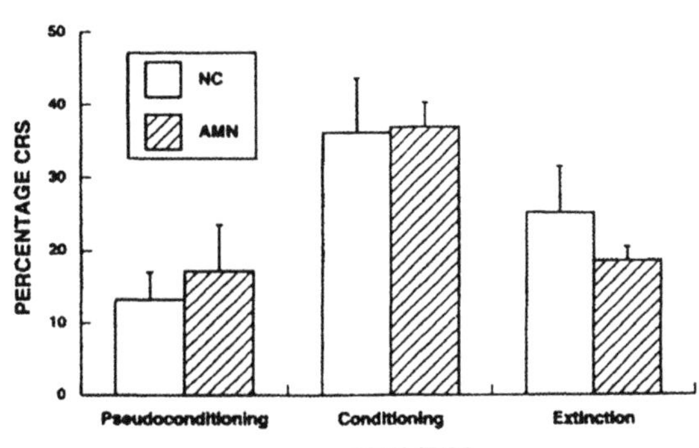

Figure 2. Mean percentage of conditioned responses for normal control participants (open bars) and amnesic patients (hatched bars) in pseudoconditioning (unpaired tones), conditioning (paired conditioned stimulus-unconditioned stimulus), and extinction (tones alone) in Gabrieli et al. (1995). In the public domain.

The data from the Gabrieli et al. study strongly indicate that delay eyeblink conditioning is fully intact in amnesic humans with bilateral medial temporal lobe lesions. Gabrieli et al. (1995) concluded that "in humans, as in rabbits, brain structures critical for declarative memory are not essential for the acquisition of elementary CS-US associations" (p. 819). Importantly, however, another study indicates that delay eyeblink conditioning is not spared in all forms of amnesia (McGlinchey-Berroth et al., 1995). In that study we compared the performance of four male Korsakoff patients, ten recovered chronic alcoholic participants, and ten normal control participants using delay conditioning procedures identical to the one described above in the Gabrieli et al. study.

As shown in Figure 3, the Korsakoff amnesics were severely impaired in acquiring CRs. They did not evidence an increase in CRs during paired CS-US conditioning trials relative to an established pre-learning baseline, while matched normal control subjects did show such an increase. This finding is in sharp contrast to the Woodruff-Pak and Gabrieli et al. studies. Unexpectedly, we discovered that recovered chronic alcoholic subjects were also impaired, albeit to a lesser extent, in acquisition of delay eyeblink conditioning relative to normal control subjects. Their overall level of acquisition was significantly less than the controls, and this was so during most learning blocks. The fact that learning in the recovered alcoholic group was depressed in a manner similar to the Korsakoff's patients suggested that the impairment in delay eyeblink conditioning was related to years of alcohol abuse and not to amnesia *per se*. As alluded to above, this impairment was likely due to cerebellar degeneration caused by the consumption of alcohol over long periods of time.

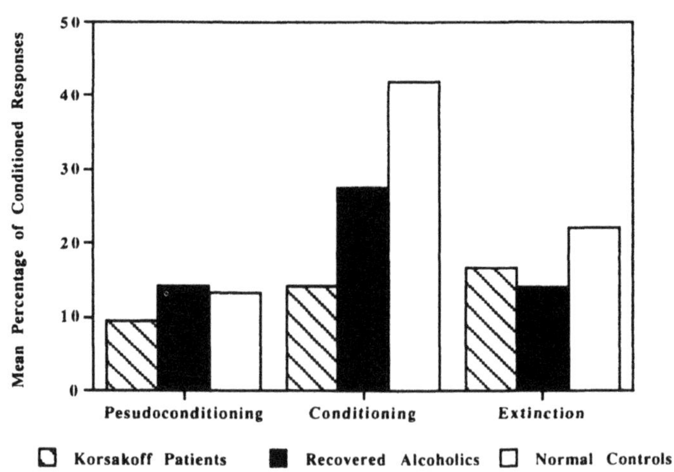

Figure 3. Mean percentage of conditioned responses for alcoholic Korsakoff patients, recovered alcoholics and control participants in McGlinchey-Berroth et al. (1995).

The possibility that the delay eyeblink conditioning impairment reported above in the McGlinchey-Berroth et al. study was due to cerebellar atrophy and not to diencephalic damage was supported by a study by Daum and Ackermann (1994). In the latter study, delay eyeblink conditioning was assessed in an amnesic patient with bilateral thalamic infarcts. The patient, T.H., was severely amnesic on both immediate and delayed tests of verbal and nonverbal material, but her attention was spared and she had a normal IQ. The CS was an 800 ms 1000 Hz, 65-dB tone and the US was a 80 ms air puff that coterminated with the tone. During each block of 10 trials, there were seven CS-US paired trials and three tone only trials. T.H.'s performance was compared to that of a control group.

Daum and Ackermann found that the number of CRs that T.H. produced was within one standard deviation of the control group across the five blocks of 10 trials, indicating unimpaired delay eyeblink conditioning in a patient with bilateral diencephalic infarcts. This finding is important because it helps to resolve the ambiguity of the McGlinchey-Berroth et al. (1995) findings,and indicates that delay eyeblink conditioning is intact in nonalcoholic diencephalic amnesia.

Taken together, the data from studies of simple delay eyeblink conditioning in amnesia are in good correspondence with the animal literature and suggest that in humans, as in animals, the cerebellum is essential for conditioning to occur. This conclusion is based, in part, on the fact that the Korsakoff amnesics in the McGlinchey-Berroth et al. study were unable to acquire CRs above a baseline level (as well as a number of other studies examining eyeblink classical conditioning in non-amnesic patients with cerebellar disorders (Daum et al., 1993; Lye et al., 1988; Topka et al., 1993; Woodruff-Pak et al., 1996a). It is curious, however, that the McGlinchey-Berroth et al. study contradicts the findings from the single case reported in Weiskrantz and Warrington (1979). Recall that their Korsakoff amnesic patient, A.S., did show evidence of acquisition. It is possible that the considerable differences in procedures and methods of analysis contributed to this difference. However, it may be more likely, although purely speculative at this point, that there is some heterogeneity in the pattern of atrophy across individuals. Since the publication of the McGlinchey-Berroth et al. paper, we have tested several more Korsakoff amnesics and have found one patient to be perfectly normal in acquisition, similar to the patient in the Weiskrantz and Warrington report. Additionally, we have tested numerous additional alcoholics and have found that some are as impaired in acquisition as the typical Korsakoff amnesic. We know from animal studies that it is the lateral interpositus nucleus that is the most critical structure for the acquisition and retention of CRs (see Thompson et al., 1983). Imaging studies would be very helpful in determining if there is atrophy in the deep nuclei in alcoholic amnesics with impaired acquisition but no atrophy in the deep nuclei in alcoholic amnesics with normal acquisition.

TRACE EYEBLANK CONDITIONING

The findings from the delay conditioning paradigm indicate that medial temporal lobe structures important for declarative memory are not essential for delay conditioning.

However, hippocampal lesions do disrupt acquisition in the trace conditioning paradigm in rabbits (Solomon et al., 1986) and can even eliminate acquisition if the hippocampectomy is relatively complete (Moyer et al., 1990). The primary difference between delay and trace conditioning is that there is a temporal separation between the CS and US in trace conditioning that necessitates the formation of an abstract link, or in Pavlov's terms, a perseverative "trace" (Pavlov, 1927) between the CS and US. Precisely why it is that the trace period seems to require hippocampal involvement is a matter of debate; some have argued that the hippocampus is involved in representing temporal information (Solomon, 1979) or temporal associations (Moyer et al., 1990), while others have suggested that the hippocampus is involved in binding together discrete pieces of information (e.g., Cohen & Eichenbaum, 1993; Eichenbaum, Otto & Cohen, 1992; Sutherland & Rudy, 1989; Wickelgren, 1979). A recent proposal has suggested that awareness is necessary for trace conditioning to occur and that the hippocampal or declarative memory system is necessary for this awareness (Clark and Squire, 1998; see also Chapter 11, this volume).

Currently, there are only two published reports of trace eyeblink conditioning in amnesic individuals. The first study was reported by Woodruff-Pak and was conducted in conjunction with the delay eyeblink conditioning investigation described earlier (Woodruff-Pak, 1993). Again, the participants were H.M. and a post encephalitic patient. The CS was a 400 ms, 1000 Hz, 80-dB tone that was delivered binaurally. The CS was followed by a 500 ms trace (blank) period after which the 100 ms corneal air puff US was delivered to the right eye. There were five testing sessions consisting of 10 blocks of 9 trials. The first trial of each block was a CS only trial, the remaining trials were CS-US pairs. Two years after trace conditioning, H.M. was brought back to the laboratory and received two additional 90 trial sessions of trace conditioning trials.

The learning curves for trace conditioning in the two amnesics and controls are presented in Figure 4. Averaging across the initial five sessions for the CS-US paired trials, H.M. produced approximately the same percentage of CRs as did his control subject (44% for H.M. compared to 49% for the control). In the tone alone trials, H.M. produced more CRs than he did in the CS-US pairs. The encephalitic patient produced a mean percentage of CRs of 46, which was considerably less than his/her control patient but was similar to H.M. and his control subject. H.M. required 91 trials to reach criterion and the encephalitic patient required 9 trials; their control subjects reached criterion in the trace task on the first trial. Neither of the two amnesics produced any short-latency alpha responses, as had been observed by Moyer et al. (1990) in rabbits. H.M. reached criterial performance in only nine trials at the two-year follow-up. It is clear from these data that the amnesic participants were able to acquire conditioned responses; in fact, both were able to reach criterial performance (i.e., produce a CR in at least eight of nine consecutive trials). These findings led Woodruff-Pak to conclude "the hippocampus is not critical for trace classical conditioning in humans" (p. 922). It is important to note, however, that while the patients did reach criterial learning, they required considerably more trials to do so than did their control subjects. Additionally, the fact that H.M. attained criterial learning so rapidly after two years following initial acquisition, in conjunction with having no recollection of the prior conditioning sessions, suggests that perhaps what trace conditioning could be learned may have been mediated by another memory system (a system that may have underlied his normal performance in delay eyeblink conditioning).

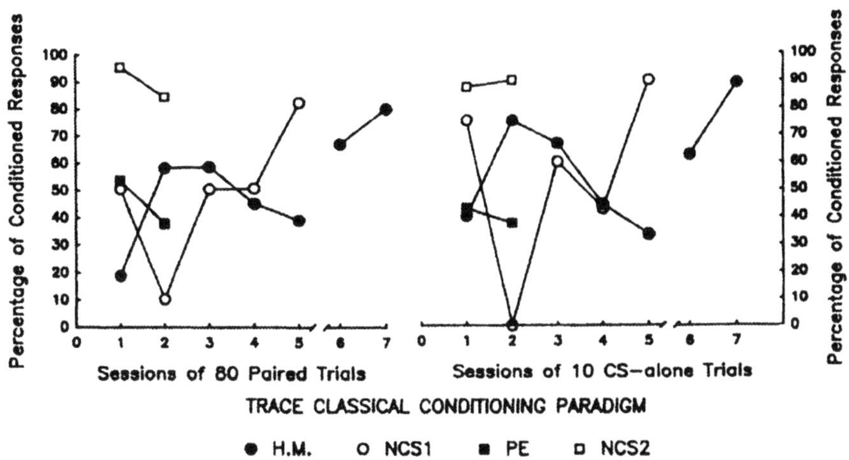

Figure 4. Percentage of conditioned responses for amnesics and control participants in the trace conditioning paradigm in Woodruff-Pak (1993) for paired conditioned stimulus-unconditioned stimulus trails (left panel) and conditioned stimulus alone trials (right panel). (From "Eyeblink classical conditioning in H.M.: Delay and trace paradigms," by D.S. Woodruff-Pak, 1993, *Behavioral Neuroscience, 107*, p.911-925. Copyright 1993 by the American Psychological Association. Reprinted with permission.)

To examine this issue further, we also conducted a trace eyeblink conditioning study with a group of seven amnesic individuals (McGlinchey-Berroth, Carrillo, Gabrieli, Brawn & Disterhoft, 1997). Four of the patients became amnesic as the result of an anoxic episode, two from encephalitis, and one from status epilepticus. CT or MRI in 5 of the 7 cases confirmed bilateral damage to the hippocampal formation. The remaining two cases had suffered anoxia and were presumed to have bilateral damage. The amnesic patients showed severe memory deficits in both the verbal and nonverbal domains as measured by the WMS-R and the Warrington Recognition Test, but had preserved intelligence and attention as revealed by the WAIS-R. All patients had been previously trained in a delay eyeblink conditioning task.

The CS in this study was an 85-dB, 1 kHz tone that was delivered binaurally over earphones for a period of 100 ms and was clearly audible to all subjects. The US was a 100 ms, corneal air puff delivered to the right eye. Trace interval was varied across three testing sessions and was either 500, 750, or 1000 ms in duration. Each subject participated in three conditioning sessions that were separated by at least two weeks. Each conditioning session consisted of 60 conditioning trials followed by 30 extinction trials in which the CS was presented alone.

The data from this study showed that patients with amnesia due to bilateral temporal lobe damage were significantly impaired in trace eyeblink conditioning. As shown in Figure 5, they were impaired relative to normal controls for each of the trace intervals.

The performances of these amnesics were compared to the baseline performances (during pseudoconditioning) in the Gabrieli et al. (1995) study. These comparisons revealed that the patients did acquire CRs above a baseline level in both the 500 and 750 ms conditions, but not in the 1000 ms condition. We suggested two possible accounts of the observed residual learning. First, as was suggested to account for the learning in the Woodruff-Pak study, performance may have been mediated by another memory system that underlied their performance in the delay conditioning task. Second, it is also possible that the residual learning reflects residual medial-temporal lobe memory function. This is supported by a comparison of the Solomon et al. (1986) data in which incomplete hippocampal lesions in rabbits produced an impairment in learning, and the Moyer et al. (1990) data in which more complete lesions eliminated acquisition all together. Also, we observed a change in the amnesics' peak CR latencies, which is a measure of each participant's ability to adaptively time the CR. On average, it was found that the amnesics' CRs peaked 50 ms earlier than the control participants. This deficit may be a more subtle manifestation of the alpha responses

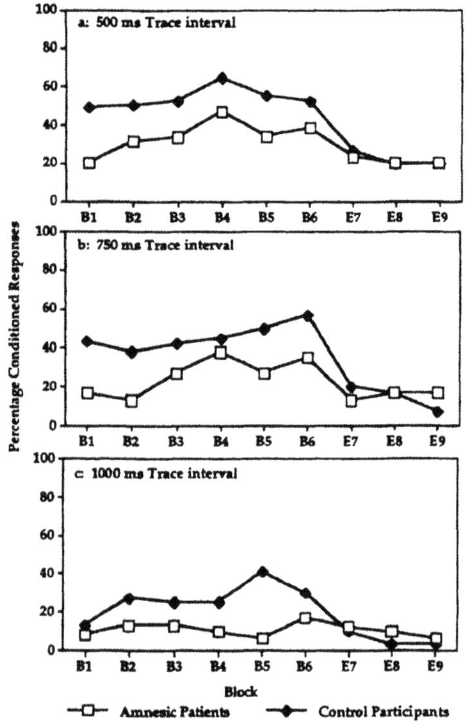

Figure 5. Mean percentage of conditioned responses in amnesic patients and control participants in trace eyeblink conditioning for the 500, 750 and 1000 ms trace intervals from McGlinchey-Berroth et al. (1997).

that have been observed in the rabbit. Additionally, McGlinchey-Berroth et al. (1997) did not observe an impairment in extinction, as has been reported in hippocampetomized rabbits (Moyer et al., 1990).

DISCRIMINATION LEARNING IN CLASSICAL EYEBLINK CONDITIONING

To summarize thus far, studies of classical eyeblink conditioning in human amnesics show that, like animals, the cerebellum is critical for learning basic CS-US associations, and that the temporal lobe memory system is critical for normal learning when the CS and the US are temporally separated. There also appear to be some interesting differences between humans and animals, primarily in the trace conditioning task. In this section, we will extend our review to examine how amnesics perform in more complex eyeblink conditioning tasks such as when there are two CSs that must be discriminated. This issue has been addressed in a number of studies that have used both the delay and the trace paradigms.

Daum and her colleagues have conducted a number of investigations examining discrimination learning in amnesia. Daum, Channon and Canavan (1989) tested three patients with severe memory disorders. Patient 1 had a history of epilepsy and alcoholism. EEG showed diffuse slowing over both hemispheres with discharging over left temporal and parietal regions, and from the anterior portion of the right temporal lobe. She was found to have low-average intelligence (WAIS-R verbal IQ = 88; performance IQ = 73), and was severely impaired for both verbal and nonverbal information after a delay. Patient 2 had suffered from encephalitis at 12 years of age. She, too, had low IQ scores (70 on both verbal and performance) and was severely amnesic based on the WMS delay measures, the Benton, and the Rey Figure. Patient 3 had suffered from epileptic seizures following febrile convulsions. CT indicated anterior hypoplasia of the right temporal lobe that was more severe than that found in the left temporal lobe. Patient 3 had a verbal IQ of 112 and a performance IQ of 70. He was severely impaired on the delay test of the Wechsler passages and on the delay test of the Rey Figure.

Patients were presented both reinforced and unreinforced trials based on a 2:1 schedule. On reinforced trials (S+), a light stimulus was presented for 6 s followed by a 1 s gap and an 800 ms, 1000 Hz, 80 dB tone. The tone was delivered binaurally over headphones. The US was an 80 ms air puff presented to the right eye that terminated with the tone. On unreinforced trials (S-), a different color light was presented followed by a 1 s gap and the same tone as on reinforced trials; there was no US delivered. The procedures differed slightly for the different patients. Patient 1 received 30 conditioning trials (20 reinforced, S+; 10 unreinforced, S-) in a repeating sequence of S+, S+, S-. Following an interview of the acquisition phase, Patient 1 then received 30 trials in which the S+ and S- were reversed. Following reversal, there was a series of extinction trials. Patients 2 and 3 received 24 reinforced (S+) trials and 12 unreinforced (S-) trials with the two trial types presented in random order. After an interview, they then received 36 reversal trials.

Collapsing across S+ and S- trials to examine overall CR acquisition, all patients showed a typical learning curve in which there was an increase in CRs across blocks of trials. These findings were taken to support the initial findings of Weiskrantz and Warrington (1979) and supported the notion of unimpaired eyeblink classical conditioning in amnesia within the context of a discrimination learning paradigm. Examination of S+ and S- trials separately revealed that during acquisition, each of the patients produced approximately the same number of CRs on both S+ and S- trials; they were not discriminating between the two trial types. The findings were similar for the discrimination reversal phase of the experiment. That is, the number of CRs was approximately equal between the S+ and the S- (with the latter being higher than the former). Extinction was observed in Patient 3, but not in Patients 1 or 2. Patient 3 was the only patient who was able to explicitly state the rule predicting reinforcement. Patient 1 and 2 had some knowledge of the different colored lights, but were unsure of the order of presentation of stimuli.

These findings suggest that while the acquisition of CRs was intact in these patients, discrimination learning and discrimination reversal were considerably impaired. The findings with regard to extinction were inconclusive. Unfortunately, because a control group was not included in this study, it was difficult to ascertain whether the acquisition (or extinction in Patient 3) was normal. A second study was thus conducted that included a control group to examine discriminative conditioning in patients with temporal lobe damage (Daum et al., 1991). Four groups of individuals participated in this study. Two groups had undergone unilateral temporal lobe resection; eight had right temporal resection and nine had left temporal resection. There were no neuropsychological data reported, so it is unclear as to the extent of these individuals' memory problems. A third group of six patients were tested who had undergone resection of frontal lobe tissue; there were three each of left and right resections. A fourth group was comprised of healthy volunteers who served as a control group.

As in the previous study, participants were presented with reinforced and unreinforced trials on a schedule of 2:1, with trials in the order of S+, S+, S-. The sequence of events for reinforced trials was: a 4 s signal light (S+), a 1 s gap, an 800 ms 1000 Hz, 65 dB tone CS, and an 80 ms air puff US that coterminated with the tone. The sequence of events for unreinforced trials was similar except that a different colored light signal was presented and there was no US.

CR frequencies were reported for each group broken out by reinforced and unreinforced trials. This analysis revealed that the percentage of CRs differed between these two trial types for the control subjects, with greater CRs during S+ trials than S- trials. This difference approached significance for the frontal resection group. In contrast, there was no significant difference in the percentage of CRs for reinforced and unreinforced trials for either the right or the left temporal lobectomy groups. Further analysis revealed that the four groups of patients did not differ in the percentage of CRs for S+ trials, but did differ significantly for S- trials. The left and right temporal groups showed higher rates of CRs for S- trials than either the frontal or the control group. With regard to awareness of stimulus contingencies, a post experimental interview indicated that all of the normal controls and all but one frontal patient was aware of the reinforcement rule. In contrast, only about half of the temporal lobectomy group could state the contingencies. To analyze possible differences between aware and unaware participants, the temporal lobectomy patients were divided based on their awareness. This analysis revealed that there was no difference in CR frequency between S+ and S- trials for those patients who were aware, but there were more CRs on S- trials than on S+ trials for those who were unaware.

In summary, the normal control subjects showed clear evidence of the acquisition of discriminative learning, as did the frontal lobectomy group but to a lesser extent. The temporal lobectomy groups, however, did not show evidence of discriminative responding to the S+ and the S-. The nature of this failure was that the temporal lobectomy patients generated an abnormally high number of CRs on S- trials. As noted by Daum et al. (1991), these findings are in accord with those from hippocampally lesioned rabbits in this paradigm (Ross, Orr, Holland & Berger, 1984). Another interesting aspect of the data was that even the aware temporal lobectomy patients were not able to show evidence of discriminative responding. Aware patients did not show a difference between S+ and S-, and the unaware patients actually showed a greater percentage of CRs on S- trials. Daum et al. speculated that this may have been due to the reinforcement schedule; that receiving two S+ trials consecutively may have made the unaware patients more likely to produce a CR on the subsequent S- trial. It was argued that the impairment in discrimination learning was not due to impaired trace conditioning, but rather due to deficits in configural cue learning (Sutherland & Rudy, 1989), impaired learning of if-then rules (Hirsh, 1974) or to a deficit in response inhibition, which has been observed in animals with hippocampal lesions (see Gray & McNaughton, 1983).

There are several aspects of the Daum et al. (1991) study that render the conclusions inconclusive with regard to the issue of discrimination learning in amnesia. First, the discrimination task itself was relatively complex. Recall that each conditioning trial began with an informative light after which a tone CS was presented followed (or not) by the US. A second issue is that the patients only had unilateral damage and it is unknown the extent of memory problems that existed in these individuals. Daum and her colleagues have subsequently conducted experiments to examine simple discrimination and reversal in unilateral temporal lobectomy patients (Daum, Channon & Gray, 1992) and bilateral amnesics (Daum, Breitenstein, Ackermann & Schugens, 1997; see Chapter 9, this volume).

Daum, Channon and Gray (Daum et al., 1992) tested 16 patients who had undergone either right (n = 8) or left (n = 8) temporal lobe resection. Their performance was compared to that of a control group consisting of 16 healthy volunteers. On a reinforced trial, a tone (CS+) was presented for 800 ms followed by an air puff US for 80 ms; the tone and the air puff terminated simultaneously. On an unreinforced trial, a tone (CS-) was presented alone. The schedule of reinforcement was 2:1. Participants also received a series of extinction trials in which participants received eight previously reinforced tones and four previously unreinforced tones.

The findings from this study were straightforward. There were no differences between the temporal lobectomy patients and control participants with regard to the first occurrence of a CR, nor did they differ in the percentage of CRs as a function of trial type. That is, the patients responded discriminatively to the CS+ and CS- to the same extent as the normal controls. In both groups there was a greater percentage of

CRs on CS+ trials than on CS- trials. There was also no difference between groups on extinction. Both showed a significant reduction in CRs during extinction compared to the final block of conditioning trials and, not surprisingly, there was a greater decrement in CRs for reinforced trials than for unreinforced trials. Daum et al. (1992) concluded that "temporal lobe lesions in man did not impair simple discrimination learning and extinction within a classical eyelid conditioning task" (p. 165). It thus appears that simple discrimination is spared, while conditional discrimination is impaired following unilateral temporal lobe lesions.

What of bilateral temporal lobe lesions and discrimination learning? This question was addressed in a later study by Daum, Breitenstein, Ackermann and Schugens (1997). Nine patients with amnesia due to either hippocampal or diencephalic damage and nine matched control participants were tested on a simple discrimination and discrimination reversal task. There was a 50-trial two-tone discrimination learning phase followed by a 50-trials two-tone reversal phase. The data revealed that, like the normal controls, amnesic patients produced a significantly greater percentage of CRs on CS+ trials than on CS- trials. During the reversal phase, however, the patients produced a similar percentage of CRs to both the CS+ and the CS- (unfortunately, it was not mentioned whether the diencephalic patients displayed the same pattern as the hippocampally damaged patients). Normal controls were able to reverse the discrimination. These data extend the previous findings of preserved simple discrimination learning to cases of bilateral medial temporal lobe or diencephalic damage and support the notion that the hippocampus is critical in more complex eyeblink conditioning paradigms such as when a learned discrimination must be reversed.

The finding of intact simple discrimination learning in amnesia does not extend to tasks in which there is a temporal separation between the CS and the US. Clark and Squire (1998; see also Chapter 11, this volume) have recently conducted an investigation of discrimination learning in amnesia using both a delay and trace paradigm. The performance of four severely amnesic patients was compared to group of 48 normal control participants on two delay conditioning tasks and two trace conditioning tasks (the amnesic patients participated in all tasks but subsets of the controls participated in only one task). Participants ranged in age from 59 to 78 (patients averaged 67.5 years; controls averaged 66.9 years). In one delay task, the CS was presented for 700 ms followed by a coterminating 100 ms US, in the second delay task, the CS was presented for 1250 ms followed by the coterminating 100 ms US. In one trace conditioning task, the CS was followed by a 500 ms blank period before US onset, in the second trace task, the CS was followed by a 1000 ms trace period. In each task, there were two CSs; on one-half of the trials the CS was paired with the US (CS+) and on one-half of the trials the CS was presented alone (CS-). There were 60 CS+ trials and 60 CS- trials. Participants also completed a true or false questionnaire following the conditioning session to evaluate their level of awareness of stimulus contingencies.

The findings from this study showed that the amnesic patients, none of whom displayed an awareness of the stimulus contingencies, acquired differential conditioning in both versions of the delay task, but were unable to acquire differential conditioning in either of the trace conditioning tasks. Further, only those control subjects who became aware of the stimulus contingencies showed differential conditioning in the trace conditioning task (a matter further discussed in Chapter 11, this volume). Awareness was not a factor in the normal controls for differential acquisition in the delay conditioning task. Interestingly, the reason for the failure to acquire differential responding was different depending on the trace interval. In the 1000 ms trace interval, amnesic patients and unaware controls failed to acquire CRs to the CS+, whereas in the 500 ms trace interval the failure was due to the more typical pattern of a high level of responding to the CS-. The failure of patients to acquire CRs at the 1000 ms interval is consistent with the McGlinchey-Berroth et al. (1997) finding that amnesic patients could not acquire CRs in a nondiscrimination trace conditioning task at that trace interval.

A final study examining discrimination learning in amnesia was conducted to assess a possible role of the hippocampal system in modulating the activity of the cerebellum (McGlinchey-Berroth, Brawn & Disterhoft, 1999). As has been reviewed in this chapter and in others in this series, the cerebellum is the structure critical for the development and retention of conditioned responses. The cerebellum is also critically involved in the timing of many aspects of cognition (see Schmahmann, 1997, for reviews). Perrett, Ruiz and Mauk (1993) addressed the possibility that the cerebellar cortex in particular is important in learning temporal associations. In that study rabbits were trained using two discriminable tone CSs that were individually associated with two different ISIs (Mauk & Ruiz, 1992). Both CSs signaled the same US. After the rabbits had learned the temporal discrimination (i.e., their CRs were appropriately timed as a function of the two CSs), they received aspiration lesions to the anterior lobe of the cerebellar cortex. After the lesions, the rabbits' CRs were no longer tied to the specific ISI; both CSs elicited similarly timed CRs that peaked at very short latencies.

While the cerebellar cortex does appear to be critical for learning temporal associations based on the findings from the Perrett et al. study, it is possible that the hippocampus and related structures may also play a role, given that these structures are involved in processing temporal information (Clark & Squire, 1998; McGlinchey-Berroth et al., 1997; Moyer et al., 1990; Solomon, 1979; Solomon et al., 1986; Woodruff-Pak, 1993). To test this possibility, we adapted the Perrett et al. task for use with our amnesic patients (McGlinchey-Berroth et al., 1999). This study included seven bilaterally damaged, medial temporal lobe amnesic patients and seven matched control subjects. There were two tone CSs. CS1 was an 85 dB, 1 kHz tone and CS2 was an 85 dB, 5 kHz tone. The tones were delivered binaurally over earphones and were presented for a total of either 450 ms or 850 ms. The US was a 100 ms, corneal air puff delivered to the right eye that coterminated with the CS.

Several findings from this study were informative with regard to a possible role of the hippocampal system in temporal discrimination learning. First, as shown in Figure 6, the peak latency of amnesic patients' CRs occurred significantly earlier than control participants in the 750 ms condition. Second, a similar trend was found in the onset latency measure. Third, amnesic patients produced significantly more short latency, nonadaptive CRs than control participants (compare to the findings from Woodruff-Pak (1993) and McGlinchey-Berroth (1997) who did not find a higher rate of alpha responses in the amnesic patients). Patients did not display such alterations in the 350

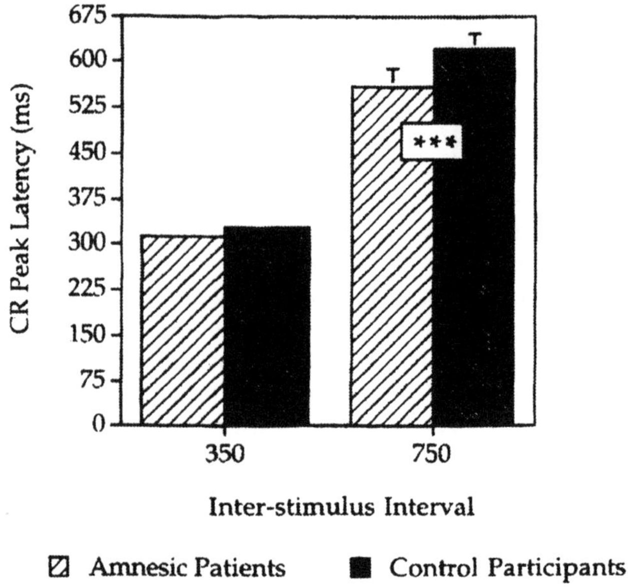

Figure 6. Mean conditioned response peak latency during temporal discrimination learning in amnesic patients and control participants from McGlinchey-Berroth et al. (1999).

ms ISI condition. It is important to note that the observed alterations in the amnesic patients were considerably more subtle than the changes observed by Perrett et al. following cerebellar cortex lesions. This difference suggests that the hippocampal system in humans may only modulate the expression of CRs that are generated by the cerebellum. McGlinchey-Berroth et al. speculated that this modulatory activity may help explain the activity observed in the hippocampus (or hippocampal system) during delay conditioning tasks in which the hippocampal activity is not critical for task performance (for example, in humans see Blaxton et al., 1996; Logan & Grafton, 1995). Fourth, patients did not show evidence of extinction in the 750 ms ISI condition; there was no difference in the percentage of CRs during conditioning trials compared to extinction trials. While such a finding has been documented in animal studies (Moyer et al., 1990), the current literature in humans has been inconclusive (Weiskrantz & Warrington, 1979) or ambiguous (Daum et al., 1989).

CONCLUSIONS

This chapter has reviewed the performance of amnesic individuals in eyeblink classical conditioning. In doing so, we have uncovered a number of findings that are in accord with the extensive animal literature, but we have also uncovered some very interesting differences that must be addressed in future work.

First is the issue of alpha or short latency responses. Hippocampally lesioned animals show a high rate of alpha responses in trace conditioning whereas bitemporal amnesics do not. In fact, Woodruff-Pak (1993) and McGlinchey-Berroth et al. (1997) found more alpha responses in the normal controls than in the amnesic patients (although the number was very small in both groups). In the McGlinchey-Berroth study, there was a slight alteration in the timing of CRs, such that they occurred significantly earlier than did controls, which may reflect a similar but more subtle deficit in humans than in rabbits. Only in the temporal discrimination task did the amnesic patients display a high rate of nonadaptive responses (McGlinchey-Berroth et al., 1999). One could speculate that alpha responses in humans only occur in highly complex tasks with a temporal component, but further work is obviously necessary to conclusively demonstrate under what conditions humans display alpha responses.

Another issue is that of extinction. The findings from the studies with amnesic humans are inconsistent and ambiguous. In Weiskrantz and Warrington (1979), one patient showed inconsistent extinction and one patient did not show extinction. Similarly in Daum, Channon and Canavan (Daum et al., 1989), one patient showed extinction (but there was not control group to evaluate whether it was normal), and two patients did not show extinction. Additionally, we have found intact extinction in simple delay conditioning (Gabrieli et al., 1995), but impaired extinction given a long ISI in a temporal discrimination task (McGlinchey-Berroth et al., 1999). Clearly the issue of extinction is highly complex and performance can vary between individuals within the same task parameters. Presently it is unclear whether such inconsistency is related to individual differences in lesion localization or size, or to factors specific to the conditioning paradigms (i.e., trace versus delay).

It would also be worthwhile to determine if the alterations in timing found in amnesic individuals would be similarly observed in hippocampally lesioned animals. Such an investigation would be beneficial in examining the possible modulatory role of the hippocampus in the temporal expression of CRs generated from the cerebellum.

In addition to these exciting differences between humans and animals, a great deal more can be learned from the study of eyeblink classical conditioning in bitemporal patients with amnesia. The examination of amnesic's performance on a number of additional classical conditioning paradigms would also yield important data regarding the correspondence of findings between species and provide additional insights for the refinement of more global theories of learning and memory.

REFERENCES

Akase, E., Alkon, D.L., & Disterhoft, J.F. (1989). Hippocampal lesions impair memory of short-delay conditioned eye blink in rabbits. *Behavioral Neuroscience, 103*(5), 935-943.

Bauer, R.M., Tobias, B., & Valenstein, E. (1993). Amnesic Disorders. In K.M. Heilman & E. Valenstein (Eds.). *Clinical Neuropsychology,* (3rd ed., pp. 523-602). New York: Oxford Press.

Berger, T., & Orr, W.B. (1983). Hippocampectomy selectively disrupts discrimination reversal conditioning of the rabbit nictitating membrane response. *Behavioral Brain Research, 8*, 49-68.

Blaxton, T.A., Zeffiro, T.A., Gabrieli, J.D.E., Bookheimer, S.Y., Carrillo, M.C., Theordore, W.H.,& Disterhoft, J.F. 1996). Functional mapping of human learning: A positron emission tomography activation study of eyeblink conditioning. *The Journal of Neuroscience, 16(12)*, 4032-4040.

Charness, N., Milberg, W., & Alexander, M.P. (1988). Teaching an amnesic a complex cognitive skill. *Brain and Cognition, 8(2)*, 253-272.

Clark, G.A., McCormick, D.A., Lavond, D.G., & Thompson, R.F. (1984). Effects of lesions of cerebellar nuclei on conditioned behavioral and hippocampal neuronal responses. *Brain Research, 291*, 125-136.

Clark, R.E., & Squire, L.R. (1998). Classical conditioning and brain systems? The role of awareness. *Science, 280*, 77-81.

Cohen, J.J., & Eichenbaum, H. (1993). *Memory, Amnesia, and the Hippocampal System.* Cambridge, MA: The MIT Press.

Cohen, N.J., & Squire, L.R. (1980). Preserved learning and retention of pattern-analyzing skill in amnesia: Dissociation of knowing how and knowing that. *Science, 210*, 207-210.

Corkin, S. (1968). Acquisition of motor skills after bilateral medial temporal-lobe excision. *Neuropsychologia, 6*, 255-265.

Daum, I., & Ackermann, H. (1994). Dissociation of declarative and nondeclarative memory after bilateral thalamic lesions: A case report. *International Journal of Neuroscience, 75*, 153-165.

Daum, I., Breitenstein, C., Ackermann, H., & Schugens, M.M. (1997). Impairment of eyeblink discrimination reversal learning in amnesia. *Society for Neuroscience Abstracts, 23(1)*, 207.

Daum, I., Channon, S., & Canavan, A.G.M. (1989). Classical conditioning in patients with severe memory problems. *Journal of Neurology, Neurosurgery, and Psychiatry, 52*, 47-51.

Daum, I., Channon, S., & Gray, J.A. (1992). Classical conditioning after temporal lobe lesions in man: Sparing of simple discrimination and extinction. *Behavioral Brain Research, 52*, 159-165.

Daum, I., Channon, S., Polkey, C.E., & Gray, J.A. (1991). Classical conditioning after temporal lobe lesions in man: Impairment in conditional discrimination. *Behavioral Neuroscience, 105*, 396-408.

Daum, I., Schugens, M., Ackermann, H., Lutzenberger, W., Dichgans, J., & Birbaumer, N. (1993). Classical conditioning after cerebellar lesions in humans. *Behavioral Neuroscience, 107*, 748-756.

Daum, I., & Schugens, M.M. (1996). On the cerebellum and classical conditioning. *Current Directions in Psychological Science, 5(2)*, 58-61.

Eichenbaum, H., Otto, T., & Cohen, N.J. (1992). The hippocampus-What does it do? *Behavioral and Neural Biology, 57*, 2-36.

Gabrieli, J D.E., Corkin, S., Mickel, S.F., & Growdon, J.H. (1993). Intact acquisition and long-term retention of mirror-tracing skill in Alzheimer's disease and in global amnesia. *Behavioral Neuroscience, 107*, 899-910.

Gabrieli, J.D.E., Keane, M.M., Zarella, M.M., & Poldrack, R.A. (1997). Preservation of implicit memory for new associations in global amnesia. *Psychological Science, 8(4)*, 326-329.

Gabrieli, J.D.E., McGlinchey-Berroth, R., Carrillo, M.C., Gluck, M.A., Cermak, L.S., & Disterhoft, J.F. (1995). Intact delay-eyeblink classical conditioning in amnesia. *Behavioral Neuroscience, 109*, 819-827.

Gabrieli, J.D.E., Milberg, W., Keane, M.M., & Corkin, S. (1990). Intact priming of patterns despite impaired memory. *Neuropsychologia, 28(5)*, 417-427.

Graf, P., & Schacter, D.L. (1985). Implicit and explicit memory for new associations in normal and amnesic subjects. *Journal of Experimental Psychology: Learning, Memory and Cognition, 11*, 501-518.

Gray, J.A., & McNaughton, N. (1983). Comparison between the behavioral effects of septal and hippocampal lesions: A review. *Neuroscience and Biobehavioral Reviews, 9*, 119-188.

Hamann, S.B., Squire, L.R., & Schacter, D.L. (1995). Perceptual thresholds and priming in amnesia. *Neuropsychology, 9(1)*, 3-15.

Harper, C. (1982). Neuropathology of brain damage caused by alcohol. *The Medical Journal of Australia, 2*, 277-282.

Harper, C.G., & Kril, J.J. (1990). Neuropathology of alcoholism. *Alcohol & Alcoholism, 25*, 207-216.

Hirsh, R. (1974). The hippocampus and contextual retrieval of information from memory: A theory. *Behavioral Biology, 12*, 421-444.

James, G.O., Hardiman, M.J., & Yeo, C.H. (1987). Hippocampal lesions and trace conditioning in the rabbit. *Behavioural Brain Research, 23*, 109-116.

Jernigan, T.L., Butters, N., DiTraglia, G. Schafer, K., Smith, T., Irwin, M., Grant, I., Schuckit, M., & Cermak, L. (1991). Reduced cerebral grey matter observed in alcoholics using magnetic resonance imaging. *Alcoholism: Clinical and Experiment Research, 15*, 418-427.

Keane, M.M., Gabrieli, J.D.E., Noland, J.S., & McNealy, S.I. (1995). Normal perceptual priming of orthographically illegal nonwords in amnesia. *Journal of the International Neuropsychological*

Society, 1, 425-433.

Lavond, D.G., Hembree, T.L., & Thompson, R.F. (1985). Effect of kainic acid lesions of the cerebellar interpositus nucleus on eyelid conditioning in the rabbit. *Brain Research, 326*, 179-182.

Lavond, D.G., Lincoln, J.C., McCormick, D.A., & Thompson, R.F. (1984). Effect of bilateral lesions of the dentate and interpositus cerebellar nuclei on conditioning of heart rate and nictitating membrane eyelid responses in the rabbit. *Brain Research, 305*, 323-330.

Lavond, D.G., McCormick, D.A., Clark, G.A., Holmes, D.T., & Thompson, R.F. (1981). Effects of ipsilateral rostral pontine recticular lesions on retention of classically conditioned nictitating membrane and eyelid responses. *Physiological Psychology, 9*, 335-339.

Lincoln, J.S., McCormick, D.A., & Thompson, R.F. (1982). Ipsilateral cerebellar lesions prevent learning of the classically conditioned nictitating membrane/eyelid response. *Brain Research, 242*, 190-193.

Logan, C.G., & Grafton, S.T. (1995). Functional anatomy of human eyeblink conditioning determined with regional cerebral glucose metabolism and positron emission tomography. *Proceedings of the National Academy of Science, (USA), 92*, 7500-7504.

Lye, R.H., O'Boyle, D.J., Ramsden, R.T., & Schady, W. (1988). Effects of a unilateral cerebellar lesion in the acquisition of eye-blink conditioning in man. *Journal of Physiology, 403*, 58.

Mauk, M.D., & Ruiz, B.P. (1992). Learning-dependent timing of Pavlovian eyelid responses: Differential conditioning using multiple interstimulus intervals. *Behavioral Neuroscience, 106*, 666-681.

McCormick, D.A., Clark, G.A., Lavond, D.G., & Thompson, R.F. (1982a). Inital localization of the memory trace for a basic form of learning. *Proceedings of the National Academy of Sciences, 79*, 2731-2742.

McCormick, D.A., Guyer, P.E., & Thompson, R.F. (1982b). Superior cerebellar peduncle lesions selectively abolish the ipsilateral classically conditioned nictitating membrane/eyelid response of the rabbit. *Brain Research, 244*, 347-350.

McCormick, D.A., Lavond, D.G., Clark, G.A., Kettner, R.E., Rising, C.E., & Thompson, R.F. (1981). The engram found?: Role of the cerebellum in classical conditioning of nictitating membrane and eyelid responses. *Bulletin of the Psychonomic Society, 18*, 103-105.

McCormick, D.A., & Thompson, R.F. (1984a). Cerebellum: Essential involvement in the classically conditioned eyelid response. *Science, 223*, 296-223.

McCormick, D.A., & Thompson, R.F. (1984b). Neuronal responses of the rabbit cerebellum during acquisition and performance of a classically conditioned nictitating membrane-eyelid response. *Journal of Neuroscience, 4*, 2811-2822.

McGlinchey-Berroth, R., Brawn, C., & Disterhoft, J.F. (1999). Temporal discrimination learning in severe amnesics reveals an alteration in the timing of eyeblink conditioned responses. *Behavioral Neuroscience, 113(1)*, 10-18.

McGlinchey-Berroth, R., Carrillo, M.C., Gabrieli, J.D.E., Brawn, C.M., & Disterhoft, J.F. (1997). Impaired trace eyeblink conditioning in bilateral medial temporal lobe amnesia. *Behavioral Neuroscience, 111*, 873-882.

McGlinchey-Berroth, R., Cermak, L.S., Carrillo, M., Armfield, S., Gabrieli, J.D.E., & Disterhoft, J.F. (1995). Impaired delay eyeblink conditioning in amnesic Korsakoff's patients and recovered alcoholics. *Alcoholism: Clinical and Experimental Research, 19(5)*, 1127-1132.

Milner, B., Corkin, S., & Teuber, H.L. (1968). Further analysis of the hippocampal amnesia syndrome: 14 year follow-up study of H. M. *Neuropsychologia, 6*, 215-234.

Moyer, J.R., Deyo, R.A., & Disterhoft, J.F. (1990). Hippocampectomy disrupts trace eye-blink conditioning in rabbits. *Behavioral Neuroscience, 104*, 243-252.

Musen, G., & Squire, L.R. (1992). Nonverbal priming in amnesia. *Memory and Cognition, 20(4)*, 441-448.

Orr, W.B., & Berger, T.W. (1985). Hippocampectomy disrupts the topography of conditioned nictitating membrane responses during reversal learning. *Behavioral Neuroscience, 99*, 35-45.

Pavlov, I.P. (1927). *Conditioned Reflexes (translated by G.V. Anrep)*. London and New York: Oxford University Press.

Port, R.L., Romano, A.G., Steinmetz, J.E., Mikhail, A.A., & Patterson, M.M. (1986). Retention and acquisition of classical trace-conditioned responses by rabbits with hippocampal lesions. *Behavioral Neuroscience, 100*, 745-752.

Ross, R.T., Orr, W.B., Holland, P.C., & Berger, T.W. (1984). Hippocampectomy disrupts acquisition and retention of learned conditioning and responding. *Behavioral Neuroscience, 98*, 211-225.

Schacter, D.L., & Church, B. (1995). Implicit memory in amnesic patients: When is auditory priming spared? *Journal of the International Neuropsychological Society, 1*, 434-442.

Schmahmann, J.D. (1997). *The Cerebellum and Cognition*. Academic Press.
Schmaltz, L.W., & Theios, J. (1972). Acquisition and extinction of a classically conditioned response in hippocampectomized rabbit (oryctolagus cuniculus). *Journal of Comparative and Physiological Psychology, 79*, 328-333.
Solomon, P.R. (1979). Temporal versus spatial information processing theories of hippocampal function. *Psychological Bulletin, 86*, 1272.
Solomon, P.R., Brett, M., Groccia-Ellison, M.E., & Oyler, C. (1995). Classical conditioning in patients with Alzheimer's Disease: A multiday study. *Psychology and Aging, 10(2)*, 248-254.
Solomon, P.R., Levine, E., Bein, T., & Pendlebury, W.W. (1991). Disruption of classical conditioning in patients with Alzheimer's Disease. *Neurobiology, 12*, 283-287.
Solomon, P.R., & Moore, J.W. (1975). Latent inhibition and stimulus generalization of the classically conditioned nictitating membrane response in rabbits (oryctolagus cuniculus) following dorsal hippocampal ablation. *Journal of Comparative and Physiological Psychology, 89*, 1192-1203.
Solomon, P.R., Stowe, G.T., & Pendlebury, W.P. (1989). Disrupted eyelid conditioning in a patient with damage to the cerebellar afferents. *Behavioral Neuroscience, 103*, 898-902.
Solomon, P.R., Vander Schaaf, E.R., Norbe, A.C., Weisz, D.J., & Thompson, R.F. (1986). Hippocampus and trace conditioning of the rabbit's nictitating membrane response. *Behavioral Neuroscience, 100*, 729-744.
Squire, L. (1987). *Memory and brain*. New York: Oxford University Press.
Steinmetz, J.E., Lavond, D.G., Ivkovich, D., Logan, C.F., & Thompson, R.F. (1992). Disruption of classical eyelid conditioning after cerebellar lesions: Damage to a memory trace system or a simple performance deficit? *Journal of Neuroscience, 12*, 4403-4426.
Sutherland, R.J., & Rudy, J.W. (1989). Configural association theory: The role of the hippocampal formation in learning, memory, and amnesia. *Psychobiology, 17*, 129-144.
Thompson, R.F. (1986). The neurobiology of learning and memory. *Science, 233*, 941-947.
Thompson, R.F., McCormick, D.A., Lavond, D.G., Clark, G.A., Kettner, R.E., & Mauk, M.D. (1983). The engram found? Inital localization of the memory trace for a basic form of associative learning. *Progress in Psychobiology and Physiological Psychology, 10*, 167-196.
Topka, H., Valls-Sole, J., Massaquoi, S.G., & Hallett, M. (1993). Deficit in classical conditioning in patients with cerebellar degeneration. *Brain, 116*, 961-969.
Torvik, A. (1985). Two types of lesions in Wernicke's encephalopathy. *Neuropathology and Applied Neurobiology, 11*, 179-190.
Torvik, A., Lindboe, C.F., & Rodge, S. (1982). Brain lesions in alcoholics. A neuropatholgical study with clinical correlations. *Journal of the Neurological Sciences, 75*, 233-248.
Warrington, E.K. (1984). *Recognition Memory Test*. Windsor: United Kingdom: NFER-Nelson.
Warrington, E.K., & Weiskrantz, L. (1968). A new method of testing long-term retention with special reference to amnesic patients. *Nature, 217*, 972-974.
Warrington, E.K., & Weiskrantz, L. (1970). The amnesic syndrome: Consolidation or retrieval? *Nature, 228*, 628-630.
Wechsler, D. (1987). *Wechsler Memory Scale-Revised (manual)*. New York: Psychological Corporation.
Weiskrantz, L., & Warrington, E.K. (1979). Conditioning in Amnesic Patients. *Neuropsychologia, 17*, 187-194.
Wickelgren, W.A. (1979). Chunking and consolidation: A theortecal synthesis of semantic networks, configuring in conditioning, S-R versus cognitive learning, normal forgetting, the amneisc syndrome and the hippocampus arousal system. *Psychological Review, 86*, 44-60.
Woodruff-Pak. (1996). Huntington's disease and eyeblink classical conditioning: Normal learning but abnormal timing. *Journal of the International Neuropsychological Society, 2(4)*, 323-334.
Woodruff-Pak, D.S. (1993). Eyeblink classical conditioning in H.M.: Delay and trace paradigms. *Behavioral Neuroscience, 107*, 911-925.
Woodruff-Pak, D.S., Finkbiner, R.G., & Sasse, D.K. (1990). Eyeblink conditioning discriminates Alzheimer's patients from non-demented aged. *Clinical Neuroscience and Neuropathology, 1*, 45-49.
Woodruff-Pak, D.S., Lavond, D.G., & Thompson, R.F. (1985). Trace conditioning: Abolished by cerebellar nuclear lesions but not lateral cerebellar cortex aspirations. *Brain Research, 348*, 249-260.
Woodruff-Pak, D.S., Papka, M., & Ivry, R.B. (1996a). Cerebellar involvement in eyeblink classical conditioning in humans. *Neuropsychology, 10*, 443-458.
Woodruff-Pak, D.S., Papka, M., Romano, S., & Li, Y.T. (1996b). Eyeblink classical conditioning in Alzheimer's disease and cerebrovascular dementia. *Neurobiology of Aging, 17(4)*, 505-512.
Yeo, C.H., Hardiman, M.J., & Glickstein, M. (1985). Classical conditioning of the nictitating membrane

response of the rabbit: II. Lesions of the cerebellar cortex. *Experimental Brain Research, 60*, 99-113.
Yeo, C.H., Hardiman, M.J., Moore, J.W., & Russell, I.S. (1984). Trace conditioning of the nictitating membrane resonse in decorticate rabbits. *Behavioural Brain Research, 11*, 85-88.

11 AWARENESS AND THE CONDITIONED EYEBLINK RESPONSE

Robert E. Clark and Larry R. Squire
University of California, San Diego

INTRODUCTION

In 1973, a symposium entitled "Classical Conditioning and the Cognitive Processes" was organized by Russell Lockhart and a series of papers were published in the journal *Psychophysiology*. The lead paper, "Cognitive factors in eyelid conditioning" was presented by David Grant, an expert in human classical conditioning. He began his paper with the following comment, "By organizing a symposium on classical conditioning and the cognitive processes, Dr. Lockhart invited the participants to fish in very deep waters (Grant, 1973, p. 75)." Grant chose this phrase because he felt that while cognition is certainly involved in eyeblink conditioning, participants accurately (or inaccurately) report all sorts of ideation, which can change over the course of a conditioning session. Determining how such cognition affects behavior seems a complex and almost intractable task. As we attempt here to address the role of awareness in human eyeblink conditioning, Grant's comment on fishing in very deep waters seems as apropos now as it was more than a quarter of a century ago. Here we describe our efforts to relate awareness to the conditioned eyeblink response and to interpret this relationship within a framework of brain memory systems. Finally, we address some of the problems that confront researchers working in this arena.

Classical conditioning of the eyeblink response, be it in rodents, rabbits, monkeys, or humans, has been categorized as an example of nondeclarative learning, that is, a type of learning and memory that is nonconscious and automatic. In fact, classical conditioning can be viewed as a quintessential example of nondeclarative learning because acquisition of the response can be acquired normally even if the subject is unaware of learning the response (Weiskrantz & Warrington, 1979; Papka, Ivry & Woodruff-Pak, 1997). Indeed, the fact that learning can occur automatically and outside of awareness is a primary reason for the widespread use of this paradigm. Classical conditioning provides a methodological platform for establishing and testing theories of basic associative learning and the variables that influence these processes (e.g. Martin & Levey, 1969). This powerful paradigm is strengthened by the oftentimes close correspondence that can be observed between findings from humans and findings from experimental non-human animals (e.g., Woodruff-Pak & Thompson, 1988).

A particular advantage of human studies is that, in addition to studying these basic associative learning processes, which are evidenced through careful examination of the response characteristics and learning curves of the conditioned eyeblink response, researchers are also able to ask humans what they learned or thought they learned during the conditioning session. Yet, at the same time, work with humans is, in a sense, a double-edged sword. With humans, there are many potentially complicating variables (language mediation, differences in intelligence, personality, and arousal/anxiety, as well as the ability to voluntarily control eyeblinks), variables that can influence or (depending on one's perspective) contaminate the analysis of the conditioned eyeblink response. Many experimentalists in human eyeblink conditioning working in the 1950s through the late 1970s, tried to ignore or eliminate these variables (e.g., Spence, 1966). However, Leonard Ross, an important contributor to the human eyeblink literature, believed that the active involvement of the human subject in the conditioning experiment could not be ignored or eliminated and must be considered and evaluated. In other words, as he eloquently stated:, "[the human subject must be recognized] as something more than a passive appendage of a conditionable eyelid" (Ross, 1965, p. 250).

In our laboratory, we have heeded Ross's admonition and begun a program to examine how a subject's knowledge of the causal fabric of the conditioning session, i.e., awareness that the conditioned stimulus (CS) predicts the occurrence of the unconditioned stimulus (US), influences performance under different conditioning protocols. This type of knowledge or awareness is a hallmark of declarative memory and could provide insight into how declarative memory works together with other memory systems of the brain to form the conditioned response.

We first summarize our recent findings regarding human eyeblink classical conditioning and the conscious knowledge that is developed during conditioning. Then we suggest how these findings might be interpreted in terms of the memory systems of the brain. We conclude with a discussion of several difficulties that arise in trying to relate awareness to conditioning performance; as well as more general methodological concerns that arise in the context of human eyeblink conditioning.

BACKGROUND

Memory is composed of several different abilities that depend on different brain systems (Squire, 1992). Declarative memory provides the capacity for conscious recollection of facts and events. Nondeclarative memory is inaccessible to conscious recollection but is expressed through performance as skills, habits, and certain forms of classical conditioning. Simple delay classical conditioning of the eyeblink response is a well-studied example of nondeclarative memory. In delay classical conditioning, the CS is presented and remains on until the US is presented. The two stimuli overlap and coterminate. Studies in the rabbit have shown that the cerebellum is essential for delay conditioning and that no other forebrain structure, including the hippocampus, is required (Thompson & Krupa, 1994).

In trace classical conditioning, the CS is presented and terminated. A silent or trace interval then follows before the presentation of the US. An interesting feature of trace eyeblink conditioning is that acquisition and retention of the conditioned response (CR) is severely disrupted in rabbits when the dorsal and ventral hippocampus is damaged conjointly (Kim, Clark & Thompson, 1995; Moyer, Deyo, & Disterhoft, 1990). When only the dorsal hippocampus is damaged, the impairment is less severe and primarily affects onset latencies (James, Hardiman & Yeo, 1987; Port, Romano, Steinmetz, Mikhail & Patterson, 1986; Solomon, Vander Schaaf, Thompson & Weisz, 1986). In the first study to examine trace conditioning in humans with hippocampal damage, normal trace conditioning was observed with a 500 ms trace interval (Woodruff-Pak, 1993). In a more recent study, humans with hippocampal damage showed no acquisition with a 1000 ms trace interval, whereas some acquisition occurred with a 500 ms trace interval (McGlinchey-Berroth, Carrillo, Gabrieli, Brawn & Disterhoft, 1997). These data suggest that the hippocampus is critical for trace conditioning (with sufficient lesion size and trace interval). Studies in rats, monkeys, and humans indicate that the hippocampus is also a critical structure for the establishment of declarative memory (Squire, 1992). Perhaps declarative memory impairment, which follows damage to the hippocampus, is related to the impairment observed in trace conditioning. Thus, an important question is why normal trace conditioning requires the hippocampus and why trace conditioning might involve declarative memory.

We reasoned that trace conditioning might differ from delay conditioning by requiring knowledge or awareness of the CS-US relationship to build up and be remembered across many trials. We adopted a two-part approach to examine this possibility. First, we tested healthy adult participants and assessed how their awareness of the CS-US relationship related to their performance in different conditioning protocols; and second, we tested amnesic patients with damage to the hippocampus. We reasoned that this group would have great difficulty in developing knowledge of the CS-US relationship and would also have difficulty with trace conditioning.

The basic design of our initial experiments was to classically condition the eyeblink response in amnesic patients and healthy volunteers and then, following conditioning, to assess with a post-conditioning questionnaire how much awareness they had about the CS-US relationship. Finally, we asked how awareness related to classically conditioned eyeblink performance. Because, as noted above, delay conditioning had been found to be independent of the hippocampus, and trace conditioning appears to be hippocampus dependent, we were particularly interested in determining how knowledge or awareness of the CS-US relationship related to both delay and trace conditioning.

AWARENESS AND TRACE OR DELAY DIFFERENTIAL CONDITIONING

In the experiments we describe here, we assessed awareness of the stimulus contingencies in both trace and delay differential classical conditioning. In the first set of experiments, awareness was a dependent variable. That is, awareness was simply measured after the conditioning session. In the second set of experiments, we attempted to make awareness an independent variable by directly manipulating it before and during the conditioning sessions.

Awareness as a Dependent Variable

We tested four amnesic patients (three men and one woman) with bilateral damage to the hippocampal formation (confirmed by magnetic resonance imaging for three of the four patients). These patients (mean age = 67.5 years and 15.6 years of education) have been tested extensively in our laboratory over the years and have severe deficits in declarative memory (Reed & Squire, 1997). We also tested 48 normal volunteers who were age and education matched to the amnesic patients.

Differential Conditioning

In our experiments we used differential conditioning. Most studies of eyeblink conditioning in both humans and animals have used a single-cue paradigm. In single-cue conditioning, a single CS is paired with the US. In other words, only one discrete CS is presented, and this CS predicts the occurrence of the US. In differential conditioning, two different CSs are presented. These CSs can be in the same modality (e.g., two tones of different frequencies) or in different modalities (e.g., a tone and a light). When differential conditioning is used, one of the CSs always precedes and predicts the US. This CS is termed the positive CS or the CS^+. The other CS is not predictive of the US and occurs alone. This CS is termed the negative CS or the CS^-. In single-cue conditioning, acquisition is reflected as an increased probability of responding to the CS during the course of training. In contrast, for differential conditioning, acquisition reflects a greater probability of responding to the CS^+ than to the CS^-. Differential conditioning is often expressed as the percentage of CRs to the CS^+ minus the percentage of CRs to the CS^-. This difference then describes the level of differential conditioning. We used differential conditioning for several reasons (that we elaborate later in this chapter). Perhaps the most important reason was that differential conditioning provides the possibility of assessing knowledge about a greater number of relationships than single-cue conditioning (e.g., the CS^+ predicts the US, the CS^- predicts the omission of the US, the CS^+ and CS^- are unrelated, etc.).

The Delay and Trace Paradigms

We used two differential delay conditioning procedures and two differential trace conditioning procedures (Figure 1). As noted above, one difference between trace and delay conditioning is that in delay conditioning the CS and US overlap; in trace conditioning, there is silent or trace interval between the offset of the CS and the onset of the US. A second difference is that the trace interval between the CS and the US increases the interval between the onset of the CS and the onset of the US. This interval is termed the inter-stimulus-interval (ISI). Because simply changing the ISI within single-cue delay conditioning influences the acquisition of the CR (e.g. Kimble, 1947; Solomon, Blanchard, Levine, Velazquez & Groccia-Ellison, 1991), it was necessary to control for the possibility that differences observed between delay and trace conditioning were due to the long ISI, not the trace interval itself. Accordingly, we used two versions of delay conditioning and two versions of trace conditioning. Each version of delay conditioning involved an ISI that matched one of the versions of trace conditioning (Figure 1).

For delay conditioning, the CS was presented for 700 ms before the presentation of a 100 ms US (Delay 700, $n = 12$), or the CS was presented for 1250 ms before US onset (Delay 1250, $n = 10$). In both versions of delay conditioning, the CS and US overlapped and coterminated. For trace conditioning, a CS was presented for 250 ms, and then a 500 ms trace interval (Trace 500, $n = 12$) or a 1000 ms trace interval (Trace 1000, $n = 14$) intervened before presentation of the US. Each normal volunteer was tested on only one of these four versions of classical conditioning. The amnesic patients were given Trace 1000 conditioning first and then 6-35 days later were given Delay 1250 conditioning.

Figure 1. Icons representing two versions of delay (A and B) and two versions of trace (C and D) conditioning. Numbers represent time in milliseconds.

Procedures for the Conditioning Session

Participants were told that they were participating in a study of how distraction affects learning and memory, and that they would view a silent movie while being distracted by tones, static noise (white noise), and airpuffs. After giving informed consent, participants were seated in a comfortable chair in a darkened room, 0.7 m from a television monitor, and shown "After the Gold Rush," which they were asked to remember for a later test. Presentation of a silent movie during the conditioning trials is standard practice in recent studies of human eyeblink conditioning.

Participants were then fitted with a pair of headphones which were used to deliver the CSs. The CSs were an 85 dB, 1 KHz tone and an 85 dB burst of white noise. A pair of modified sunglasses held a nozzle for delivering the US (a 3 psi air puff to the left eye) and also held an infrared phototransistor for measuring the eyeblink. The phototransistor emitted an infrared beam and measured the amount of beam reflected back. When the eye is completely open, most of the infrared beam is absorbed by the pupil. When the eyelid closes across the cornea, more of the beam is reflected back to the sensor. As a result, a graded voltage change occurs at the phototransistor's output, which essentially transduces an eyeblink response into an electrical signal. This signal is relayed into a computer for storage and analysis (see Clark & Zola, 1998, for more hardware details).

During the movie, 120 conditioning trials occurred at an ITI of 10-15 sec. Each 20-trial block consisted of 10 CS+ trials and 10 CS- trials. The order of the CS+ and CS- trials was random, except that neither trial type occurred more than twice consecutively. Each stimulus served equally often as CS+ and CS- within each subject group. For the amnesic patients, the CS+ and CS- were reversed for the second conditioning session.

Immediately after conditioning, participants took a true/false test that asked about the content of the movie and other aspects of the conditioning session. Figure 2 shows for each group the average number of correct responses out of 10 questions that were asked about the silent movie. As expected, the controls had little difficulty with these questions, whereas the amnesic patients failed to score above chance. The critical questions were 17 additional items concerning the temporal relationships between the CS^+, the CS^- and the US. These questions progressed from general to more specific (e.g., True or False; I believe the air puff usually came immediately before the tone; I believe the tone usually came immediately before the static noise; I believe the static noise and air puff were always closely related in time; I believe the tone predicted when the air puff would come). Participants responded to the test items in a fixed order and were not permitted to change earlier answers.

Scoring the Awareness Questionnaire

To determine if participants were aware of the CS^+, CS^- and US relationships, we asked whether they scored significantly better than chance on the questions that asked about the temporal relationships between the stimuli. This calculation was based on the binomial probability distribution, indicating that correctly answering 13 of 17 true/false questions by chance would occur only 5% of the time (i.e., $p = .05$). Thus, if an individual scored 13 or higher, we could say with 95% confidence that this individual had some awareness of the stimulus contingencies. Accordingly, individuals scoring 13 or higher were designated as aware of the relationships among the stimuli, and individuals who did not score significantly above chance (< 13 test items correct out of 17) were designated as unaware. Figure 3 shows for each group the average number of correct responses out of 17 for those designated as aware and unaware of the stimulus contingencies.

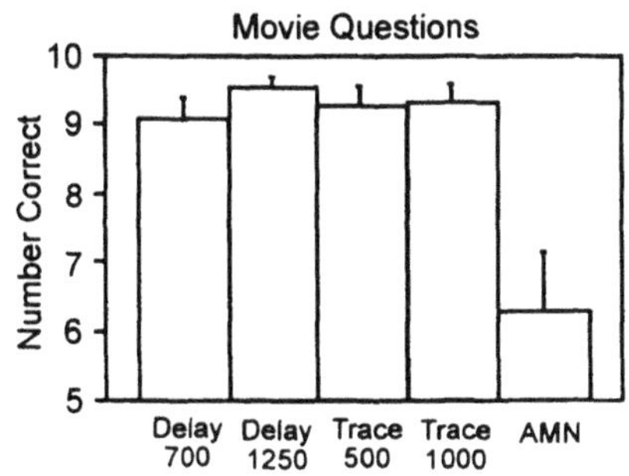

Figure 2. Number of correct responses to 10 true/false questions about the content of the silent movie that participants watched during the conditioning procedure.

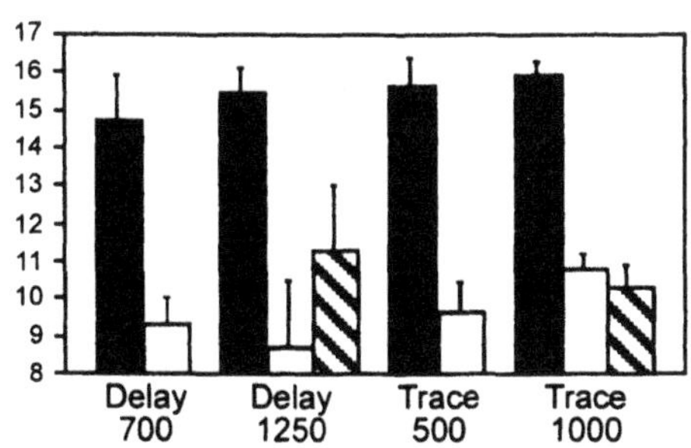

Figure 3. Number of correct responses to 17 true/false questions about the temporal relationships between the CS+, CS-, and the US. The black bars are the scores of controls who were aware of the CS-US relationship, the white bars are the scores of controls who were unaware of the CS-US relationship, and the hatched bars are the scores for four amnesic patients.

Acquisition of Classical Eyeblink Conditioning

We next compared the acquisition of classical eyeblink conditioning for the aware and unaware groups on each version of the task. Knowledge of the stimulus contingencies was not related to performance on either version of delay conditioning (Figure 4). Normal volunteers acquired delay conditioning whether they were knowledgeable about the CS-US associations or not. The amnesic patients also acquired delay conditioning and were indistinguishable from the normal volunteers.

In contrast to the results for delay conditioning, knowledge of the stimulus contingencies was a crucial factor in both versions of trace conditioning. Individuals who developed knowledge of the CS-US associations performed significantly better than those who failed to develop knowledge of the stimulus contingencies (Figure 5). Interestingly, unaware individuals in the Trace 500 group failed to show differential conditioning because of sustained high rates of responding to the CS^-. This finding indicated that even unaware individuals in the Trace 500 group could exhibit high rates of CRs; however, they failed to develop discriminative CRs (i.e., more CRs in response to the CS^+ than CRs to the CS^-). In contrast, unaware individuals in the Trace 1000 group failed to exhibit a significant number of CRs to either the CS^+ or the CS^-. That is, unaware individuals in the Trace 1000 group failed to demonstrate any acquisition at all. Finally, the amnesic patients, none of whom became aware of the CS-US associations, were unable to acquire differential trace conditioning and their pattern of behavior was similar to that of the unaware individuals in the Trace 1000 paradigm.

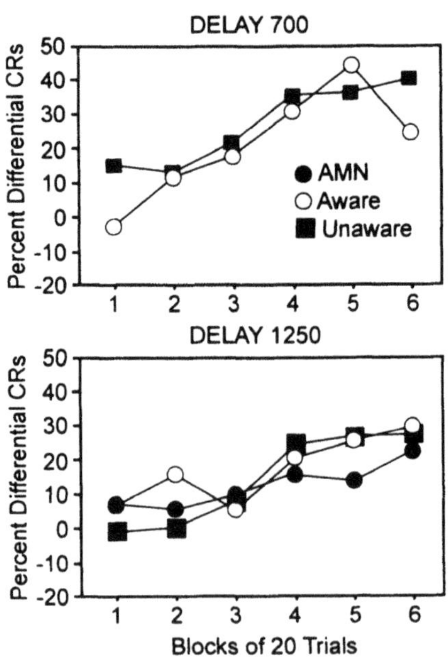

Figure 4. Performance of aware and unaware controls, together with amnesic patients, on the two versions of delay conditioning.

Because these amnesic patients have significant memory impairment, we wondered if perhaps they had become aware of the CS-US associations but simply forgot them by the time they responded to the questionnaire immediately following their conditioning session. Therefore, immediately following the completion of the questionnaire the patients were given a series of 49 additional conditioning trials.

During this series of conditioning trials they were asked the same set of questions that they had just attempted to answer in the questionnaire (one question between each trial). These questions included the 17 critical questions that asked about the relationships between the stimuli. Presenting these questions during the conditioning session failed to improve their scores on the questionnaire and also failed to improve their differential trace conditioning performance (Clark & Squire, 1998).

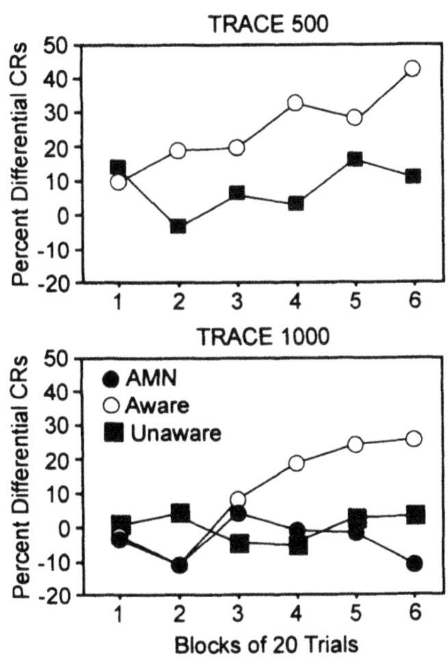

Figure 5. Performance of aware and unaware controls, together with amnesic patients, on the two versions of trace conditioning.

The Manipulation of Awareness

The findings just described suggest that trace conditioning differs from delay conditioning in that, if trace conditioning is to occur, conscious knowledge of the stimulus contingencies must develop during the conditioning session. This observation raises an interesting "chicken and egg problem." For trace conditioning, one can ask which comes first, awareness of the stimulus contingencies and then successful conditioning, or successful conditioning and then awareness of the stimulus contingencies? In other words, one possibility is that awareness of the stimulus contingencies is a critical factor for successful trace conditioning. Yet, an alternative possibility is that successful trace conditioning leads to the awareness of the stimulus contingencies. We examined this issue by manipulating awareness directly in four different experiments. First, we reasoned that if awareness of the stimulus contingencies is a prerequisite for trace conditioning, then preventing awareness should prevent trace conditioning. Second, preventing awareness should not affect delay conditioning because awareness of the stimulus contingencies is not related to delay conditioning. Third, providing awareness of the stimulus contingencies before conditioning should facilitate trace conditioning. Fourth, we asked whether providing knowledge about the stimulus contingencies is sufficient on its own to support trace conditioning or whether the knowledge also has to be accessible during the conditioning session (Clark & Squire, 1999).

Procedures

Except where noted, the procedures for these experiments were identical to those described above. We tested 38 older adults (mean age = 66.7) and assigned them to one of four groups. For two of the groups, we attempted to reduce or eliminate the possibility of becoming aware of the relationships between the CS^+, the CS^-, and the US. Accordingly, we engaged participants in a secondary, attention-demanding task during either differential trace conditioning (Trace-Distraction, n = 9) or during differential delay conditioning (Delay-Distraction, n = 12). In a third group (Trace-Knowledge, n = 8), we promoted awareness of the CS-US associations by thoroughly explaining the CS^+, CS^-, and US relationships to each participant before differential trace conditioning. For the fourth group (Trace-Knowledge-Distraction, n = 9), we also thoroughly explained the relationships between the CS+, CS- and US before conditioning. This group then engaged in the secondary task during differential trace conditioning.

The Secondary, Attention-demanding Task

Rather than have the participants simply watch a silent movie during the conditioning session, we asked them to watch a computer screen where single digits were presented (once every 1.5 seconds for a 1-second duration) throughout the conditioning session. Participants were asked to press a button when they saw 3 odd digits consecutively (Mulligan & Hartman, 1996). We reasoned that this ongoing task might prevent the participants from focusing on the conditioning stimuli and their relationship to one another.

Promoting Awareness

To promote awareness of the conditioning protocol in the Trace-Knowledge and Trace-Knowledge-Distraction groups, the relationships between the CS^+, CS^- and US were thoroughly explained prior to conditioning. The experimenter then asked questions to confirm that participants understood the protocol. The Trace-Knowledge group then watched a silent movie (After The Gold Rush) while they received trace conditioning. The Trace-Knowledge-Distraction group engaged in the secondary digit-detection task during trace conditioning.

Following the conditioning session, participants were given the same true/false questionnaire (omitting questions about the movie) that was described above, which asked about various aspects of the conditioning session including how well they understood the stimulus contingencies. Again, critical questions were the 17 items concerning the temporal relationships between the CS^+, the CS^- and the US.

Table 1 shows the average number of correct items on the 17-item questionnaire for the 4 groups. The two groups that engaged in the distraction task, without being given knowledge about the task (Trace-Distraction and Delay-Distraction) scored numerically worse than all other groups (9.1 and 12.8, respectively). The Trace-Distraction group did not score above chance, though the Delay-Distraction group was able to develop some awareness of the stimulus contingencies and scored above chance.

Group	Scores	S.E.M.
Trace-Distraction (9)	09.1	1.5
Delay-Distraction (12)	12.8	0.7
Trace-Knowledge (8)	16.0	0.6
Trace-Knowledge-Distraction (9)	13.9	1.0

Table 1. Table shows the average scores of participants in each group on the 17 questions that asked about the temporal relationships between the CS+, the CS-, and the US. The numbers in parentheses show the number of participants in each group. S.E.M. = standard error of the mean.

Figure 6 shows the differential conditioning performance of the Trace-Distraction group. For comparison purposes, the figure also shows the performance of the aware and unaware participants from our first set of studies (from Figure 5), who were trained with the same trace conditioning protocol but without the distraction task. The Trace-Distraction group did not acquire differential conditioning and performed similarly to the subgroup of participants in the earlier study who did not become aware of the stimulus contingencies (awareness score for that subgroup = 10.7; awareness for Trace-Distraction group = 9.1).

Figure 7 shows the conditioning performance of the Delay-Distraction group in comparison to the performance of the participants from our previous study (Figure 4), who were trained with the same delay conditioning protocol but without the distraction task. The Delay-Distraction group was not affected by the distraction task and acquired delay conditioning at the same rate as the group that was not distracted. Thus, awareness of the stimulus contingencies was unrelated to conditioning performance, and the distraction task did not affect conditioning.

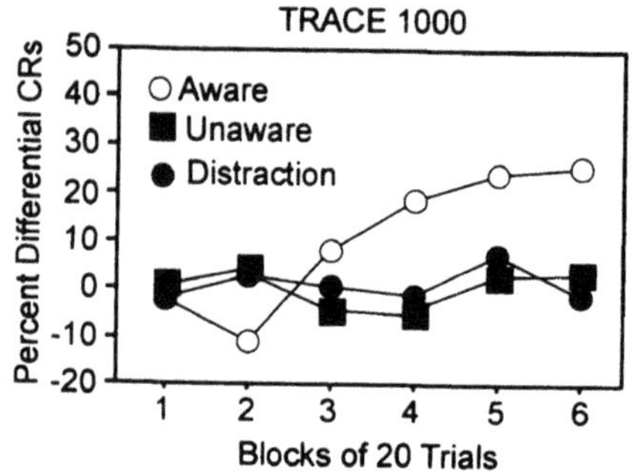

Figure 6. Performance of aware and unaware participants who watched a movie during trace conditioning (aware and unaware) and a group of participants who were distracted during trace conditioning (distraction).

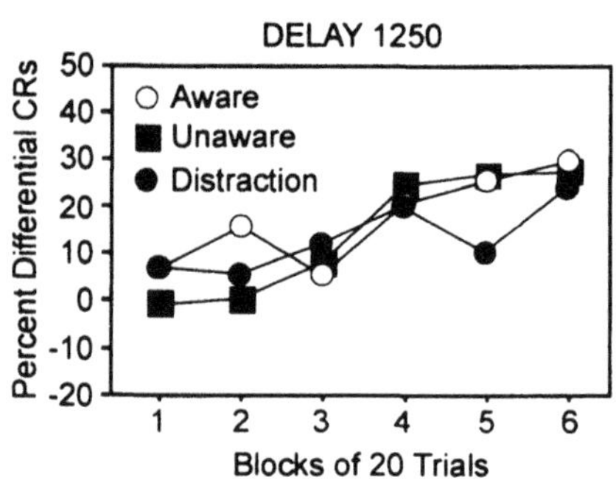

Figure 7. Performance of participants who watched a movie during delay conditioning (aware and unaware) and participants who performed a secondary task during delay conditioning (distraction).

The two groups that were given knowledge about the stimulus contingencies before the conditioning session (Trace-Knowledge and Trace-Knowledge-Distraction) were able to express that knowledge in the post-session questionnaire (awareness scores of 16.0 and 13.9, respectively, Table 1). Both scores were significantly above chance. Figure 8 shows the performance of the Trace-Knowledge group together with the aware and unaware participants from Figure 5, who were tested in the identical fashion but without any explanation about the stimulus contingencies. Participants in the Trace-Knowledge group performed significantly better than the unaware individuals from the previous study (block 6 scores: $t13 = .3$, $p < 0.01$). The Trace-Knowledge group and the aware participants performed similarly during the four final blocks of training. However, the Trace-Knowledge group performed better than the aware group during the first two blocks of training. The high level of differential responding during the first two blocks of conditioning (40 trials) likely occurred because the instructions sensitized participants to the CS+.

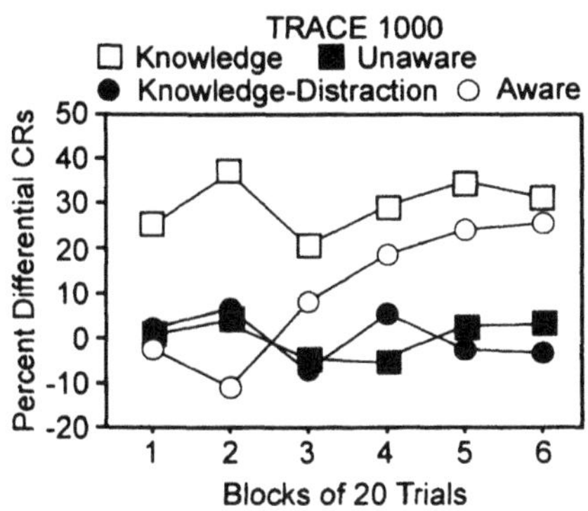

Figure 8. Performance of participants who watched a movie during trace conditioning (aware and unaware), participants who were provided knowledge of the stimulus relationships before trace conditioning and then watched a movie during conditioning (knowledge), and participants who were provided knowledge of the stimulus relationships before trace conditioning and then performed a secondary task during conditioning (knowledge-distraction).

Figure 8 also shows the performance of the Trace-Knowledge-Distraction group. The nine participants in this group failed to exhibit differential trace conditioning, even though six of the nine scored 13 or higher on the 17 relationship questions. The three other individuals in this group apparently forgot the stimulus contingencies during the conditioning session (scoring less than 13 of 17 correct). There were no differences in eyeblink conditioning performance between those who scored well and those who scored poorly on the questionnaire. As a group, they conditioned significantly worse than the group that was provided knowledge of the stimulus contingencies but not distracted (Trace-Knowledge) and no better than the group that was distracted during trace conditioning without having prior knowledge of the stimulus contingencies (Trace-Distraction). Thus, having knowledge about the stimulus contingencies is not sufficient to support the acquisition of trace conditioning. Individuals must also be able to have access to their knowledge, or be able to use their knowledge during the conditioning session itself.

The findings just described suggest that awareness of the stimulus contingencies is a prerequisite for trace classical eyeblink conditioning and not simply a result of successful conditioning. Preventing awareness by engaging the participants in an attention-demanding task prevented awareness of the stimulus contingencies and also prevented the acquisition of differential trace conditioning (Trace-Distraction group). This critical requirement for awareness appears unique to trace conditioning, because awareness of the stimulus contingencies is not critical for delay conditioning (Clark & Squire, 1998; Papka, Ivry & Woodruff-Pak, 1997). Indeed, the same distraction task that prevented trace conditioning had no effect on delay conditioning (Delay-Distraction group, Figure 7). Further, informing participants of the stimulus contingencies before conditioning (Trace-Knowledge group) resulted in successful differential trace conditioning. Finally, informing participants of the stimulus contingencies before conditioning and then distracting them during conditioning prevented trace differential conditioning (Trace-Knowledge-Distraction group). In the latter group, trace conditioning did not occur, even though after conditioning, six of nine participants were aware of the stimulus contingencies as demonstrated by their performance on the post-conditioning questionnaire. Yet these same six individuals obtained a score of only -3 % in block 6 of conditioning. This result suggests that simply being aware of the stimulus contingencies is not sufficient for trace conditioning. Knowledge of the stimulus contingencies must be available for trial-to-trial use during the conditioning session itself.

BRAIN SYSTEMS

Trace conditioning may require declarative knowledge because the trace interval between the CS and the US makes it difficult to process the CS-US relationship in an automatic, reflexive way. The present findings indicate that knowledge of the stimulus relationships is critical for successful trace conditioning and that performance during trace conditioning can be altered by promoting or preventing awareness. Though trace conditioning is dependent on the hippocampus, trace conditioning also depends on the cerebellum (Woodruff-Pak, Lavond & Thompson, 1985). Thus, the CR in trace conditioning, as in delay conditioning, requires a cerebellar circuit. In delay conditioning, because the CS is present during the presentation of the US, the cerebellum has access to the CS and US information concurrently. For trace conditioning, the silent interval between the offset of the CS and the onset of the US may make it difficult for the cerebellum to form a motor memory. It is interesting to note that electrophysiological studies have indicated that no residual activity survives in the cerebellum for longer than 300 ms following the termination of an input pulse (Eccles, Ito & Szentagothai, 1967). In our paradigm, the US followed the offset of the CS by 1000 ms. This circumstance suggests that the cerebellum could not, independent of other neural structures, maintain a representation of the CS across the trace interval. If however, the hippocampus and neocortex (which also appears to be critical for trace conditioning; Kronforst-Collins & Disterhoft, 1997) have represented the stimulus contingencies, then processed information about the CS could be sent to the cerebellum, perhaps at a time during the trial that is optimal for cerebellar plasticity (i.e., immediately before and during the US). An interesting possibility is that in trace conditioning, the cerebellum receives reformatted information from the hippocampus, such that CS and US information arrive at the cerebellum in the temporally overlapping fashion that the cerebellum can use. A pathway has been described from the hippocampus to the cerebellum by way of the retrosplenial cortex and pontine nuclei (Berger, Weikart, Bassett & Orr, 1986).

Another interesting issue concerns stimulus-stimulus (S-S) learning and stimulus-response (S-R) learning. During some forms of classical conditioning (e.g., tone CS--shock US), rapidly developing receptive field plasticity in the primary auditory cortex occurs in response to the CS (Bakin & Weinberger, 1990). This rapidly acquired association is between the CS and the US and has been interpreted as S-S learning or declarative memory (Weinberger, 1998). It may be that this type of plasticity is similar to our measure of awareness in humans and is dependent on the hippocampus. In other words, S-S learning may provide the declarative knowledge that the CS is associated with, or predictive of the US. By contrast, S-R learning is the association between the CS and the US as it relates to the formation of an appropriate conditioned response. This conditioned response is more slowly acquired and is a precisely timed response specific to the US. In classical conditioning of the eyeblink response, the S-R association is the domain of the cerebellum. During conditioning, an individual may acquire both an S-S association (linking the CS and US) and an S-R association (developing a CR in response to the CS that is specific to the US). Thus, the eyeblink conditioned response itself would be formed and driven by the cerebellum and would be a product of the S-R association. It may be that during delay conditioning, the cerebellum is capable of making the critical S-R association, and S-S learning would be superfluous. However, the trace interval in trace conditioning may make it difficult or impossible for the cerebellum to make the S-R association unless other brain structures, including the hippocampus, have also made the S-S association. In this case, the S-S association would allow the hippocampus to work with the cerebellum to establish the critical S-R association and to form the conditioned response. This would explain why awareness of the conditioning contingencies (S-S association) is not critical for delay conditioning but is critical for successful trace conditioning.

ISSUES THAT REMAIN TO BE RESOLVED

Though the series of studies outlined here have helped illuminate the role of different brain systems in delay and trace classical conditioning, several issues remain to be resolved. Some of these issues have recently been discussed (LaBar & Disterhoft, 1998). Here we consider some of the more important difficulties and suggest critical follow-up studies as well as new methods that are needed to facilitate progress.

Differential Conditioning

In our studies, we used differential conditioning and not single-cue conditioning. Single-cue conditioning is more commonly used in both humans and experimental animals. There are several reasons why experimentalists might choose to study differential conditioning. For example, one might wish to examine stimulus generalization (how does acquisition to one CS generalize to a different, but similar CS), or to examine the development of inhibitory sets, which refers to the notion that participants actively learn to inhibit responding to the CS^-. One reason we used differential conditioning was to control for nonassociative processes that may influence conditioning. For example, increased responding to a CS could be due to sensitization. Sensitization is an increase in responding due to experience with the US and not to the pairing of the CS and US. An individual may respond more to the CS because the experience with the US has increased responsiveness to all stimulus presentations. A differential conditioning paradigm allows the effects of sensitization to be distinguished from the effects of associative learning. Sensitization would be expected to affect the CS^+ and the CS^- trials similarly, which would result in greater responding to both the CS^+ and the CS^-, but no increase in differential conditioning. Another related issue is that some individuals have a tendency to emit more spontaneous blinks than others, which can be thought of as natural eyeblink responses unrelated to the CS or US. Individuals with high spontaneous blink rates will appear to show more conditioned responses, i.e., a higher level of conditioning than individuals with lower spontaneous blink rates. Yet there may be no actual difference in the extent to which these groups have associated the CS with the US. In differential conditioning, spontaneous blinks would be randomly and equally distributed among CS^+ and CS^- trials and would not contribute to differential conditioning.

There was an additional, important reason why we used differential conditioning. Compared to single-cue conditioning, in differential conditioning there are more possible relationships among the stimuli that a participant can become aware of during the conditioning session. For example, in single-cue conditioning, the only valid relationship is that the CS predicts the US. In contrast, with differential conditioning, the participant has the possibility of learning that the CS^+ predicts the US, that the CS^- does not predict the US, and that the CS^+ and CS^- are unrelated. Thus, in differential conditioning it is possible to obtain a wide range of awareness scores that can then be evaluated against differential conditioning performance. While the differential conditioning paradigm has this distinct advantage, it may place a greater cognitive demand on the participant than single-cue conditioning (Ross & Nelson, 1973). Accordingly, it is not obvious that the results from differential conditioning experiments would necessarily generalize to single-cue conditioning (LaBar & Disterhoft, 1998). We are currently evaluating this possibility by examining the relationship between awareness and single-cue trace conditioning (for preliminary findings, see Woodruff-Pak, 1999).

Conditioning in Older Adult Participants

In our experiments, we have studied older adults averaging 66.9 years of age. These individuals could then be compared to the amnesic patients (average age = 67.5). We also reasoned that older subjects would be advantageous for studying the relationship between awareness and conditioning. In order to relate awareness of the stimulus contingencies to eyeblink performance, it is important that some individuals fail to become aware of the stimulus contingencies and that others do become aware of these contingencies. It seemed to us that younger subjects (e.g., the college sophomores that often participate in behavioral studies) may all become aware of these relationships. As it turned out, our older participants did achieve a wide range of awareness scores and in this sense provided suitable participants. However, it is also true that older individuals condition more poorly than younger subjects (Woodruff-Pak & Thompson, 1988; Solomon, Pomerlau, Bennett, James & Morse, 1989). Accordingly, it will be important to determine how well our findings from older adults generalize to young adults. It is possible that young adults would condition more successfully, be more immune to distraction, and acquire more awareness than older adults. If so, it might prove difficult in young adults to manipulate awareness and to study its relevance to conditioning.

Recently, this issue has been examined using our differential conditioning protocols (Delay 700, Delay 1250, Trace 500 and Trace 1000) and our awareness questionnaires (M-G. Knuttinen & J.F. Disterhoft, personal communication, January 5, 1999). Older and younger participants were compared. Younger participants all became aware of the stimulus contingencies and all showed evidence of differential conditioning in both versions of the delay and trace conditioning protocols. Interestingly, the older participants showed evidence of differential conditioning in both versions of delay conditioning, but they demonstrated no evidence of differential conditioning in either version of trace conditioning. Additionally, the older participants all failed to become aware of the stimulus contingencies. These results with older individuals are fully consistent with our findings in that knowledge of the stimulus contingencies was not critical for differential delay conditioning. In addition, individuals who failed to become aware of these contingencies also failed at differential trace conditioning. It is unclear why in the Knuttinen and Disterhoft study, none of the older participants became aware (and none showed differential trace conditioning), whereas in our studies, 46% of our older subjects became aware (and conditioning scores correlated with awareness). This difference cannot be accounted for by the method of assessing awareness, because the same questionnaire was employed in both laboratories. The explanation could lie in differences in the populations tested, or in other details of the conditioning protocols (e.g., the discriminability of the CS^+ and CS^- that were used).

THE IMPORTANCE OR THE SPECIFIC RESPONSE SYSTEM UNDER STUDY

The purpose in measuring awareness is to correlate awareness with a learned response. But in so doing, it is important to keep in mind that how awareness relates to a learned response may vary greatly depending on what type of response is being measured. For example, consider a situation where a yellow light always predicts a blue light, and participants are asked to push a button whenever they believe the blue light will be presented. In this case, the learned button push would be expected to be highly correlated with awareness that the yellow light predicts the blue light, because the button push itself has never been directly reinforced. Therefore, the learned button push should be driven by this awareness and by a voluntary motor response. A less obvious example comes from autonomic classical conditioning. Here, an individual may be presented, for example, with a tone CS and a shock US. The US will elicit autonomic responses such as a change in heart rate or an increase in skin conductance. There is a large literature on awareness and autonomic conditioning, suggesting that awareness is critical for conditioning to occur (e.g., Dawson, 1973). Importantly, the conditioned autonomic response in these studies depends on a different neural system than the conditioned eyeblink response, with the amygdala being a critical component (Kapp, Frysinger, Gallagher & Haselton, 1979; Lavond, Kim & Thompson, 1993). By contrast, the cerebellum is critical for eyeblink conditioning (Lavond, Kim & Thompson, 1993; Thompson & Krupa, 1994). A reliance on studies of autonomic conditioning that have examined the relationship between awareness and learning could be misleading if one is interested in the relationship between awareness and the conditioned eyeblink response. The two paradigms involve different brain systems and the relationship of the learned response to awareness is different in the two cases (see Powell, McLaughlin & Chachich, 1999).

MEASURING AWARENESS IN EYEBLINK CONDITIONING

Post-Conditioning Questions

Post-conditioning questions provide a way to assess awareness after conditioning has occurred. This method is advantageous because the questioning can have no impact on conditioning itself. There are two forms of post-conditioning tests--recall questionnaires and recognition questionnaires. Recall questionnaires are general questions that can be answered with a free-form response. For example, "Tell me about the tone and the air puff; did you notice any relationship between them?" Recognition questionnaires typically involve multiple-choice or true/false questions. For example, "true or false, I believe the tone predicted when the air puff would come." A series of such questions can be constructed to evaluate fully how well the participant has understood the contingencies of the conditioning experiment. We used these types of questions with the rationale that participants who have a good understanding of the contingencies should be able to answer all of the questions regardless of how they are asked. Questions of this nature are advantageous because it is possible to calculate what chance performance is and to determine if performance is significantly above chance.

In comparing the relative merits of recall and recognition questionnaires for assessing awareness in classical conditioning experiments, Dawson (1973) concluded that recognition questionnaires are superior to recall tests because they are more sensitive to the presence of awareness. Nevertheless, both kinds of tests have advantages. Recognition tests may be more sensitive to detecting awareness and are easy to score and quantify. However, recall tests may provide additional information. Also, participants might become confused by the recognition questions but still demonstrate good understanding of the stimulus relationships when simply asked to explain them.

A difficulty with all post-conditioning interviews is that a participant may become aware of the conditioning contingencies but then forget them or become confused by the questions. In addition, the questions themselves might cause the participant to reflect on the session and correctly identify the stimulus relationships, even if the participant was unaware of them during the conditioning session. In our questionnaire, we attempted to minimize this possibility by having the questions progress from fairly general to more specific. We also prevented the participants from returning to previous questions to make their answers more congruent with later answers. Another useful approach would be to follow the recognition test with a structured interview designed to evaluate what the participants understood about the stimulus relationships. One could ask the participants when they became aware of these relationships and whether they might have become aware while filling out the questionnaire.

Concomitant Measures of Awareness

Concomitant measures of awareness are measures that assess awareness during the conditioning session itself. It has been argued that such measures may be superior to post-conditioning questionnaires because they are less vulnerable to retrospective recall errors. They also allow the development of awareness to be temporally correlated with conditioning (Dawson, 1973). Concomitant measures usually require that an individual report verbally, during the conditioning session, what they believe the stimulus contingencies to be or what their probability estimates are for the occurrence of the US based on the presentation of the CS. However, these measures are not without problems. Having individuals purposefully engage in reporting their perceptions of the causal nature of the conditioning session may fundamentally change the nature of the task and make it difficult to reasonably compare to conditioning sessions where concomitant measures are not used. Individuals may become more focused on the stimuli and engage in rigorous hypothesis testing and may become more motivated to behaviorally "solve" the experimental procedures (LaBar & Disterhoft, 1998; Baeyens, Eelen & Van den Bergh, 1990). In any case, one can compare the conditioning that occurs when concomitant measures of awareness are taken with the conditioning that occurs when such measures are not taken, and thereby determine directly whether or not the measurement procedure influences conditioning.

THE NATURE OF THE LEARNED EYEBLINK RESPONSE. IS IT CONDITIONED OR VOLUNTARY?

In eyeblink conditioning, the responses are considered to be reflexive in nature. First, the unconditioned response (UR) is the automatic, "reflexive," reaction to the puff of air that is delivered to the eye. With repeated pairing of a CS and US a learned, conditioned response develops. This response is also thought to be reflexive and, as such, does not require cognitive involvement. Nevertheless, though an eyeblink response can be involuntary, clearly the eyeblink response can also be brought under voluntary control. If individuals become aware of the stimulus contingencies, they are also in a position to voluntarily blink their eyes to avoid the air puff. This circumstance has caused concern among experimentalists because it has been argued, at least since the 1940s, that the processes and characteristics of responses that are voluntary are very different from those that are involuntary or reflexive (Coleman & Webster, 1988). Some means of identifying voluntary responses needed to be developed so that they could either be discarded as contaminants or analyzed separately. There is a long and storied history of experimental and methodological efforts to deal with this problem during the 1950's and 1960's (for reviews, see Coleman, 1985; Coleman & Webster, 1988; Coleman & Webster, 1990).

Two criteria have emerged for identifying voluntary responses. The first was based on the slope of the response. Voluntary responses were believed to be more rapid and thus to have a characteristically steeper slope than a conditioned response (Hartman & Ross, 1961). The second was based on response latency. Voluntary responses were believed to have a short onset latency (which also involved a steep slope), and eye closure was maintained until the onset of the US (Spence & Taylor, 1951). Today, studies in humans seldom address this issue directly and only rarely indicate if methods were used to identify voluntary responses. Those studies that do address this issue have typically used the latency criterion (e.g., Daum et al., 1993). In our studies we have also used this latency criterion because of the likelihood that the peak amplitude of true conditioned responses tends to occur at about the time of the US (Martin & Levey, 1969).

Despite these improvements, there is not consensus about the most appropriate methods for detecting voluntary responses. The only large-scale study to test the validity of these two criteria (slope and latency) found that neither was fully satisfactory for discriminating voluntary responses from conditioned responses (Goodrich, 1966). Though the problem may well be less acute in studies using a short ISI (because there is less time to voluntarily blink), in our studies and in others that have used longer ISIs (e.g., McGlinchey-Berroth, Carrillo, Gabriell, Brawn & Disterhoft, 1997), the issue of voluntary blinks needs to be considered.

In our studies we attempted to remove responses that appeared to be voluntary blinks by using a latency criterion. The remaining responses had the characteristics of conditioned responses. For example, voluntary responses are believed to involve full eyelid closure, whereas the average amplitudes of the CRs in our studies were typically less than a complete eyeblink. Further, the mean latencies of the CR peaks were longer than the short-latency (< 300 ms) responses that are common in voluntary eyeblinks. Finally, most participants were unable to report how they had responded to the CS^{+}, which further suggests that they were not blinking voluntarily.

Though these findings suggest that the responses scored as CRs were actual CRs and not voluntary responses, it would be best to have an independent method for making this determination. In years past, responses had to be scored by hand, and determining the response characteristics of each eyeblink was a laborious task. Today, one can digitize the eyeblink waveform for rigorous computer analysis. For example, in addition to simply detecting eyeblinks, the computer can calculate onset latencies, peak latencies, amplitudes, area under the response curve, slope, and the number of separate response peaks. By having the computer compare the characteristics of eyeblinks from individuals in a voluntary response group with the eyeblinks from individuals in a conditioned response group, it may be possible to identify measures that reliably sort the two response types. The voluntary response group would be individuals who have been instructed to blink their eyes when they hear a tone, but who are not presented with an air puff (clearly voluntary responses). The conditioned response group would be individuals who are given paired CS and US trials but instructed not to blink (they could be given an incentive not to blink as has been done previously; Goodrich, 1966). In this case any eyeblinks that do occur would more likely be conditioned responses.

A study like the one just described would depend on having a precise and accurate electronic description of the eyeblink waveforms. One way to obtain a precise description of the waveform is to use a minitorque potentiometer, first used by Spence and Taylor (1951), which involves attaching a thin thread to the eyelid. This method has become the standard for studies of eyeblink conditioning in rabbits. A different, less intrusive technique has been adopted in contemporary human conditioning studies. The eyeblink is transduced by an infrared emitter/detector (Thompson, et al., 1994). These devices have become popular because they are easy to put in place, nothing is directly attached to the eyelid, and it is possible to carry out an experiment without drawing an individual's attention to the fact that the eyeblink response is of interest. The method is indirect in that it relies on the amount of infrared light that is reflected from the eye at various degrees of eyelid closure (Clark & Zola, 1998). Accordingly, some distortion in the measure can occur from eye movements that occur in the absence of eyeblinks, and from altered amplitudes and slopes due to changes in the subject's head position or angle of gaze (these distortions result from changes in the angle and distance of the detector relative to the eyelid; R. Clark, unpublished observations).

CONCLUSION

Classical conditioning of the eyeblink response in both humans and experimental animals has provided an enormous amount of information about basic associative learning. There is no limit in sight to how far conditioning studies can advance understanding of associative learning and its neural substrates. We have demonstrated the utility of comparing delay and trace differential conditioning in combination with awareness measures in healthy volunteers and amnesic patients. Our findings suggest how brain memory systems may participate and interact in the formation of new memories. Though many technical and theoretical challenges remain to be addressed, it is clear that the human eyeblink classical conditioning paradigm is a powerful tool that can be used to advance understanding of brain memory systems and the cognitive factors that influence them.

REFERENCES

Baeyens, F., Eelen, P., & Van den Bergh, O. (1990). Contingency awareness in evaluative conditioning: A case for unaware affective-evaluative learning. *Cognition and Emotion*, *4*, 4-18.

Bakin, J.S., & Weinberger, N.M. (1990). Classical conditioning induces CS-specific receptive field plasticity in the auditory cortex of the guinea pig. *Brain Research, 536*, 271-286.

Berger, T.W., Berry, S.D., & Thompson, R.F. (1986). Role of the hippocampus in classical conditioning of aversive and appetitive behaviors. In R.L. Isaacson & K.H. Pribram (Eds.), *The Hippocampus, Vols. II and IV*, pp. (203-239). New York: Plenum Press.

Berger, T.W., Weikart, C.L., Bassett, J.L., & Orr, W.B. (1986). Lesions of the retrosplenial cortex produce deficits in reversal learning of the rabbit nictitating membrane response: Implications for potential interactions between hippocampal and cerebellar brain systems. *Behavioral Neuroscience, 100*, 802-809.

Clark, R.E., & Squire, L.R. (1998). Classical conditioning and brain systems: A key role for awareness. *Science, 280*, 77-81.

Clark, R.E., & Squire, L.R. (1999). Human eyeblink classical conditioning: Effects of manipulating awareness of the stimulus contingencies. *Psychological Science, 10*, 14-18.

Clark, R.E., & Zola, S. (1998). Trace eyeblink classical conditioning in the monkey: A nonsurgical method and behavioral analysis. *Behavioral Neuroscience, 112*, 1062-1068.

Coleman, S.R. (1985). The problem of volition and the conditioned reflex. Part I: Conceptual background. 1900-1940. *Behaviorism, 13*, 99-124.

Coleman, S.R., & Webster, S. (1988). The problem of volition and the conditioned reflex. Part II. Voluntary-responding subjects, 1951-1980. *Behaviorism, 16*, 17-49.

Coleman, S.R., & Webster, S. (1990). The decline of a research speciality: Human-eyelid conditioning in the late 1960's. *Behavior and Philosophy, 18*, 19-42.

Dawson, M.E. (1973). Can classical conditioning occur without contingency learning? A review and evaluation of the evidence. *Psychophysiology, 10*, 82-86.

Daum, I., Schugens, M.M, Ackermann, H., Lutzenberger, W., Dichgans, J., & Birbaumer, N. (1993). Classical conditioning after cerebellar lesions in humans. *Behavioral Neuroscience, 107*, 748-756.

Eccles, J.C., Ito, M., & Szentagothai, J. (1967). *The Cerebellum as a Neuronal Machine*. New York: Springer-Verlag.

Goodrich, K.P. (1966). Experimental analysis of response slope and latency as criteria for characterizing voluntary and nonvoluntary responses in eyeblink conditioning. *Psychological Monographs, 80*, 1-34.

Grant, D.A., (1973). Cognitive Factors in Eyelid Conditioning. *Psychophysiology, 10*, 75-81.

Hartman, T.F., & Ross, L.E. (1961). An alternative criterion for the elimination of "voluntary" responses in eyelid conditioning. *Journal of Experimental Psychology, 61*, 334-338.

James, G.O., Hardiman, M.J., & Yeo, C.H. (1987). Hippocampal lesions and trace conditioning in the rabbit. *Behavioural Brain Research, 23*, 109-116.

Kapp, B.S., Frysinger, R., Gallagher, M., & Haselton, J. (1979). Amygdala central nucleus lesions: Effects on heart rate conditioning in the rabbit. *Physiolology & Behavior, 23*, 1109-1117.

Kim, J.J., Clark, R.E., & Thompson, R.F. (1995). Hippocampectomy impairs the memory of recently, but not remotely, acquired trace eyeblink conditioned responses. *Behavioral Neuroscience, 109*, 195-203.

Kimble, G.A. (1947). Conditioning as a function of the time between conditioned and unconditioned stimuli. *Journal of Experimental Psychology, 37*, 1-15.

Kronforst-Collins, M. A., & Disterhoft, J. F. (1997). Lesions of the caudal area of the rabbit medial prefrontal cortex impair trace eyeblink conditioning. *Society for Neuroscience Abstract. 23*, 782.

LaBar, K.S., & Disterhoft, J.F. (1998). Conditioning, awareness, and the hippocampus. *Hippocampus*,

8, 620-626.

Lavond, D.G., Kim, J.J., & Thompson, R.F. (1993). Mammalian brain substrates of aversive classical conditioning. *Annual Review of Psychology, 44*, 317-342.

Martin, I., & Levey, A.B. (1969). *The Genesis of the Classical Conditioned Response*. Oxford: Pergamon.

McGlinchey-Berroth, R., Carrillo, M.C., Gabrieli, J.D.E., Brawn, C.M., & Disterhoft, J.F. (1997). Impaired trace eyeblink conditioning in bilateral, medial-temporal lobe amnesia. *Behavioral Neuroscience, 111*, 873-882.

Moyer, J.R., Deyo, R.A., & Disterhoft, J.F. (1990). Hippocampectomy disrupts trace eye-blink conditioning in rabbits. *Behavioral Neuroscience, 104*, 243-252.

Papka, M., Ivry, R.B., & Woodruff-Pak, D.S. (1997). Eyeblink classical conditioning and awareness revisited. *Psychological Science, 8*, 404-408.

Port, R.L., Romano, A.G., Steinmetz, J.E., Mikhail, A.A., & Patterson, M.M. (1986). Retention and acquisition of classical trace conditioned responses by rabbits with hippocampal lesions. *Behavioral Neuroscience, 100*, 745-752.

Powell, D.A., McLaughlin, J., & Chachich, M. (1999). Autonomic and sematic nervous system effects in eyeblink classical conditioning. In D.S. Woodruff-Pak & J.E. Steinmetz (Eds.), *Eyeblink Classical Conditioning, Volume I: Animal Models*. Boston: Kluwer Academic Publishers.

Reed, J.M., & Squire, L.R. (1997). Impaired recognition memory in patients with lesions limited to the hippocampal formation. *Behavioral Neuroscience, 111*, 667-675.

Ross, L.E. (1965). Eyelid conditioning as a tool in psychological research: Some problems and prospects. In W.F. Prokasy (Ed.), *Classical conditioning*, (pp. 249-268). New York: Appleton-Century-Crofts.

Ross, L.E., & Nelson, M.N. (1973). The role of awareness in differential conditioning. *Psychophysiology, 10*, 91-94.

Solomon, P.R., Blanchard, S., Levine, E., Velazquez, E., & Groccia-Ellison, M. (1991). Attenuation of age-related conditioning deficits in humans by extension of the interstimulus interval. *Psychology and Aging, 6*, 36-42.

Solomon, P.R., Pomerleau, D., Bennett, L., James, J., & Morse, D.L. (1989). Acquisition of the classically conditioned eyeblink response in humans over the lifespan. *Psychology and Aging, 4*, 34-41.

Solomon, P.R., Vander Schaaf, E.R., Thompson, R.F., & Weisz, D.J. (1986). Hippocampus and trace conditioning of the rabbit's classically conditioned nictitating membrane response. *Behavioral Neuroscience, 100*, 729-744.

Spence, K.W. (1966). Cognitive and drive factors in the extinction of the conditioned eyeblink response in human subjects. *Psychological Review, 73*, 445-458.

Spence, K.W., & Taylor, J. (1951). Anxiety and strength of the UCS as determiners of the amount of eyelid conditioning. *Journal or Experimental Psychology, 42*, 183-188.

Squire, L.R. (1992). Memory and the hippocampus: A synthesis from findings with rats, monkeys, and humans. *Psychological Review, 99*, 195-231.

Thompson, R.F., & Krupa, D.J. (1994). Organization of memory traces in the mammalian brain. *Annual Review of Neuroscience, 17*, 519-549.

Weinberger, N.M. (1998). Physiological memory in primary auditory cortex: Characteristics and mechanisms. *Neurobiology of Learning and Memory, 70*, 226-251.

Weiskrantz, L., & Warrington, E.K. (1979). Conditioning in amnesic patients. *Neuropsychologia, 17*, 187-194.

Woodruff-Pak, D.S. (1993). Eyeblink classical conditioning in H.M.: Delay and trace paradigms. *Behavioral Neuroscience, 107* 911-925.

Woodruff-Pak, D.S. (1999). New directions for a classical paradigm: Human eyeblink conditioning. *Psychological Science, 10*, 1-3.

Woodruff-Pak, D.S., Lavond, D.G., & Thompson, R.F. (1985). Trace conditioning: Abolished by cerebellar nuclear lesions but not lateral cerebellar cortex aspirations. *Brain Research, 348*, 249-260.

Woodruff-Pak, D.S., & Thompson, R.F. (1988). Classical conditioning of the eyeblink response in the delay paradigm in adults aged 18-83 years. *Psychology and Aging, 3*, 219-229.

12 CAN EYEBLINK CLASSICAL CONDITIONING PROVIDE A FOUNDATION FOR INTEGRATING CLINICAL SCIENCE AND COGNITIVE-NEUROSCIENCE IN THE STUDY OF PSYCHOPATHOLOGY?

Richard M. McFall, Jo Anne Tracy,
Sushmita S. Ghose and Joseph E. Steinmetz
Indiana University

INTRODUCTION

Examining a psychological problem from multiple perspectives can be a powerful strategy when it involves empirical tests, carried out at one or more levels, of predictions deduced from theories at any of the levels. Theory-driven research of this type, explicitly testing predicted relationships *across levels*, potentially can improve the theories at all levels. For example, a great deal is known at the neurological level about the brain circuitry involved in eyeblink classical conditioning (EBCC). At the same time, leading clinical theories hypothesize that anxiety disorders are acquired and maintained through classical and operant conditioning. If the clinical theories are correct, persons suffering from anxiety disorders should condition differently than normals. In an eyeblink-conditioning paradigm, for example, they might condition more rapidly and/or extinguish more slowly. Thus, by combining our knowledge and theories from the two levels, in this way, we should be able to test our etiological theories of anxiety disorders. Furthermore, if the predicted differences are found, then our knowledge about the neural circuitry involved in classical conditioning should provide strong clues about the neurological correlates of anxiety disorders. Finally, if clinical theories of anxiety disorders are supported by evidence from classical conditioning studies, this would reflect favorably on the basic theory at the neurological level.

Unfortunately, integrative research of this type is less common than one might expect. In this chapter, we consider some of the philosophical and historical obstacles to such work; then we present examples of EBCC studies from our own laboratory, focused on obsessive-compulsive disorder, a particular form of anxiety disorder, to illustrate the promise of this approach; and finally we point to future directions for integrative research employing EBCC paradigms to study clinical problems.

It is fashionable for clinical psychologists to give lip service to the idea that clinical theory and practice should be integrated with the basic theories, methods, and knowledge from the rest of psychological science.[1] For example, leading textbooks in abnormal psychology tout the "biopsychosocial model" of psychopathology as though it were a viable and coherent integration of research and theory from three separate perspectives—biological, psychological, and social. Such texts give the impression that the integration already has been achieved, and that it has led to significant advances in our ability to assess, predict, explain, and treat psychological disorders. In reality, however, no such integrated model exists and, consequently, no such clinical breakthroughs have occurred. For most clinical psychologists, the goal of integration remains more of an abstract ideal than a concrete guide to action. In part, this is because psychologists have not dealt squarely and effectively with the obstacles to integration. Integration is achievable, in principle, but only if these obstacles can be overcome first.

Philosophical Obstacles to Integration

We can identify at least two major types of obstacles. The most fundamental and daunting is philosophical: Specifically, theorists must integrate the psychological and biological perspectives in ways that avoid fatal philosophical flaws, such as dualism, reductionism, or indeterminacy (Popper, 1962). For example, it is indefensibly dualistic for us to reify our psychological and biological constructs as though they represented two separate realities—the mind and the body. For reasons we will explain, it also is unacceptably reductionistic, as well as dualistic, for us to talk about our biological constructs as though they were the "true underlying causes" or "substrates" for our psychological constructs. Furthermore, interactionist theories, in which everything supposedly interacts with everything else through multiple, complex, causal pathways, are hopelessly underspecified and thus indeterminant (McFall & Townsend, 1998). Such theories represent untestable, pseudo-scientific "just-so stories" that give the illusion of explaining everything while offering no risky predictions, hence explaining virtually nothing.

The solutions to such philosophical problems require conceptual discipline; yet, as Meehl (1973; 1978) observed, psychologists too often seem plagued by a muddle-headedness that allows them to fall into conceptual traps. Long ago, Wendell Johnson (1946) charted a course around the problems of dualism, reductionism, and indeterminacy. He explained that different theoretical frameworks—e.g., biological, psychological, social—actually represent different conceptual levels of analysis, often for the very same events. The conceptions at different levels—from microscopic to macroscopic—do not represent separate "realities" (this would be dualistic). Nor are conceptions at molecular levels inherently closer to "reality" or "truth" than conceptions at more molar levels (this would be reductionistic).

To the extent that different levels of analysis provide different ways of construing the *same* events, they may be capturing the same relationships using the different terms from each level. Thus, their explanatory power may not be additive, but may be "nested" or redundant. Imagine, for instance, two persons describing the same object: one says it is "10 bananas, 5 oranges, and 3 apples in a dish"; the other says it is "a bowl of fruit." Clearly, the information contained in these two descriptions is not independent and additive, although each perspective may be superior to the other for specific purposes. Explanatory levels can be treated as independent or incrementally informative only after their contributions have been assessed empirically.

Similarly, we should not assume that explanations offered at different conceptual levels necessarily are interactive. How do "10 bananas, 5 oranges, and 3 apples" and "a bowl of fruit" interact, for instance? Indeed, we should be leery of vague multifactorial explanations; their complexity expands multiplicatively with the addition of each new factor, rapidly yielding too many free parameters to be falsifiable. Cronbach (1975) warned that interaction models are like halls of mirrors: the number of potential factors is endless, and each additional factor expands the model's complexity multiplicatively (these concerns relate to the problem of indeterminacy). Occam's razor, or parsimony, is fundamental to the construction of useful theoretical models.

Finally, no single conceptual level is capable of answering all questions equally well. Each is designed to illuminate its own theoretical questions; each has its own particular focus and range of convenience; and the "validity" of each is judged by its specific utility—that is, by how well it does what it was designed to do. In short, the purpose of scientific theory is to reduce uncertainty, and good theory enhances our ability to predict, control, and explain events *within the theory's specified domain* (Johnson, 1946; Popper, 1962).

Consistent with Johnson's explanation, Meehl, Klann, Schmieding, Breimeier, and Schroeder-Slomann (1958) offered the following resolution of the classic mind-body problem:

> ..the mental processes of man are conceived by the psychologist, first of all, as *events* (i.e., not *things*); and secondly, the "things" which participate in these events...(note, not "produce" or "underlie," but *constitute*)...are material entities. ...thought, passion, love, guilt, etc., are not produced by the body...rather they are all literally *activities* of living tissue...actions by the human machine. ...if you ask., "Where does the mind go when the body dies?" this question cannot make any sense... Such a question is like asking, "Where does the timekeeping go when a watch is smashed?" Answer: Nowhere, because timekeeping is not a thing but an event, and in this smashed watch, events of that kind no longer take place. ...The *word* "mind" is, grammatically, a noun, but it refers to acts and dispositions. The monistic view can be succinctly expressed by the analogical equation Mind : Brain :: Timekeeping : Watch :: Function : Structure :: Event : Thing (pp.159-160).

Miller (1996) proposed a similar resolution to these philosophical problems (even using the timekeeping analogy) in his presidential address to the Society for Psychophysiological Research, an organization of psychologists for whom these philosophical issues are a special concern, given their reliance on psychophysiological methods to study psychopathology. Miller highlighted the logical problems involved in making causal inferences across conceptual levels when the key processes or mechanisms linking the levels are unknown. We may be able to establish correlational and predictive relationships across levels (e.g., increased cortical activation is associated with increased attention), but must be cautious about inferring from these associations that events at one level "cause" or "explain" events at the other level.

Organisms function as whole entities, even though they can be viewed and analyzed simultaneously at multiple levels. For example, anxiety may be associated with changes in both attention and cortical activation. Manipulations that affect attention also may be associated with changes in cortical activation and anxiety, just as manipulations that affect cortical activation are likely to be associated with changes in attention and anxiety. Thus, we can describe a person's functioning at one point in time in terms of anxiety (at a clinical level), increased attention (at a cognitive level), and electrochemical cortical activities (at a neurological level); but we must not lose sight of the fact that these are different descriptions of a single, whole organism, not distinct and independent "things." We also can describe associations among anxiety, attention, and brain activity; but lacking an overarching conceptual framework capable of explaining these associations within a common language, we are limited to correlational statements. Even when associations across levels are time-lagged, such that one is a reliable antecedent to and predictor of the other, the link remains correlational, not causal, in the absence of a common explanatory theory. In short, when working toward an integrated clinical-cognitive-neuroscience model (which is the primary focus of this chapter), we must avoid using language carelessly, implying a deeper understanding than is warranted.

Assuming that we step carefully around such philosophical pitfalls, however, it is possible to advance knowledge on several fronts simultaneously by investigating the same events from two or more conceptual perspectives. This kind of integration is realistic. The simplest example is the search for biological "markers" (correlates, predictors) of psychological disorders. Such markers can inform our theories at both the biological level and the psychological level. For instance, a great deal is known at the descriptive level about the symptoms that define specific psychological disorders (e.g., anxiety, autism, depression, schizophrenia, etc.). If neurological correlates of these symptom patterns are found, these "markers," in turn, can be used to improve the precision of our classification system at the symptom level. Simultaneously, these "markers" also can be used to refine biological theories about the antecedents, concomitants, and related processes comprising the nomological net that defines the disorder (Cronbach & Meehl, 1955; MacCorquodale & Meehl, 1948).

Thus, philosophical issues need not pose insurmountable obstacles to an integration across levels within psychology. Provided that we are cognizant of potential traps and proceed cautiously, studying problems from multiple levels simultaneously could be a very fruitful research strategy.

Historical Obstacles to Integration

The second obstacle to integrating clinical psychology with the rest of psychology is historical: The "two worlds" of psychology (Cronbach, 1957)—that is, the applied and the basic—have evolved along two independent and diverging trajectories. Although these worlds share the label "psychology," they tend to differ fundamentally in their theoretical questions; their research aims, strategies, and methods; and their epistemological traditions. Perhaps the fault line between these two worlds existed from the very beginning of the discipline; however, the split only became evident and worrisome toward the middle of the 20th century. As clinical psychology was emerging as a recognized sub-specialty within psychology, Woodworth (1937) drew attention to the schism, and warned about its potential dangers. Subsequent events proved that his fears were not unfounded (Sechrest, 1992). The rate of separation between the applied and basic worlds accelerated following WWII. With encouragement from the Veterans Administration, the United States Public Health Service, and the American Psychological Association, universities poured fresh resources into doctoral training programs that redefined clinical psychology as a *profession* of "scientist-practitioners." This professional focus fostered an over-emphasis on practice and guild issues, and a neglect of basic science. Meanwhile, the rest of the discipline stayed the course of training basic scientists.

Prototypic psychologists from these two worlds now take very different approaches to the study of their phenomena. On the one hand, basic psychological researchers live in a world aimed at deriving nomothetic principles, or "laws of behavior." They regard the variability associated with individual differences as "error" or "noise"—a nuisance to be minimized or eliminated through stimulus control and data aggregation. Their experimental methods rely on random assignment of subjects to experimental conditions; precise manipulation of one or more independent variables, typically within the constraints of a laboratory; collection of large samples of target events (not necessarily from large numbers of subjects); systematic observation and objective recording of publicly observable events (eschewing introspective verbal self-reports of private events); representation of these events in quantitative measurement models; and statistical evaluation of the fit between the observed events and theoretical predictions. Precision and interpretability are considered prerequisites to generalizability; therefore, higher priority is given to stimulus control (i.e., internal validity) than to stimulus representativeness (i.e., external validity) (Campbell & Stanley, 1963).

On the other hand, individual differences are at the center of the clinical psychologist's world. Between-subject variability usually is the phenomenon of primary interest, not a nuisance to be eliminated. Furthermore, clinical psychologists typically study the deviant behaviors found in individuals suffering from various forms of psychopathology. By definition, these are low-base-rate events at the extreme tails of distributions. Because clinical subjects are members of predefined groups, they cannot be assigned randomly to their condition. This means that clinical researchers usually cannot employ true experimental designs to investigate etiological questions about psychological disorders, but necessarily are limited to investigating the correlates of the individual differences associated with the pathological conditions. Although nothing prevents clinical investigators from assessing these correlates under tightly controlled laboratory conditions, tradition has led to a preference for more "naturalistic" approaches in which higher priority is given to "ecological validity" (external validity) than to stimulus control (internal validity). When disorders are studied in a clinical setting, the focus tends to be idiographic, aimed at the assessment, diagnosis, prediction, and treatment of individual clients. Because pathological conditions tend to be viewed as private, unobservable, emotional or cognitive states, clinical investigators traditionally have relied on introspective self-report methods of measuring these subjective phenomena. Finally, many clinicians rely on intuitive clinical judgments, as opposed to more objective, actuarial, quantitative inferential methods (Matarazzo, 1990; Peterson, 1996). This intuitive epistemology is unwarranted, according to virtually all of the empirical evidence (Dawes, Faust & Meehl, 1989; Grove & Meehl, 1996; Meehl, 1954).

Bridging the historical differences between these two worlds of psychology is a challenge for proponents of integration, but not an impossibility. Indeed, when psychology was still in its infancy, integrative work was commonplace; psychological pioneers seemed to move with ease between the two worlds. For example, in the very first psychology laboratory, established by Wundt in Leipzig, in 1879, reaction time experiments explored both stimulus effects and, indirectly, the nature of human consciousness. In 1883, while serving as an assistant in Wundt's laboratory, James McKeen Cattell noted systematic individual differences in reaction times regardless of stimulus modality. He studied these differences by averaging each subject's reaction times across many trials with different stimuli. Because he was unable to manipulate the personal characteristic of interest, he relied on correlational methods, rather than experimental methods. Thus, Wundt and Cattell somehow were able to integrate smoothly their basic studies of stimulus modality effects with their studies of individual differences (Boring, 1957).

Binet was another pioneer who carried out research in both worlds—correlational studies of intelligence and experimental studies of memory and judgment—without sensing any conflict (Cairns & Ornstein, 1979). Binet's integrated approach to psychology reflected his awareness that different research problems and questions call for different research strategies and tools; yet knowledge gleaned from each approach, in turn, can cast reflected light on other problems and questions. We see no inherent reason why a similar integration could not be achieved by contemporary psychologists. The two worlds of psychology seem to exist largely as unfortunate by-products of parochial tensions arising from historically rooted differences in training and tradition.

Integration is Possible

We believe that the philosophical and historical obstacles can be overcome, and that integration is both feasible and desirable. In the remainder of this chapter, we provide examples of contemporary work that is making progress toward this goal. First, we highlight the strengths of the Eyeblink Classical Conditioning (EBCC) paradigm as a foundation for integrative research. Then we describe specific applications of the paradigm in studies of specific clinical disorders. Finally, we suggest some promising future directions for integrative clinical-cognitive-neuroscience research. Our overarching aims are two-fold: We hope to convince readers that the abstract goal of integrating clinical science with cognitive-neuroscience not only is possible, but also is a promising and worthwhile effort. In addition, we hope to show that the EBCC paradigm provides an excellent conceptual and methodological foundation upon which to build such an integrative structure.

CLINICAL IMPLICATIONS OF EYEBLINK CLASSICAL CONDITIONING IN HUMANS AND NONHUMANS

The venerable EBCC paradigm certainly is not the only approach capable of promoting integration. Other approaches have attracted considerable attention in recent years, including psychophysiological measures (e.g., electrodermal response, heart rate, event-related potential, electromyography, pupilography); brain imaging techniques (CAT scans, PET scans, fMRI); and various cognitive or motor tasks (eye tracking, finger tapping, Stroop Test, Wisconsin Card Sort, dichotic listening). In our view, however, the EBCC paradigm has inherent strengths that make it an especially appealing choice.

One the EBCC paradigm's greatest strengths is its focus on a dependent variable—*associative learning* within a *classical conditioning* framework—that is a psychological variable of importance in its own right. Other approaches tend to focus on dependent variables that are chosen as surrogates for, or indirect indicators of, otherwise inaccessible psychological constructs. For example, EEG recordings of event-related potentials provide samples of electrical activity at the scalp. These, in turn, yield time-linked wave forms that are, among other things, gross reflections of brain activity in response to variations in experimental stimuli. The resulting indices, such as the P300 wave, are of little intrinsic interest except as they may provide veiled clues about psychological variables of interest. Such indirect measures, like three-cushion billiards shots, tend to be error-prone. In contrast, the EBCC paradigm takes a straight shot at measuring directly a key psychological variable of interest—the acquisition rate, timing, amplitude, and other characteristics of a simple learned motor response.

After decades of research, there now is an extensive literature describing the use of eyeblink conditioning to assess learning in human and nonhuman subjects, and documenting the parallels in performance between these two populations. At the same time, there is an extensive literature, primarily with animals, establishing the neural circuitry involved in such conditioning. In the process of building this body of knowledge, investigators also have developed an impressive array of technical tools for controlling stimuli, recording responses, and analyzing and interpreting data. In short, eyeblink conditioning (at the psychological level) and its neurological correlates (at the biological level) are so well understood, and the dimensions of the experimental paradigm are so well established, that investigators now should be able to use the leverage provided by this knowledge and know-how to illuminate important clinical problems.

The work with humans, which began early in this century, has focused primarily on defining the behavioral characteristics of conditioned responses under varying circumstances. Investigators have mapped in detail how variations in the paradigm affect learning and other cognitive processes. Among other things, this research with humans has examined different aspects of conditioned and unconditioned responses; has investigated the influence of different timing parameters; has studied discrimination learning and other versions of the paradigm; and has explored how subject factors, such as anxiety, correlate with patterns of learning (Baron & Connor, 1960; Grant & Adams, 1944; Hilgard, Campbell & Sears, 1937; Hobson, 1968; Ominsky & Kimble, 1966; Spence & Farber, 1953).

In the 1970s and 1980s, studies of eyeblink conditioning in animals, particularly rabbits, not only identified the learning characteristics of eyeblink conditioning in nonhumans (Gormezano, Schneiderman, Deaux & Fuentes, 1962; Kehoe, 1982; Kehoe, 1983; Kehoe & Napier, 1991a; Kehoe & Napier, 1991b), but also delineated the neuroanatomical and neurophysiological correlates of conditioning and other neuromodulatory factors (Berger & Thompson, 1978; Berry & Swain, 1994; Chapman, Steinmetz Thompson, 1988; Lavond, McCormick, Clark, Holmes & Thompson, 1981; McCormick, Clark, Lavond & Thompson, 1982; Steinmetz, Lavond & Thompson, 1989; Steinmetz & Sengelaub, 1992; Thompson, 1989a; Thompson, 1989b). Because the behavioral patterns in nonhumans closely paralleled those observed in humans, this neuroanatomical research with animals also illuminated, by analogy, the neural circuitry of conditioning in humans. This neurological research established, for example, that the cerebellum and associated brainstem circuitry are necessary for successful eyeblink conditioning, and that the basal ganglia and hippocampal structures play a significant modulatory role (Berger & Thompson, 1982; Berger, Weikart, Bassett & Orr, 1986; Krupa, Thompson & Thompson, 1993; Lavond & Steinmetz, 1989; McCormick & Thompson, 1984; White, Miller, White, Dike & Steinmetz, 1994).

In short, eyeblink conditioning is so well understood—at both the behavioral and neural levels—and the associations *across these levels* also are so well documented that eyeblink conditioning now represents an exceptional platform for an integrative clinical-cognitive-neuroscience investigation into psychopathology. This research can take two forms: (a) exploratory research aimed at finding conditioning "markers" of psychological disorders, or (b) theory-driven research aimed at testing specific predictions about conditioning and extinction, cognitive processing, and neurological functioning in specific clinical populations.

For example, although a great deal is known about the behavioral symptoms of persons with clinical diagnoses such as anxiety, depression, or autism, less is known about the cognitive and neurological correlates of these symptoms. Using the leverage of the EBCC paradigm, however, investigators can look for specific learning patterns ("markers") that distinguish between persons with and without diagnostic symptoms. Such group-specific conditioning patterns, in turn, would provide promising clues about possible neurological factors associated with the disorders.

Many psychological theories of clinical disorders make reference to learning histories, cognitive processes, and neurological deficits. Too often, however, these theories have not been put at risk of falsification in rigorous empirical tests. Given what we now know about learning, cognition, and neural processing in the EBCC paradigm, however, this paradigm should provide an excellent platform for testing specific predictions derived from clinical theories of psychopathology. Even when a theory's predictions are not crystal clear, the theory-driven approach still should be useful by allowing investigators to take a "strong inference" (Platt, 1964) approach to sorting out the plausible options.

EBCC and the Search for Markers of Psychopathology

Increasingly, the EBCC paradigm is being used with success as a tool for investigating specific psychopathological disorders in humans (Steinmetz, 1999; Woodruff-Pak, 1999). The most common use, thus far, has been as a tool for discovering markers for specific clinical disorders. Typically, eyeblink conditioning patterns found in persons diagnosed with a pathological condition are compared with those found in normal controls. Because so much is known about the neuroanatomical structures involved in eyeblink conditioning, virtually any reliable between-group differences can provide strong clues about the likely neurological dysfunctions associated with the disorder. This use of the EBCC paradigm is not atheoretical; theory is essential to making reasonable inferences about the neurological implications of the markers. This approach differs from the theory-testing approach described in the next section, however, because it does not require that investigators start with theoretical preconceptions about which markers might be found. Any and all group differences in learning are treated as potentially useful windows to brain pathologies associated with particular disorders.

Note that this approach examines a clinical disorder at two levels simultaneously, with the information supplied by the markers at one level (eyeblink conditioning patterns) being interpreted in the light of theories at the other level (models of neurological dysfunction in psychopathology). But the interplay between levels can be bi-directional. Just as EBCC markers may point to neurological concomitants of a disorder, the inferred neurological concomitants may point, in return, to new predictions about likely learning patterns, which then can be tested in the EBCC paradigm. This reciprocal interplay across levels of analysis is one of the benefits of taking an integrated clinical-cognitive-neuroscience approach to studying psychopathology. The EBCC paradigm facilitates this kind of integration while minimizing the dangers of falling into philosophical or historical traps.

Over the last decade, the marker approach has been used to study a growing list of disorders, including amnesia, autism, and Down's syndrome (Sears, Finn & Steinmetz, 1994; Woodruff-Pak, 1993; Woodruff-Pak, Papka & Simon, 1994). It also has been used to study neurodegenerative diseases, including Parkinson's, Alzheimer's, and Huntington's (Daum et al., 1995; Woodruff-Pak, 1990; Woodruff-Pak & Papka, 1996). For example, anterograde amnesia is an explicit memory disorder associated with bilateral medial-temporal lobe circuits. Because eyeblink conditioning is believed to occur independently of the medial-temporal circuits, the EBCC paradigm can serve as a probe to determine the extent to which the disorder differentially affects implicit and explicit learning. Thus far, the evidence shows that patients suffering from anterograde amnesia maintain their ability to construct new motor memories, even while showing no awareness of having done so (Hamann & Squire, 1995; Squire, 1986; Squire, 1987). For example, profoundly amnesic patients have been shown to learn and retain eyeblink conditioning at normal levels (Gabrieli et al., 1995), whereas victims of discrete cerebellar damage are completely unable to learn simple eyeblink conditioning, even though their explicit learning abilities remain intact (Daum et al., 1993).

One of the key features of the conditioned eyeblink response is its precise timing. In a well-conditioned subject, the peak amplitude of the blink response (CR) will coincide precisely with the presentation of the air puff (US). This is true regardless of whether the US occurs 200 ms or 1500 ms following the CS. This exquisite CR timing generally is thought to be an expression of cerebellar function (Ivry, Keele & Diener, 1988), although at least one human study suggests that other brain structures may influence CR timing. Knowledge about the neural structures involved in CR timing has been invaluable in interpreting distinctive patterns of CR timing found in two disorders: Huntington's disease and autism.

Patients with Huntington's disease show a normal unconditioned eyeblink response (UR) to the air puff (US) and display the same rate of CR acquisition as healthy control subjects. However, Huntington's patients differ significantly from controls in the timing of their CR, showing a significantly shorter latency, which results in the CR being mistimed to the US (Woodruff-Pak & Papka, 1996). This marker of conditioning performance in Huntington's patients informs and supports what is known about both eyeblink conditioning and Huntington's disease at the neurological level. In general, it supports the view that Huntington's involves the degeneration of the basal ganglia and cerebral cortex, but spares the cerebellum and hippocampus (Woodruff-Pak & Papka, 1996).

Research by Sears et al. (1994) on autism provides another example of using the EBCC paradigm to help illuminate the neurological correlates of a psychopathological disorder. Children diagnosed with autism show more rapid eyeblink conditioning than normal controls, but these conditioned responses are poorly timed, with the peak response occurring prior to the presentation of the US. This distinctive pattern of acquisition correlates with the finding that autistic children have a particular deficit in their cerebellar Purkinje cells (Ritvo et al., 1986). The neurological interpretations of the conditioning markers found in autistic patients, as well as those found in Huntington's patients, are supported by findings from the experimental animal literature (Perrett, Ruiz & Mauk, 1993; White et al., 1994), where both cerebellar cortex lesions and basal ganglia lesions have led to maladaptive, poorly timed eyeblink CRs.

Clearly, this approach to studying psychopathology is a promising direction for future research. It illustrates the cross-fertilization and fruitful interplay that can come from examining phenomena simultaneously from the clinical science and cognitive-neuroscience perspectives, looking for convergence between markers of clinical disorders and theories of neural functioning.

EBCC Tests of Predictions from Learning Theory Models of Psychopathology

Although few investigators to date have used eyeblink conditioning to test learning theory predictions about clinical disorders, we expect this strategy to become more common in the future as more investigators become aware of its advantages. To illustrate, we first will describe theory-driven research from our laboratory focused on anxiety disorders; then we will discuss potential applications of the EBCC paradigm to similar theory-driven research with other clinical disorders.

The Diagnostic and Statistical Manual of Mental Disorders (DSM-IV) (American Psychiatric Association, 1994) identifies *anxiety disorders* as one of the major categories of psychopathology, subsuming thirteen specific disorders (e.g., panic disorder, several types of phobia, obsessive-compulsive disorder, posttraumatic stress disorder, etc.). The core feature of all these disorders, of course, is the presence of anxiety symptoms, which tend to be situational and usually are triggered by specific stimuli. Most psychological theories regard these anxiety symptoms as learned responses, with the stimulus-response associations acquired and maintained through a combination of classical (Pavlovian) and instrumental (operant) conditioning.

This formulation was set forth by Mowrer (1960), for example, in his two-factor theory of anxiety disorders: Initially, a neutral stimulus is paired with an unconditioned stimulus (US) that elicits an unconditioned response (UR) of anxiety. Through associative learning, the neutral stimulus becomes a conditioned stimulus (CS) capable of eliciting a conditioned anxiety response (CR). In an attempt to avoid the CS and escape from the discomfort of anxiety, the individual engages in instrumental avoidance behavior, which is negatively reinforced when it leads to a temporary reduction in or avoidance of the anticipated anxiety.

Conditioned anxiety and avoidance responses are acquired more readily to some stimuli than to others, perhaps because at one time these stimulus-specific responses may have had survival value for the species. According to the evolutionary view, humans and nonhumans alike are "prepared" to acquire conditioned responses to certain salient stimuli (Cook & Mineka, 1990; Seligman, 1971). In clinical patients, however, these conditioned responses are maladaptive, not adaptive. They have become so severe, distressing, generalized, time consuming, and unreasonable that they interfere significantly with daily functioning.

The related issues of biological preparedness and stimulus salience have received considerable attention in the animal research (Flaherty, 1985). The evidence that some stimuli are more salient than others, or function more readily as conditioned stimuli, means that the choice of CS-US pairing is not an arbitrary matter. For example, rats readily acquire an association between a light or tone and a foot shock, but not an association between an odor and a foot shock. Yet odor is a better CS than either a tone or light for conditioned taste aversion (Garcia & Koelling, 1966). Classical conditioning theory does not predict that any two randomly selected stimuli can become associated through repeated pairing. On the contrary, the theory imposes constraints, linked to such factors as salience, modality, timing, continuity, and contiguity (Gormezano, Kehoe & Marshall, 1983; Rescorla, 1988). Such constraints may explain why certain stimuli (e.g., fear of snakes and spiders; obsessions about contamination) and responses (e.g., avoidance of crowded places; compulsive handwashing or checking) are over-represented in the symptom patterns of persons with anxiety disorders.

The current treatment of choice for anxiety disorders—exposure with response prevention (ERP)—is linked to the two-factor learning theory (Foa & Kozak, 1985). ERP is designed specifically to bring about the extinction of avoidance responses to the conditioned stimuli. If the conditioned stimuli do not pose genuine threats, then repeated exposure to these stimuli (while preventing escape and avoidance responses) should lead to an absence of the anticipated aversive consequences, which should lead gradually to an extinction of the conditioned anxiety and avoidance responses.

For anxiety disorders ranging from simple phobia to obsessive-compulsive disorder, ERP treatments have been shown to be effective for about 75% of the patients who complete treatment (e.g., (Craske & Barlow, 1993; Stanley & Turner, 1995). Effectiveness typically is defined as at least a 60% reduction in symptoms, not complete remission (Foa & Tillmans, 1980). Because patients tend to find the exposure component of ERP aversive, drop-out rates can be 25% or higher (Foa & Tillman, 1980). Unfortunately, the treatment-outcome studies do not provide direct tests of the underlying two-factor theory of anxiety disorders. Treatments may be effective even though they are based on misguided or invalid theories. The underlying theory of anxiety disorders still needs to be tested in its own right.

To our surprise, we could find no direct experimental tests of the two-factor conditioning model of anxiety disorders. Of course, most psychologists are familiar with Watson and Rayner's (1920) famous demonstration of classical conditioning, in which Baby Albert acquired fear and avoidance of a stuffed toy after the toy was paired a few times with a loud noise. Over the years, more than 25 studies with humans have provided indirect support for the hypothesized role of classical conditioning in fear acquisition (Beidel & Turner, 1991). There also is an extensive animal literature on fear acquisition (Kim & Fanselow, 1992; LeDoux, 1996; Maren, DeCola & Fanselow, 1994; Thompson et al., 1987), providing additional analogue support for the conditioning model of anxiety disorders. Nevertheless, there are no direct laboratory tests of the conditioning model of anxiety disorders in humans. Therefore, we undertook such tests in our lab, using the EBCC paradigm.

Our research focused on one class of anxiety disorders: obsessive-compulsive disorder (OCD). OCD is characterized by intrusive, unwanted, and uncontrollable thoughts and images that the individual recognizes as irrational and self-generated (the *obsessive* feature), and by uncontrollable urges to engage in repetitive irrational behaviors or mental acts aimed at avoiding or reducing the anxiety elicited by the obsessions (the *compulsive* feature). For a person to be diagnosed with OCD, the obsessions and compulsions must disrupt the person's daily functioning and be experienced as distressing, excessive, and unreasonable (American Psychiatric Association, 1994).

OCD once was considered rare, but recent epidemiological survey data indicate a lifetime prevalence rate of 2 - 3% in the U.S. (American Psychiatric Association, 1994; Karno, Golding, Sorenson & Burnam, 1988; Rasmussen & Eisen, 1991). There is a high co-morbidity between OCD and several other disorders, including major depression, simple phobia, eating disorders, alcohol dependence, and panic disorder (Black & Noyes, 1990; Crino & Gavin, 1996; DiNardo & Barlow, 1990; Rasmussen

& Eisen, 1991). The reasons for these associations are unknown, however.

Common obsessions include fears of contamination, concerns about unintentionally harming others, distress over asymmetry or disorder, thoughts about acting out aggressive or horrific impulses, and distress over intrusive sexual images. In an effort to suppress or neutralize such obsessions, the person may engage in compulsive thoughts or actions. Examples of compulsive mental acts are praying, counting, and silent verbal rituals. Examples of overt behaviors are repetitive hand washing, checking, and motor rituals. These compulsive thoughts and actions seldom are pleasurable; their aim is to prevent or reduce anxiety. Persons diagnosed with OCD recognize, at some level, that their obsessions and compulsions are excessive and unreasonable, yet they feel powerless to control them (American Psychiatric Association, 1994).

Against the background of this clinical description, we attempted to delineate the predictions that followed logically from the conditioning theory of OCD. Immediately, a number of questions arose. For instance, if most persons experience traumatic events in their lives, why do only 3% develop OCD? We considered two possibilities: (a) this might be due to individual differences in learning histories, with OCD patients being exposed to different stimuli and different conditioning experiences than normals; or (b) this might be due to individual differences in the way persons react to essentially equivalent learning histories. (These two possibilities are not exhaustive, of course, but represent a reasonable contrast and a logical starting place.) Relevant to the first possibility, investigators have examined retrospectively the lives of OCD patients in search of differential exposure to traumatic events or unique conditioning histories that might account for their acquisition of OCD symptoms. Thus far, these searches have yielded weak support for the role of trauma (DiNardo & Barlow, 1990; Ost, 1987).

Regarding the second possibility, investigators have looked for individual differences that might explain why two persons exposed to the similar events might respond differently, one developing OCD, the other not. Cognitive theorists, for example, have suggested that differences in cognitive styles and coping strategies may mediate individual differences in conditioning (Reed, 1977; Sher, Frost & Otto, 1983). We took another tack. Rather than look to third variables to explain *assumed group differences in conditionability*, we started with the more fundamental prior question: Do persons with symptoms of OCD actually perform differently than normal controls in a classical conditioning paradigm? If so, how? Do symptomatic persons simply condition more readily than normals? Do they extinguish more slowly? Do they show deficits in discrimination learning by overgeneralizing the category of conditioned stimuli? Do their conditioned responses differ from those of normals in intensity, timing, consistency, or some other way? Perhaps they do not differ fundamentally from normals in their rate or pattern of conditioning, but differ in arousal level, attention, or other variables that yield group differences in conditioning only under specific circumstances. Perhaps they do not condition differently in response to neutral stimuli, such as tones, but condition differently in response to specific types of "prepared" stimuli. Unfortunately, learning models of OCD are ambiguous about the specific group differences we should expect. They lead us to expect individual differences in conditionability, but offer little guidance about which of these possibilities explains why only 3% of the population acquires OCD symptoms.

Two Studies

We took a theory-driven approach to exploring these possibilities, starting by testing the simplest explanations first. We hypothesized that persons with OCD symptoms would differ from normal controls in the rates and patterns of their acquisition and extinction of conditioned eyeblinks to neutral tones in a simple EBCC paradigm (Tracy, Ghose, Stecher, McFall & Steinmetz, 1999). Essentially, we were testing the notion that OCD is related to fundamental differences in conditionability.

Participants in both studies were college undergraduates from introductory psychology classes, pre-screened on the Maudsley Obsessional-Compulsive Inventory (MOCI; Hodgson & Rachman, 1977), a self-report measure of OCD behaviors. Our non-clinical OCD sample was drawn from students scoring in the top 4% on this measure; our control group was drawn randomly (matching for sex) from students scoring in the bottom 75%. Previous research has shown that non-clinical participants who admit to high rates of obsessions and compulsions are similar to clinically diagnosed OCD patients (Frost, Sher & Green, 1986; Rachman & deSilva, 1978). Moreover, our selection ratio of 4% was close to the population prevalence rates of 3% for OCD.

Both studies used a standard delay paradigm (500 ms tone CS, 100 ms air puff US, 400 ms ISI), consisting of 10 blocks of 10 paired acquisition trials followed by three additional blocks of 10 tone-alone extinction trials. The inter-trial interval varied from 10 to 20 sec, with a mean of 15. Concurrent with the conditioning procedure, participants engaged in a background task. The only difference between studies one and two was the nature of this background task. In study one, it was an active visual search task; in study two, it was a passive picture viewing task. Both tasks involved attending to images on a computer screen and making a keyboard response to each image; however, the visual search task was more arousing, requiring vigilance and involving the risk of errors, whereas the picture viewing task was neither demanding nor arousing.

The visual search task consisted of computer presentations of a series of 5 x 5 matrices of randomly arranged letters—blue Os and green Ds. Fifty percent of the matrices contained an errant green O. Participants' task was to determine for each matrix whether it contained a green O, responding as quickly as possible by pressing either Y (yes) or N (no) on the computer keyboard. The picture viewing task, which replaced the visual search task in study two, consisted of computer presentations of a series of neutral pictures (e.g., landscapes, teddy bears, candy, views from outer space). Participants simply indicated whether or not they liked each picture by pressing Y (yes) or N (no) on the computer keyboard. In both studies, the timing of the background task and conditioning task were independent.

Analyses of study one's eyeblink conditioning data uncovered no between-group differences. The groups did not differ significantly in percentage of participants reaching the conditioning criterion; number of trials to criterion; percentage of conditioned responses; mean latency to peak conditioned response; mean amplitude of peak response; or mean amplitude of unconditioned response. In contrast, analyses of study two's data revealed clear between-group differences: The OCD group acquired the conditioned eyeblink response significantly more rapidly than the control group did; the OCD group also showed a significantly greater decrease in UR amplitudes over blocks than did the control group. Figure 1 graphically displays the eyeblink amplitude and timing curves for each group, averaged for each block of conditioning trials, for each study. The curves for the OCD group in studý two differ clearly from the curves in the other three panels. In study two only, the OCD group showed evidence of conditioning within the first five trials of the very first block, and showed a corresponding drop in UR amplitude starting with the same early trials. Thus, the results from study two support the learning-theory model of OCD, which predicts that persons with OCD should acquire classically conditioned responses more rapidly than normals. There was no support for the hypothesis that persons with OCD might extinguish more slowly than normals.

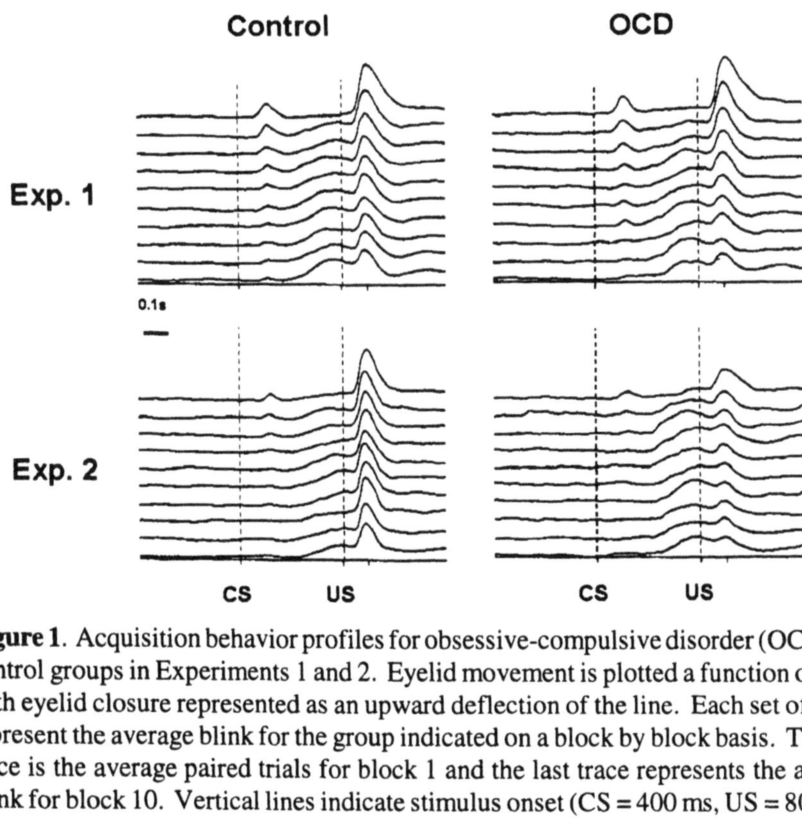

Figure 1. Acquisition behavior profiles for obsessive-compulsive disorder (OCD) and control groups in Experiments 1 and 2. Eyelid movement is plotted a function of time, with eyelid closure represented as an upward deflection of the line. Each set of traces represent the average blink for the group indicated on a block by block basis. The first trace is the average paired trials for block 1 and the last trace represents the average blink for block 10. Vertical lines indicate stimulus onset (CS = 400 ms, US = 800 ms). Small blinks within 200 ms of the CS onset are alpha responses. Blinks that occur 200-400 ms after the CS onset are conditioned responses.

Support for the learning model, however, was dependent on the background task. The OCD and normal groups conditioned at the same rate when exposed to the demanding visual search task; both groups performed better under this task than under the picture viewing task. The overall percentage of conditioned responses for both groups was 75%, which is well above the level typically reported in the human eyeblink literature. Under the less demanding picture viewing task, the overall percentage of conditioned responses declined for both groups, but this decline was greater for the normal group than for the OCD group. Moreover, the OCD group still managed to reach its asymptotic level of conditioned responses within the first five trials of the first block!

Taken together, the two studies indicate that background tasks can have a significant impact on conditioning. This means that prior conclusions concerning background tasks—for example, that they exert little influence on conditioning except when they involve the same neural circuitry (Papka, Ivry, & Woodruff-Pak, 1995)—need to be revisited. Previous research had focused on the possibility that background tasks may interfere with the acquisition of conditioned responses; our studies raise the possibility that some tasks actually may facilitate conditioning.

Future Directions

Future studies will examine, among other things, how conditioning is affected by the different levels and types of arousal created by different background tasks. In addition, we now are testing other learning theory explanations for OCD. For example, learning theory suggests that OCD symptoms may develop when persons fail to discriminate between genuinely dangerous stimuli (e.g., life threatening germs) and similar-but-safe stimuli (e.g., normal germs on doorknobs). If so, persons with OCD should perform differently than normals in a two-tone discrimination-learning version of the EBCC paradigm. We currently are testing this possibility.

Posttraumatic stress disorder, panic disorder, agoraphobia, and simple phobia are examples of other anxiety disorders assumed to be acquired through conditioning. Theoretical accounts specific to these disorders need to be studied systematically using the EBCC paradigm. In addition, classical conditioning has been implicated in the etiology of other DSM-IV disorders, including alcohol and substance abuse, antisocial personality disorder, bulimia nervosa, depression, paraphilia, and sexual dysfunctions (see Emmelkamp, 1994). The EBCC paradigm could be used to test specific predictions about the role of conditioning in each of these clinical problems.

For instance, according to theories of antisocial personality disorder (APD), persons with APD are deficient, relative to normals, in their rate of acquisition for conditioned anxiety and avoidance responses (Lykken, 1957). Eysenck (1960) proposed that such conditioning deficits explain why persons with APD fail to acquire many of the essential components of conscience and socialized behavior. Research tends to support this hypothesis, especially for conditioned inhibition of responses paired with the anticipation of punishment (Fowles, 1993; Fowles & Missel, 1994; Hare, 1978). Thus, in a discrimination conditioning paradigm, APD participants should learn more slowly than normal participants to inhibit responses to the CS- when it is an aversive stimulus.

Bulimia nervosa is another clinical disorder that could be studied. According to learning theories, specific food- and body-related cues have become conditioned stimuli for anxiety and avoidance in persons with this disorder. To test this hypothesis in the EBCC paradigm, for example, photos presented on a computer screen of high/low-fat foods or heavy/thin female bodies might serve as the conditioning stimuli (CS+/CS-) in a discrimination conditioning paradigm. Female participants pre-selected to represent bulimia nervosa should acquire this discrimination more rapidly than controls if the conditioning cues in the photos (e.g., fat content; body size) are more salient for the bulimic participants.

One final example: Paraphilia is another clinical disorder that could be studied with the EBCC paradigm. Paraphilia is characterized by a persistent pattern of sexual behaviors in which unusual objects, rituals, or situations are required for full sexual satisfaction (American Psychiatric Association, 1994). Fetishism is one form of paraphilia in which a person's sexual interest is focused on inanimate objects, such as clothing, shoes, jewelry, body parts, or odors (Abel, Blanchard, & Barlow, 1981). Learning models assume that fetishism results from the pairing of inanimate objects with sexual arousal and gratification. Although it is unclear why only certain individuals develop such patterns, one possibility is that persons who develop fetishes condition more readily than normals. Consistent with this individual-differences view, theorists have suggested (Bailey, Gaulin, Agyei, & Gladue, 1994; Money, 1986) that men are more likely than women to develop paraphilias because men rely more than women do on visual sexual stimuli for arousal (i.e., they find these stimuli more salient). Using a compound conditioned stimulus (CCS) version of the EBCC paradigm, it would be possible not only to test whether men with fetishes condition differently than normal men do, but also to test whether men condition more rapidly to visual stimuli than women do. In the CCS paradigm, two stimuli initially serve as a compound CS. After a conditioned response has been established to both stimuli, one is removed, and conditioned responses to the lone CS are recorded. Reports in the animal literature indicate that the amplitude of the eyeblink is reduced by 50% following removal of the compound CS (Kehoe & Schreurs, 1986). Using this paradigm to explore fetishism, male and female participants initially might be presented with a compound conditioning stimulus consisting of sexual pictures and a tone. Later, the tone would be removed, leaving only the sexual pictures to serve as the CS. Women should show a greater reduction in eyeblink amplitude than men to this manipulation. Men with a fetish should show a smaller reduction than normal men.

IMPLICATIONS FOR INTEGRATION

Essentially the same EBCC paradigm—with its variety of well-developed procedures aimed at addressing different questions—can be used to investigate a wide range of clinical disorders. Using a common experimental platform has the advantage of permitting theoretically informative comparisons of results across studies and populations. Investigators should be just as interested in detecting conditioning patterns that discriminate among the various disorders as in finding markers that discriminate between clinical populations (Chapman & Chapman, 1989). The long-term goal should be to identify the distinctive conditioning patterns that define each clinical disorder (Campbell & Fiske, 1959). This knowledge should have major theoretical and practical implications for psychological science—at all levels of analysis. It would help psychopathologists devise more precise taxonomies of clinical disorders. It would help clinical scientists improve their ability to assess, predict, treat, and explain clinical phenomena. It would direct cognitive scientists' attention to low-base-rate phenomena that eventually must be incorporated into theories of cognitive processing. And it would direct neuroscientists' attention to the most promising neural structures and processes to investigate in connection with clinical disorders.

The EBCC paradigm already has yielded promising clues about the neural and cognitive correlates of clinical disorders, such as autism, Alzheimer's, and Huntington. It also has given us a fruitful method of testing clinical theories about the etiology of disorders such as OCD. We expect that future research of this sort, focused on other clinical problems, will provide additional enlightenment. Best of all, perhaps, the work reviewed in this chapter demonstrates the power of pursuing an integrated approach to clinical problems.

Viewing clinical problems simultaneously from two or more levels of analysis allows investigators to document consistent patterns of association *among the levels of analysis*. If we triangulate—viewing clinical problems from the three perspectives of clinical symptoms, cognitive processing, and neural functioning—the combination becomes as stable as a three-legged stool; that is, otherwise flimsy and unstable pieces of separate information are combined to form a solid, integrated structure. Thus, for a given clinical disorder, the more successfully we identify systematic relationships among patients' symptomatic behaviors, their distinctive patterns of learning under varying circumstances, and their neural functioning, the more confidence we have in the validity of our theories *at all levels.*

This kind of integration requires a recognition that each level of analysis makes its own, distinctive contribution to the whole; that the whole remains a cohesive, mutually reinforcing structure of separate parts; and that our integrated knowledge is a woven fabric, the intertwined threads of the warp and woof spun by looking at the same problems from different perspectives. In the long term, this kind of integrated model is our best hope of developing effective methods of assessing, predicting, preventing, and treating specific clinical disorders.

NOTE

1. Our characterizations of clinical psychology and neuroscience are heuristic generalizations aimed at sharpening each group's prototype features and highlighting group differences. Clearly, these stereotypes do not apply to all group members. After all, two of the authors (RMM & SSG) are clinical scientists; two (JAT & JES) are neuroscientists.

REFERENCES

Abel, G.G., Blanchard, E.B., & Barlow, D.H. (1981). Measurement of sexual arousal in several paraphilias: The effects of stimulus modality, instructional set, and stimulus content. *Behaviour Research and Therapy, 19*, 25-33.

American Psychiatric Association (1994). *Diagnostic and Statistical Manual of Mental Disorders, 4th edition (DSM-IV)*. Washington, D.C.: American Psychiatric Association.

Bailey, J. M., Gaulin, S., Agyei, Y., & Gladue, B. A. (1994). Effects of gender and sexual orientation on evolutionarily relevant aspects of human mating psychology. *Journal of Personality and Social Psychology, 66*, 1081-1093.

Baron, M.R., & Connor, J.P. (1960). Eyelid conditioned responses with various levels of anxiety. *Journal of Experimental Psychology, 60*(5), 310-313.

Beidel, D.C., & Turner, S.M. (1991). Anxiety disorders. In M. Hersen & S. M. Turner (Eds.), *Adult Psychopathology and Diagnosis* . New York: John Wiley & Sons, Inc.

Berger, T.W., & Thompson, R.F. (1978). Identification of pyramidal cells as the critical elements in hippocampal neuronal plasticity during learning. *Proceedings of the Nattional Academy of Science (USA), 75*, 1572-1576.

Berger, T.W., & Thompson, R.F. (1982). Hippocampal cellular plasticity during extinction of classically conditioned nictitating membrane behavior. *Behavioural Brain Research, 4*, 63-76.

Berger, T.W., Weikart, C.L., Bassett, J.L., & Orr, W.B. (1986). Lesions of the retrosplenial cortex produce deficits in reversal learning of the rabbit nictitating membrane response: Implications for potential interactions between hippocampal and cerebellar brain systems. *Behavioral Neuroscience, 100*, 802-809.

Berry, S.D., & Swain, R.A. (1994). Water deprivation optimizes hippocampal activity and facilitates nictitating membrane conditioning. *Journal of Neuroscience, 103*(1), 71-76.

Black, D.W., & Noyes, R. (1990). Comorbidity and obsessive-compulsive disorder. In J. D. Maser & C. R. Cloninger (Eds.), *Comorbidity of Mood and Anxiety Disorders* (pp. 305-316). Washington, DC: American Psychiatric Press, Inc.

Boring, E.G. (1957). *A History of Eexperimental Psychology* (2nd ed.). New York: Appleton-Century-Crofts.

Cairns, R.B., & Ornstein, P.A. (1979). Developmental psychology. In E. Hearst (Ed.), *The First Century of Experimental Psychology* (pp. 459-510). Hillsdale, NJ: Lawrence Erlbaum.

Campbell, D.T., & Fiske, D.W. (1959). Convergent and discriminant validation by multitrait-multimethod matrix. *Psychological Bulletin, 56*, 81-105.

Campbell, D.T., & Stanley, J.C. (1963). *Experimental and Quasi-experimental Designs for Research*. Chicago: Rand-McNally.

Chapman, L.J., & Chapman, J.P. (1989). Strategies for resolving the heterogeneity of schizophrenics and their relatives using cognitive measures. *Journal of Abnormal Psychology, 98*, 357-366.

Chapman, P.F., Steinmetz, J.E., & Thompson, R.F. (1988). Classical conditioning does not occur when direct stimulation of the red nucleus or cerebellar nuclei is the unconditioned stimulus. *Brain Research, 442*, 97-104.

Cook, M., & Mineka, S. (1990). Selective associations in the observational conditioning of fear in rhesus monkeys. *Journal of Experimental Psychology: Animal Behavior Processes, 16*(4), 372-389.

Craske, M.G., & Barlow, D.H. (1993). Panic disorder and agoraphobia. In D. H. Barlow (Ed.), *Clinical Handbook of Psychological Disorders* (Vol. 2nd). New York: Guilford.

Crino, R.D., & Gavin, A. (1996). Obsessive-compulsive disorder and Axis I comorbidity. *Journal of Anxiety Disorders, 10*(1), 37-46.

Cronbach, L.J. (1957). The two disciplines of scientific psychology. *American Psychologist, 12*, 671-684.

Cronbach, L.J. (1975). Beyond the two disciplines of scientific psychology. *American Psychologist, 30*, 116-127.

Cronbach, L.J., & Meehl, P.E. (1955). Construct validity in psychological tests. *Psychological Bulletin, 52*, 281-302.

Daum, I., Chugens, M.M., Spieker, S., Poser, U., Schonle, P.W., & Birbaumer, N. (1995). Memory and skill acquisition in parkinson's disease and frontal lobe dysfunction. *Cortex, 31*, 413-432.

Daum, I., Schugens, M.M., Achermann, H., Lutzenberger, W., Dichgans, J., & Birbaumer, N. (1993). Classical conditioning after cerebellar lesions in humans. *Behavioral Neuroscience, 107*, 748-756.

Dawes, R. M., Faust, D., & Meehl, P. E. (1989). Clinical versus actuarial judgement. *Science, 243*, 1668-1674.

DiNardo, P.A., & Barlow, D.H. (1990). Syndrome and symptom co-occurrence in the anxiety disorders. In J. D. Maser & C. R. Cloninger (Eds.), *Comorbidity of Mood and Anxiety Disorders* (pp. 205-230). Washington, DC: American Psychiatric Press, Inc.

Emmelkamp, P.M.G. (1994). Behavior therapy with adults. In A.E. Bergin & S.L. Garfield (Eds.), *Handbook of Psychotherapy and Behavior Change* (4th ed., pp. 379-427). New York: Wiley.

Eysenck, H. J. (1960). *Behavior Therapy and the Neuroses: Readings in Modern Methods of Treatment*

Derived from Learning Theory. New York: Pergamon.

Flaherty, C.F. (1985). *Animal Learning and Cognition*. New York: Alfred A. Knopf.

Foa, E.B., & Kozak, M.J. (1985). Treatment of anxiety disorders: Implications for psychopathology. In A. H. Tuma & J.D. Maser (Eds.), *Anxiety and Anxiety Disorders* (pp. 421-452). Hillsdale, NJ: Erlbaum.

Fowles, D.C. (1993). Electrodermal activity and antisocial behavior: Empirical findings and theoretical issues. In J.C. Roy, W. Boucsein, D. Fowles, & J. Gruzelier (Eds.), *Progress in Electrodermal Research* . London: Plenum.

Fowles, D.C., & Missel, K.A. (1994). Electrodermal hyporeactivity, motivation, and psychotherapy: Theoretical issues. In D.C. Fowles, P. Sutker, & S.H. Goodman (Eds.), *Progress in Experimental Personality and Psychopathology Research*. New York: Springer.

Frost, R. O., Sher, K. J., & Green, T. (1986). Psychopathology and personality characteristics of nonclinical compulsive checkers. *Behaviour Research and Therapy, 24*(2), 133-143.

Gabrieli, J.D., McGlinchey-Berroth, R., Carrillo, M.C., Gluck, M.A., Cermak, L.S., & Disterhoft, J.F. (1995). Intact delay-eyeblink classical conditioning in amnesia. *Behavioral Neuroscience, 109*(5), 819-27.

Garcia, J., & Koelling, R.A. (1966). Relation of cue to consequence in avoidance learning. *Psychonomic Science, 4*(123-124).

Gormezano, I., Kehoe, E.J., & Marshall, B.S. (1983). Twenty years of classical conditioning research with the rabbit. In J.M. Sprague & A.N. Epstein (Eds.), *Progress in Psychobiology and Physiological Psychology, Vol. 10* (pp. 197-275). NY: Academic Press.

Gormezano, I., Schneiderman, N., Deaux, E., & Fuentes, I. (1962). Nictitating membrane: Classical conditioning and extinction in the albino rabbit. *Science, 138*, 33-34.

Grant, D.A., & Adams, J.K. (1944). "Alpha" conditioning in the eyelid. *Journal of Experimental Psychology, 34*, 136-141.

Grove, W.M., & Meehl, P.E. (1996). Comparative efficience of informal (subjective, impressionistic) and formal (mechaical, algorithimic) prediction procedure: The clinical-statistical controversy. *Psychology, Public Policy, and Law, 2*, 293-323.

Hamann, S.B., & Squire, L.R. (1995). On the Acquisition of new declarative knowledge in amnesia. *Behavioral Neuroscience, 109*(6), 1027-1044.

Hare, R.D. (1978). Electrodermal and cardiovascular correlates of sociopathy. In R.D. Hare & D. Schalling (Eds.), *Psychopathic Behaviour: Approaches to Research* . New York: Wiley.

Hilgard, E.R., Campbell, A.A., & Sears, W.N. (1937). Conditioned discrimination: The development of discrimination with and without verbal report. *American Journal of Psychology, XLIX*, 564-580.

Hobson, G.N. (1968). Effects of UCS adaptation upon conditioning in low and high anxiety men and women. *Journal of Experimental Psychology, 76*(3), 360-363.

Hodgson, R.J., & Rachman, S. (1977). Obsessive-compulsive complaints. *Behaviour Research and Therapy, 15*, 389-395.

Ivry, R.B., Keele, S.W., & Diener, H.C. (1988). Dissociation of the lateral and medial cerebellum in movement timing and movement execution. *Experimental Brain Research, 73*, 167-180.

Johnson, W. (1946). *People in Quandries: The Semantics of Personal Adjustment*. New York: Harper Brothers.

Karno, M., Golding, J.M., Sorenson, S.B., & Burnam, M.A. (1988). The epidemiology of obsessive-compulsive disorder in five U.S. communitites. *Archives of General Psychiatry, 45*, 1094-1099.

Kehoe, E.J. (1982). Overshadowing and summation in compound stimulus conditioning of the rabbit's nictitating membrane response. *Journal of Experimental Psychololology: Animal Behavior, 8*, 313-328.

Kehoe, E.J. (1983). CS-US contiguity and CS intensity in conditioning of the rabbit's nictitating membrane response to serial compound stimuli. *Journal of Experimental Psychology: Animal Behavior, 9*, 307-319.

Kehoe, E.J., & Napier, R.M. (1991a). In the blink of an eye: Real-time stimulus factors in delay and trace conditioning of the rabbit's nictitating membrane response. *Quarterly Journal of Experimental Psychology [B]., 43*, 257-277.

Kehoe, E.J., & Napier, R.M. (1991b). Temporal specificity in cross-modal transfer of the rabbit nictitating membrane response. *Journal of Experimental Psychology: Animal Behavior, 17*, 26-35.

Kehoe, J.E., & Schreurs, B.G. (1986). Compound conditioning of the rabbit's nictitating membrane response: Test trial manipulations. *Bulletin of the Psychonomic Society, 24*(1), 79-81.

Kim, J.J., & Fanselow, M.S. (1992). Modality-specific retrograde amnesia of fear. *Science, 256*, 675-677.

Krupa, D.J., Thompson, J.K., & Thompson, R.F. (1993). Localization of a memory trace in the mammalian brain. *Science, 260*, 989-991.
Lavond, D.G., McCormick, D.A., Clark, G.A., Holmes, D.T., & Thompson, R.F. (1981). Effects of ipsilateral rostral pontine reticular lesions on retention of classically conditioned nictitating membrane and eyelid responses. *Physiological Psychology, 9*, 335-339.
Lavond, D.G., & Steinmetz, J.E. (1989). Acquisition of classical conditioning without cerebellar cortex. *Behavioural Brain Research, 33*, 113-164.
LeDoux, J. (Ed.). (1996). *Emotional Networks and Motor Control: A Fearful View, (Vol. 107).* Elsevier Science.
Lykken, D.T. (1957). A study of anxiety in the sociopathic personality. *Journal of Abnormal and Social Psychology, 55*, 6-10.
MacCorquodale, K., & Meehl, P.E. (1948). On the disctinction between hypothetical constructs and intervening variables. *Psychological Review, 55*, 95-107.
Maren, S., DeCola, J.P., & Fanselow, M.S. (1994). Water deprivation enhances fear conditioning to contextual, but not discrete, conditional stimuli in rats. *Behavioral Neuroscience, 106*(3), 645-649.
Matarazzo, J. (1990). Psychological assessment versus psychological testing: Validation from Binet to the school, clinic, and courtroom. *American Psychologist, 45*, 999-1017.
McCormick, D.A., Clark, G.A., Lavond, D.G., & Thompson, R.F. (1982). Initial localization of the memory trace for a basic form of learning. *Proceedings of the National Academy of Science (U.S.A.), 79*, 2731-2735.
McCormick, D.A., & Thompson, R.F. (1984). Cerebellum: essential involvement in the classically conditioned eyelid response. *Science, 223*, 296-299.
McFall, R.M., & Townsend, J.T. (1998). Foundations of psychological assessment: Implications for cognitive assessment in clinical science. *Psychological Assessment, 10*(4), 316-330.
Meehl, P.E. (1954). *Clinical Versus Statistical Prediction: A Theoretical Analysis and a Review of the Evidence*. Minneapolis: University of Minnesota Press.
Meehl, P.E. (1973). *Psychodiagnosis: Selected Papers*. New York: Norton.
Meehl, P.E. (1978). Theoretical risks and tabular asterisks: Sir Karl, Sir Ronald and the slow progress of soft psychology. *Journal of Consulting and Clinical Psychology, 46*, 806-834.
Meehl, P.E., Klaan, R., Schmieding, A., Breimeier, K., & Schroeder-Slomann, S. (1958). *What, Then, is Man?* St. Louis: Concordia Publishing House.
Miller, G.A. (1996). How we think about cognition, emotion and biology in psychopathology. *Psychophysiology, 33*, 615-628.
Money, J. (1986). *Lovemaps: Clinical Concepts of Sexual/Erotic Health and Pathology, Paraphilia, and Gender Transposition*. New York: Irvington.
Mowrer, O.H. (1960). *Learning Theory and Behavior*. New York: John Wiley and Sons.
Ominsky, M., & Kimble, G.A. (1966). Anxiety and eyelid conditioning. *Journal of Experimental Psychology, 71*(3), 471-472.
Ost, L.G. (1987). Age of onset in different phobias. *Journal of Abnormal Psychology, 96*, 223-229.
Papka, M., Ivry, R.B., & Woodruff-Pak, D.S. (1995). Selective disruption of eyeblink classical conditioning by concurrent tapping. *NeuroReport, 6*(11), 1493-1497.
Perrett, S.P., Ruiz, B.P., & Mauk, M.D. (1993). Cerebellar cortex lesions disrupt learning-dependent timing of conditioned eyelid responses. *The Journal of Neuroscience, 13*, 1708-1718.
Peterson, D.R. (1996). Making psychology indispensable. *Applied & Preventive Psychology, 5*, 1-8.
Platt, J.R. (1964). Strong inference. *Science, 146*, 347-353.
Popper, K. (1962). *Conjectures &Refutations*. New York: Basic Books.
Rachman, S., & deSilva, P. (1978). Abnormal and normal obsessions. *Behaviour Research and Therapy, 16*, 233-248.
Rasmussen, S.A., & Eisen, J.L. (1991). Phenomenology of OCD: Clinical subtypes, heterogeneity and coexistence. In J. Zohar, T. Insel, & S. Rasmussen (Eds.), *The Psychobiology of Obsessive Compulsive Disorder*. New York: Springer.
Reed, G.F. (1977). Obsessional cognition: Performance on two numerical tasks. *British Journal of Psychiatry, 130*, 184-185.
Rescorla, R.A. (1988). Behavioral studies of Pavlovian conditioning. *Annual Review of Neuroscience, 11*, 329-352.
Ritvo, E., Freeman, B.J., Scheibel, A., Duong, T., Robinson, H., Guthrie, D., & Ritvo, A. (1986). Lower Purkinje cell counts in the cerebella of four autistic subjects: Initial finding of the UCLA-NSAC Autopsy Research report. *American Journal of Psychiatry, 143*, 862-866.

Sears, L.L., Finn, P.R., & Steinmetz, J.E. (1994). Abnormal classical eye-blink conditioning in autism. *Journal of Autism and Developmental Disorders, 24*(6), 737-751.

Sechrest, L. (1992). The past future of clinical psychology: A reflection on Woodworth (1937). *Journal of Consulting and Clinical Psychology, 60*(18-23).

Seligman, M. (1971). Phobias and preparedness. *Behavioral Therapy, 2*, 307-320.

Sher, K.J., Frost, R.O., & Otto, R. (1983). Cognitive deficits in compulsive checkers: An exploratory study. *Behaviour Research and Therapy, 21*(4), 357-363.

Spence, K.W., & Farber, I.E. (1953). Conditioning and extinction as a function of anxiety. *Journal of Experimental Psychology, 45*, 57-63.

Squire, L.R. (1986). Mechanisms of memory. *Science, 232*, 1612-1619.

Squire, L.R. (1987). *Memory and Brain*. New York: Oxford University Press.

Stanley, M.A., & Turner, S.M. (1995). Current status of pharmacological and behavioral treatment of obsessive-compulsive disorder. *Behavioral Therapy, 26*(1), 163-186.

Steinmetz, J.E. (1999). A renewed interest in human classical eyeblink conditioning. *Psychological Science, 10*(1), 24-25.

Steinmetz, J.E., Lavond, D.G., & Thompson, R.F. (1989). Classical conditioning in rabbits using pontine nucleus stimulation as a conditioned stimulus and inferior olive stimulation as an unconditioned stimulus. *Synapse, 3*, 225-233.

Steinmetz, J.E., & Sengelaub, D.R. (1992). Possible conditioned stimulus pathway for classical eyelid conditioning in rabbits. I. Anatomical evidence for direct projections from the pontine nuclei to the cerebellar interpositus nucleus. *Behavioral Neural Biology, 57*, 103-115.

Thompson, R.F. (1989a). The essential memory trace circuit and the essential reinforcement system for a basic form of associative learning. In T. Archer & L.-G. Nilsson (Eds.), *Aversion, Avoidance and Anxiety: Perspectives on Aversively Motivated behavior* (pp. 251-264). Hillsdale, NJ: Lawrence Erlbaum.

Thompson, R.F. (1989b). Neural circuit for classical conditioning of the eyelid closure response. In J.H. Byrne & W.O. Berry (Eds.), *Neural Models of Plasticity* (pp. 160-177). New York: Academic Press.

Thompson, R.F., Donegan, N.H., Clark, G.A., Lavond, D.G., Lincoln, J.S., Madden, J., IV, Mamounas, L.A., Mauk, M.D., & McCormick, D.A. (1987). Neuronal substrates of discrete, defensive conditioned reflexes, conditioned fear states, and their interactions in the rabbit. In I. Gormezano, W.F. Prokasy, & R.F. Thompson (Eds.), *Classical Conditioning* (pp. 371-399). Hillsdale,NJ: Erlbaum.

Tracy, J.A., Ghose, S.S., Stecher, T., McFall, R.M., & Steinmetz, J.E. (1999). Classical conditioning in a non-clinical obsessive-compulsive population. *Psychological Science, 10*, 9-13.

Watson, J.B. (1924). *Psychology from the Standpoint of a Behaviorist*. Philadelphia: J.B. Lippincott Company.

White, I.M., Miller, D.P., White, W., Dike, G.L., & Steinmetz, J.E. (1994). Neuronal activity in rabbit neostriatum during classical eyelid conditioning. *Experimental Brain Research, 99*, 179-190.

Woodruff-Pak, D.S., Finkbiner, R.G., Sasse, D.K. (1990). Eyeblink conditioning discriminates Alzheimer's patients from non-demented aged. *NeuroReport, 1*, 45-48.

Woodruff-Pak, D.S. (1993). Eyeblink classical conditioning in H.M.: Delay and trace paradigms. *Behavioral Neuroscience, 107*(6), 911-925.

Woodruff-Pak, D.S. (1999). New directions for a classical paradigm: Human eyeblink conditioning. *Psychological Science, 10*(1), 1-3.

Woodruff-Pak, D.S., & Papka, M. (1996). Huntington's desease and eyeblink conditioning: Normal learning by abnormal timing. *Neuropsychology, 11*(4), 474-487.

Woodruff-Pak, D.S., Papka, M., & Simon, E.W. (1994). Eyeblink classical conditioning in Down's Syndrome, fragile X syndrome, and normal adults over and under age 35. *Neuropsychology, 8*(1), 14-24.

Woodworth, R.S. (1937). The future of clinical psychology. *Journal of Consulting Psychology, 1*, 4-5.

APPENDIX: BIBLIOGRAPHY OF HUMAN EYEBLINK CONDITIONING (1899-1985)

Isidore Gormezano
University of Iowa

1899

Zwaardemaker, H., & Lans, L.J. (1899). Uber ein Stadium relativer Unerregdarkeit als Ursache des intermitterenden Charakters des Lidschlagrefiexes. *Centbl. F. Psysiol., 13,* 325-329.

1910

Weiss, O. (1910-1911). Die zeitliche Dauer Des Lidscniages. *Zsch. F. Psychol. U. Psysiol. D. Sinnersorg, 45, Abstract II.* 307-312.

1913

Dodge, R. The refractory phase of the normal wink reflex. *American Journal of Psychology, 913, 24,* 1-7.

1922

Carson, H. (1922). The conditioned eyelid reaction. *Journal of Experimental Psychology, 5,* 153-195.

1923

Carson, H. (1923). A note on the conditioned eyelid reaction. *Journal of Experimental Psychology, 6,* 82-83.

1924

Carson, H. (1924). The concept of backward association. *American Journal of*

Psychology, 35, 217-221.

1925

Carson, H. (1925). General aspects of the conditioned response. *Psychology Review, 32,* 285-231.

1927

Blout, W.P. (1927). Studies of the movements of animals: Blinking. *Quarterly Journal of Experimental Psychology, 18,* 111-126.
Dodge, R. (1927). Protopraxic and epicritic stratification of human adjustments.. *American Journal of Psychology, 39,* 145-157.
Ponders E., & Kennedy, W.P. (1927). On the act of blinking. *Quarterly Journal of Experimental Physiology, 18,* 89-110.

1930

Allison, L.W. (1930). Apparatus for studying eyelid responses. *American Journal of Psychology, 42,* 632-635.
Switzer, S.A. (1930). Backward conditioning of the lid reflex. *Journal of Experimental Psychology, 13,* 76-97.

1931

Hilgard, E.R. (1931). Conditioned eyelid reactions to a light to a light stimulus based upon the reflex wink to sound. *Psychological Monographs, 41,*184.
Peak, H. (1931). Modification of the lid-reflex by voluntarily induced sets. *Psychological Monographs, 42,* 188.
Peterson, J., & Allison, L.W. (1931). Controls of the eye-wink mechanism. *Journal of Experimental Psychology, 14,* 144-155.

1932

Allison, L.W., & Peterson, J. (1932). An experimental study of reflex and voluntary eyelid responses. *Journal of Experimental Psychology, 15,* 56-72.
Cohen, L. H. (1932). Periodicity of recovery during the refractory phase of the eyelid reflex. *Journal of Experimental Psychology, 15,* 436-446.
Cohen, L.H. (1932). Negative adaptation and refractory phase in the yelid reflex. *Journal of Experimental Psychology, 15,* 447-454.
Cohen, L.H. (1932). The effect of refractory phase upon negative adaptation of

primary reflex response. *Journal of Experimental Psychology, 15,* 455-457.
Peak, H. (1932). Intensity of stimulation and the amplitude and latency of the lid reflex: Includes analysis/quantitative relationships under relaxed and voluntary instructed sets. *American Journal of Psychology, 44,* 785-788.
Telford, C.W., & Anderson, B.O. (1932). The normal wink reflex: Its facilitation and inhibition. *Journal of Experimental Psychology, 15,* 235-266.

1933

Cason, H., & Katcher, N. (1933). An attempt to condition breathing and eyelid responses to a subliminal electric stimulus. *Journal of General Psychology, XVL, 6,* 183-184.
Cohen, L.H., Hilgard, E.R., & Wendt, G.R. (1933). Sensitivity to light in a case of hysterical blindness studied by reinforcement-inhibition and conditioning methods. *Yale Journal of Biology and Medicine, 6,* 61-67.
Hilgard, E.R. (1933). Modification of reflexes and conditioned reaction. *Journal of General Psychology, 9,* 210-215.
Hilgard, E. R. (1933). Reinforcement and inhibition of eyelid reflexes. *Journal of General Psychology, VIII, I,* 85-113.
Hilgard, E.R., & Wendt, G.R. (1933). The problem of reflex sensitivity to light studied in the case of hemianopsia. *Yale Journal of Biology and Medicine, 5,* 375.
Miller, J. (1933). Report on the conditioned eyelid reaction. *Unpublished study on file in the Psychological Laboratory of Oberlin College.*
Peak, H. (1933). An evaluation of the concepts of reflex and voluntary behavior. *Psychological Review, 40,* 71-89.
Peak, H. (1933). Reflex and voluntary reaction of the eyelid. *Journal of General Psychology, 8,* 130-156.
Shipley, W.C. (1933). An apparent transfer of conditioning. *Journal of General Psychology, 8,* 382-391.

1934

Bernstein, A.L. (1934). Temporal factors in the formation of conditioned eyelid reactions in human subjects. *Journal of General Psychology, 10,* 173-197.
Carson, H. (1934). Dr. Hilgard on the conditioned eyelid reaction. *Journal of Experimental Psychology, 17,* 894-899.
Cason, H. (1934). The rate of verbal activities in the conditioning of human subjects. *Psychological Review, 41,* 563-571.
Hilgard, E.R. (1934). The latency of conditioned eyelid reactions: A reply to Dr. Cason. *Journal of Experimental Psychology, 17,* 899-908.
Newhall, S.M., & Halverson, H.M. (1934). Eye-movements correlated with innervation of the orbicularis oculi. *Journal of General Psychology, XI,* 387-400.
Shipley, W.C. (1934). Studies of inhibitions in conditioned responses. *Journal of General Psychology, 11,* 46-64.

Switzer, S.A. (1934). Anticipatory and inhibitory characteristics of delayed conditioned reactions. *Journal of Experimental Psychology, 17,* 603-620.

1935

Biel, W.C. (1935). Attempted modifications of the eyelid reflex to light by the conditioning technique. *Psychological Bulletin, 32,* 527.

Carson, H. (1935). Backward conditioned eyelid responses. *Journal of Experimental Psychology, XVII, 5,* 599-610.

Hilgard, E.R., & Marquis, D.G. (1935). Acquisition, extinction and retention of conditioned lid responses to light in dogs. *Journal of Comparative Psychology, 19,* 29-58.

Kline, L.W., & Kohler, H.M. (1935). A comparison of the conditioning of muscular responses which vary in their degree of voluntary control. *American Journal* of *Psychology, 47,* 129-138.

1936

Campbell, A.A., & Hilgard, E.R. (1936). Individual differences in ease of conditioning. *Journal of Experimental Psychology, XIX,* 561-571.

Carson, H. (1936). Sensory conditioning. *Journal of Experimental Psychology, 19,* 572-591.

Hilgard, E.R., & Campbell, A.A. (1936). The course of acquisition and retention of conditioned eyelid responses in man (UCS as puff of air). *Journal of Experimental Psychology, XIX, 2,* 227-247.

Hilgard, E.R., & Marquis, D.G. (1936). Conditioned eyelid responses in monkeys with a comparison of dog: monkey and man. *Psychological Monographs, 47,* 186-198.

Marquis, D.G., & Hilgard, E.R. (1936). Conditioned lid responses to light in dogs after the removal of the visual cortex. *Journal of Comparative Psychology, 22,* 157-178.

Miller, J., & Cole, L.E. (1936). The influence of a "voluntary" reaction upon the development and the extinction of the conditioned eyelid reaction. *Journal of Genetic Psychology, 48,* 405-440.

Neet, C.C. (1936). A comparison of verbal, manual, and conditioned response methods in the determination of auditory intensity thresholds. *Journal of Experimental Psychology, 19,* 401-416.

1937

Hilgard, E.R., & Biel, W.C. (1937). Reflex sensitization and conditioning of eye-lid responses at intervals near simultaneity. *Journal of General Psychology, 16,* 223-234.

Hilgard, E.R., & Campbell, A.A. (1937). Vincent curves of conditioning. *Journal of Experimental Psychology, 21,* 310-319.
Hilgard, E.R., Campbell, A.A., & Sears, W.N. (1937). Conditioned discrimination: The development of discrimination with and without verbal report. *American Journal of Psychology, XLIX,* 564-580.
Marquis, D.G., & Hilgard, E.R. (1937). Conditioned responses to light in monkeys after removal of the occipital lobes. *Brain, 60,* 1-12.
Rodnik, E.H. (1937). Does the interval of delay of conditioned responses possess inhibitory properties? *Journal of Experimental Psychology, 20,* 507-527.

1938

Campbell, A.A. (1938). The inter-relations of two measures of conditioning in man. *Journal of Experimental Psychology, 22,* 225-243.
Hilgard, E.R. (1938). An algebraic analysis of conditioned discrimination in man. *Psychological Review, 45, 6,* 472-496.
Hilgard, E.R., Campbell, R.K., & Sears, W.N. (1938). Conditioned discrimination: The effect of knowledge of stimulus-relationships. *American Journal of Psychology, LI,* 498-506.
Hilgard, E.R., & Humphreys, L.G. (1938). The retention of conditioned discrimination in man. *Journal of General Psychology, 19,* 111-125.
Hilgard, E.R., & Humphreys, L.G. (1938). Effect of supporting and antagonistic voluntary instructions of conditioned discrimination. *Journal of Experimental Psychology, 22,* 291-304.
Hughes, B., & Schlosberg, H. (1938). Conditioning in the white rate. IV: The conditioned lid reflex. *Journal of Experimental Psychology, 23,* 641.650.
Porter, J.M. Jr. (1938). The modification of conditioned eyelid responses by successive series of non-reinforced elicitations. *Journal of General Psychology, 19,* 307-323.
Porter, J.M. Jr. (1938). Backward conditioning of the eyelid response. *Journal of Experimental Psychology, 23,* 403-410.

1939

Beck, L.H. (1939). Conditioning and the coordination of movements. *Journal of General Psych*ology, 20, 375-397.
Calvin, J.S. (1939). Decremental factors in conditioned response learning. *Ph.D. Dissertation*, Yale University.
Cole, L.E. (1939). A comparison of the factors of practice and knowledge of experimental procedures in conditioning the eyelid response of human subjects. *Journal of General Psychology, 20,*349-373.
Grant, D.A. (1939). The influence of attitude on the conditioned eyelid response. *Journal of Experimental Psychology, 25,* 333-346.
Grant, D.A. (1939). A study of patterning in the conditioned eyelid response.

Journal of Experimental Psychology, 25, 445-461.
Humphreys, L.G. (1939). The effect of random alternation of reinforcement on the acquisition and extinction of conditioned eyelid reactions. *Journal of Experimental Psychology, 25,* 141-158.
Lumsdaine, A.A. (1939). Conditioned eyelid responses as mediating generalized conditioned finger reactions. *Psychological Bulletin, 36,* 650.
Marquis, D.G., & Porter, J.M. Jr. (1939). Differential characteristics of conditioned eyelid responses established by reflex and voluntary reinforcement. *Journal of Experimental Psychology, 24,* 347-365.
Martino, G. (1939). The conditioned reflex of blinking. *Journal of Neurophysiology, 2,* 173-177.
Miller, J. (1939). The effect of facilitory and inhibitory attitudes on eyelid conditioning. *Psychological Bulletin, 36,* 577-578.
Porter, J.M. Jr. (1939). Experimental extinction as a function of the interval between successive non-reinforced elicitations. *Journal of General Psychology, 20,* 109-134.

1940

Hilgard, E.R., & Grant, D.A. (1940). Sensitization as a supplement to association in eyelid conditioning. *Psychological Bulletin, 37,* 478-479.
Humphres, L.G. (1940). Distributed practice in the development of the conditioned eyelid reaction. *Journal of General Psychology, 22,* 379-479.
Lumsdaine, A.A. (1940). Criteria of the ease and extent of conditioning. *Psychological Bulletin, 37,* 592-593.
Miller, J. (1940). Conditioned eyelid responses to serial stimulation. *Psychological Bulletin, 37,* 593.

1941

Carter, L.F. (1941). Intensity of conditioned stimulus and rate of conditioning. *Journal of Experimental Psychology, 28,* 481-490.
Grant, D.A. (1941). Sensitization and association in eyelid conditioning. *Ph.D. Dissertation,* Stanford University.
Grant, D.A., & Kreuzer, H.I. (1941). The function of generalized response sets during repeated electric shock stimulation. *Journal of General Psychology, 24,* 21-38.
Long, L.D. (1941). An investigation of the original response to the conditioned stimulus. *Archives of Psychology,* 359.
Lumsdaine, A.A. (1941). Measures of individual differences in susceptibility to conditioning. *Journal of Experimental Psychology, 28,* 428-435.

1942

Cole, L.E., Woodbury, C.B., & Philleo, C. (1942). The effect of order and rate of presentation of stimuli upon the establishment of a conditioned discrimination. *Journal of General Psychology, 26,* 35-49.

Metzner, C.A. (1942). The influence of preliminary stimulation upon human eyelid responses during conditioning and during subsequent heteromodal generalization. *Ph.D. Dissertation*, The University of Wisconsin.

Peak, H. (1942). Dr. Courts on the influence of muscular tension on the lid reflex. *Journal of Experimental Psychology, 30,*515-517.

Weber, H., & Wendt, G.R. Conditioning of eyelid closure with various conditions of reinforcement. *Journal of Experimental Psychology, 30,* 114-124.

1943

Grant, D.A. (1943). Sensitization and association in eyelid conditioning. *Journal of Experimental Psychology, 32,* 201-212.

Grant, D.A. (1943). The pseudo-conditioned eyelid response. *Journal of Experimental Psychology, 32,* 139-149. (See Abstract in *Psychological Bulletin,* 1940).

Humphreys, L.G. (1943). Measures of strength of conditioned eyelid responses. *Journal of General Psychology, 29,* 101-111.

King, H.E., & Landis, C. (1943). A comparison of eyelid responses conditoned with reflex and voluntary reinforcement in normal individuals and in psychiatric patients. *Journal of Experimental Psychology, 33,* 210-220.

1944

Grant, D.A., & Adams, J.K. (1944). "Alpha" conditioning in the eyelid. *Journal of Experimental Psychology, 34,* 136-141.

Morgan, J.J.B., & Morgan, S.S. (1944). Infant learning as a developmental index. *Journal of General Psychology, 65,* 281-289.

1945

Grant, D.S. (1945). A sensitized eyelid reaction related to the conditioned eyelid response. *Journal of Experimental Psychology, 35,* 393-402.

Reynolds, B. (1945). The acquisition of a trace conditioned response as function of the magnitude of the stimulus trace. *Journal of Experimental Psychology, 35,*15-30.

Reynolds, B. (1945). Extinction of trace conditioned responses as a function of the spacing of trials during the acquisition and extinction series. *Journal of Experimental Psychology, 35,* 91-95.

1946

Grant, D.A., and Norris, E.B. (1946). Dark adaptation as a factor in the sensitization or the Beta response of the eyelid to light. *Journal of Experimental Psychology, 36,* 390-397.

McDonald A. (1946). The effect of adaptation to the unconditioned stimulus upon the formation of conditioned avoidance responses. *Journal of Experimental Psychology, 36,* 1-12.

1947

Grant, D.A., & Norris, E.B. (1947). Eyelid conditioning as influenced by the presence of sensitized Beta-responses. *Journal of Experimental Psychology, 37,* 423-433.

Grant, D.A., Norris, E.B., & Boissard, S. (1947). Dark adaptation and the pseudo-conditioned eyelid response. *Journal of Experimental Psychology, 37,* 434-439.

Kimble, G.A. (1947). Conditioning as a function of the time between conditioned and unconditioned stimuli. *Journal of Experimental Psychology, 37,* 1-15.

1948

Grant D.A., Hake, H.w., & Schneider, D.E. (1948). Effects of pre-testing with the conditioned stimulus upon extinction of the conditioned eyelid response. *American Journal of Psychology, LXI,* 243-246.

Grant, D.A., Norris, E.B., & Hornseth, J.P. (1948) Sensitization of the Beta response under verbally induced inhibitory set and counter-reinforcement. *American Journal of Psychology, LXI,* 66-72.

Grant, d.A., & Schneider, D.E. (1948). Intensity of the conditioned stimulus and strength of conditioning. I. The conditioned eyelid response to light. *Journal of Experimental Psychology, 38,* 690-696.

Hake, H.W. (1948). Generalization and discrimination in the conditioned eyelid response to sound. *MS Thesis,* The University of Wisconsin.

Norris, E.B., & Grant, D.A. (1948). Eyelid conditioning as affected by verbally induced inhibitory set and counter reinforcement. *American Journal of Psychology, LXI,* 37-49.

Passey, G.E. (1948). The influence of intensity of unconditioned stimulus upon acquisition of a conditioned response. *Journal of Experimental Psychology, 38,* 420-428.

1949

Grant, D.A., Hornseth, J.P., & Hake, H.W. (1949). Sensitization of the Beta response as a function of the wavelength of the stimulus. *Journal of Experimental*

Psychology, 39, 195-199.
Grant, D.A., & Schneider, D.E. (1949). Intensity of the conditioned stimulus and strength of conditioning: II. The conditioned galvanic skin response to an auditory stimulus. *Journal of Experimental Psychology, 39,* 35-40.
Tinker, M.A. (1949). Involuntary blink rate and illumination intensity in visual work. *Journal of Experimental Psychology, 39,* 558-560.

1950

Grant, D.A., Riopelle, A.J., & Hake, H.W. (1950). Resistance to extinction and the pattern of reinforcement. II. Alternation of reinforcement and the conditioned eyelid response. *Journal of Experimental Psychology, 40,* 53-60.
Myers, J.A. (1950). An experimental investigation of the effect of varying the time between the onsets of the conditioned and unconditioned stimuli on the conditioned eyelid response. *Ph.D. Dissertation,* University of Iowa, 1950.
Spence, K.W., & Norris, E.B. (1950). Eyelid conditioning as a function of the inter-trial interval. *Journal of Experimental Psychology, 40,* 716-720.

1951

Grant, D.A., & Hake, H.W. (1951). Dark adaptation and the Humphreys random reinforcement phenomenon in human eyelid conditioning. *Journal of Experimental Psychology, 42,* 417-423.
Grant, D.A., Hake, H.W., Riopelle, A.J., & Kostlan, A. (1951). Effects of repeated pretesting with conditioned stimulus upon extinction of the conditioned eyelid response to light. *American Journal of Psychology, 64,* 247-251.
Hake, H.W., Grant, D.A., & Hornseth, J.P. (1951). Resistance to extinction and the pattern of reinforcement. III. The effect of trial patterning in verbal conditioning. *Journal of Experimental Psychology, 41,* 221-225.
Hilgard, E.R., Jones, L.V., & Kaplan, S.J. (1951). Conditioned discrimination as related to anxiety. *Journal of Experimental Psychology, 42,* 94-99.
Logan, F.A. (1951). A comparison of avoidance and nonavoidance eyelid conditioning. *Journal of Experimental Psychology, 42,* 390-393.
Murdock, B.B. Jr. (1951). Forward and backward conditioning of the eyelid with a coordinated voluntary response. *The American Journal of Psychology, 64,* 94-98.
Spence, K.W., Taylor, J.A. (1951). Anxiety and strength of the UCS as determiners of the amount of eyelid conditioning. *Journal of Experimental Psychology, 42,* 183-188.
Taylor, J.A. (1951). The relationship of anxiety to the conditioned eyelid response. *Journal of Experimental Psychology, 41,* 81-92.
Hake, H.W., & Grant, D.A. Resistance to extinction and the pattern of reinforcement. II. Effect of successive alternation of blocks of reinforced and unreinforced trials upon the conditioned eyelid response to light. *Journal of Experimental Psychology, 41,* 216-220.

1952

Baron, M.R. (1952). The effect of long intertrial intervals on the limit of eyelid conditioning. (Extension of Spence and Norris). *Journal of Experimental Psychology, 44,* 438-441.

Grant, D.A., & Schipper, L.M. (1952). The acquisition and extinction of conditioned eyelid responses as a function of the percentage of fixed ratio random reinforcement. *Journal of Experimental Psychology, 43,* 313-320.

Grant, D.A., Schipper, L.M., & Ross, B.M. (1952). The effect of intertrial interval during acquisition on extinction of the condioned eyelid response following partial reinforcement. *Journal of Experimental Psychology, 44,* 203-210.

Vandermeer, S., & Amsel, A. (1952). Work and rest factors in eyelid conditioning. *Journal of Experimental Psychology, 43,* 261-266.

1953

McAllister, W.R. (1953). Eyelid conditioning as a function of the CS-UCS interval. *Journal of Experimental Psychology, 45,* 417-422.

McAllister, W.R. (1953). The effect on eyelid conditioning of shifting the CS-UCS interval. *Journal of Experimental Psychology, 45,* 423-428.

Meyer, D.R., Banrick, H.P., & Fitte, P.M. (1953). Incentive, anxiety, and the human blink rate. *Journal of Experimental Psychology, 45,* 183-187.

Spence, K.W. (1953). Learning and performance in eyelid conditioning as a function of intensity of the UCS. *Journal of Experimental Psychology, 45,* 57-63.

Spence, K.W., & Farber, I.E. (1953). Conditioning and extinction as a function of anxiety. *Journal of Experimental Psychology, 45,* 116-119.

Spence, K.W., & Taylor, J.A. (1953). The relation of conditioned response strength to anxiety in normal, neurotic, and psychotic subjects. *Journal of Experimental Psychology, 45,* 265-272.

1954

Franks, C.M. (1954). An experimental study of conditioning as related to mental abnormality. *Ph.D. Dissertation.* University of London.

Spence, K.W., & Beecroft, R.S. (1954). Differential conditioning and level of anxiety. *Journal of Experimental Psychology, 48,* 399-403.

Spence, K. W., & Farber, I.E. (1954). The relation of anxiety to differential eyelid conditioning. *Journal of Experimental Psychology, 47,* 127-134.

Spence, K.W., Farber, I.E., & Taylor, E. (1954). The relation of electric shock and anxiety to level of performance in eyelid conditioning. *Journal of Experimental Psychology, 48,* 404-408.

Taylor, E. (1954). Generalization of the conditioned eyelid resonse to an auditory stimulus varying in intensity. *Ph.D. Dissertation.* University of Iowa.

Taylor, J.A., & Spence, K.W. (1954). Conditioning level in the behavior disorders.

Journal of Abnormal and Social Psychology, 49, 497-502.

1955

Franks, C.M. (1955). The establishment of a conditioning laboratory for the investigation of personality and cortical functioning. *Nature, 175,* 984-985.
Franks, C.M., & Laverty, S.G. (1955). Sodium amytal and eyelid conditioning. *Journal of Mental Science, 101,* 654-663.
Franks, C.M., & Withers, W.C.R. (1955). Photoelectric recording of eyelid movements. *American Journal of Psychology, 68,* 467-471.
Kimble, G.A., Mann, L.I., & Dufort, R.H. (1955). Classical and instrumental eyelid conditioning. *Journal of Experimental Psychology, 49,* 407-417.
Warren, A.B., & Grant, D.A. The relation of conditioned discrimination to the MMPI pd personality variable. *Journal of Experimental Psychology, 49,* 23-27.
Vooks, V.W. (1955). Gradual strengthening of S-R connections or increasing number of S-R connections. *Journal of Psychology, 39,* 289-299.

1956

Franks, C.M. (1956). Conditioning and personality. *Journal of Abnormal and Social Psychology, 52,* 143-150.
Galloway, T.F., & Butler, F.A. (1956). Conditioned eyelid response to tone as an objective test of hearing. *Journal of Speech and Hearing Disorders, 21,* 47-55.
Kimble, G.A., & Dufort, R.H. (1956). The associative factor in eyelid conditioning. *Journal of Experimental Psychology, 52,* 386-391.
Taylor, J.A. (1956). Level of conditioning and intensity of the adaptation stimulus. *Journal of Experimental Psychology, 51,* 127-130.

1957

Franks, C.M. (1957). Effect of food, drink and tobacco deprivation on the conditioning of the eyeblink response. *Journal of Experimental Psychology, 53,* 117-120.
Goodrich, K.P., Ross, L.E., & Wagner, A.R. (1957). Performance in eyelid conditioning following interpolated presentations of the UCS. *Journal of Experimental Psychology, 53,* 214-217.
Cynther, M.D. (1957). Differential eyelid conditioning as a function of stimulus simularity and strength of response to the CS. *Journal of Experimental Psychology, 53,* 408-416.
King, D.C., & Michels, K.M. Muscular tension and the human blink rate. *Journal of Experimental Psychology, 53,* 113-116.

1958

Bartholowmew, A.A., Franks, C.M., & Marley, E. (1958). Susceptibility to methylpentynol: Eyelid conditioning and PGR response. *Journal of Mental Science, 104,* 1167-1173.

Boneau, C.A. (1958). The interstimulus interval and the latency of the conditioned eyelid response. *Journal of Experimental Psychology, 56,* 464-471.

Das, J.P. (1958). Conditioning and hypnosis. *Journal of Experimental Psychology, 56,* 110-113.

Dufort, R.H., & Kimble, G.A. (1958). Ready signals and the effect of interpolated UCS presentations in eyelid conditioning. *Journal of Experimental Psychology, 56,* 1-7.

Franks, C.M., & Trouton, P. (1958). Effects of amobarbitol sodium and dexamphetamine sulfate on the conditioning of the eyeblink response. *Journal of Comparative and Physiological Psychology, 51,* 220-222.

Grant, D.A., Hunter, H.G., & Patel, A.S. (1958). Spontaneous recovery of the conditioned eyelid response. *Journal of General Psychology, 59,* 135-141.

Grice, G.R., & Davis, J.D. (1958). Mediated stimulus equivalence and distinctiveness in human conditioning. *Journal of Experimental Psychology, 55,* 565-571.

Howat, M.G., & Grant, D.A. (1958). Influence or intertrial interval during extinction of spontaneous recovery of conditioned eyelid responses. *Journal of Experimental Psychology, 56,* 11-15.

McAllister, W.R., & McAllister, D.E. (1958). Effect of knowledge of conditioning upon eyelid conditioning. *Journal of Experimental Psychology, 55,* 579-583.

Prokasy, W.F. (1958). Extinction and spontaneous recovery of conditioned eyelid responses as a function of amount of acquisition and extinction training. *Journal of Experimental Psychology, 56,* 319-324.

Prokasy, W.F., Grant, D., & Myers, N.A. (1958). Eyelid conditioning as a function of unconditioned stimulus intensity and intertrial interval. *Journal of Experimental Psychology, 55,* 242-246.

Reynolds, W.F. (1958). Acquisition and extinction of the conditioned eyelid response following partial and continuous reinforcement. *Journal of Experimental Psychology, 55,* 335-341.

Runquist, W.N., Spence, K.W., & Stubbs, D.W. (1958). Differential conditioning and intensity of the UCS. *Journal of Experimental Psychology, 55,* 51-55.

Shagass, C., & Kerenyi, A.B. (1958). Neurophysiologic studies of personality. *Journal of Nervous and Mental Disease, 126,* 141-147.

Spence, K.W., & Runquist, W.N. (1958). Temporal effects of conditioned fear on the eyelid reflex. *Journal of Experimental Psychology, 55,* 613-616.

1959

Atkinson, C.J. (1959). The use of the eyelid reflex as an operant in audiometric testing. *Journal of Experimental Analysis Behavior, 2,* 212.

Braun, H.W., & Geiselhart, R. (1959). Age difference in the acquisition and

extinction of the conditioned eyelid response. *Journal of Experimental Psychology, 57,* 386-388.
Caldwell, D.F., & Cromwell, R.L. (1959). The relationship of manifest anxiety and electric shock to eyelid conditioning. *Journal of Experimental Psychology, 57,* 348-349.
Church, R.M., & Pfaffman, C. (1959). A respondent-conditioning apparatus for the student laboratory. *Journal of American Psychology, 72,* 267-270.
Franks, C.M., & Leigh, P. The theoretical and experimental application of a conditioning model to a consideration of bronchial asthma in man. *Journal of Psychosomatic Research, 4,* 88-89.
Goodrich, K.P., Ross, L.E., & Wagner, A.R. Supplementary report: Effect of interpolated UCS trials in eyelid conditioning without a ready signal. *Journal of Experimental Psychology, 58,* 319-320.
O'Connor, N., & Rawnsley, K. Two types of conditioning in psychotics and normals. *Journal of Abnormal and Social Psychology, 58,* 157-161.
Ross, L.E. (1959). The decremental effect of partial reinforcement during acquisition of the conditioned eyelid response. *Journal of Experimental Psychology, 57,* 74-82.
Ross, L.E., & Hunter, J.J. (1959). Habit strength parameters in eyelid conditioning as a function of UCS intensity. *Psychological Record, 9,* 103-107.
Runquist, W.N., & Ross, L.E. (1959). The relation between physiological measures of emotionality and performance in eyelid conditioning. *Journal of Experimental Psychology, 57,* 329-332.
Runquist, W.N., & Spence K.W. (1959). Performance in eyelid conditioning as a function of UCS duration. *Journal of Experimental Psychology, 57,* 249-252.
Runquist, W.N., & Spence, K.W. (1959). Performance in eyelid conditioning related to changes in muscular tension and physiological measures of emotionality. *Journal of Experimental Psychology, 58,* 417-422.
Spence, K.W., & Ross, L.E. (1959). A methodological study of the form and latency of eyelid responses in conditioning. *Journal of Experimental Psychology, 58,* 376-381.

1960

Baron, M.R., & Connor, J.P. (1960). Eyelid conditioned responses with various levels of anxiety. *Journal of Experimental Psychology, 60,* 310-313.
Beeman, E.Y., Hartman, T.F., & Grant, D.A. (1960). Supplementary report: Influence of intertrial interval during extinction on spontaneous recovery of conditioned eyelid responses. *Journal of Experimental Psychology, 59,* 279-280.
Grant, D.A., McRarling, C., & Gormezano, I. (1960). Temporal conditioning and the effect of interpolated UCS presentations in eyelid conditioning. *Journal of General Psychology, 63,* 249-257.
Grice, G.R., & Davis, J.D. (1960). Effect of concurrent responses on the evocation and generalization of the conditioned eyeblink. *Journal of Experimental Psychology, 59,* 391-395.

Hansche, W.J., & Grant, D.A. (1960). Onset versus termination of a stimulus as the CS in eyelid conditioning. *Journal of Experimental Psychology, 59,* 19-26.

Hartman, T.F., Grant, D.A., & Ross, L.E. (1960). An investigation of the latency of "instructed voluntary" eyelid responses. *Psychological Reports, 7,* 305-311.

Hartman, T.f., & Grant, D.A. (1960). Effect of intermittent reinforcement on acquisition, extinction, and spontaneous recovery of the conditioned eyelid response. *Journal of Experimental Psychology, 60,* 89-96.

McAllister, W.R., & McAllister, D.E. (1960). The influence of the ready signal and unpaired UCS presentations on eyelid conditioning. *Journal of Experimental Psychology, 60,* 30-35.

McAllister, W.R., & McAllister, D.E. (1960). The "ready" signal in eyelid conditioning. *American Journal of Psychology, 73,* 444-447.

Prokasy, W.F., Jr., & Chambliss, J.D. (1960). Temporal conditioning: Negative results. *Psychological Reports, 7,* 539-542.

Ross, L.E., & Spence, K.W. (1960). Eyelid conditioning performance under partial reinforcement as a function of UCS intensity. *Journal of Experimental Psychology, 59,* 379-382.

Spence, K.W., & Wevant, R.G. (1960). Conditioning performance of high and low-anxious Ss in the absence of a warning signal. *Journal of Experimental Psychology, 59,* 146-149.

Trapold, M.A., & Spence, K.W. (1960). Performance changes in eyelid conditioning as related to the motivational and reinforcing properties of the UCS. *Journal of Experimental Psychology, 59,* 209-213.

Walker, E.G. (1960). Eyelid conditioning as a function of intensity of conditioned and unconditioned stimuli. *Journal of Experimental Psychology, 59,* 303-311.

1961

Beeman, E.Y., & Grant, D.A. (1961). Delayed extinction and spontaneous recovery following spaced and massed acquisition of the eyelid CR. *Journal of General Psychology, 65,* 293-300.

Cromwell, R.L., Pack, B.E., & Forshee, J.G. (1961). Studies in activity level: V. The relationship among eyelid conditioning, intelligence, activity level, and age. *American Journal of Mental Deficiency, 65,* 744-748.

Field, J.G., & Brengelman, J.C. (1961). Eyelid conditioning and three personality parameters. *Journal of Abnormal Psychology, 63,* 517-523.

Froseth, J.Z., & Grant, D.A. (1961). Influence of intermittent reinforcement upon acquisition, extinction, and spontaneous recovery in eyelid conditioning with fixed acquisition series. *Journal of General Psychology, 64,* 225-232.

Ross, L.E. (1961). Conditioned fear as a function of CS-UCS and probe stimulus intervals. *Journal of Experimental Psychology, 61,* 265-273.

Spence, K.W., & Goldstein, H. (1961). Eyelid conditioning performance as a function of emotion-producing instructions. *Journal of Experimental Psychology, 62,* 291-294.

Spence, K.W., & Trapold, M.A. (1961). Performance in eyelid conditioning as a function of reinforcement schedules and changes in them. *Proceedings of the National Academy of Science, 47,* 1860-1868.

1962

Champion, R.A. (1962). Stimulus-response contiguity in classical aversive conditioning. *Journal of Experimental Psychology, 64,* 35-39.

Franks, V., & Franks, C.M. (1962). Classical conditioning procedures as an index of vocational adjustment among mental defectives. *Perceptual Motor Skills, 14,* 241-242.

Gormezano, I., & Moore, J.W. (1962). Effects of instructional set and UCS intensity on the latency, percentage, and form of the eyelid response. *Journal of Experimental Psychology, 63,* 487-494.

Gormezano, I., Moore, J.W., & Deaux, E. (1962). Supplementary report: Yoked comparisons of classical and avoidance eyelid conditioning under three UCS intensities. *Journal of Experimental Psychology, 64,* 551-552.

Hartman, T.F., & Grant, D.A. (1962). Effects of pattern of reinforcement and verbal information of acquisition, extinction, and spontaneous recovery of the eyelid CR. *Journal of Experimental Psychology, 63,* 217-226.

Hartman, T.F., & Grant, D.A. (1962). Differential eyelid conditioning as a function of the CS-UCS interval. *Journal of Experimental Psychology, 64,* 131-136.

Kimble, G.A. (1962). Classical conditioning and the problem of awareness. Supplement to *Journal of Personality, 30,* 27-45.

Klinger, B.I., & Prokasy, W.F.Jr. (1962). A note on MAS score and the ready signal in classical eyelid conditioning. *Psychological Reports, 10,* 829-830.

Logan, F.A., & Wagner, A.R. (1962). Supplementary report: Direction of change in CS in eyelid conditioning. *Journal of Experimental Psychology, 64,* 325-326.

Passey, G.E., & Burns, T.C. (1962). Influence of variable reinforcement upon acquisition of the conditioned eyelid response. *Psychological Reports, 11,* 547-552.

1963

Franks, C.M. (1963). Personality and eyeblink conditioning seven years later. *Acta Psychologica, 21,* 295-312.

Franks, C.M. (1963). Ease of conditioning and spontaneous recovery from experimental extinction. *British Journal of Psychology, 54(4),* 351-357.

Goodrich, K.P., Markowitz, J., & Wall, D.M. (1963). Differential eyeblink conditioning in voluntary and nonvoluntary subjects. *Psychological Reports, 13,* 723-730.

Kimble, G.A., & Pennypacker, H.S. (1963). Eyelid conditioning in young and aged subjects. *Journal of Genetic Psychology, 103,* 283-289.

Krauss, H.H., & Prokasy, W.F. (1963). On intertrial interval discrimination in classical conditioning. *Psychological Reports, 12,* 138.

Moore, J.W., & Gormezano, I. (1963). Effects of omitted versus delayed UCS on classical eyelid conditioning under partial reinforcement. *Journal of Experimental Psychology, 65,* 248-257.

Passey, G.E., & Hoelle, D.F. (1963). Influence of distribution shape on variable reinforcement effects in eyelid conditioning. *Psychological Reports, 13,* 731-733.

Passey, G.E., & Sekyra, F. (1963). Variable reinforcement versus constant reinforcement in eyelid conditioning. *Psychological Reports, 13,* 99-102.

Prokasy, W.F.Jr., & Whaley, F.L. (1963). Intertrial interval range shift in classical eyelid conditioning. *Psychological Reports, 12,* 55-58.

Spence, K.W. (1963). Cognitive factors in the extinction of the conditioned eyelid response in humans. *Science, 140,* 1224-1225.

Sweetbaum, H.A. (1963). Comparison of the effects of introversion-extroversion and anxiety of conditioning. *Journal of Abnormal Social Psychology, 66(3),* 249-254.

1964

Abbott, D.W., & Price, L.E. (1964). Stimulus generalization of the conditioned eyelid response to structurally similar nonsense syllables. *Journal of Experimental Psychology, 68,* 368-371.

Baker, B., & Loess, H. (1964). Suggestibility and performance in eyelid conditioning. *Psychonomic Science, 1,* 137-138.

Franks, C.M. (1964). A replication is a replication is not a replication. *Psychological Reports, 15,* 550.

Goodrich, K.P. (1964). Invariance of eyeblink conditioning over conditions of spatial variance in a visual CS. *Psychological Reports, 15,* 467-470.

Goodrich, K.P. (1964). Effect of a ready signal on the latency of voluntary responses in eyelid conditioning. *Journal of Experimental Psychology, 67,* 496-498.

Gormezano, I., & Moore, J.W. (1964). Yoked comparisons of contingent and noncontingent US presentations in human eyelid conditioning. *Psychonomic Science, 1,* 231-232.

Hickok, C.W., & Grant, D.A. (1964). Effects of pattern of reinforcement and verbal information on acquisition and extinction of the eyelid CR. *Journal of General Psychology, 71,* 279-289.

Issa, I. (1964). The effect of attitudinal factors on the relationship between conditioning and personality. *British Journal of Social and Clinical Psychology, 3(2),* 113-119.

Levy, C.M., Grant, D.A., & Clark, A.H. (1964). Reversal of conditioned discrimination of the eyelid response. *Journal of Experimental Psychology, 67,* 80-82.

Loess, H. (1964). Effect of unpaired UCS presentations on performance in eyelid conditioning. *Psychological Reports, 15,* 439-444.

Ludvigson, H.W. (1964). Chlorpromazine and d-amphetamine in eyelid conditioning. *Psychological Reports, 14,* 402.

Ludvigson, H.W. (1964). Comments on "A replication is a replication in not a replication." *Psychological Reports, 15,* 1002.

Mattson, M., & Moore, J.W. (1964). Intertrial responding and CS intensity in classical eyelid conditioning. *Journal of Experimental Psychology, 68,* 369-401.

Moore, J.W. (1964). Differential eyelid conditioning as a function of the frequency and intensity of auditory CSs. *Journal of Experimental Psychology, 68,* 250-259.

Moore, J.W., & Newman, F.L. (1964). On-trial and intertrial responding in eyelid conditioning as a function of US-intensity, percentage reinforcement, and the similarity between the CS and inter-trial stimulus. *Psychonomic Science, 1,* 213-214.

Moore, J.W. (1964). Comparisons of classical and instrumental eyelid conditioning: A reply to Kimble. *Psychological Reports, 14,* 966.

Nicholls, M.F., & Kimble, G.A. (1964). Effect of instructions upon eyelid conditioning. *Journal of Experimental Psychology, 67,* 400-402.

Norman, D.A., Goodrich, K.P., & Markowitz, J. (1964). An AC-amplification system for recording eyeblinks and other movements. *American Journal of Psychology, 77,* 127-128.

Passey, G.E., & Sekyra, F. (1964). Geometric and arithmetic means as indices of UCS intersity with variable reinforcement. *Journal of Experimental Psychology, 67,* 7-10.

Pennypacker, H.S. (1964). External inhibition of the conditioned eyelid reflex. *Journal of Experimental Psychology, 67,* 33-40.

Pennypacker, H.S. (1964). Measurement of the conditioned eyelid reflex. *Science, 144,* 1248-1249.

Porter, J.J., Engle, R.G., Brady, K.R., & Knopp, S.H. (1964). CS duration and task instructions as determiners of extinction of the conditioned eyelid response. *Psychonomic Science, 1,* 375-376.

Price, L.E., Vandament, W.E., & Abbott, D.W. (1964). Effects of a ready signal condition on acquisition and extinction of the conditioned eyelid response. *Journal of Experimental Psychology, 68,* 516-518.

Ross, L.E., Koski, C.H., & Yaeger, J. (1964). Classical eyelid conditioning of the severely retarded: Partial reinforcement effects. *Psychonomic Science, 1,* 253-254.

Spence, K.W., Homzie, M.J., & Rutledge, E.F. (1964). Extinction of the human eyelid CR as a function of the discriminability of the change from acquisition to extinction. *Journal of Experimental Psychology, 67,* 545-552.

Spence, K.W. (1964). Anxiety (Drive) level and performance in eyelid conditioning. *Psychological Bulletin, 61,* 129-139.

Spence, K.W., & Spence, J.T. (1964). Relation of eyelid conditioning to manifest axiety, extraversion, and rigidity. *Journal of Abnormal Social Psychology, 68,* 144-149.

Spence, K.W., and Rutledge, E. (1964). The effect of overlearning on the rats of extinction of the eyelid CR. *Psychonomic Science, 1,* 315-316.

Trapold, M.A., Homzie, M., & Rutledge, E. (1964). Backward conditioning and UCR latency. *Journal of Experimental Psychology, 67,* 387-391.

Vandament, W.E., & Price, L.E. (1964). Primary stimulus generalizatin under different percentages of reinforcement in eyelid conditioning. *Journal of Experimental Psychology, 67,* 162-167.

1965

Burstein, K.R. (1965). The influence of UCS upon the acquisition of the conditioned eyelid response. *Psychonomic Science, 2,* 303-304.

Burstein, K.R. (1965). Effect of UCS intensity upon the acquisition of conditioned responses acquired under a lengthened interstimulus interval. *Journal of Experimental Psychology, 70,* 147-150.

Colman, S.R., Newman, F.L., & Moore, J.W. (1965). Terrace's "Fading-in" of CS- in differential eyelid conditioning. *Psychonomic Science, 3,* 467-468.

Dufort, R.H., & Rollins, H.A. (1965). Acquisition of the conditioned eyelid response under different ready-signal conditions. *Psychonomic Science, 3,* 81-82.

Fishbein, D.H. (1965). Studies in efficiency: Muscle-action patterns in reaction time as related to inhibition of eyelid conditioning. *Journal of Personality and Social Psychology, 2,* 180-187.

Gormezano, I. (1965). Yoked comparisons of classical and instrumental conditioning of the eyelid response: An addendum on "voluntary responders." In W.F. Prokasy (Ed.), *Classical Conditioning.* New York: Appleton-Century-Crofts, pp. 47-70.

Hansche, W.J., & Grant, D.A. (1965). A comparison of instrumental reward and avoidance training with classical reinforcement technique in conditioning the eyelid response. *Psychonomic Science, 2,* 305-306.

Hartmann, T.F. (1965). Dynamic transmission, elective generalization, and semantic conditioning. In W.F. prokasy (Ed.), *Classical Conditioning.* New York: Appleton-Century-Crofts, pp. 90-106.

Herron, E.W. (1965). Personality factors associated with the acquisition of the conditioned eyelid response. *Journal of Personality and Social Psychology, 2,* 775-777.

Hickock, C.W., Grant, D.A., & North, J.A. (1965). Differential eyelid conditioning of voluntary form responders. *Psychonomic Science, 3,* 583-584.

Homzie, M.J., & Weiss, G. (1965). UCS intensity and the associative strength of the eyelid CR with a masked conditioning procedure. *Journal of Experimental Psychology, 69,* 101-103.

Keehn, J.D. (1965). Operant eyelid conditioning of severely retarded children. *Psychonomic Science, 3,* 585-586.

Keehn, J.d., Lloyd, K.e., Hibbs, M., & Johnson, D. (1965). Operant eyeblink conditioning without awareness: A preliminary report. *Psychonomic Science, 2,* 357-358.

MacDonald, G.E., Levine, G.J., & Amsel, A. (1965). The effects of CR-contingent UCW presentations in eyelid conditioning. *Psychonomic Science, 3,* 225-226.

Martin, I., & Levey, A.B. (1965). Efficiency of the conditioned eyelid response. *Science, 150,* 781-783.

McPherson, F.M. (1965). Comment on Eysenck's account of some Aberdeen studies of introversion-extraversion and eyeblink conditioning. *British Journal of Psychology, 56(4),* 483-484.

Meiselman, H.L., & Moore, J.W. The effects of percentage reinforcement, UCS duration, and experience with procedure on the conditioned eyelid response.

Psychonomic Science, 3, 335-336.
Moore, J.W., & Newman, F.L. (1965). Intertrial stimuli and differentiation of the conditioned eyelid response. *Psychonomic Science, 3,* 341-342.
Muir, R.W., & Runquist, W.N. (1965). Extended differential conditioning of the classically conditioned eyeblink reflex. *Psychonomic Science, 3,* 581-582.
Novak, D.J., & Grant, D.A. (1965). Semantic generalization of the conditioned eyelid response with two types of training. *Psychological Reports, 17,* 731-738.
Perry, S.L., & Moore, J.W. (1965). The partial-reinforcement effect sustained through blocks of continuous reinforcement in classical eyelid conditioning. *Journal of Experimental Psychology, 69,* 158-161.
Porter, J.J., & Senkowski, P.C. (1965). The effects of task instructions and instructed or uninstructed CS on the eyelid response. *Psychonomic Science, 3,* 257-258.
Price, L.E., Abbott, D.W., & Vandament, W.E. (1965). Effects of CS and UCS change on extinction of the conditioned eyelid response. *Journal of Experimental Psychology, 69,* 437-438.
Prokasy, W.F. (1965). Classical eyelid conditioning, experimenter operations, task demands, and response shaping. In W. F. Prokasy (Ed.). *Classical Conditioning.* New York: Appleton-Century-Crofts, pp. 208-225.
Prokasy, W.F. (1965). An application of a three-state all-or-none model to human eyelid conditioning data. *Psychonomic Science, 3,* 349-350.
Prokasy, W.F. (1965). Stimulus fluctuation, reactive inhibition, and time between trials in classical eyelid conditioning. *Journal of Experimental Psychology, 70,* 464-472.
Ross, L.E. (1965). Eyelid conditioning as a tool in psychological research: Some problems and prospects. In W.F. Prokasy (Ed.) *Classical Conditioning.* New York: Appleton-Century-Crofts, pp. 249-268.
Ross, L.E., & Hartman, T.F. (1965). Human eyelid conditioning: The recent experimental literature. *Genetic Psychological Monographs, 71,* 93-136.
Runquist, W.N., & Towart, E. (1965). Further evidence for intrasession decrements in eyelid conditioning. *Psychological Reports, 17,* 891-897.
Runquist, W.N., & Muir, W.R. (1965). Intrasession decrements in the performance of the classically conditioned eyelid reflex. *Journal of Experimental Psychology, 70,* 520-525.
Runquist, W.N., & Evans, J.F. (1965). Inhibitory effects of post trial stimulation on classical eyelid conditioning under partial reinforcement. *Psychonomic Science, 3,* 579-580.
Spence, K.W. (1965). Individual differences in human eyelid conditioning. *Psychonomic Science, 3,* 333-334.

1966

Abbott, D.W. (1966). Effects of meaningfulness of structurally similar CVCs on stimulus generalization of eyelid closure. *Journal of Experimental Psychology, 71,* 511-515.
Boice, R., & Boice, C. (1966). An inverse effect of UCS intensity upon partially reinforced eyelid conditioning. *Psychonomic Science, 5,* 69-70.

Brownfield, E.D., & Keehn, J.D. (1966). Operant eyelid conditioning in trisomy-18. *Journal of Abnormal Psychology, 71,* 413-415.

Chen, W-Y. (1966). The effect of the intensity of UCS upon eyelid conditioning. *Acta Psychologica Taiwanica, 8,* 64-68.

Eysenck, H.J. (1966). A reply to McPherson's comments on the Aberdeen conditioning studies. *British Journal of Psychology, 57(3-4),* 419-421.

Fishbein, H.D., & Gormezano, I. (1966). Effects of differential instructions, differential payoffs, and the presence or absence of feedback on the percentage, latency, and amplitude of the conditioned eyelid response. *Journal of Experimental Psychology, 71,* 535-538.

Fishbein, H.D., & LeBlanc, M. (1966). Classical eyelid conditioning as a function of interstimulus interval and correction procedure for "spontaneous" blinking. *Proceedings of the 74th Annual Convention of the American Psychological Association,* 63-64.

Fleming, R.A., & Grant, D.A. (1966). A comparison of rate and contingency of classical and instrumental reinforcement upon the acquisition theory of CS intensity. *Journal of Experimental Psychology, 72,* 488-491.

Goodrich, K.P. (1966). Elemental analysis of response slopes and latency as criteria for characterizing voluntary and nonvoluntary responses in eyeblink conditioning. *Pysycological Monographs, 80(14),* 1-34.

Grice, G.R., Masters, L., & Kohfeld, D.L. (1966). Classical conditioning without discrimination training: A test of the generalization theory of CS intensity. *Journal of Experimental Psychology, 72,* 510-513.

Hobson, G.N. (1966). Ethanol inhibition of formation of conditioned eyeblink responses in man. *Psychol-pharmacologia, 9(2),* 93-100.

Jaffee, C.L., Millman, E., & Gorman, B. (1966). An attempt to condition an eyeblink response to verbal deception. *Psychological Reports, 19,* 421-422.

Levy, C.M. (1966). Effect of intrastimulus agreement and conflict upon conditioned discrimination and reversal of the eyelid response. *Journal of Experimental Psychology, 72,* 76-84.

Lin, P-f. (1966). Classical aversive conditioning as a function of reaction latency. *Acta Psychologica Taiwanica, 8,* 57-63.

Lintz, L.M., & Fitzgerald, H.E. (1966). Apparatus for eyelid conditioning in infants. *Journal of Experimental Child Psychology, 4,* 276-279.

Lipkin, S.G., & Moore, J.W. (1966). Eyelid trace conditioning, CS intensity, CS-UCS interval, and a correction for "spontaneous" blinking. *Journal of Experimental Psychology, 72,* 216-220.

Marlatt, G.A., Lilie, D., Selvidge, B.D., Sipes, M.D., & Gormezano, I. (1966). Cross-modal generalization to tone and light in human eyelid conditioning. *Psychonomic Science, 5,* 59-60.

Martin, I., & Levey, A.B. (1966). Latency of the eyelid UCR during conditioning. *Life Sciences,* 17-26

Moore, J.W., & Newman, F.L. (1966). Intertrial stimuli and generalization of the conditioned eyelid response. *Journal of Experimental Psychology, 71,* 414-419.

Ominsky, M., & Kimble, G.A. (1966). Anxiety and eyelid conditioning. *Journal of Experimental Psychology, 71,* 471-472.

Perlmuter, L.C. (1966). Effects of CS manipulations on the conditioned eyelid response: compounding, generalization, the inter-CS-interval, and pre-exposure. *Psychonomic Monographs Supplements, 1,* 271-286.

Prokasy, W.F., & Allen, C.K. (1966). Drive times habit in human eyelid conditioning. *Psychonomic Science, 5,* 155-156.

Ross, L.E. (1966). Classical conditioning and discrimination learning research with the mentally retarded. *International Review Research Mental Retardation, 1,* 21-54.

Spain, B. (1966). Eyelid conditioning and arousal in schizophrenic and normal subjects. *Journal of Abnormal Psychology, 71,* 260-266.

Spence, K.W., & Platt, J.R. (1966). UCS intensity and performance in eyelid conditioning. *Psychological Bulletin, 65,* 1-10.

Spence, K.W. (1966). Extinction of the human eyelid CR as a function of presence or absence of the UCS during extinction. *Journal of Experimental Psychology, 71,* 642-648.

Spence, K.W., & Deaux, E. (1966). Conditioning (habit growth) in the absence of CRS. *Psychonomic Science, 6,* 61-62.

Spence, K.W., & Spence, J.T. (1966). Sex and anxiety differences in eyelid conditioning. *Psychological Bulletin, 65,* 137-142.

Spence, K.W. (1966). Cognitive and drive factors in the extinction of the conditioned eyeblink response in human subjects. *Psychological Review, 73,* 445-458.

Turner, B.B. (1966). Effects of a ready signal upon eyelid conditioning. *Journal of Experimental Psychology, 72,* 11-14.

Zimbardo, P.G. (1966). The cognitive control of motivation. *Transactions of the New York Academy of Sciences, 28(7),* 902-921.

1967

Berman, J., Williams, C.D., & Schneiderman, N. (1967). Warning signal as a component of a compound stimulus in human eyelid conditioning. *Psychonomic Sciences, 9,* 541-542.

Borrowman, E.B., North, J.A., & Grant, D.A. (1967). Stimulus reinforcement incongruity in differential eyelid conditioning with verbal stimuli. *Journal of General Psychology, 76,* 43-48.

Bunde, D.C., & Grant, D.A. (1967). Classical differential eyelid conditioning and the compatibility of the reinforcement contingencies to verbal conditioned stimuli that express a command. *Psychonomic Bulletin, 1,* 16.

Burstein, K.R. (1967). UCS intensity and eyelid conditioning: Another look. *Psychonomic Science, 7,* 81-82.

Burstein, K.R. (1967). Comment on Suboski. *Psychonomic Science, 8,* 547.

Cerekwicki, L.E., & Grant, D.A. (1967). Delay of positive reinforcement in instrumental eyelid conditioning. *Journal of Experimental Psychology, 75,* 360-364.

Cobb, N.J., Price, L.E., & Abbott, D.W. (1967). Effects of stimulus change and drive level on extinction of the conditioned eyelid response. *Psychological Reports, 20,*

775-778.

Deaux, E, & Deaux, K.K. (1967). Effect of extinction trials on spontaneous blinking. *Psychonomic Science, 7,* 73-74.

Dufort, R.H. (1967). Eyelid conditioning as a function of UCS duration with drive equated. *Journal of Experimental Psychology, 74,* 321-323.

Fishbein, H.D., & LeBlanc, M. (1967). Human eyelid conditioning as a function of interstimulus interval. *Journal of Experimental Psychology, 75,* 130-133.

Fishbein, H.D. (1967). Effects of differential instructions and number of acquisition trials on extinction and reacquisition of the conditioned-eyelid response. *Journal of Experimental Psychology, 75,* 126-129.

Fishbein, H.D. (1967). Effects of differential instructions, differential feedback, and UCS intensity on the conditioned eyelid response. *Journal of Experimental Psychology, 75,* 56-63.

Fishbein, H.D. (1967). CS intensity and CS-UCS interval effects in eyelid conditioning. *Psychonomic Bulletin, 1,* 16.

Franks, C.M. (1967). A longitudinal conditional eyeblink reflex study of four adult men. *Australian Journal of Psychology, 19(2),* 125-132.

Gold, D. (1967). The effect of generalized and specific expectancies upon eyelid conditioning. *Psychonomic Science, 8,* 147-148.

Grant, D.A., Levey, C.M., Thompson, J., Hickok, C.W., & Bunde, D.C. (1967). Transfer of differential eyelid conditioning through successive discriminations. *Journal of Experimental Psychology, 75,* 246-254.

Grice, G.R., Hunter, J.J., Kohfeld, D.L., & Masters, L. (1967). Order of presentation, CS intensity, and response latency. *Journal of Experimental Psychology, 74,* 581-585.

Hickok, C.W., Grant, D.A., & North, J.A. (1967). Factors in the reversal of differential conditioning of the human eyelid response. *Journal of General Psychology, 76,* 125-137.

Homzie, M.J. (1967). Performance in classical eyelid conditioning as a function of lengthening the CS-UCS interval. *Psychonomic Science, 7,* 211-212.

Jonnson, J.T., & Heal, L.W. (1967). CS-UCS interval in differential eyelid conditioning with retardates. *Psychonomic Science, 9,* 327-328.

Keehn, J.D. (1967). Experimental studies of "the unconscious". Operant conditioning of unconscious eyeblinking. *Behavior Research and Therapy, 5,* 95-102.

Leonard, T.B. III, Kimble, G.A., & Perlmuter, L.C. (1967). Eyelid conditioning at low US intensities and eyeblink threshold. *Psychonomic Science, 9,* 187-188.

Levy, A.B., & Martin, I. (1967). Reflex sensitivity and the conditioned eyelid response. *Psychonomic Science, 8,* 153-154.

Lintz, L.M., Fitzgerald, H.E., & Brackbill, Y. (1967). Conditioning the eyeblink response to sound in infants. *Psychonomic Science, 7,* 405-406.

Massaro, D.W., & Moore, J.W. (1967). Differential classical and avoidance eyelid conditioning. *Journal of Experimental Psychology, 75,* 151-157.

Payne, R.W., Netley, C.T., & Sloane, R.B. (1967). Rigidity, drive and conditioning in neurotics. *British Journal of Psychology, 58(1-2),* 111-126.

Perlmuter, L.C., & Leonard, T.B. III. (1967). Effect of binaural and alternating CSs on eyelid conditioning. *Psychological Reports, 20,* 359-365.

Plapp, J.M. (1967). Hypnosis, conditioning, and physiological responses. *Proceedings 75th Annual Convention of the American Psychological Association, 2,* 141-142.

Prokasy, W.F. (1967). Unconditioned stimulus intensity and asymptotic performance in human eyelid conditioning. *Psychonomic Science, 8,* 149-150.

Prokasy, W.F., Carlton, R.A., & Higgins, J.D. (1967). Effects of nonrandom intermittent reinforcement schedules in human eyelid conditioning. *Journal of Experimental Psychology, 74,* 282-288.

Ross, L.E., Wilcox, S.M., & Maver, M.J. (1967). A simple eyelid conditioning masking task and its effect on differential conditioning. *Psychonomic Science, 9,* 333-334.

Ross, L.E., Headrick, M.W., & McKay, D.B. (1967). Classical eyelid conditioning of young mongoloid children. *Journal of Mental Deficiency, 72,* 21-29.

Schumsky, D.A., Richman, C.L., & Trinder, J. (1967). Free operant conditioning of the human eyelid. *Psychonomic Science, 8,* 237-238.

Spence, K.W., & Platt, J.R. (1967). Effects of partial reinforcement on acquisition and extinction of the conditioned eyeblink in a masking situation. *Journal of Experimental Psychology, 74,* 259-263.

Suboski, M.D., Greenner, R.T., & Pappas, P. (1967). The law of effect and the origin of the classically conditioned eyelid response. *Canadian Journal of Psychology, 21(5),* 409-415.

Suboski, M.D. (1967). UCS intensity and the latency of the classically conditioned eyelid response. *Journal of Experimental Psychology, 74,* 31-35.

Suboski, M.D. (1967). UCS intensity in eyelid conditioning. *Psychonomic Science, 8,* 63-64.

Vandament, W.E. (1967). Differential eyelid conditioning to stimulus compounds as a function of temporal relations between stimuli. *Psychological Reports, 21,* 161-168.

1968

Brackbill, Y., Lintz, L.M., & Fitzgerald, H.E. (1968). Differences in the autonomic and somatic conditioning in infants. *Psychosomatic Medicine, 30,* 193-200.

Cerekwicki, L.E., Grant, D.A., & Porter, E.C. (1968). The effect of number and relatedness of verbal discriminanda upon differential eyelid conditioning. *Journal of Verbal Learning and Verbal Behavior, 7,* 847-853.

Davidson, P.O., Payne, R.W., & Sloane, R.B. (1968). Conditionability in normals and neurotics. *Journal of Experimental Research in Personality, 3,* 107-113.

Fishbein, H.D., & Levy, S. (1968). Suppressin of the UCR in human eyelid conditioning as a function of CS intensity. *British Journal of Psychology, 59(3),* 273-276.

Fleming, R.A., Grant, D.A., North, J.A., & Levy, C.M. (1968). Arithmetic correctness as the discriminandum in classical and differential eyelid conditioning. *Journal of Experimental Psychology, 77,* 286-294.

Fleming, R.A., Grant, D.A., & North, J.A. (1968). Truth and falsity of verbal statements as conditioned stimuli in classical and differential eyelid conditioning. *Journal of Experimental Psychology, 78,* 178-180.

Felming, R.A., Cerekwicki, L.E., & Grant, D.A. (1968). "Appropriateness" of the stimuli-reinforcement contingency in instrumental differential conditioning of the eyelid response to the arithmetic concept of "right" and "wrong". *Journal of Experimental Psychology, 77,* 295-300.

Grant, D.A. (1968). Adding communication to the signalling property of the CS in classical conditioning. *Journal of General Psychology, 79,* 147-175.

Higgins, J.D., & Prokasy, W.F., Jr. (1968). The effects of transition probability of reinforcement in intermittent reinforcement schedules in human eyelid conditioning. *Psychonomic Science, 12,* 69-70.

Hobson, G.N. (1968). Effects of UCS adaptation upon conditioning in low and high anxiety men and women. *Journal of Experimental Psychology, 76,* 360-363.

Homzie, M.J. (1968). Separate-phase differential eyelid conditioning within the context of a masking procedure. *Journal of Experimental Psychology, 76,* 630-635.

Hug, J.J., & Porter, J.J. (1968). Interaction of habit (H) and drive (D) in classical eyelid conditioning: H and D as a function of UCS intensity. *Journal of Experimental Psychology, 77,* 150-154.

Kimble, G.A., Leonard, T.B. III, & Perlmuter, L.C. (1968). Effects of interstimulus interval and discrimination learning in eyelid conditioning using between-and within-Ss designs. *Journal of Experimental Psychology, 77,* 652-660.

Levey, A.B., & Martin, I. (1968). Shape of the conditioned eyelid response. *Psychological Review, 75,* 398-408.

Minnegerode, F.A., & O'Connell, D.C. (1968). US intensity and nonreinforcement technique in eyelid conditioning. *Psychonomic Science, 12,* 371-372.

Ohlrich, E.S., & Ross, L.E. (1968). Acquisition and differential conditioning of the eyelid response in normal and retarded children. *Journal of Experimental Child Psychology, 6,* 181-193.

Ominsky, M. (1968). Differential instructions and interstimulus interval in eyelid conditioning. *Psychonomic Science, 12,* 51-52.

Ominsky, M. (1968). Instructions and interstimulus interval in eyelid conditioning. *Psychonomic Science, 12,* 49-50.

Ominsky, M., & Posnick, G.M. (1968). The effect of paired neutral stimuli on the acquisition and extinction of the classical eyeblink response. *Psychonomic Science, 10,* 67-68.

Perlmuter, L.C., Kimble, G.A., & Leonard, T.B. III. (1968). Effect of a simultaneous conditioning procedure upon subsequent extintion and acquisition. *Journal of Experimental Psychology, 77,* 648-651.

Porter, J.J., & Hug, J.J. (1968). The interaction of habit (H) and drive (D) in classical eyelid conditioning: H as a function of UCS intensity and trials, D as a function of UCS intensity and anxiety. *Psychonomic Science, 10,* 399-400.

Prokasy, W.F., & Harsanyi, M.A. (1968). Two-phase model for human classical conditioning. *Journal of Experimental Psychology, 78,* 359-368.

Prokasy, W.F., Higgins, J.D., & Carlton, R.A. (1968). Sequential effects in

differential human eyelid conditioning. *Psychonomic Science, 12,* 58.
Suboski, M.D., & Greenner, R.T. (1968). Ready signal and definition of a CR in classical eyelid conditioning. *Psychological Reports, 23,* 995-1001.
White, B.L., & Clark, K.R. (1968). Apparatus for eliciting and recording the eyeblink response in human infants. *Perceptual and Motor Skills, 27,* 959-964.

1969

Bernstein, A.L., & Rutledge, E.F. (1969). Simultaneous performance in eyelid conditioning and probability learning as a function of puff intensity. *Journal of Experimental Psychology, 79,* 22-26.
Cerekwicki, L.E., Kantowitz, B.H., & Grant, D.A. (1969). Replicability of and optimal delay of reinforcement result in instrumental eyelid conditioning. *Journal of Experimental Psychology, 79,* 189-190.
Fishbein, H.D., Jones, P.D., & Silverthorne, C. (1969). CS intensity and CS-UCS interval effects in human eyelid conditioning. *Journal of Experimental Psychology, 81,* 109-114.
Fishbein, H.D., & Rees, J.F. (1969). The interaction effects of CS intensity and CS-UCS interval in human eyelid conditioning. *British Journal* of Psychology, 60(3), 357-361.
Foth, D.L., & Runquist, W.N. (1969). Differential eyelid conditioning to verbal stimuli varying in formal similarity. *Journal of Experimental Psychology, 80,* 9-13.
Gold, D.P. (1969). Effect of the experimenter in human eyelid conditioning. *Psycnonomic Science, 17,* 232-233.
Grant, D.A., Kroll, N.E.A., Kantowitz, B., Zajano, M.J., & Solberg, K.B. (1969). Transfer of eyelid conditioning from instrumental to classical reinforcement and vice versa. *Journal of Experimental Psychology, 82,* 503-510.
Hobson, G.N. (1969). UCS adaptation in eyeblink conditioning experiments. *Journal of Experimental Psychology, 80,* 386-387.
Kelly, D., & Martin, I. (1969). Autonomic reactivity, eyelid conditioning and their relationship to neuroticism and extraversion. *Behavioral Research Therapy, 3,* 233-244.
Kelly, M.R. (1969). The Shor Personal Experiences Questionnaire: some personality variables and college achievement. *Australian Journal of Psychology, 21(1),* 85-89.
Kessler, R.S., Williams, C.D., & Schneiderman, N. (1969). Extinction of human eyelid conditioning as a function of components of a masking procedure. *Psychonomic Science, 17,* 337-338.
Kwaterski, S.E., & Moore, J.W. (1969). Differential eyelid conditioning based on opposing instrumental contingencies. *Journal of Experimental Psychology, 79,* 547-551.
Lin, P-F. (1969). The effect of the interpolated UCS alone trials on classical aversive conditioning. *Acta Psychologica Taiwanica, 11,* 71-77.
Martin, I., Marks, I.M., & Gelder, M. (1969). Conditioned eyelid responses in phobic

patients. *Behavior Research Therapy, 7,* 115-124.
Mayer, M.J., & Ross, L.E. (1969). The effects of stimulus complexity, interstimulus interval and masking task conditions in differential eyelid conditioning. *Journal of Experimental Psychology, 81,* 469-474.
Moore, J.W., Newman, F.L., & Glasgow, B. (1969). Intertrial cues as discriminative stimuli in human eyelid conditioning. *Journal of Experimental Psychology, 79,* 319-326.
Nagalakshmi, W.V., & Marthy, H.N. (1969). Relation of conditioned response strength to anxiety in normals, neurotics and psychotics. *Transactions of All-Inda Institute Mental Health, 7,* 65-73.
Newman, F.L., & Woodhouse, J. (1969). Differential eyelid conditioning: Establishing differential responding prior to varying the probability of reinforcement. *Journal of Experimental Psychology, 80,* 146-149.
Ost, J.W.P., Hill, R.E., & Naleski, J. (1969). Human eyelid conditioning: The interaction of reinforcement schedule and CS-US interval length. *Psychonomic Science, 14,* 259-260.
Piers, E.V., & Hirchner, e.P. (1969). Eyelid conditioning and personality: Positive results from nonpartisans. *Journal of Abnormal Psychology, 74,* 336-339.
Prokasy, W.F., & Kumofer, K.L. (1969). Conditional probability of reinforcement and sequential behavior in human conditioning with intermittent reinforcement schedules. *Psychonomic Science, 14,* 49-50.
Prokasy, W.F., Allen, C.K., & Dey, M.K. (1969). Discrimination gradients in human eyelid conditioning. *Psychonomic Science, 14,* 191-192.
Prokasy, W.F., & Kumpfer, K. (1969). One-and two-operator versions of the threshold model applied to the performances of Vs and Cs in human eyelid conditioning. *Journal of Experimental Psychology, 80,* 231-236.
Prokasy, W.F., & Allen, C.K. (1969). Instructional sets in human differential eyelid conditioning. *Journal of Experimental Psychology, 80,* 271-278.
Schnur, P., & Ksir, C.J. (1969). Latent inhibition in human eyelid conditioning. *Journal of Experimental Psychology, 80,* 388-389.
Silverthorne, C.P., & Fishbein, H.D. (1969). A comparison of five acquisition procedures in human eyelid conditioning. *Proceedings of the 77th Annual Convention of the American Psychology Association, 4(1),* 67-68.
Suboski, M.D., & Khosla, S. (1969). UCS intensity and instructional set in classical eyelid conditioning: Discrimination conditioning and signal detection analysis. *Canadian Journal of Psychology, 23,* 389.401.
Vandament, W.E. (1969). Response latency as a function of interstimulus interval in conditioned eyelid discrimination. *Journal of Experimental Psychology, 82,* 561-565.
Vandament, W.E. (1969). Differential eyelid conditioning as a function of CS-UCS interval and distance separating the CSs. *Psychological Reports, 25,* 407-411.
Wilcox, S.M., & Ross, L.E. (1969). Differential classical eyelid conditioning as a function of CS intensity, CS rise time, and interstimulus interval. *Journal of Experimental Psychology, 82,* 272-278.

1970

Bunde, D.C., Grant, D.A., & Frost, M.R. (1970). Differential eyelid conditioning to stimuli that express a response-related command or convey reinforcement related information. *Journal of Verbal Learning and Verbal Behavior, 9,* 346-355.

Foth, D.I., & Runquist, W.N. (1970). Effects of unconditioned stimulus intensity and schedules of 50% partial reinforcement in human classical eyelid conditioning. *Journal of Experimental Psychology, 84,* 244-247.

Gendreau, P. (1970). Effect of two days monotonous confinement on conditioned eyelid frequency and topography. *Perceptual and Motor Skills, 31,* 291-293.

Hupka, R.B., Kwaterski, S.E., & Moore, J.W. (1970). Conditioned diminution of the UCR: Differences between the human eyeblink and the rabbit nictitating membrane. *Journal of Experimental Psychology, 83,* 45-51.

Lloyd, K.E., Russel, H.K., & Garmize, L.M. (1970). Operant eyelid conditioning in trisomy 18: Replication and extension. *Journal of Abnormal Psychology, 75,* 338-341.

Peterson, G.B., & Newman, F.L. (1970). Differential human eyelid conditioning as a function of the probability of reinforcement and CS similarity. *Journal of Experimental Psychology, 85,* 318-320.

Rees, J.F., & Fishbein, H.D. (1970). Test of the TSD model in human eyelid conditioning: A priori probability and payoff manipulations. *Journal of Experimental Psychology, 83,* 291-298.

Sommer, F.G., & Ling, D. (1970). Auditory testing of newborns using eyeblink conditioning. *Journal of Auditory Research, 10,* 292-295.

Vandament, W.E. (1970). Generalization and ISI in human eyelid conditioning. *Psychological Reports, 26,* 717-718.

1971

Allen, C.K., & Barnum, A.R. (1971). Differential eyelid conditioning as a function of the probability of reinforcement of the conditioned stimuli. *Psychonomic Science, 22,* 251-252.

Barratt, E.S. (1971). Psychophysiological correlates of classical differential eyelid conditioning among subjects selected on the basis of impulsiveness and anxiety. *Biological Psychiatry, 3,* 339-346.

Fitgerald, H.E., & Brackbill, Y. (1971). Tactile conditioning of an autonomic and somatic response in young infants. *Conditioned Reflex, 6,* 41-51.

Furedy, J.J. (1971). Cross-modal differentiation under identical reinforcement schedules, and UCS-intensity effects in human classical eyelid conditioning. *Canadian Journal of Psychology, 25,* 7-23.

Gendreau, P., & Suboski, M.D. (1971). Intelligence and age in discrimination conditioning of the eyelid response. *Journal of Experimental Psychology, 89,* 379-382.

Gendreau, P., & Suboski, M.D. (1971). Classical discrimination eyelid conditioning in primary psychopaths. *Journal of Abnormal Psychology, 77,* 242-246.

Gormezano, I., & Gernald, C.D. (1971). Human eyelid conditioning with paraorbital shock as the US. *Psychonomic Science, 25,* 88-90.
Perry, L.C., Ornstein, P.A., & Grant, D.A. (1971). A test of associative generalization of the conditioned eyelid response. *Psychonomic Science, 23,* 319-320.
Ross, S.M., & Ross, L.E. (1971). Comparison of trace and delay classical eyelid conditioning as a function of interstimulus interval. *Journal of Experimental Psychology, 91,* 165-167.
Schmusky, D.A., Trinder, J., & Richmann, CL. (1971). Human operant eyelid conditioning: Auditory vs. visual reinforcing signal. *Psychonomic Science, 22,* 359-360.

1972

Gendreau, P. (1972). Effects of methamphetamine on well-practiced discrimination conditioning of the eyelid response. *Psychopharmacologia, 25,* 112-116.
Grice, G.R., Hendriksen, K., & Speixx, J.M. (1972). Response mediated generalization in eyelid conditioning with reduced conflicting information. *Journal of Experimental Psychology, 92,* 398-404.
Prokasy, W.F. (1972). Developments with the two-phase model applied to human eyelid conditioning. In A.H. Black and W.F. Prokasy (Eds.), *Classical Conditioning II.* New York: Appleton-Century-Croft, pp. 119-147.
Ross, S.M. (1972). Trace and delay classical eyelid conditioning in severely and profondly retarded subjects as a function of interstimulus interval. *American Journal of Mental Deficiency, 77,* 39-45.
Suboski, M., & Litner, J. (1971). Partial reinforcement and instructional set in discrimination conditioning of the eyelid response. *Canadian Journal of Psychology, 26,* 117-126.
Werden, D., & Ross, L.E. (1971). A comparison of trace and delay classical conditioning performance of normal children. *Journal of Experimental Child Psychology, 14,* 126-132.

1973

Gordon, W.C., & Dufort, R.H. (1973). The effect of a ready signal on the relationship between habit and drive variables in human eyelid conditioning. *Bulletin of Psychonomic Society, 1,* 117-118.
Grant, D.A. (1973). Cognitive factors in eyelid conditioning. *Psychophysiology, 10,* 75-81.
Grant, D.A. (1973). Reification and reality in conditioning paradigms: Implications of results when modes of reinforcement are changed. In F.J. McGuigan and D.B. Lumsden (Eds.), *Contemporary Approaches to Conditioning and Learning.* Washington, D.C.: V.H. Winston.
Newman, F.L., Francis, J.C., West, A., & Covey, D. (1971). Differential eyelid

conditioning: The generalization of reinforcement and of nonreinforcement. *Psychonomic Society Bulletin, 1,* 433-436.
Ross, L.E., & Nelson, M.N. (1971). The role of awareness in differential conditioning. *Psychophysiology, 10,* 91-94.
Schnurr, B.C. & Runquist, W.N. (1971). Acquisition and extinction of human eyelid conditioned response as a function of schedule of reinforcement and unconditioned stimulus intensity under two masked conditioning procedures. *Journal of Experimental Psychology, 101,* 398-401.

1974

Hellige, J.B., & Grant, D.A. (1974a). Eyelid conditioning performance when the mode of reinforcement is changed from classical to instrumental and vice versa. *Journal of Experimental Psychology, 102,* 710-719.
Hellige, J.B., & Grant, D.A. (1974b). Response rate and development of response topography in eyelid conditioning under different conditions of reinforcement. *Journal of Experimental Psychology, 103,* 574-582.
Levey, A.B., & Martin, I. (1974). Sequence of response development in human eyelid conditioning. *Journal of Experimental Psychology, 102,* 678-686.
Little, A.H. (1974). A comparative study of trace and delay conditioning in the human infant. *Dissertation Abstracts International, 34,* 5224-5225.
Mosley, J.L., Bakal, D.A., & Pilek, V. (1974). Conditioned eyelid response, peripheral vasoconstriction, and attention in retarded and nonretarded individuals. *American Journal of Mental Deficiency, 78,* 694-703.
Murray, H.G., & Carruthers, B.C. (1974). Human eyelid conditioning with airpuff vs. infraorbital shock as the UCS. *Canadian Journal of Psychology, 28,* 269-287.
Nelson, M.N., & Ross, L.E. (1974). Effects of masking tasks on differential eyelid conditioning: A distinction between knowledge of stimulus contingencies and attentional or cognitive activities involving them. *Journal of Experimental Psychology, 102,* 1-9.
Osborne, B., Roach, T., Gendreau, L., & Gendreau, P. (1974). An electrode hookup for human eyelid conditioning. *Behavioral Research Methods and Instrumentation, 6,* 416-418.
Prokasy, W.F., Williams, W.C., Lee, W.Y.M., & Kumpfer, K.L. (1974). Two-phase model analysis of the effects of interstimulus interval and masking task in human aversive classical conditioning. *Memory and Cognition, 2,* 206-210.
Putman, L.E., Ross, L.E., & Graham, F.K. (1974). Cardiac orienting during "good" and "poor" differential eyelid conditioning. *Journal of Experimental Psychology, 102,* 563-573.
Ross, S.M., Ross, L.E., & Werden, D. (1974). Trace and delay differential classical eyelid conditioning in human adults. *Psychonomic Society Bulletin, 3,* 224-226.
Ross, L.E., Ferreira, M.C., & Ross, S.M. (1974). Backward masking of conditioned stimuli, effects on differential and single-cue classical conditioning performance. *Journal of Experimental Psychology, 103,* 603-613.
Weckowicz, T.E., Nutter, R., & Gibbs, J.T. (1974). The effect of tranylcypromine

(Parnate) on eyelid conditioning and paired associate learning in depressed patients. *Pavlovian Journal of Biological Science, 9,* 122-123.

Zajano, M.J., Grant, D.A., & Schwartz, M. (1974). Transfer of differential eyelid conditioning: Effects of semantic and formal features of verbal stimuli. *Journal of Experimental Psychology, 103,* 1147-1152.

Zajano, M.J., & Grant, D.A. (1974). Response topography in the acquisition of differential eyelid conditioning. *Journal of Experimental Psychology, 103,* 1115-1123.

1975

Agathon, M. (1975). A note on the conditioned reflex. Studies of schizophrenia in France. *Pavlovian Journal of Biological Science, 10,* 142-144.

Albin, J.B. (1975). Delay and trace conditioning in normal and retarded individuals: The role of US mode and US intensity. *Dissertation Abstracts International,* 6063.

Allen, J.A. (1975). An examination of the reltionships between orienting response level, voluntary responders, and conditioners. *Dissertation Abstracts International, 36,* 464.

Clark, P.M., & Albino, R.C. (1975). Extraversion, attention, and eyeblink conditioning. *Journal of Behavioral Science, 2,* 183-191.

Collins, M.J. (1975). Classical conditioning of differential eyelid responses to verbal and nonverbal stimuli in aphasic and normal adults. *Dissertation Abstracts International, 35,* 6175.

Hellige, J. (1975). Hemispheric processing differences revealed by differential conditioning and reaction time performance. *Journal of Experimental Psychology, 104,* 309-326.

Leonard, D.W. (1975). Partial reinforcement effects in classical aversive conditioning in rabbits and human beings. *Journal of Comparative and Physiological Psychology, 88,* 596-608.

Mosley, J.L. (1975). Acquisition and extinction of the human eyelid conditioned response as related to intellectual functioning. *Journal of Mental Deficiency, 81,* 41-48.

Perry, L.C. (1975). Verbal discrimination learning theory and differential eyelid conditioning to related words at three interstimulus intervals. *Bulletin of the Psychonomic Society, 7,* 299-302.

1977

Cyamada, T. (1977). Inhibitory effects of a ready signal on eyelid conditioning. *Tohoku Psychologica Folia, 36,* 9-14.

Follyk, S. (1977). Classical eyelid conditioning in retarded and nonretarded adults. *Dissertation Abstracts International, 37,* 5349-5350.

Grice, G.R. (1977). Information processing dynamics of human eyelid conditioning.

Journal of Experimental Psychology, General, 106, 71-93.

Ison, J.R., & Ash, B. (1977). Effects of experience on stimulus-produced reflex inhibition in the human. *Bulletin of the Psychonomic Society, 10*, 467-468.

Kadlac, J.A., & Grant, D.A. (1977). Eyelid response topography in differential interstimulus interval conditioning. *Journal of Experimental Psychology, Human Learning Memory, 3*, 345-355.

Nelson, M.N. (1977). Cardiac orienting during differential and single-cue eyelid conditioning in severely and profoundly retarded children. *Dissertation Abstracts International, 37*, 3652.

Perry, L.C., Grant, D.A., & Schwartz, M. (1977). Effects of noun imagery and awareness of discriminative cue upon differential eyelid conditioning to grammatical and ungrammatical phrases. *Memory Cognition, 5*, 423-429.

1978

Codey, W.J., & Grant, D.A. (1978). Biasing the development of response topography with nonspecific positive and negative evocative verbal stimuli. *Journal of Experimental Psychology, Human Learning and Memory, 4*, 175-186.

Hulstijn, W. (1978). The orienting reaction during human eyelid conditioning following preconditioned exposures to the CS. *Psychological Research, 40*, 77-88.

1979

Cyamada, T. (1979). Effects of preexposure to a ready signal on human eyelid conditioning. *Tohoku Psychologica Folia, 38*, 75-82.

Kadlac, J.A. (1979). Individual differences and levels-of-processing tasks in differential eyelid conditioning: Response frequency, topography, cardiac orienting, and sequential effects. *Dissertation Abstracts International, 39*, 4617.

Kadlac, J.A. (1979). Cognitive factors affecting sequential dependencies in differential eyelid conditioning. *Pavlovian Journal of Biological Science, 14*, 191-198.

Perry, L.C., Brown, R.M., & Perry, D.G. (1979). Interactive effects of cognitive involvement and response topography upon differential eyelid conditioning to conceptual discriminada. *American Journal of Psychology, 92*, 401-412.

Prokasy, W.F., & Williams, W.C. (1979). Information processing and the decremental effect of intermittent reinforcement schedules in human conditioning. *Bulletin of the Psychonomic Society, 14*, 57-60.

Weiskrantz, L., & Warrington, E.K. (1979). Conditioning in amnesic patients. *Neuropsychologia, 17*, 187-194.

1980

Benish, W.A., & Grant, D.A. (1979). Intrastimulus conflict in differential eyelid conditioning. *Bulletin of the Psychonomic Society, 15,* 428-430.
Benish, W.A., & Grant, D.A. (1979). Hemispheric processing in differential classical eyelid conditioning. *Bulletin of the Psychonomic Society, 15,* 433-444.
Benish, W.A., & Grant, D.A. (1979). Subject awareness in differential classical eyelid conditioning. *Bulletin of the Psychonomic Society, 15,* 431-432.

1981

Jones, J., Eysenck, H., Marrin, I., & Levey, A. (1981). Personality and the topography of the conditioned eyelid response. *Personality Individual Differences, 2(1),* 61-83.
Yamasaki, K., & Miyata, Y. (1981). An investigation of voluntary responses in human classical eyelid conditioning. *Psychologia: An International Journal of Psychology in the Orient, 24,* 146-156.

1982

Baer, P., & Faher, M. (1982). Cognitive factors in the concurrent differential conditioning of eyelid and skin conductance responses. *Memory and Cognition, 10,* 135-140.
Dostalek, C., et al. (1982). Development of latency of eyelid conditioned reflexes in man. *Activitas Nervosa Superior, 24,* 168-169.
Hardwick, C., & Lobb, H. (1982). Eyelid conditioning and intellectual level: Effects of contextual change on extinction. *The American Journal of Mental Deficiency, 87(3),* 325-331.
Hyskova, F. et al. (1982). Character of acquisition curve of conditioning and personality. *Activitas Nervosa Superior, 24(3),* 169-170.

1983

Beyrs, J., Freka, G., Martin, I., & Levey, A.B. (1983). The influence of psychoticism and extraversion on classical conditioning using a paraorbital shock UCS. *Personality of Individual Differences, 4(3),* 275-283.
Freka, G., Beyts, J., Levey, A.B., & Martin, I. (1983). The role of awareness in human conditioning. *Pavlovian Journal of Biological Science, 18,* 69-76.
Freka, G., Beyts, J., Levey, A., & Martin, I. (1983). The influence of psychoticism on classical conditioning. *Personality of Individual Differences, 4(2),* 189-197.

1984

Little, A.H., Lipsitt, L.P., & Rovee-Collier, C. (1984). Classical conditioning and retention of the infants eyelid response: Effects of age and inter-stimulus interval. *Journal of Experimental Child Psychology, 37(3),* 512-524.

Willer, Jean-Claude, Boulu, P., & Bratzlavsky, M. (1984). Electrophysiological evidence for crossed digosynaptic trigemino-facial connections in normal man. *Journal of Neurology, Neurosurgery and Psychiatry, 47(1),* 87-90.

1985

Hoffman, H.S., Cohen, M.E., & deVido, C.J. (1985). A comparison of classical eyelid conditioning in adults and infants. *Infant Behavior and Development, 8(3),* 247-254.

Perruchet, P. (1985). A pitfall for the expectancy theory of human eyelid conditioning. *Pavlovian Journal of Biological Science*, 20(4), 163-170.

Perruchet, P. (1985). Expectancy for airpuff and conditioned eyeblinks in humans. *Acta Psychologica, 58(1),* 31-44.

INDEX

D

H

I

K

L

M

N

V

W

www.ingramcontent.com/pod-product-compliance
Ingram Content Group UK Ltd.
Pitfield, Milton Keynes, MK11 3LW, UK
UKHW020135160926
475607UK00003B/55

9780792377276